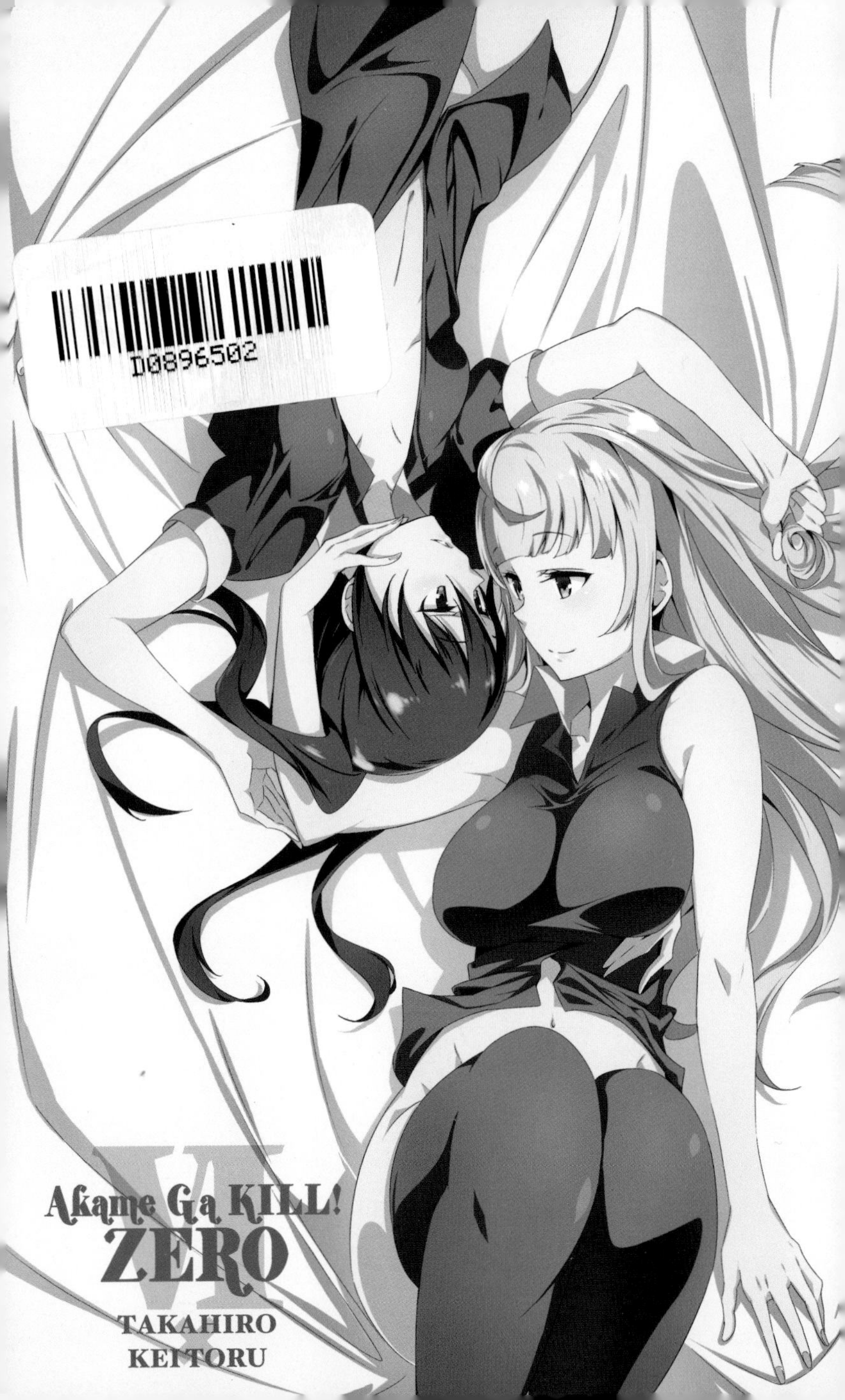
VI
Akame Ga KILL!
ZERO
TAKAHIRO
KEI TORU

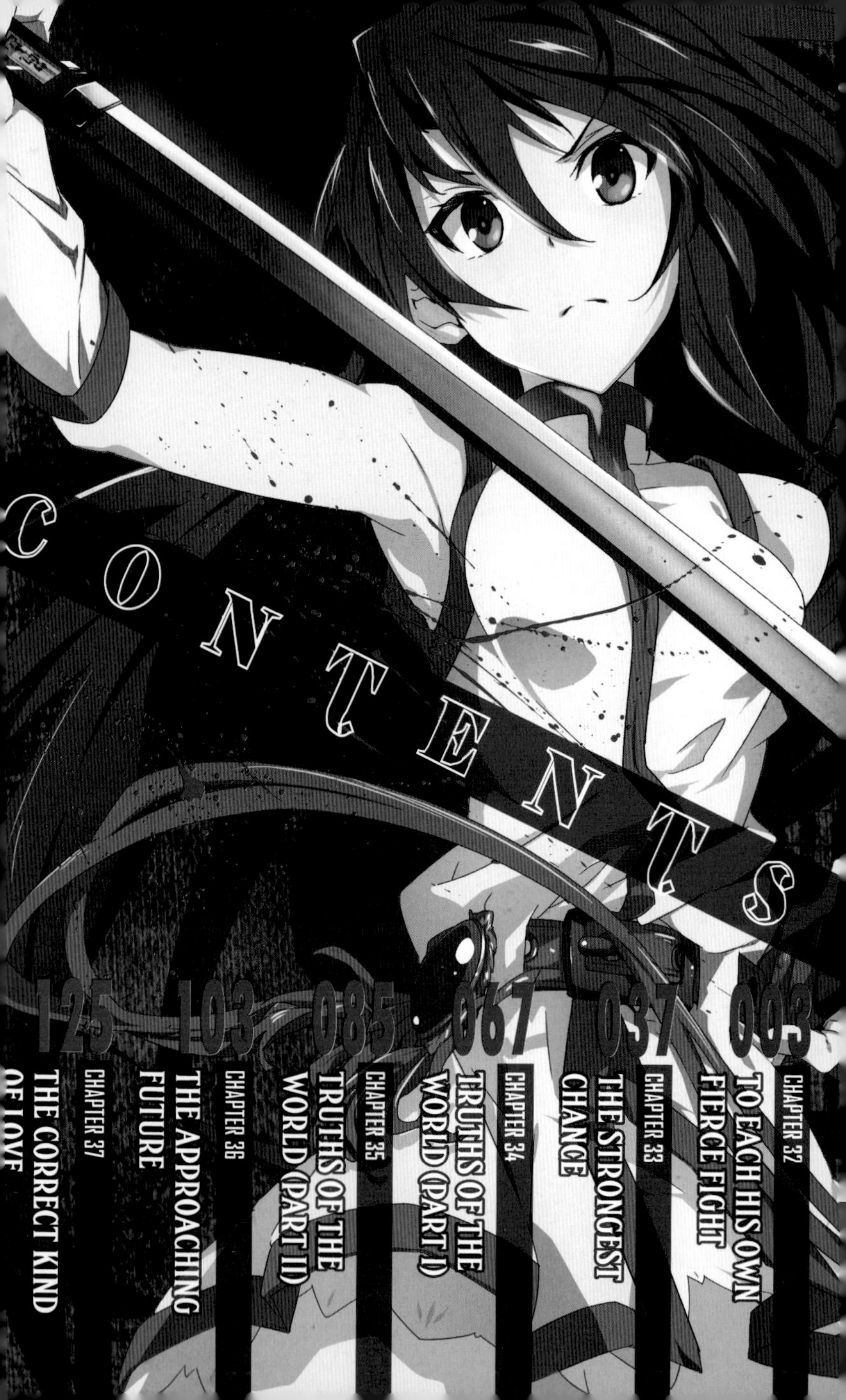

CONTENTS

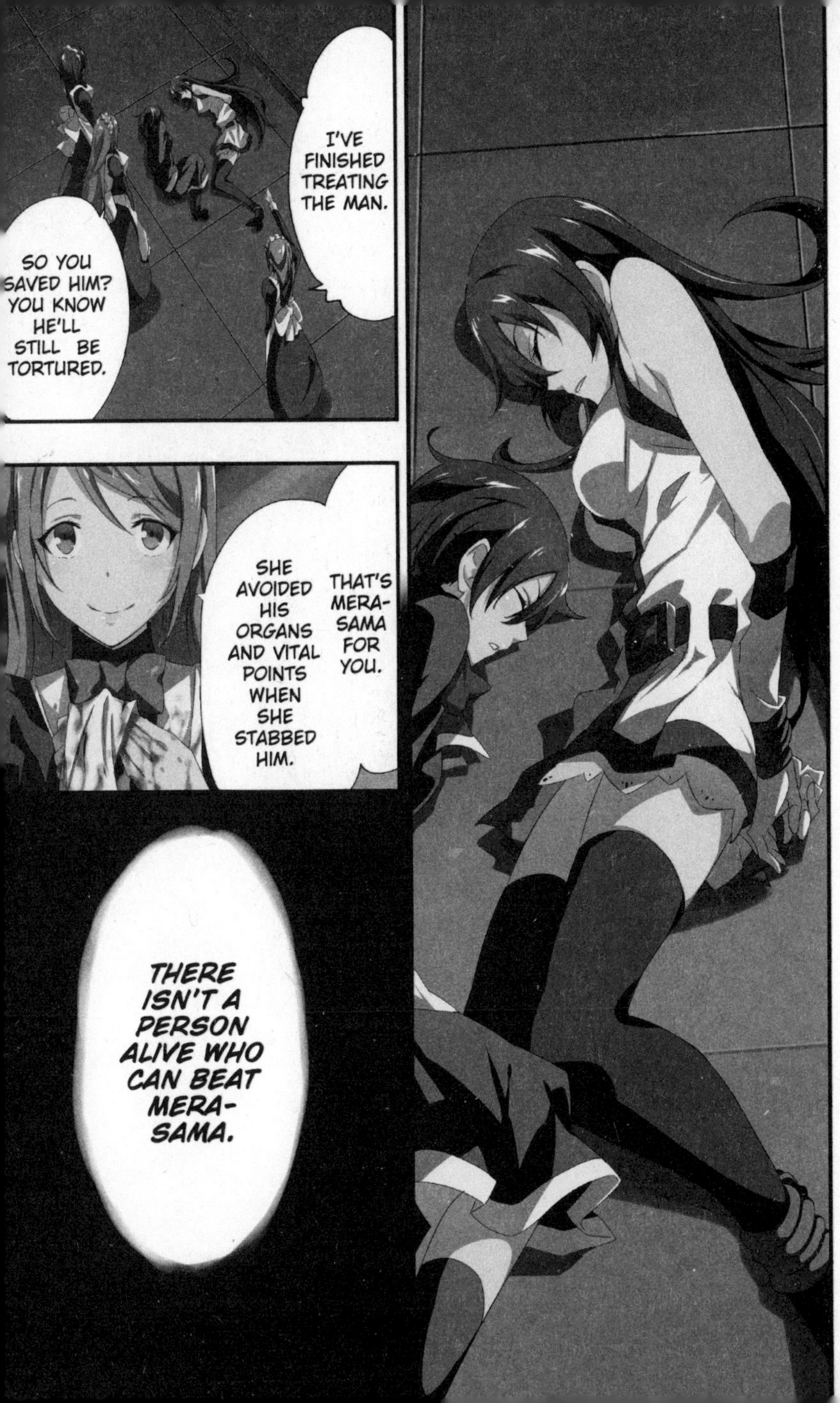
I'VE FINISHED TREATING THE MAN.
SO YOU SAVED HIM? YOU KNOW HE'LL STILL BE TORTURED.
THAT'S MERA-SAMA FOR YOU.
SHE AVOIDED HIS ORGANS AND VITAL POINTS WHEN SHE STABBED HIM.
THERE ISN'T A PERSON ALIVE WHO CAN BEAT MERA-SAMA.

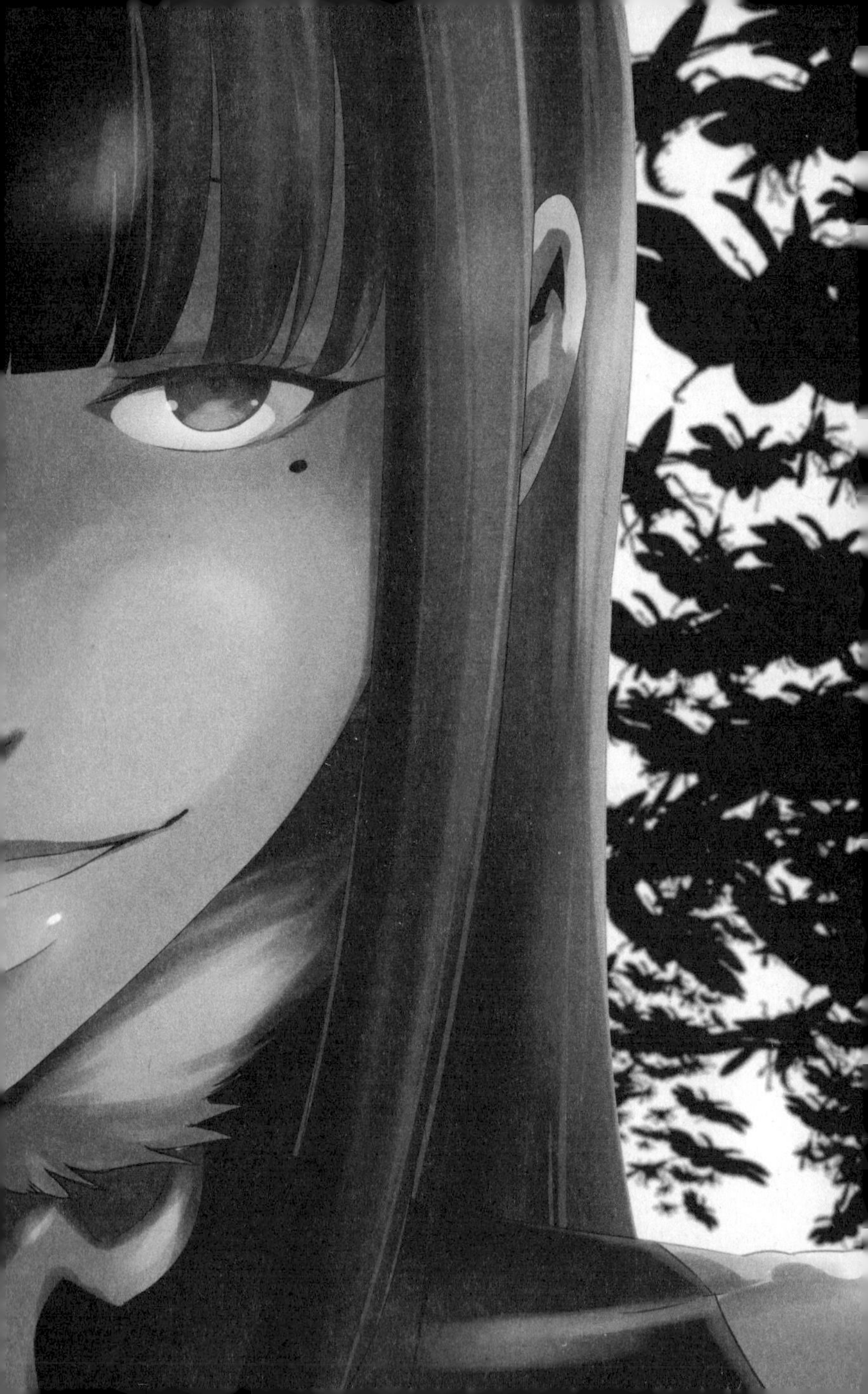

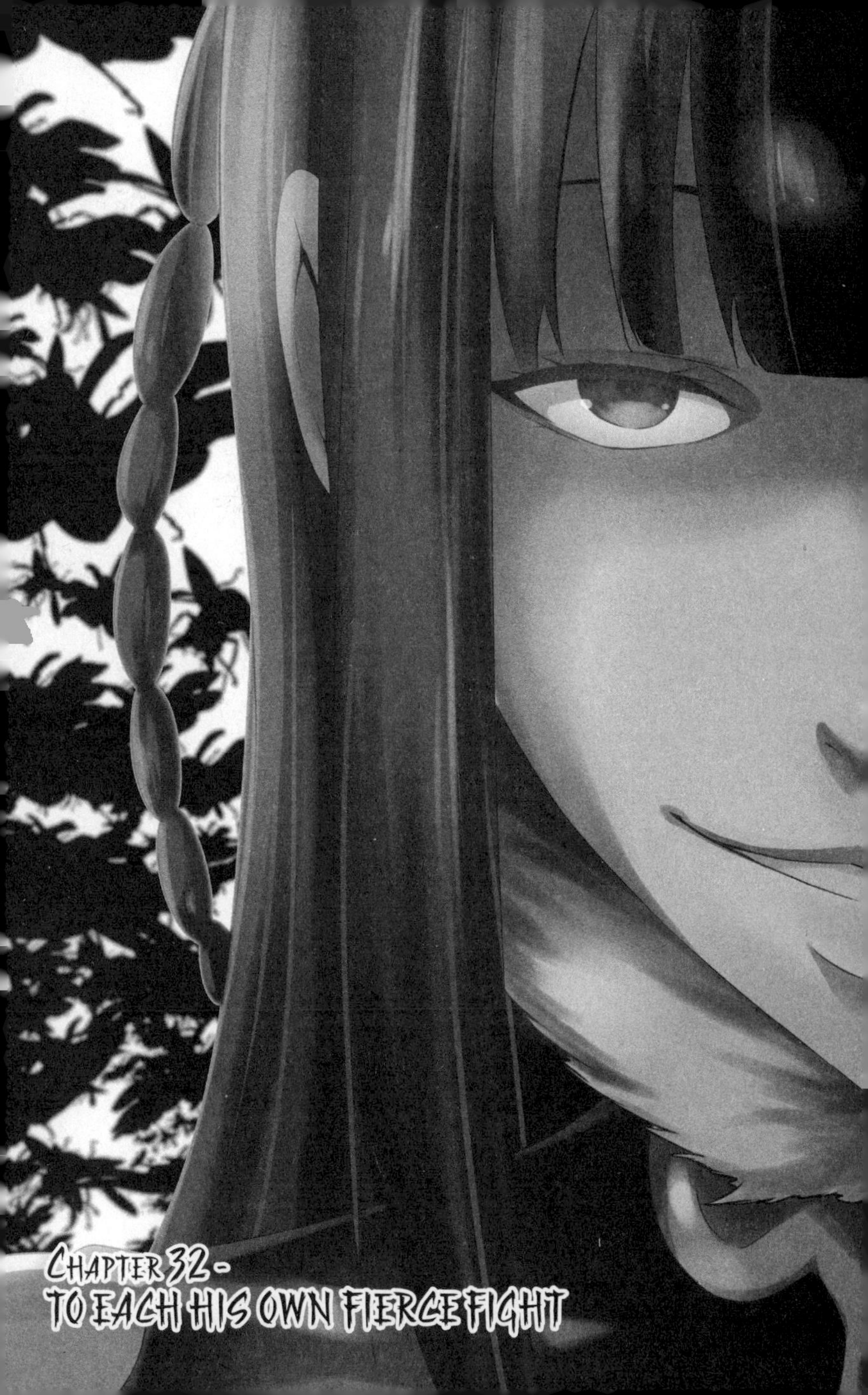
Chapter 32 -
To Each His Own Fierce Fight

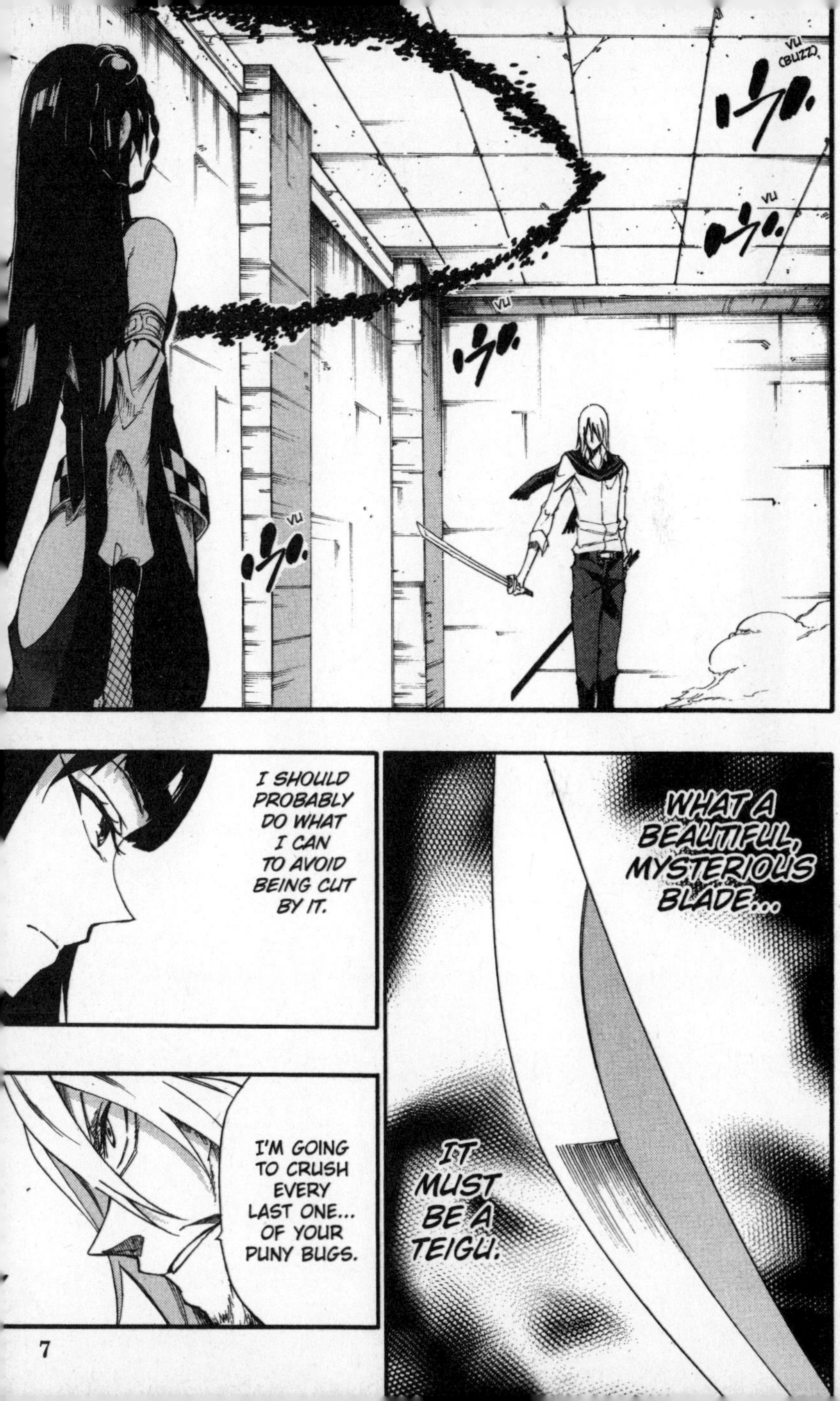
VU (BUZZ)
VU
VU
VU
WHAT A BEAUTIFUL, MYSTERIOUS BLADE...
IT MUST BE A TEIGU.
I SHOULD PROBABLY DO WHAT I CAN TO AVOID BEING CUT BY IT.
I'M GOING TO CRUSH EVERY LAST ONE... OF YOUR PUNY BUGS.

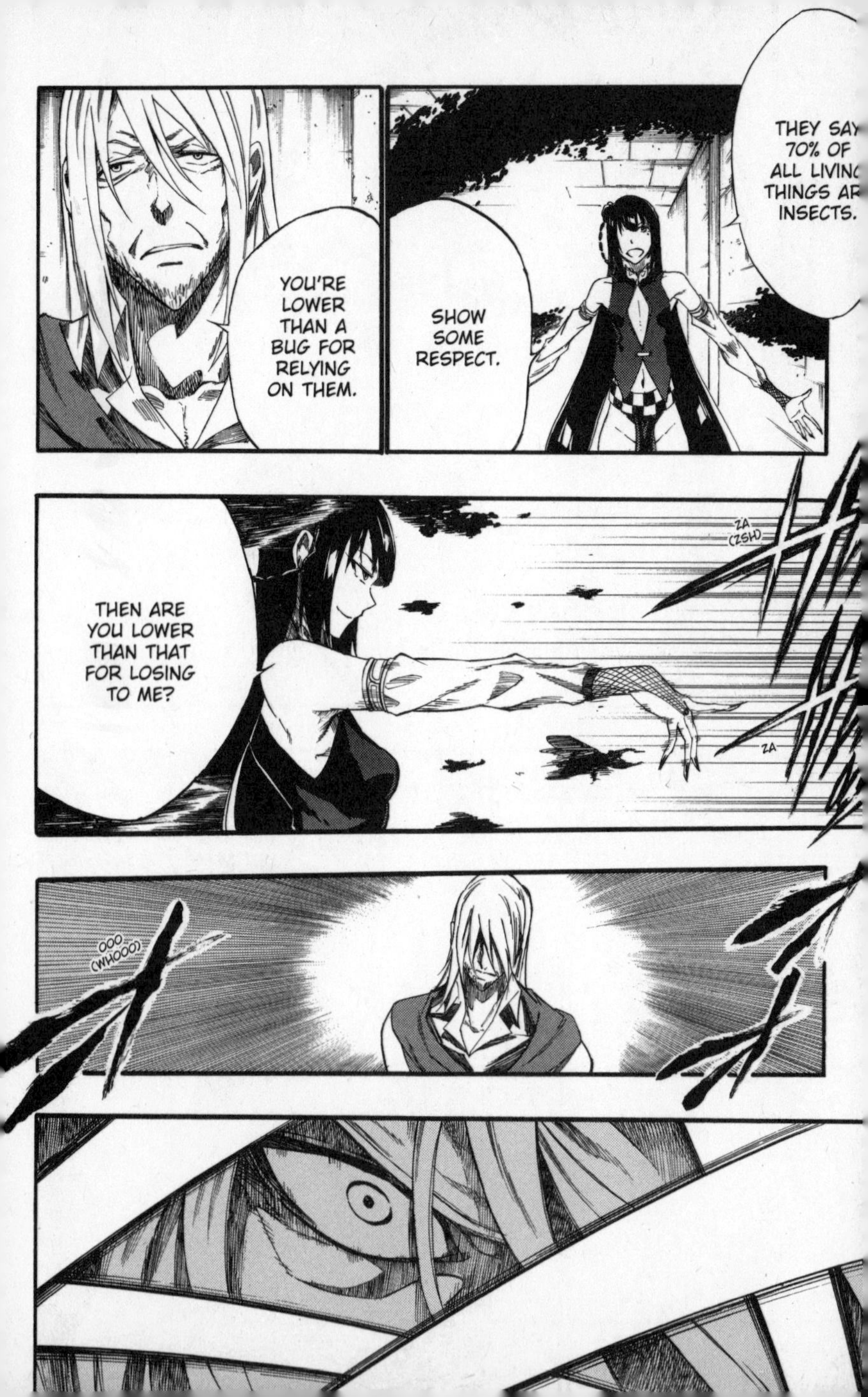
THEY SAY 70% OF ALL LIVING THINGS ARE INSECTS.
SHOW SOME RESPECT.
YOU'RE LOWER THAN A BUG FOR RELYING ON THEM.
ZA (ZSH)
ZA
THEN ARE YOU LOWER THAN THAT FOR LOSING TO ME?
OOO (WHOOO)

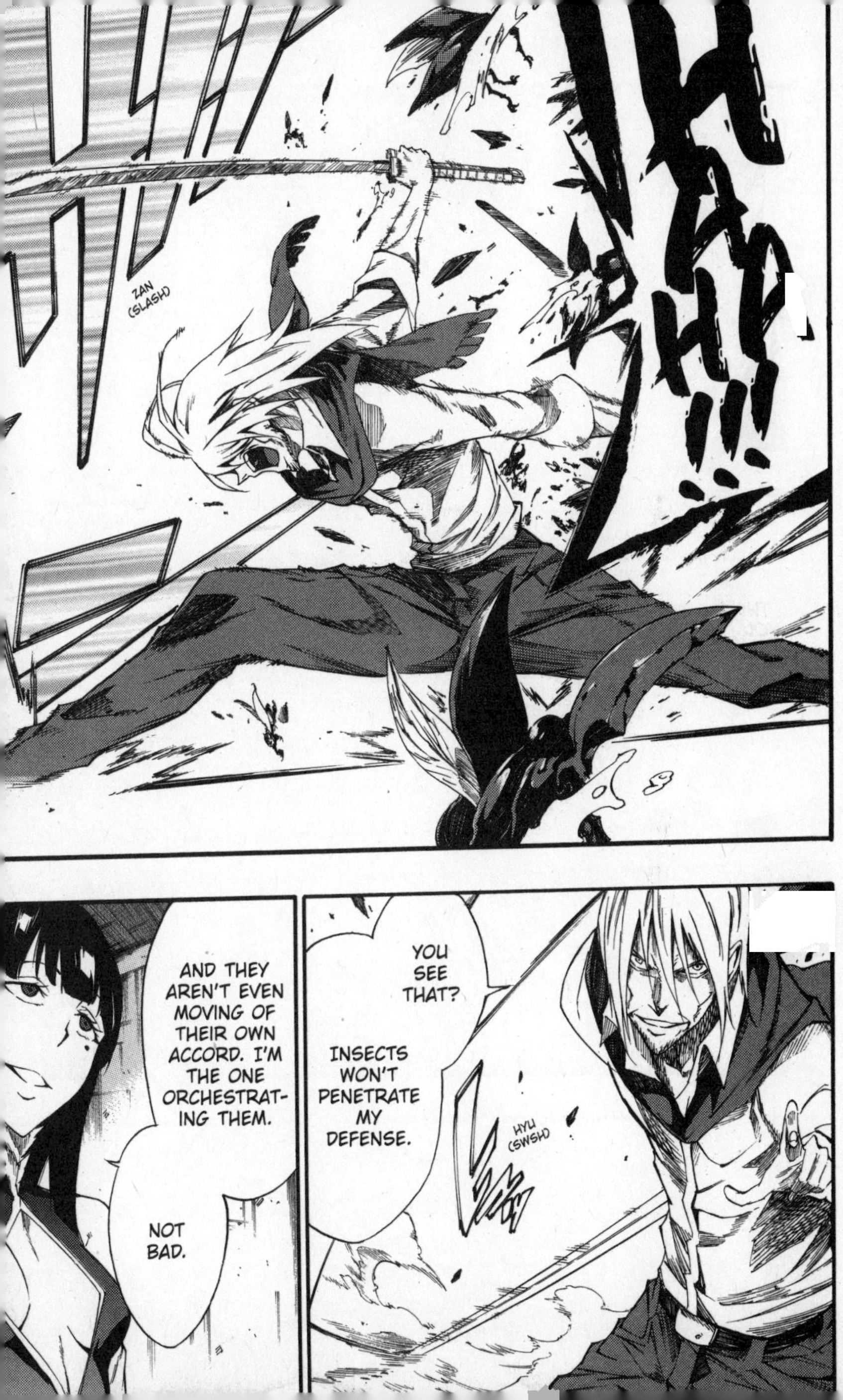
ZAN (SLASH)
YOU SEE THAT?
INSECTS WON'T PENETRATE MY DEFENSE.
HYU (SWSH)
AND THEY AREN'T EVEN MOVING OF THEIR OWN ACCORD. I'M THE ONE ORCHESTRATING THEM.
NOT BAD.

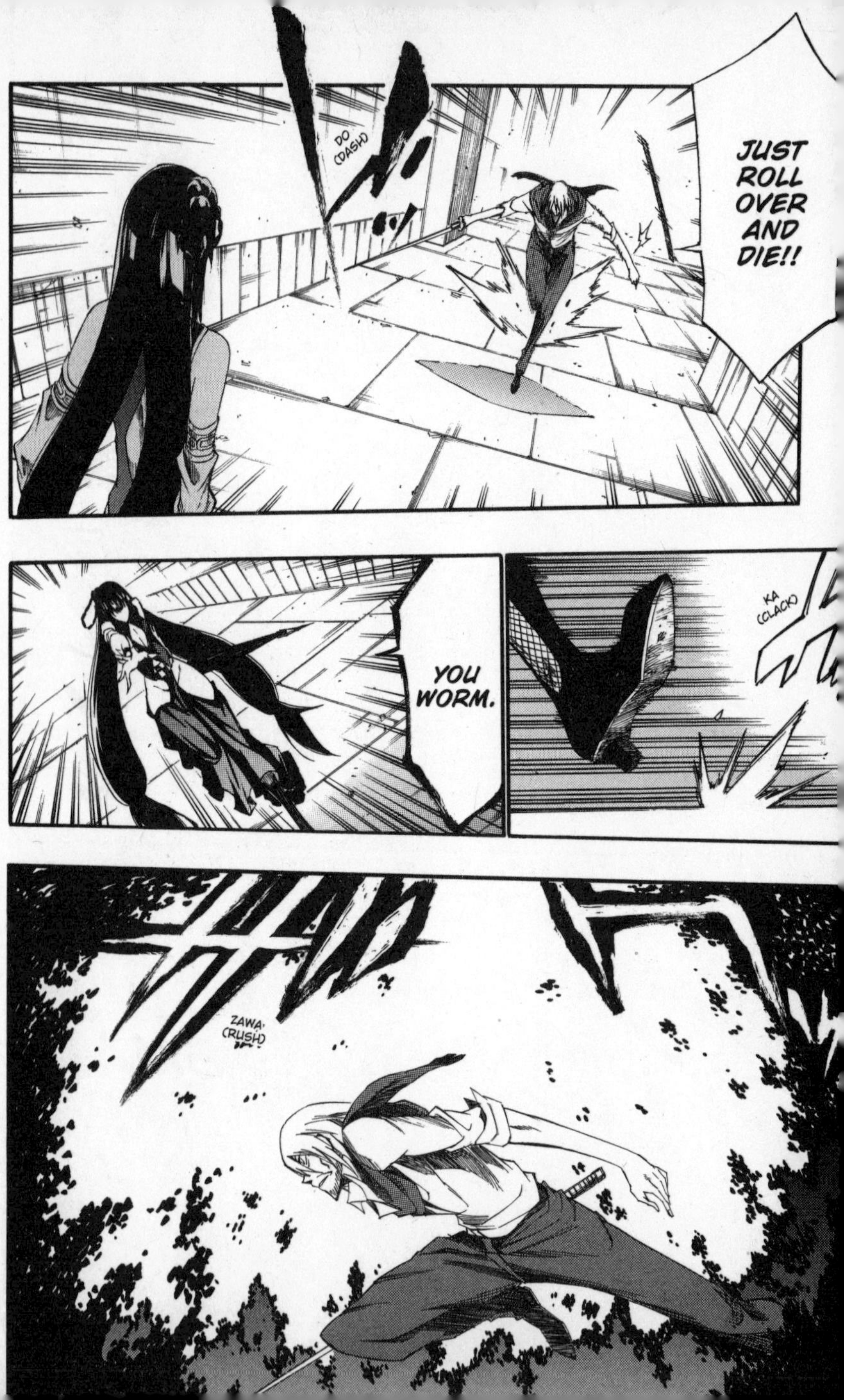
JUST ROLL OVER AND DIE!!
DO (DASH)
KA (CLACK)
YOU WORM.
ZAWA (CRUSH)

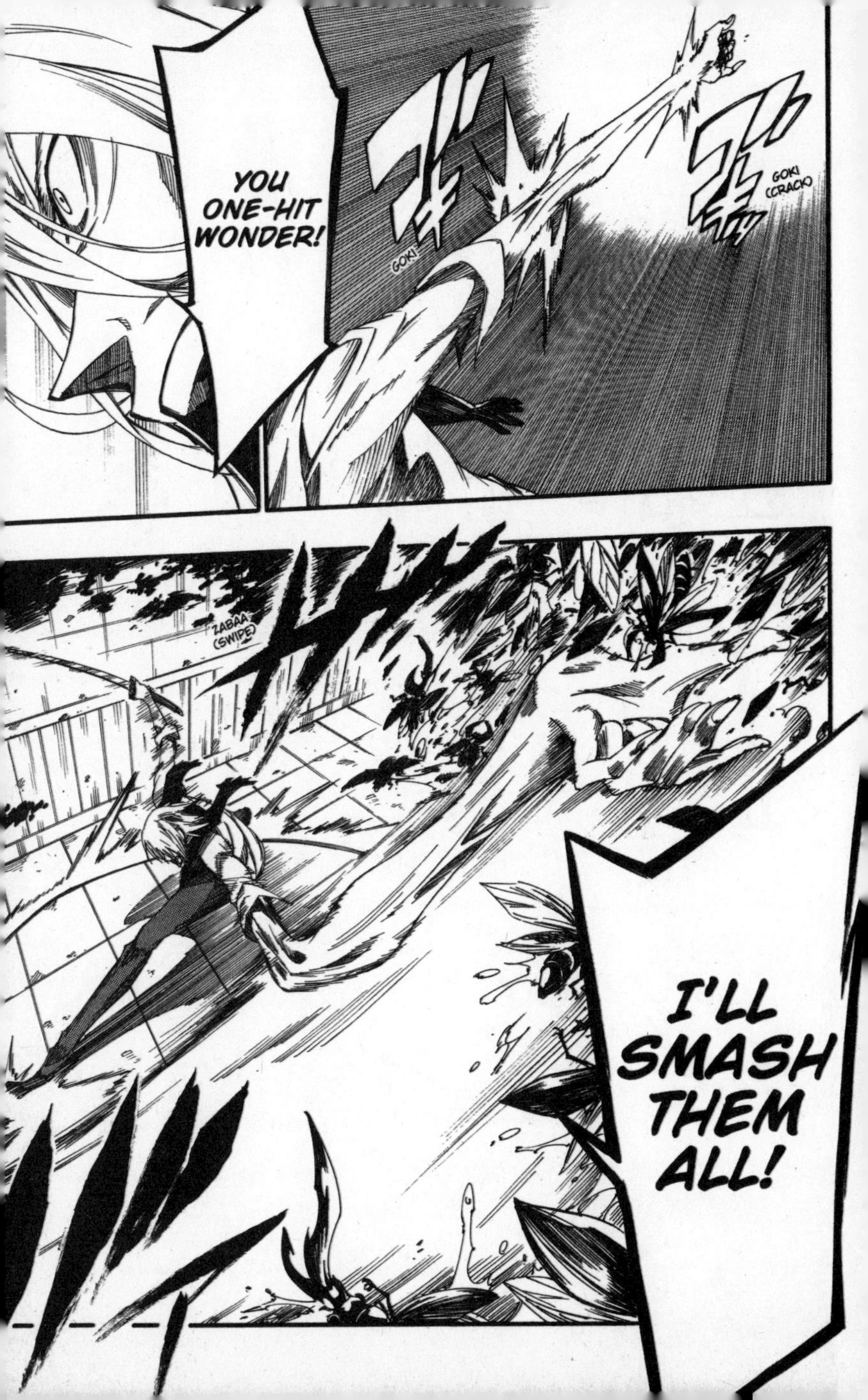
GOKI (CRACK)
GOKI!
YOU ONE-HIT WONDER!
I'LL SMASH THEM ALL!
ZABAA (SWIPE)

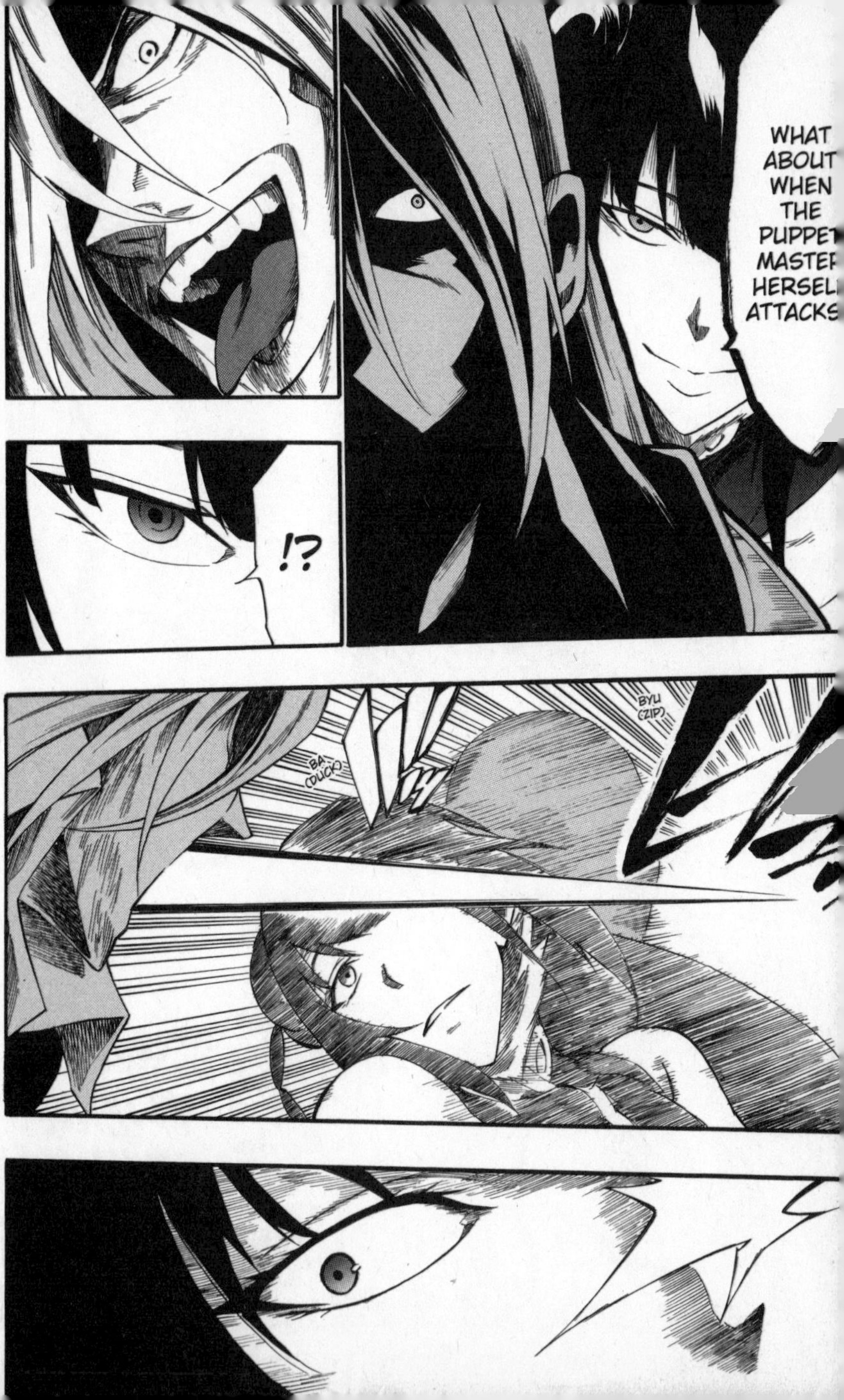
WHAT ABOUT WHEN THE PUPPET MASTER HERSELF ATTACKS
!?
BYU (ZIP)
BA (DUCK)

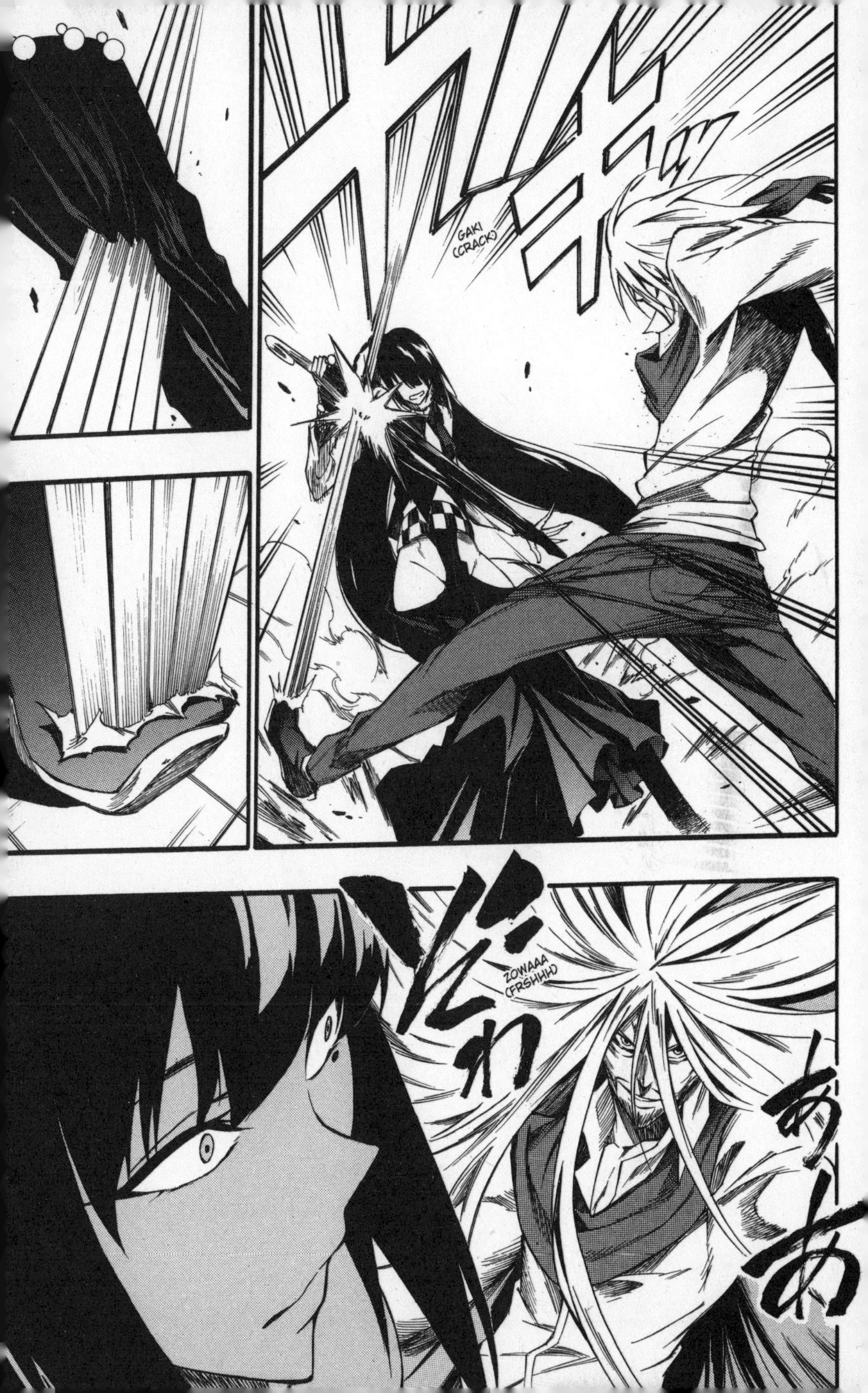
GAKI (CRACK)
ZOWAAA (FRSHHH)

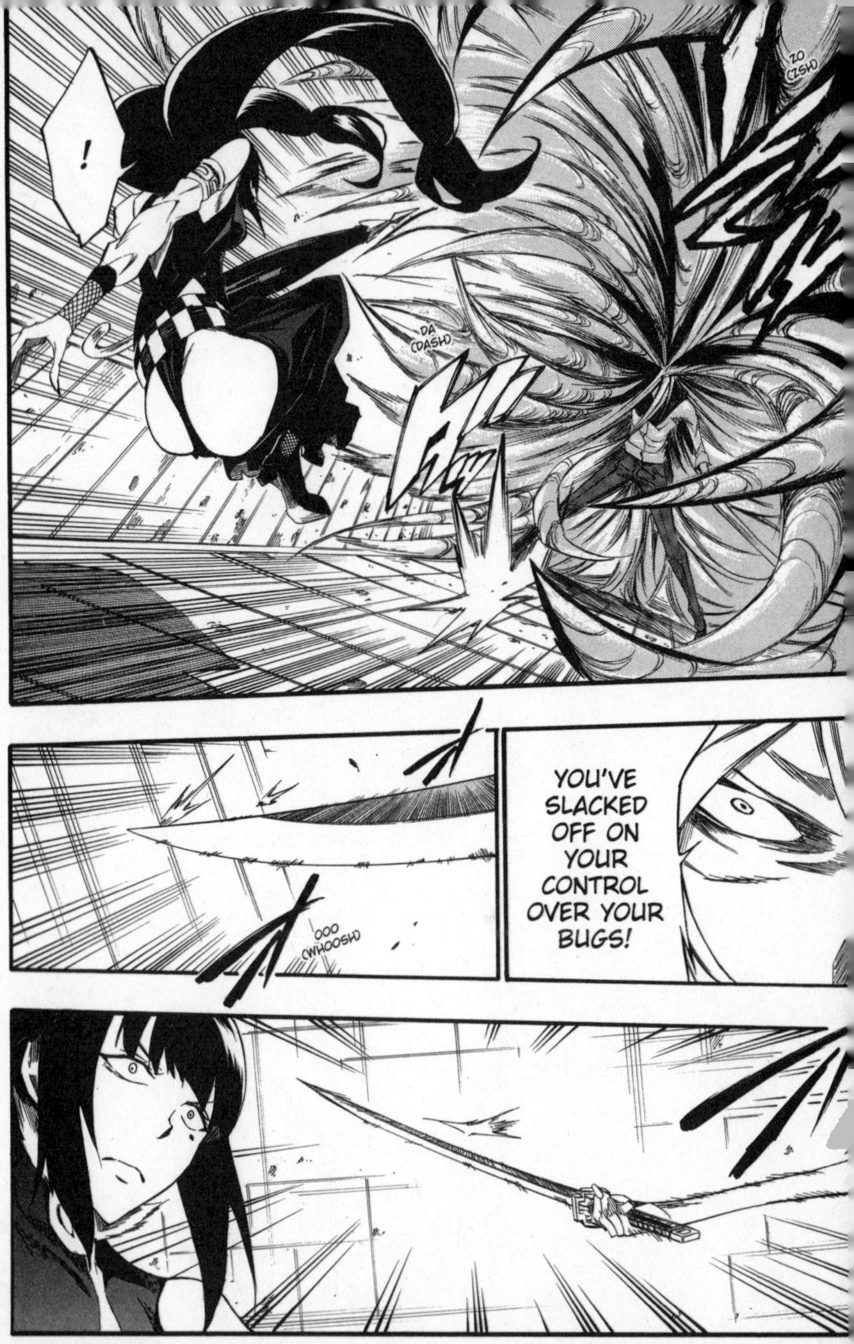
ZO (ZSH)
DA (DASH)
!
YOU'VE SLACKED OFF ON YOUR CONTROL OVER YOUR BUGS!
OOO (WHOOSH)

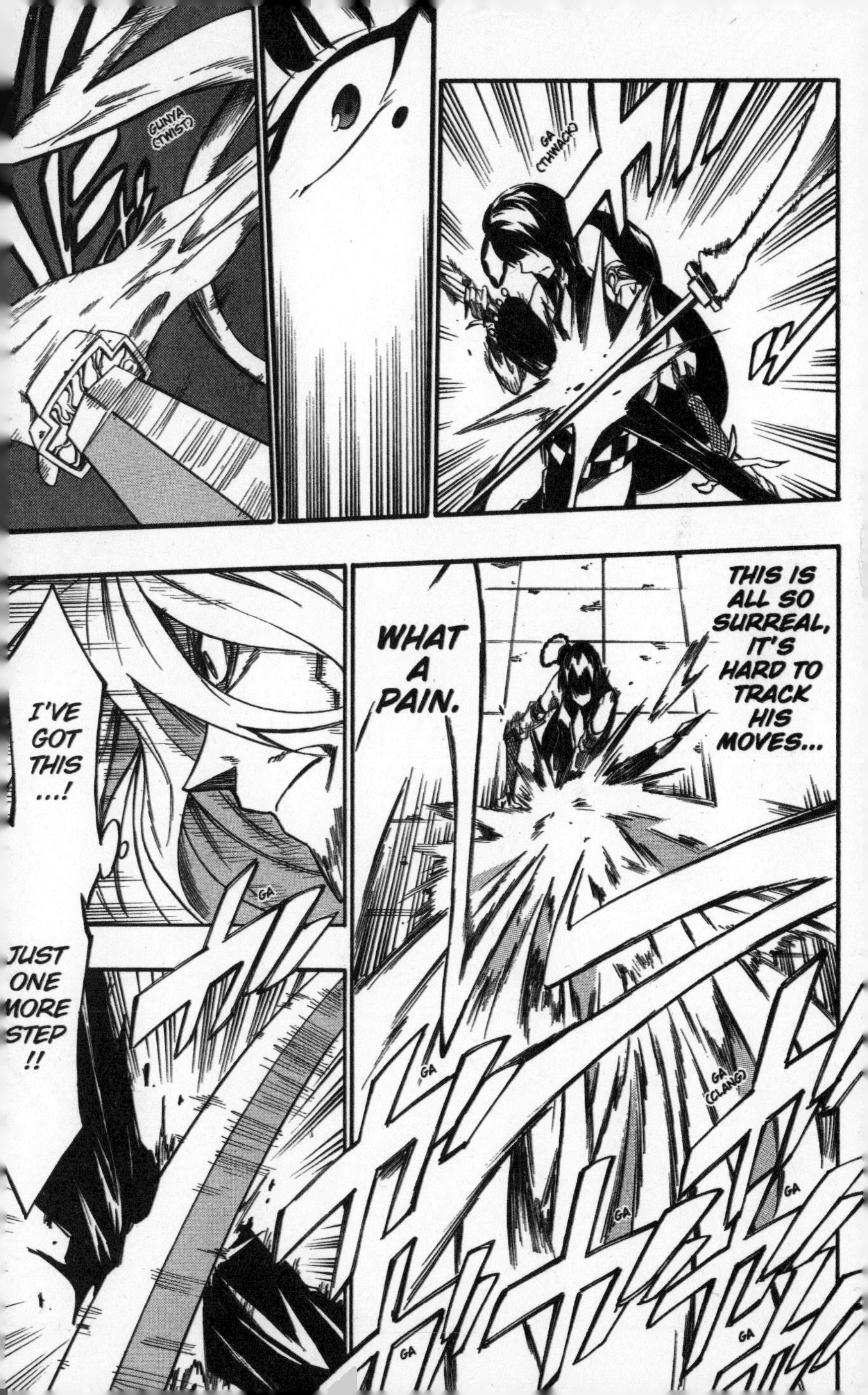
GA (THWACK)
GUNYA (TWIST)
THIS IS ALL SO SURREAL, IT'S HARD TO TRACK HIS MOVES...
WHAT A PAIN.
I'VE GOT THIS ...!
JUST ONE MORE STEP !!
GA
GA
GA (CLANG)
GA
GA
GA
GA

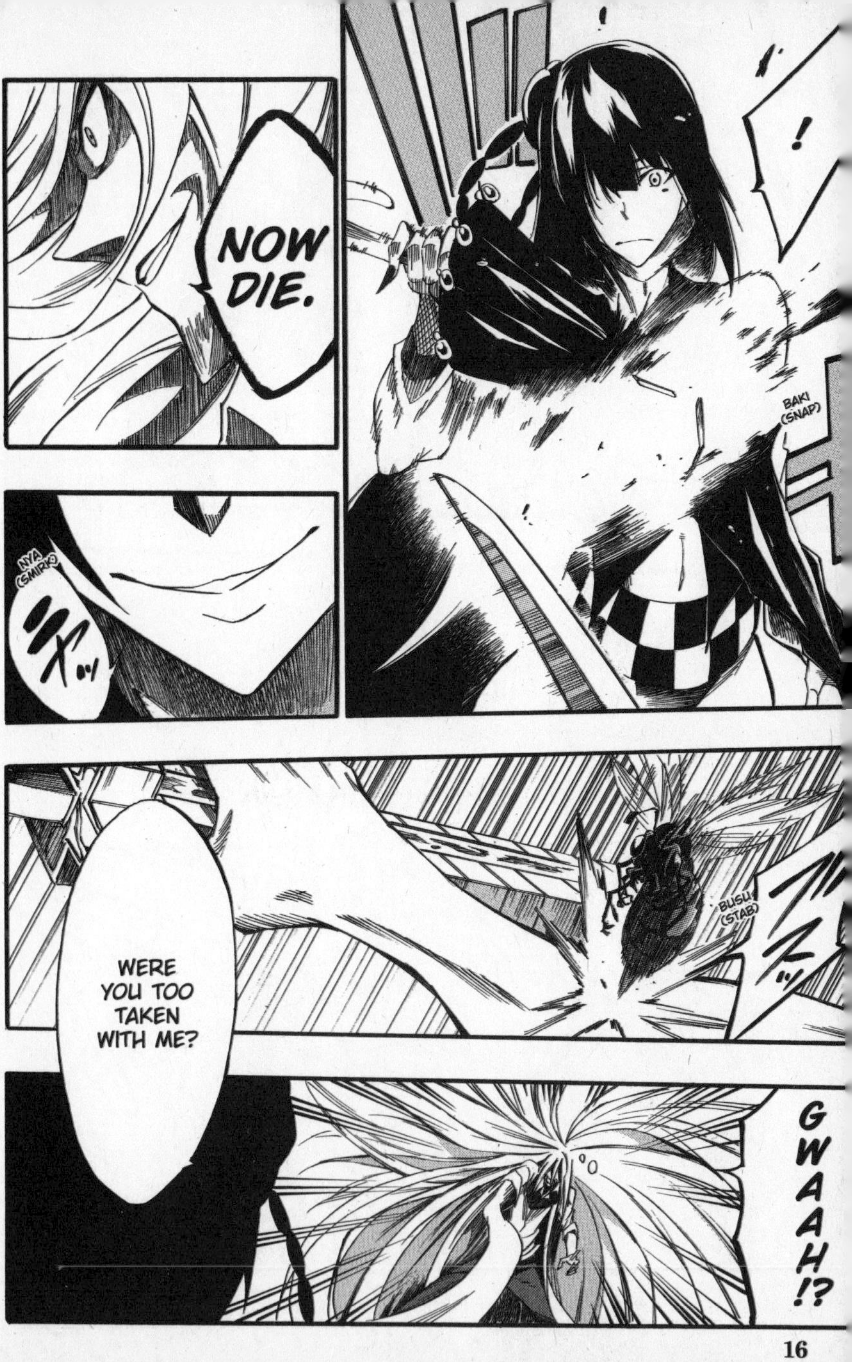
!
BAKI (SNAP)
NOW DIE.
NYA (SMIRK)
BUSU (STAB)
WERE YOU TOO TAKEN WITH ME?
GWAAAH!?

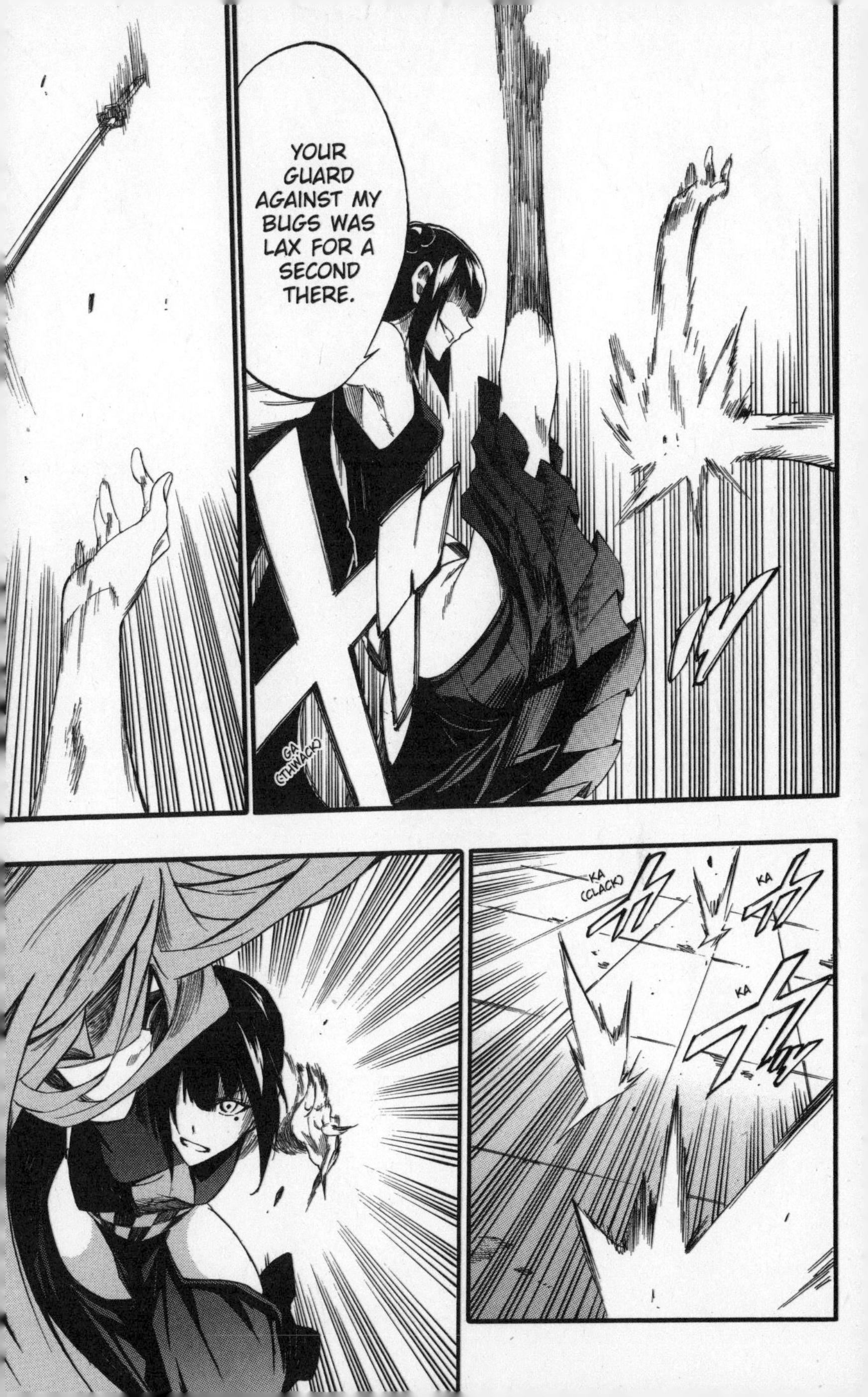
YOUR GUARD AGAINST MY BUGS WAS LAX FOR A SECOND THERE.
GA (THWACK)
KA (CLACK)
KA
KA

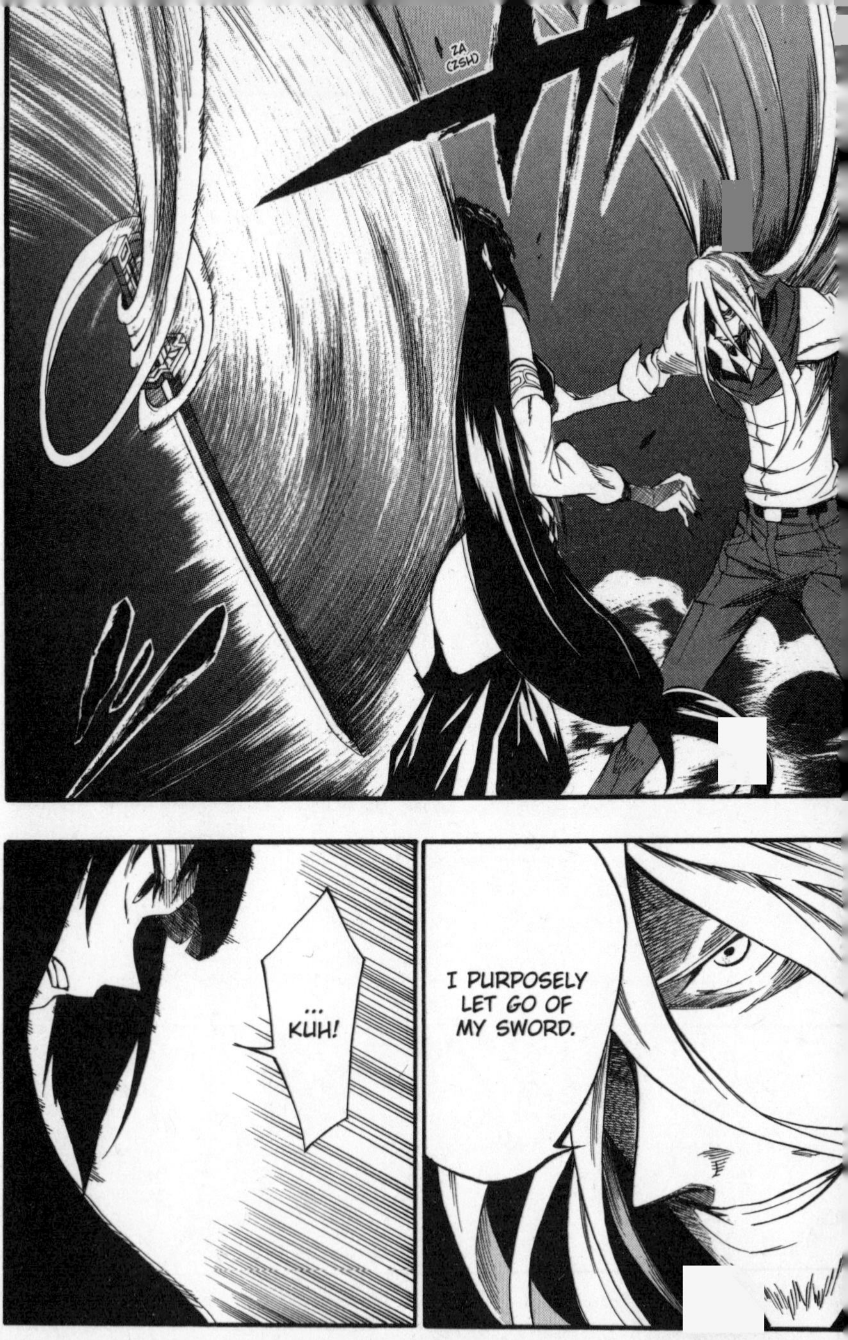
ZA
(ZSH)
I PURPOSELY LET GO OF MY SWORD.
... KUH!

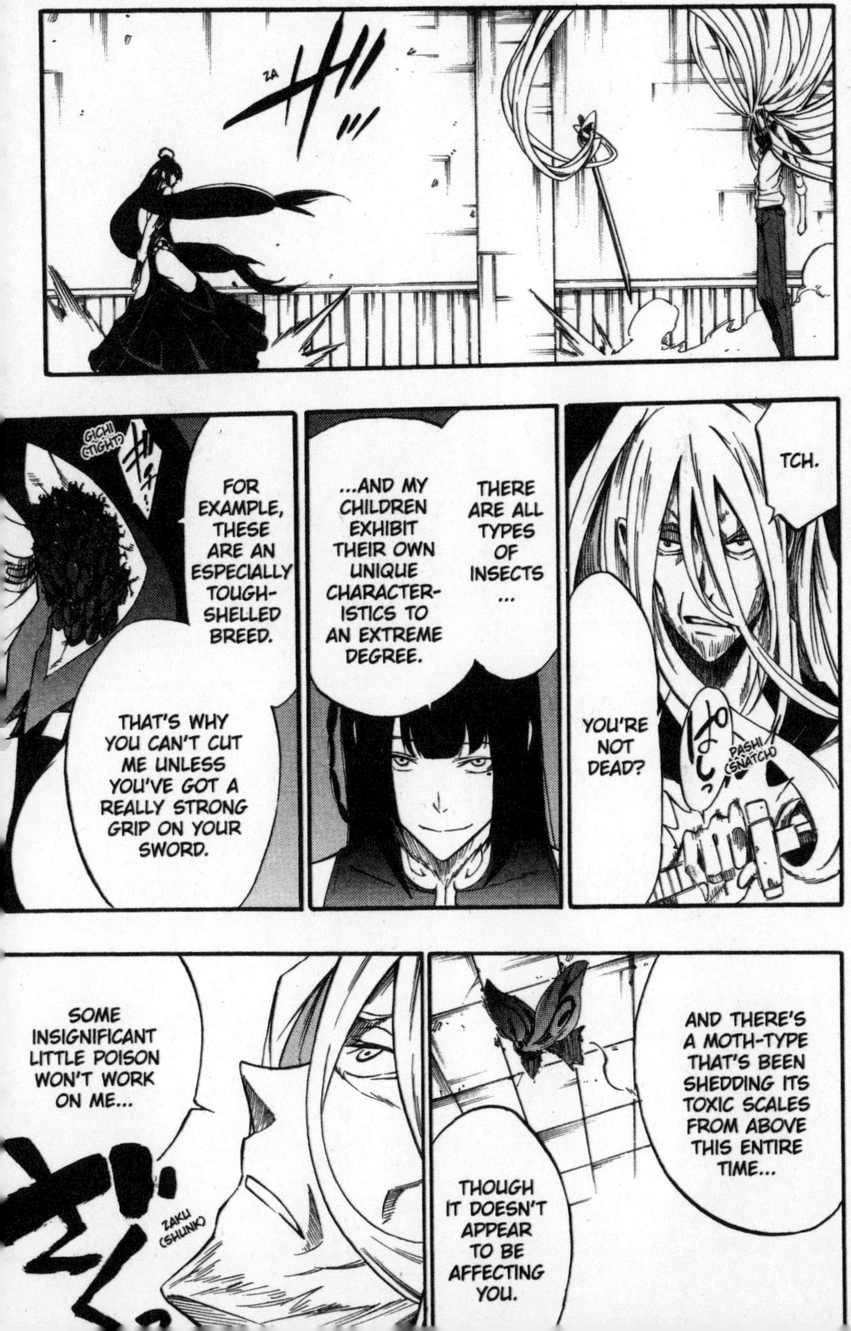
ZA
TCH.
YOU'RE NOT DEAD?
PASHI (SNATCH)
THERE ARE ALL TYPES OF INSECTS...
...AND MY CHILDREN EXHIBIT THEIR OWN UNIQUE CHARACTER-ISTICS TO AN EXTREME DEGREE.
GICHI (TIGHT)
FOR EXAMPLE, THESE ARE AN ESPECIALLY TOUGH-SHELLED BREED.
THAT'S WHY YOU CAN'T CUT ME UNLESS YOU'VE GOT A REALLY STRONG GRIP ON YOUR SWORD.
AND THERE'S A MOTH-TYPE THAT'S BEEN SHEDDING ITS TOXIC SCALES FROM ABOVE THIS ENTIRE TIME...
THOUGH IT DOESN'T APPEAR TO BE AFFECTING YOU.
SOME INSIGNIFICANT LITTLE POISON WON'T WORK ON ME...
ZAKU (SHUNK)

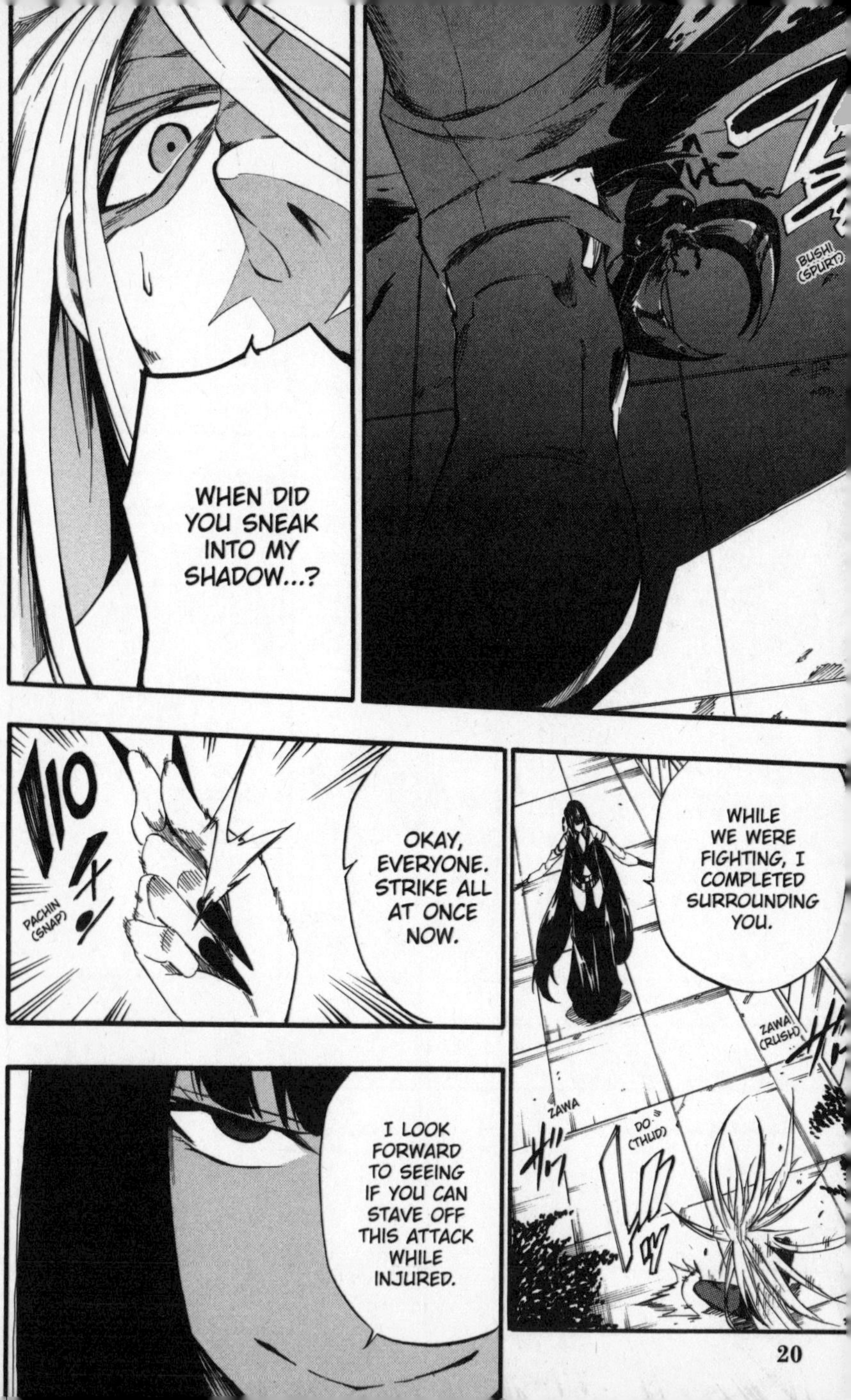
BUSHI (SPURT)
WHEN DID YOU SNEAK INTO MY SHADOW...?
WHILE WE WERE FIGHTING, I COMPLETED SURROUNDING YOU.
ZAWA (RUSH)
ZAWA
DO (THUD)
OKAY, EVERYONE. STRIKE ALL AT ONCE NOW.
PACHIN (SNAP)
I LOOK FORWARD TO SEEING IF YOU CAN STAVE OFF THIS ATTACK WHILE INJURED.

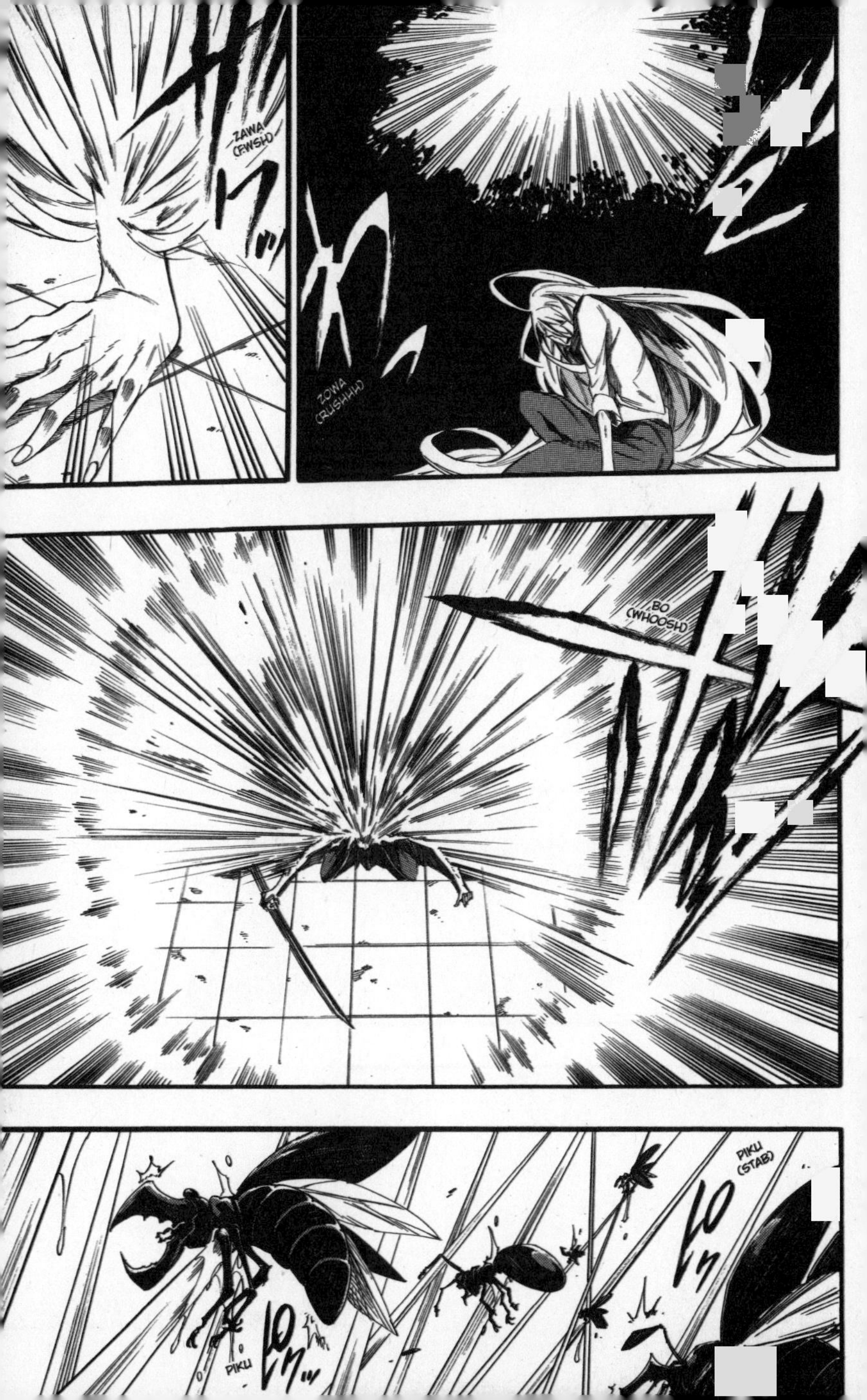
ZOWA
(RUSHHH)
ZAWA
(FWSH)
BO
(WHOOSH)
PIKU
(STAB)
PIKU

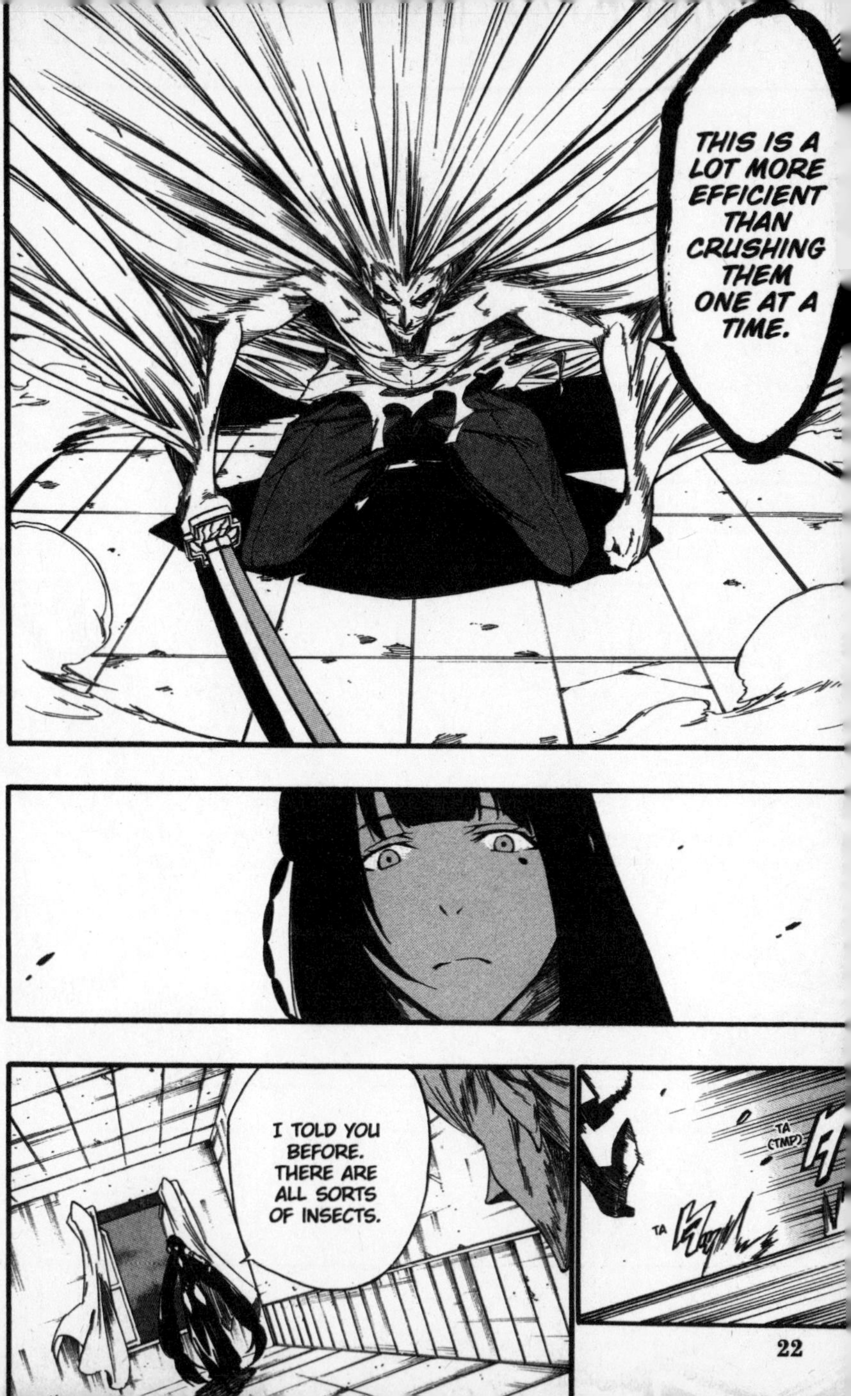
THIS IS A LOT MORE EFFICIENT THAN CRUSHING THEM ONE AT A TIME.
I TOLD YOU BEFORE. THERE ARE ALL SORTS OF INSECTS.
TA (TMP)
TA

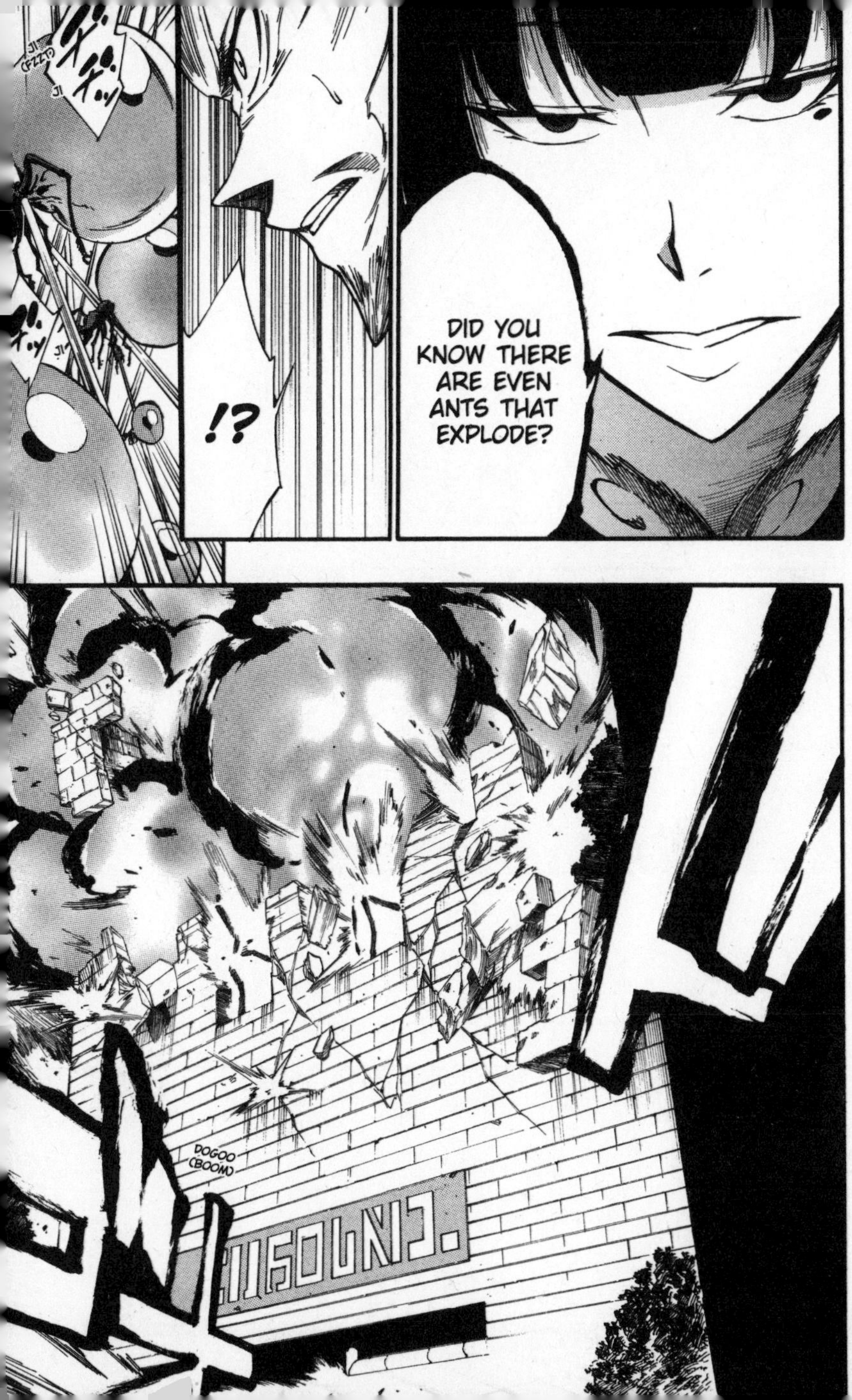
DID YOU KNOW THERE ARE EVEN ANTS THAT EXPLODE?
!?
JI (FZZT)
JI
JI
DOGOO (BOOM)

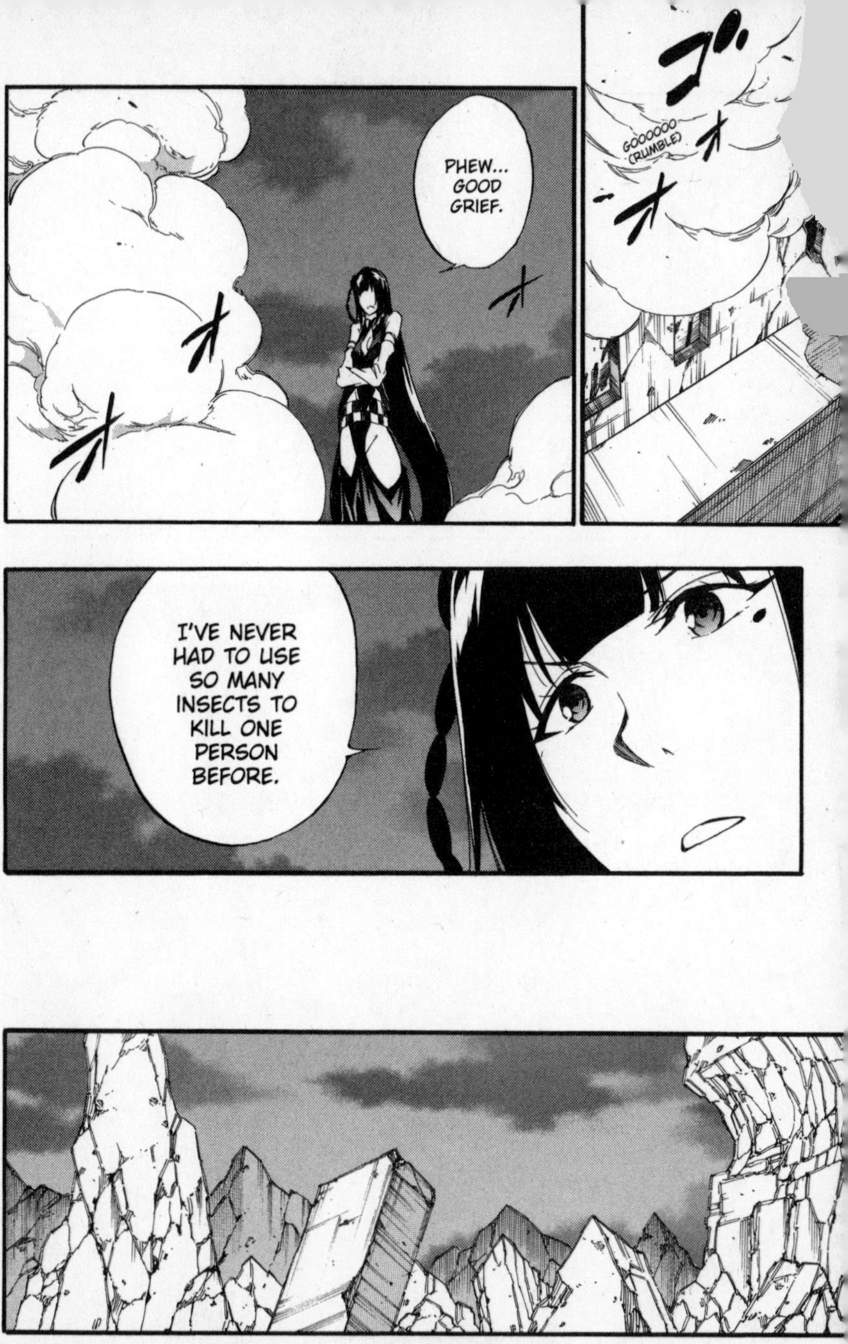

GOOOOOO (RUMBLE)
PHEW... GOOD GRIEF.
I'VE NEVER HAD TO USE SO MANY INSECTS TO KILL ONE PERSON BEFORE.

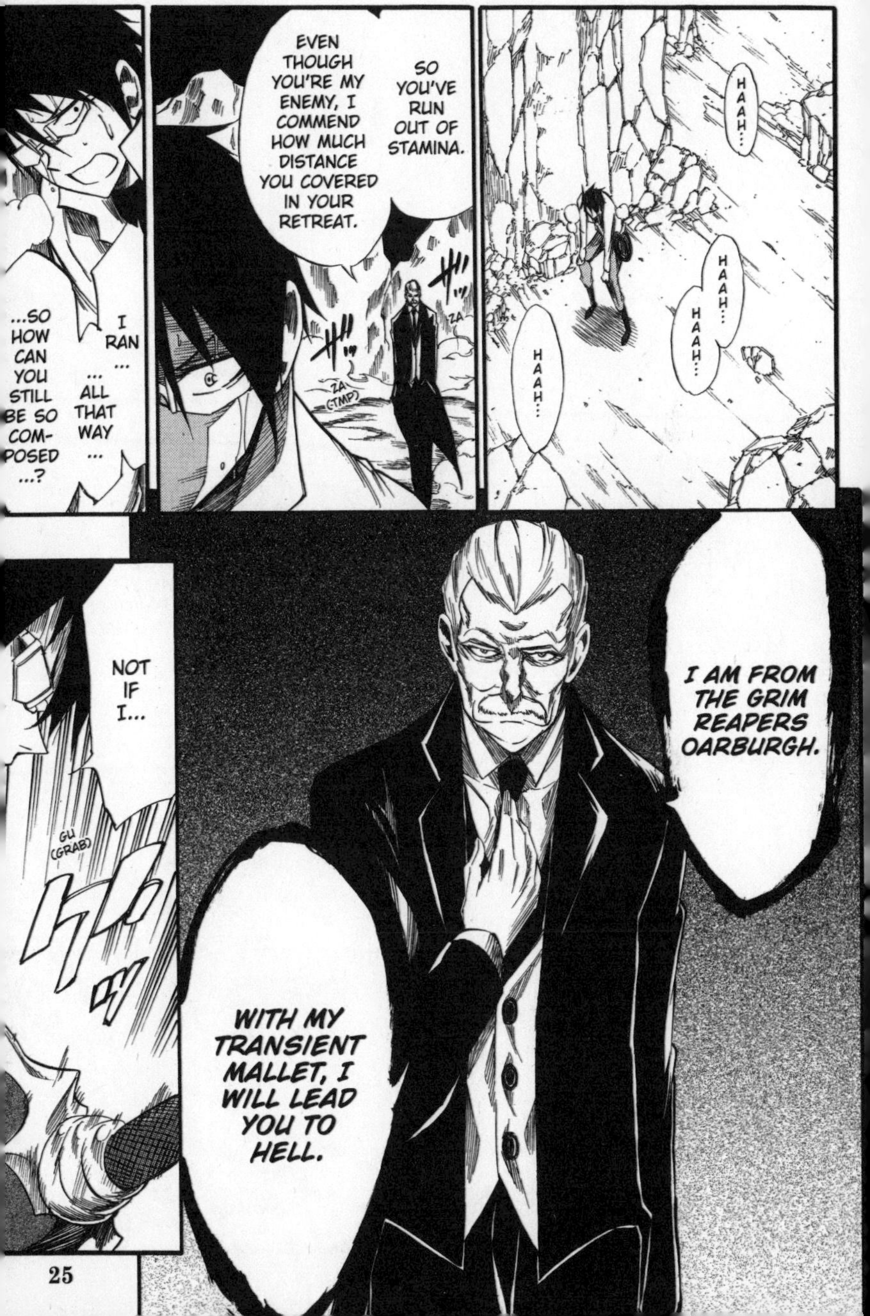
HAAH...
HAAH...
HAAH...
HAAH...
SO YOU'VE RUN OUT OF STAMINA.
EVEN THOUGH YOU'RE MY ENEMY, I COMMEND HOW MUCH DISTANCE YOU COVERED IN YOUR RETREAT.
ZA
ZA (TMP)
I RAN... ...ALL THAT WAY...
...SO HOW CAN YOU STILL BE SO COMPOSED...?
I AM FROM THE GRIM REAPERS OARBURGH.
WITH MY TRANSIENT MALLET, I WILL LEAD YOU TO HELL.
NOT IF I...
GU (GRAB)

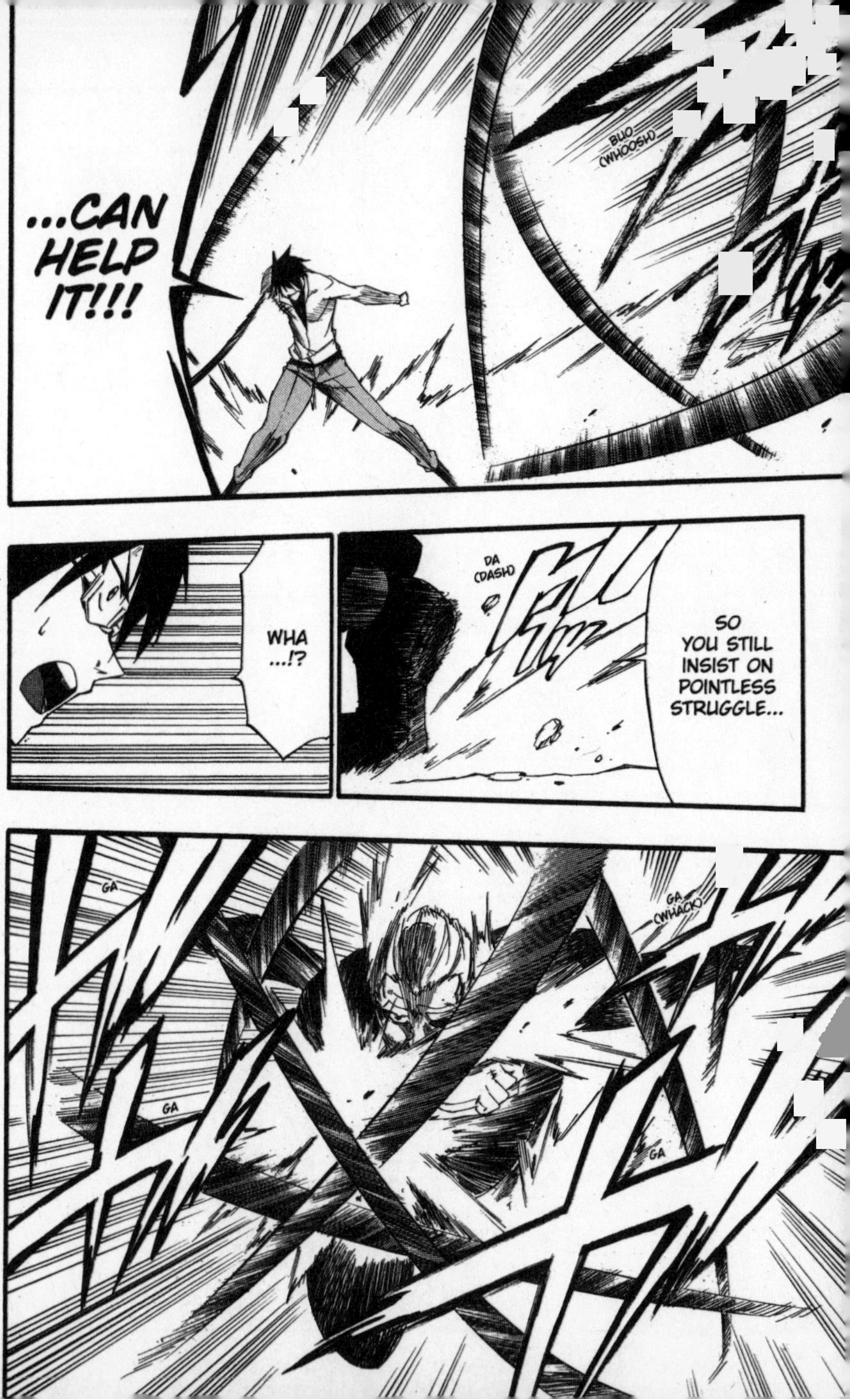
BUO (WHOOSH)
...CAN HELP IT!!!
SO YOU STILL INSIST ON POINTLESS STRUGGLE...
DA (DASH)
WHA ...!?
GA (WHACK)
GA
GA
GA

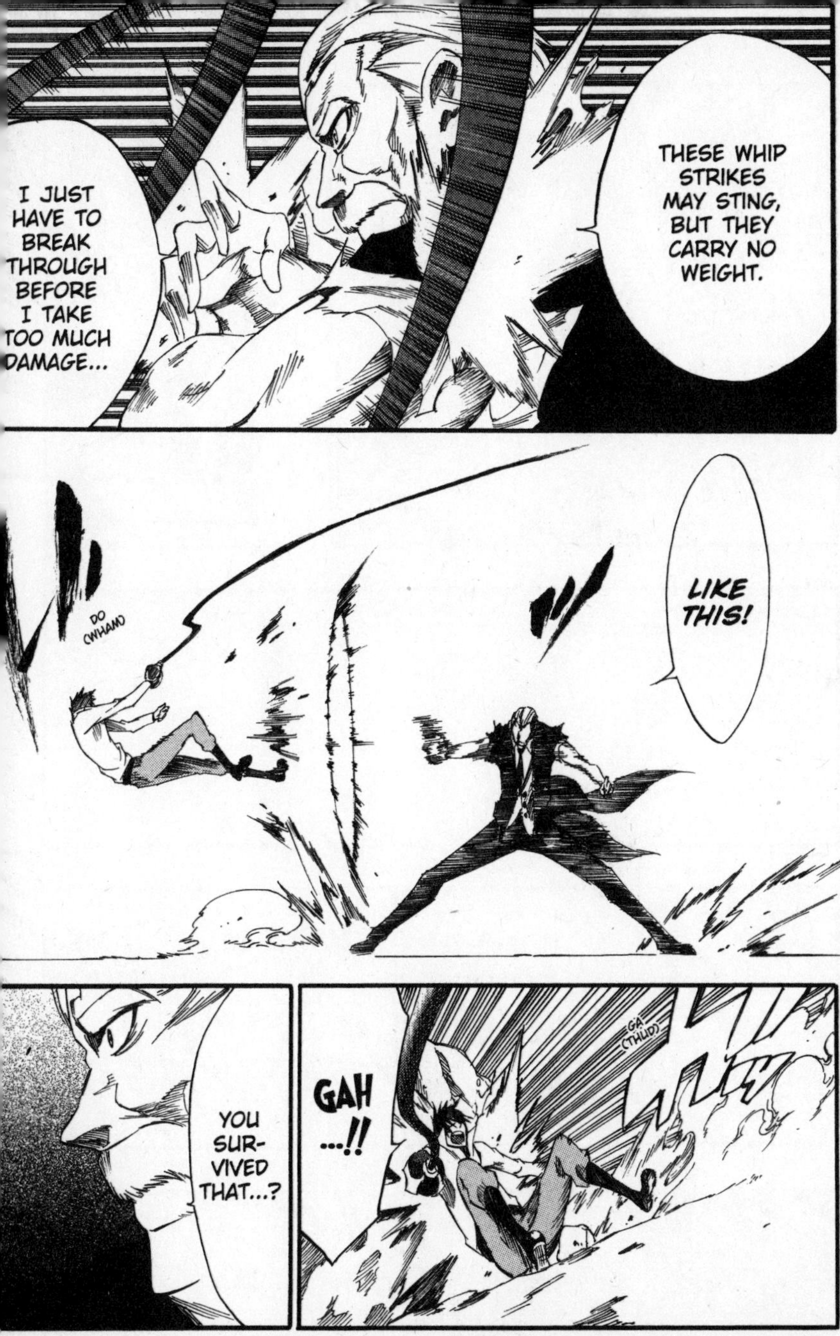

THESE WHIP STRIKES MAY STING, BUT THEY CARRY NO WEIGHT.
I JUST HAVE TO BREAK THROUGH BEFORE I TAKE TOO MUCH DAMAGE...
LIKE THIS!
DO (WHAM)
GA (THUD)
GAH ...!!
YOU SURVIVED THAT...?

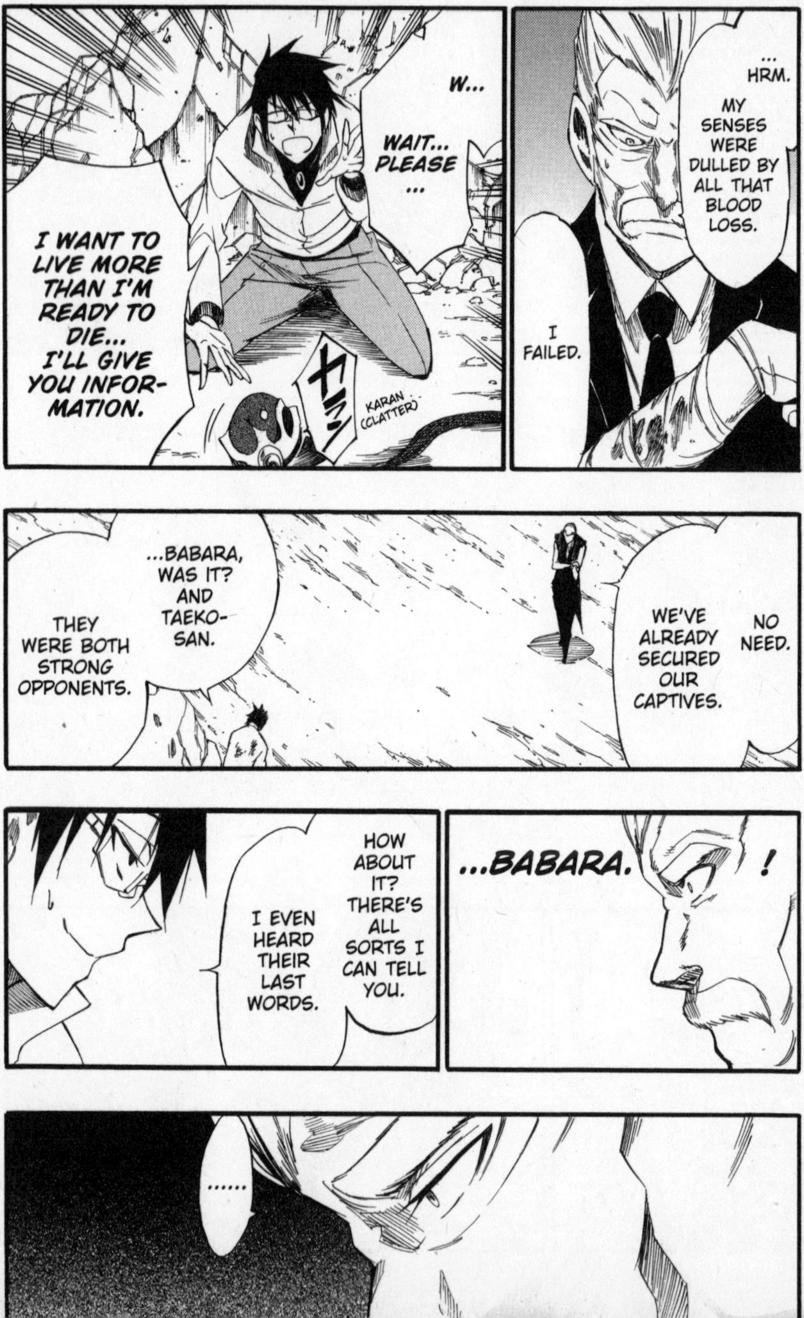

... HRM.
MY SENSES WERE DULLED BY ALL THAT BLOOD LOSS.
I FAILED.
W...
WAIT... PLEASE ...
I WANT TO LIVE MORE THAN I'M READY TO DIE... I'LL GIVE YOU INFORMATION.
KARAN (CLATTER)
NO NEED.
WE'VE ALREADY SECURED OUR CAPTIVES.
...BABARA, WAS IT? AND TAEKO-SAN.
THEY WERE BOTH STRONG OPPONENTS.
...BABARA.
!
HOW ABOUT IT? THERE'S ALL SORTS I CAN TELL YOU.
I EVEN HEARD THEIR LAST WORDS.
......

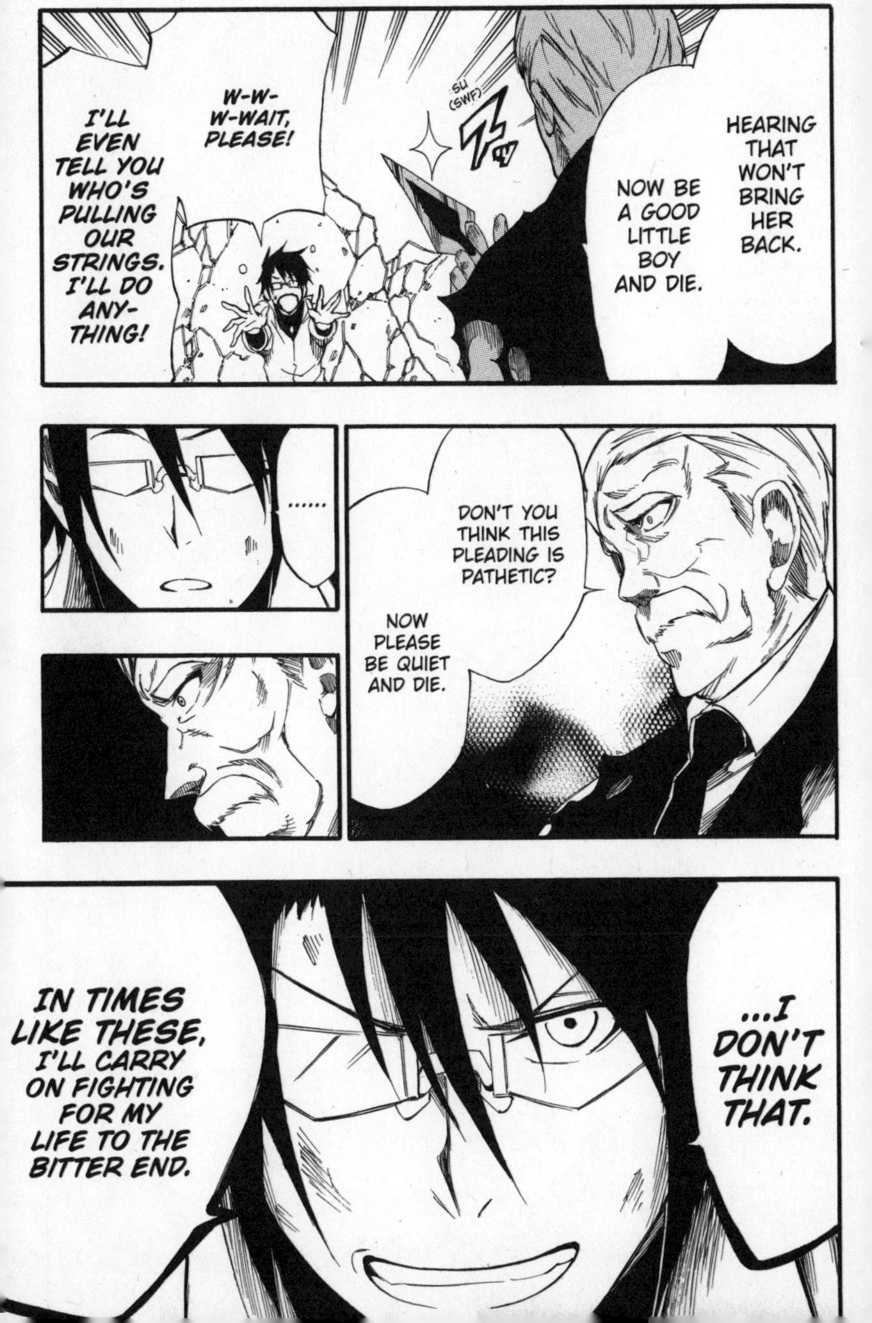
HEARING THAT WON'T BRING HER BACK.
NOW BE A GOOD LITTLE BOY AND DIE.
SU (SWF)
W-W-W-WAIT, PLEASE!
I'LL EVEN TELL YOU WHO'S PULLING OUR STRINGS. I'LL DO ANY-THING!
DON'T YOU THINK THIS PLEADING IS PATHETIC?
NOW PLEASE BE QUIET AND DIE.
......
...I DON'T THINK THAT.
IN TIMES LIKE THESE, I'LL CARRY ON FIGHTING FOR MY LIFE TO THE BITTER END.

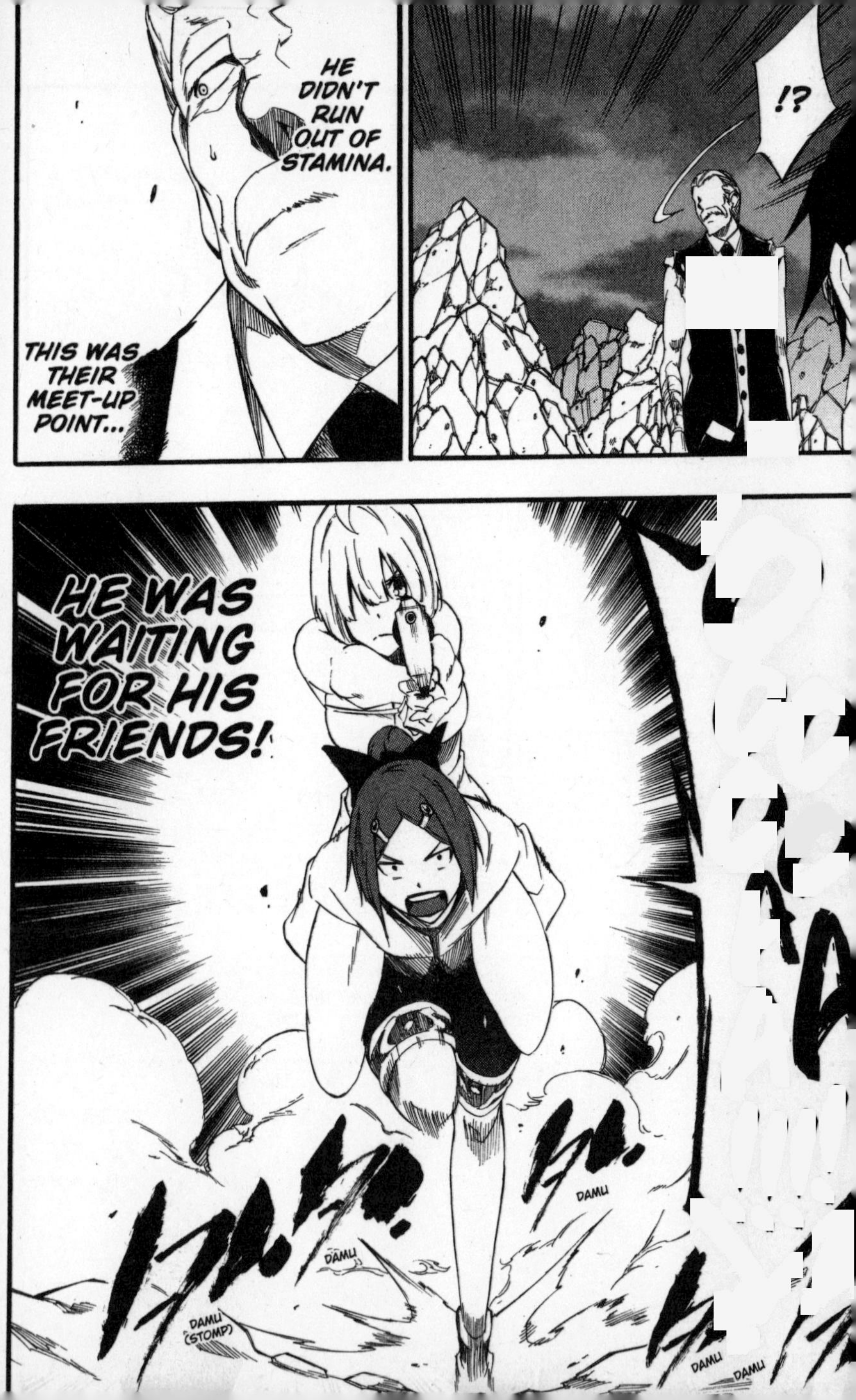
!?
HE DIDN'T RUN OUT OF STAMINA.
THIS WAS THEIR MEET-UP POINT...
HE WAS WAITING FOR HIS FRIENDS!
DAMU
DAMU
DAMU
DAMU
DAMU
DAMU (STOMP)

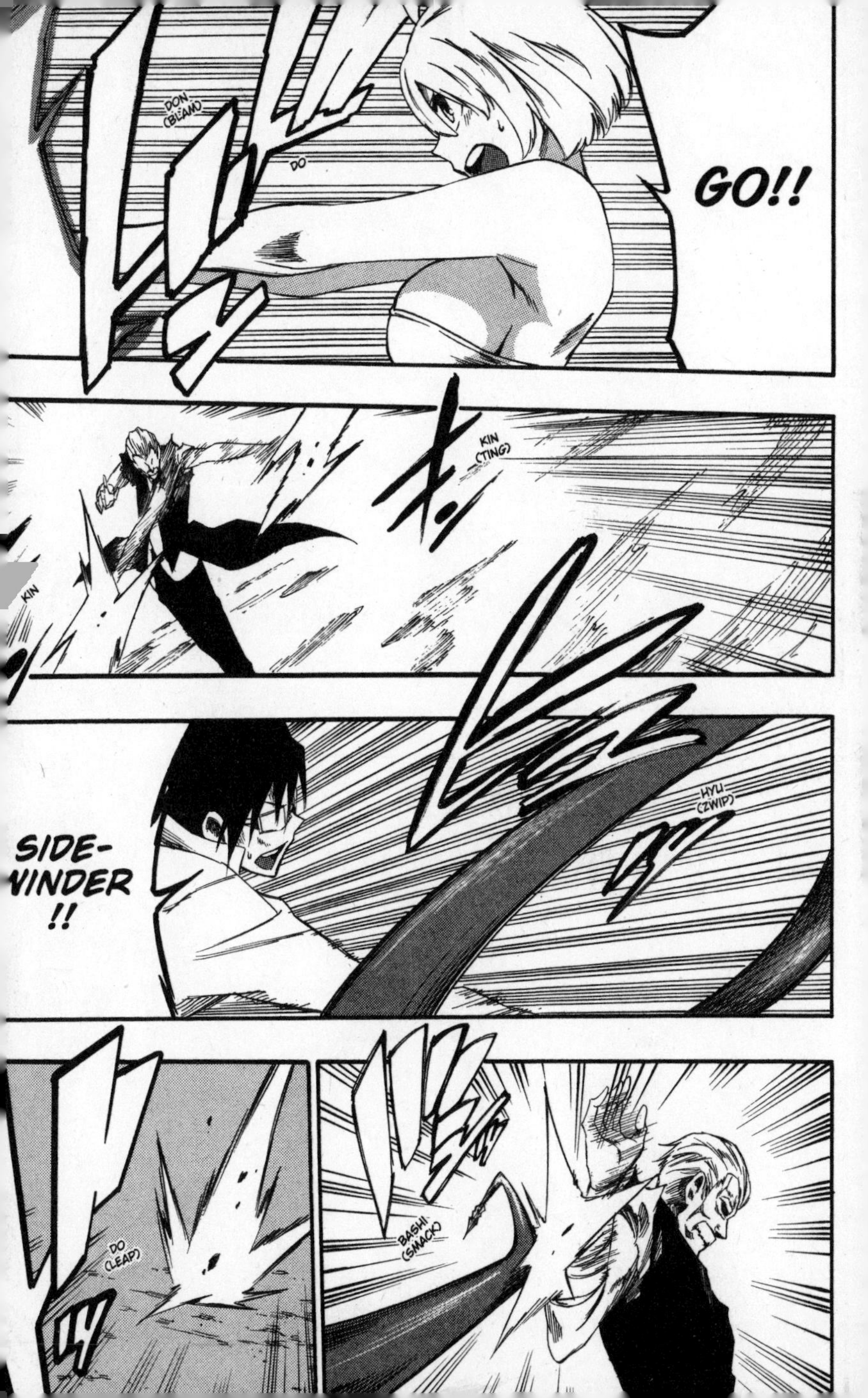
GO!!
DON (BLAM)
DO
KIN (TING)
KIN
SIDE-
WINDER
!!
HYU (ZWIP)
DO (LEAP)
BASHI (SMACK)

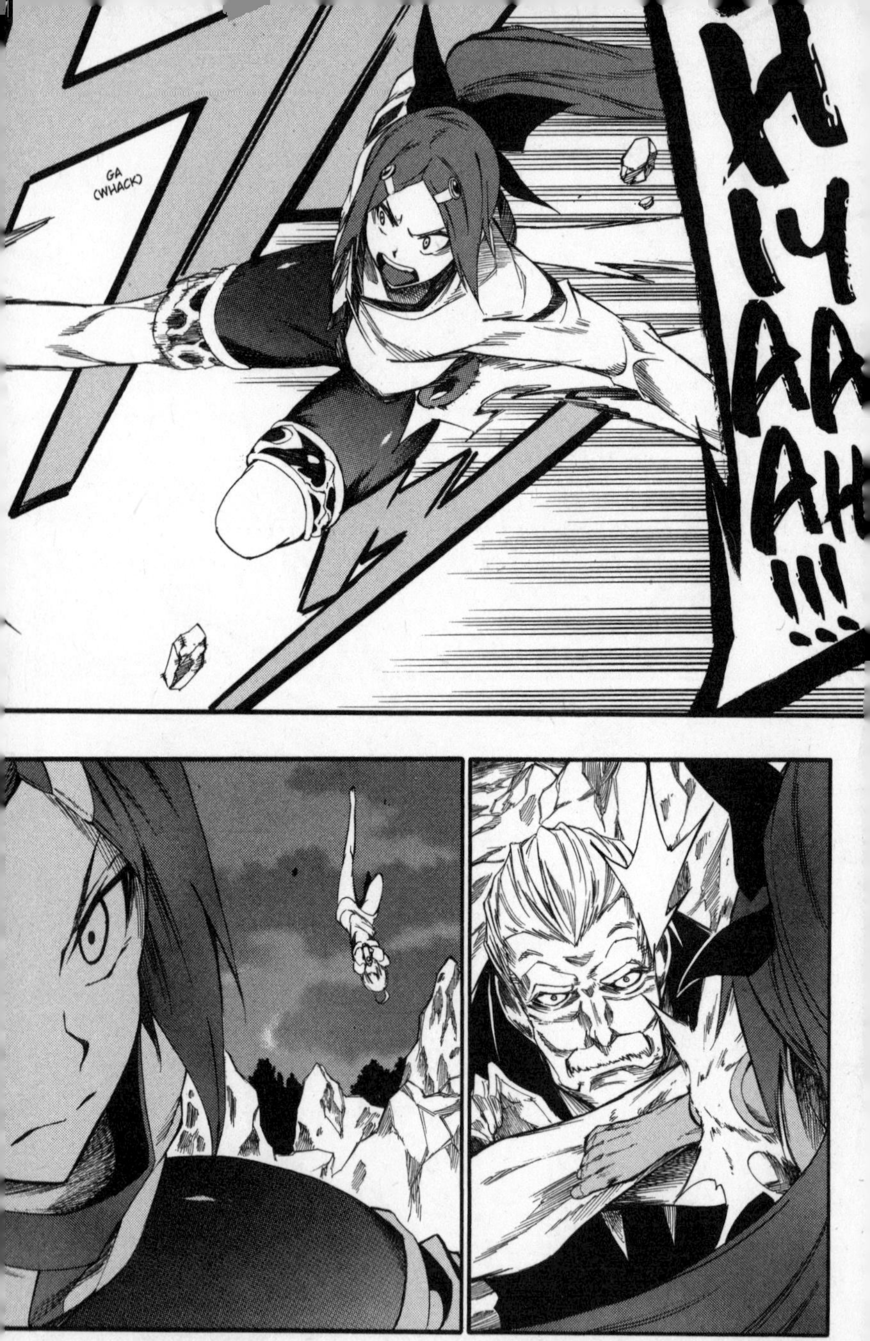
HIYAAAH!!!
GA
(WHACK)

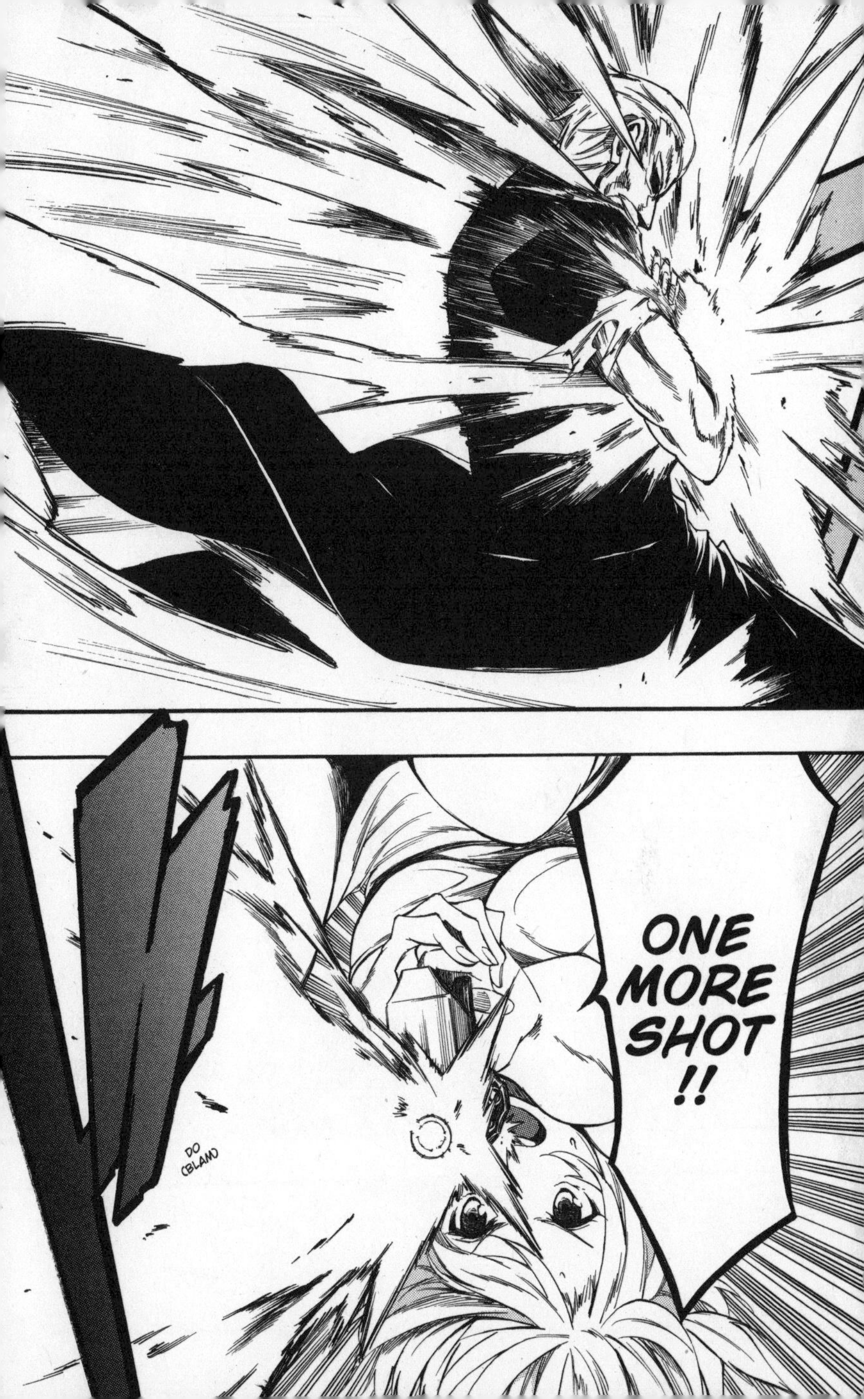
ONE MORE SHOT !!
DO (BLAM)

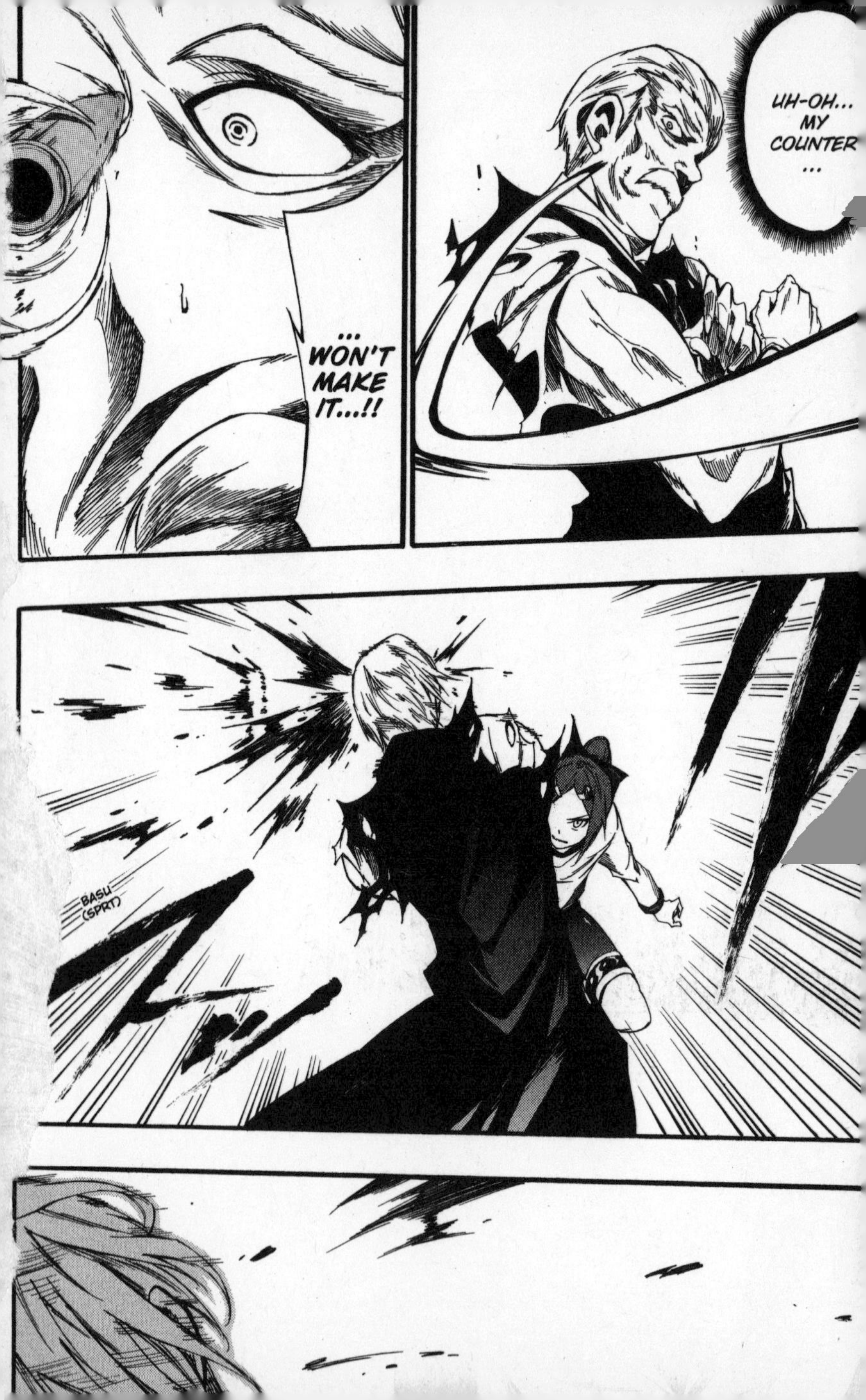
UH-OH... MY COUNTER ...
... WON'T MAKE IT...!!
BASU (SPRT)

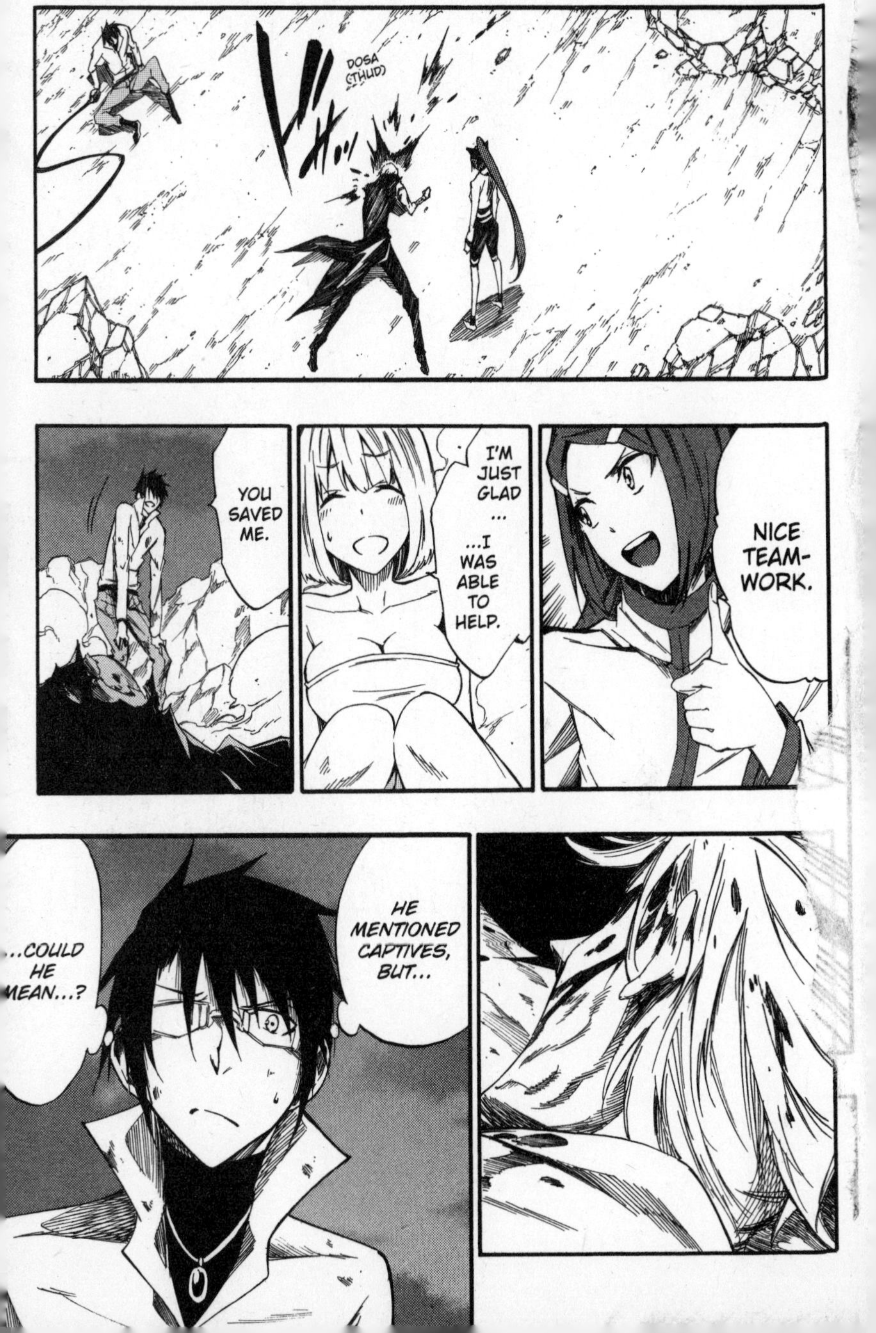
DOSA (THUD)
NICE TEAM-WORK.
I'M JUST GLAD ...
...I WAS ABLE TO HELP.
YOU SAVED ME.
HE MENTIONED CAPTIVES, BUT...
...COULD HE MEAN...?

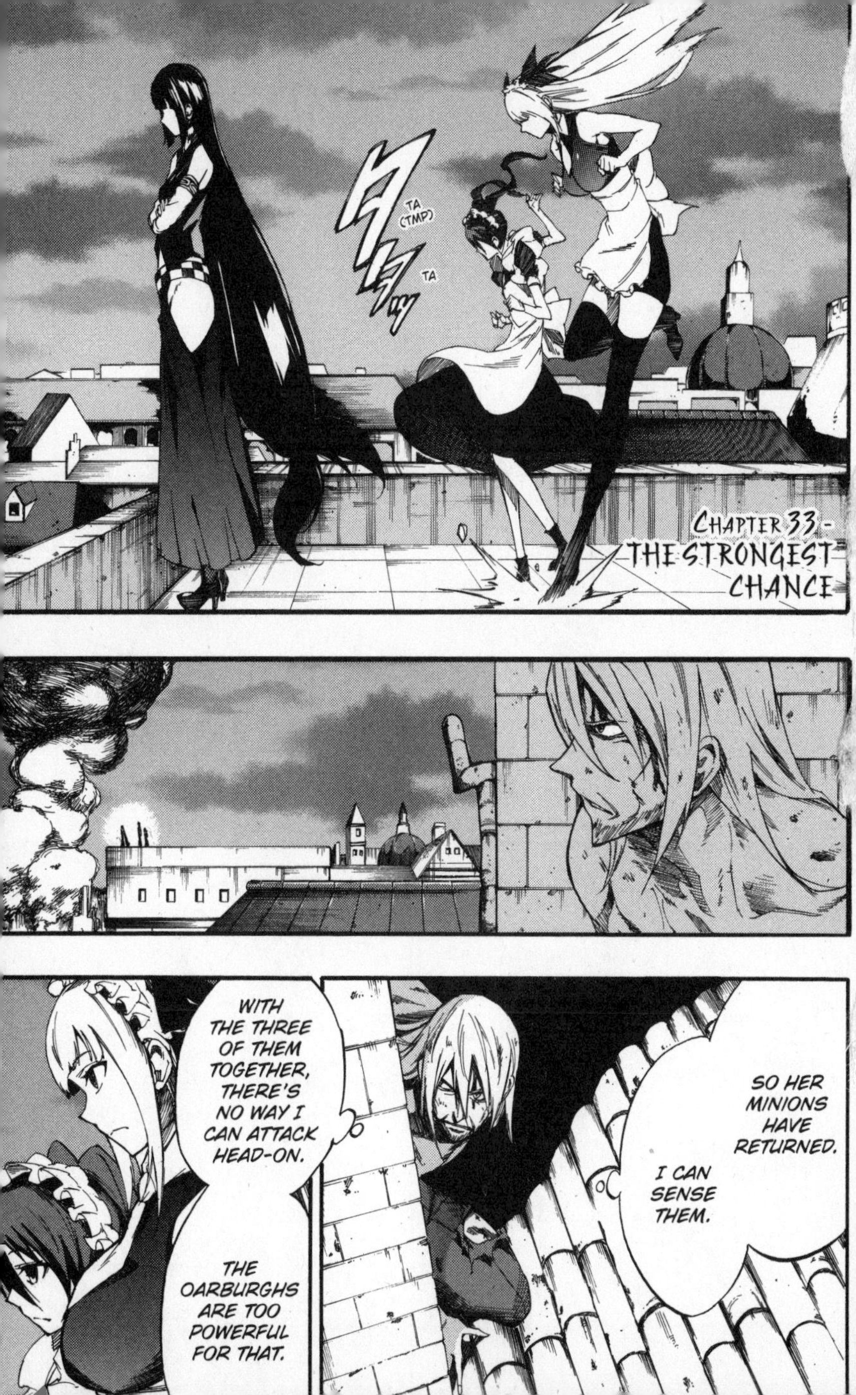

TA (TMP)
TA
CHAPTER 33 - THE STRONGEST CHANCE
SO HER MINIONS HAVE RETURNED.
I CAN SENSE THEM.
WITH THE THREE OF THEM TOGETHER, THERE'S NO WAY I CAN ATTACK HEAD-ON.
THE OARBURGHS ARE TOO POWERFUL FOR THAT.

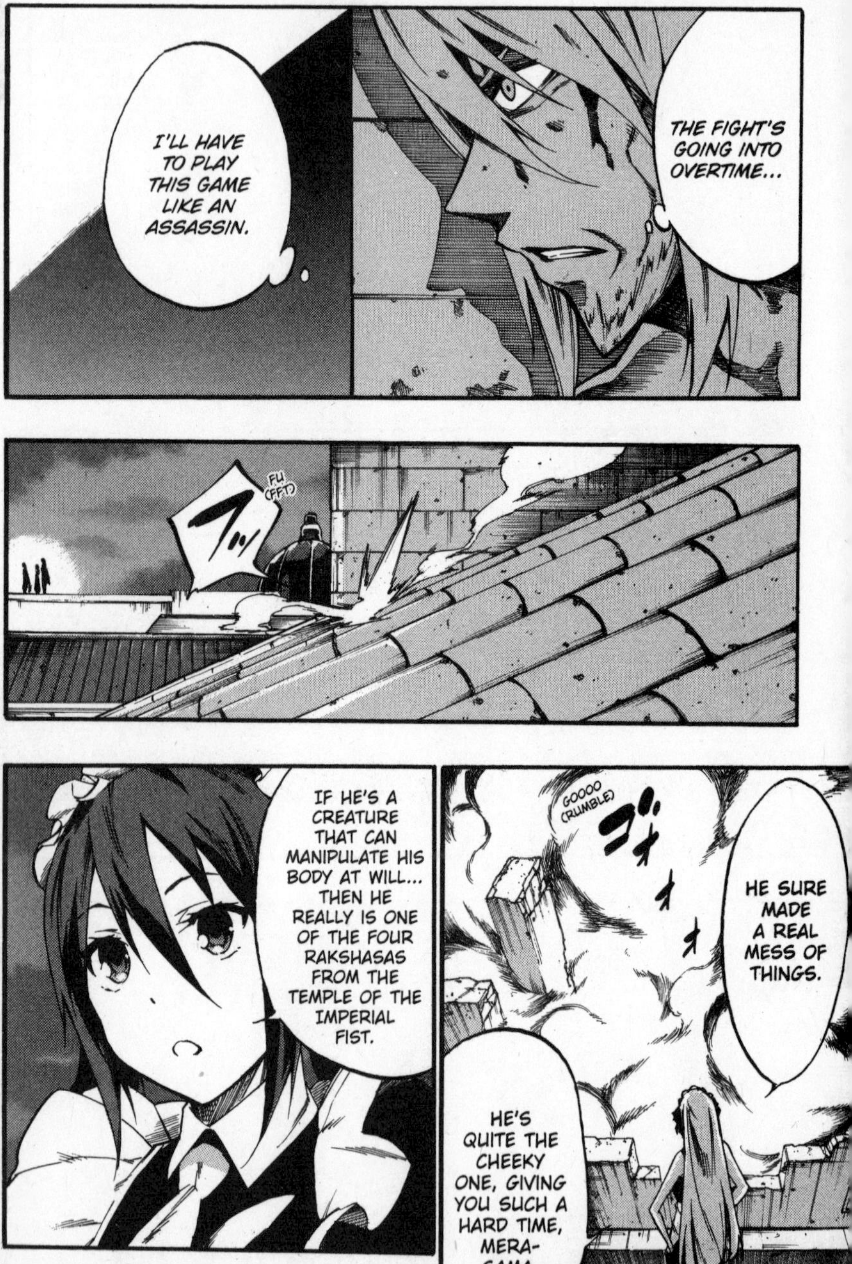
THE FIGHT'S GOING INTO OVERTIME...
I'LL HAVE TO PLAY THIS GAME LIKE AN ASSASSIN.
FU (PFFT)
GOOOO (RUMBLE)
HE SURE MADE A REAL MESS OF THINGS.
HE'S QUITE THE CHEEKY ONE, GIVING YOU SUCH A HARD TIME, MERA-SAMA.
IF HE'S A CREATURE THAT CAN MANIPULATE HIS BODY AT WILL... THEN HE REALLY IS ONE OF THE FOUR RAKSHASAS FROM THE TEMPLE OF THE IMPERIAL FIST.

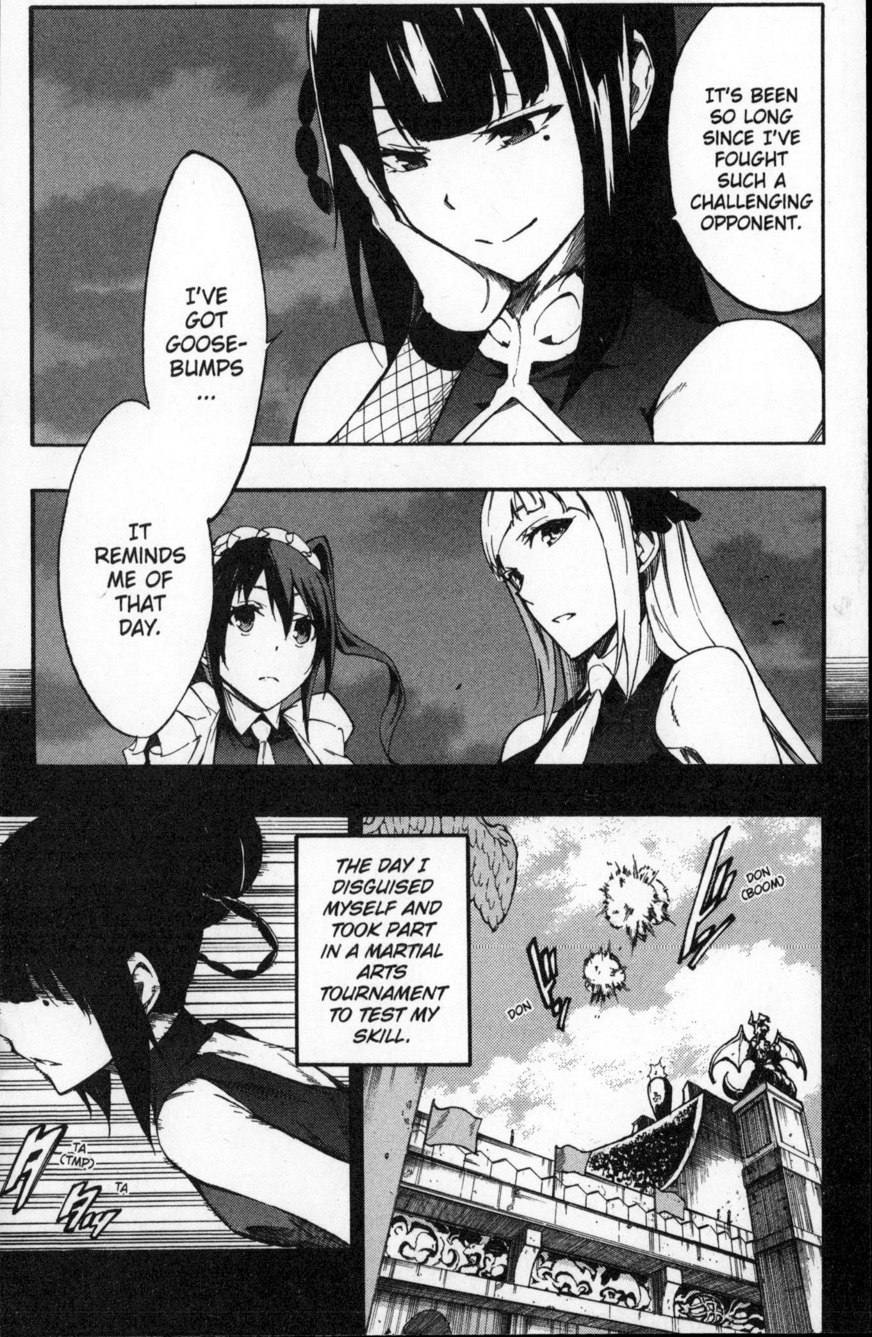
IT'S BEEN SO LONG SINCE I'VE FOUGHT SUCH A CHALLENGING OPPONENT.
I'VE GOT GOOSE-BUMPS ...
IT REMINDS ME OF THAT DAY.
THE DAY I DISGUISED MYSELF AND TOOK PART IN A MARTIAL ARTS TOURNAMENT TO TEST MY SKILL.
DON (BOOM)
DON
TA (TMP)
TA

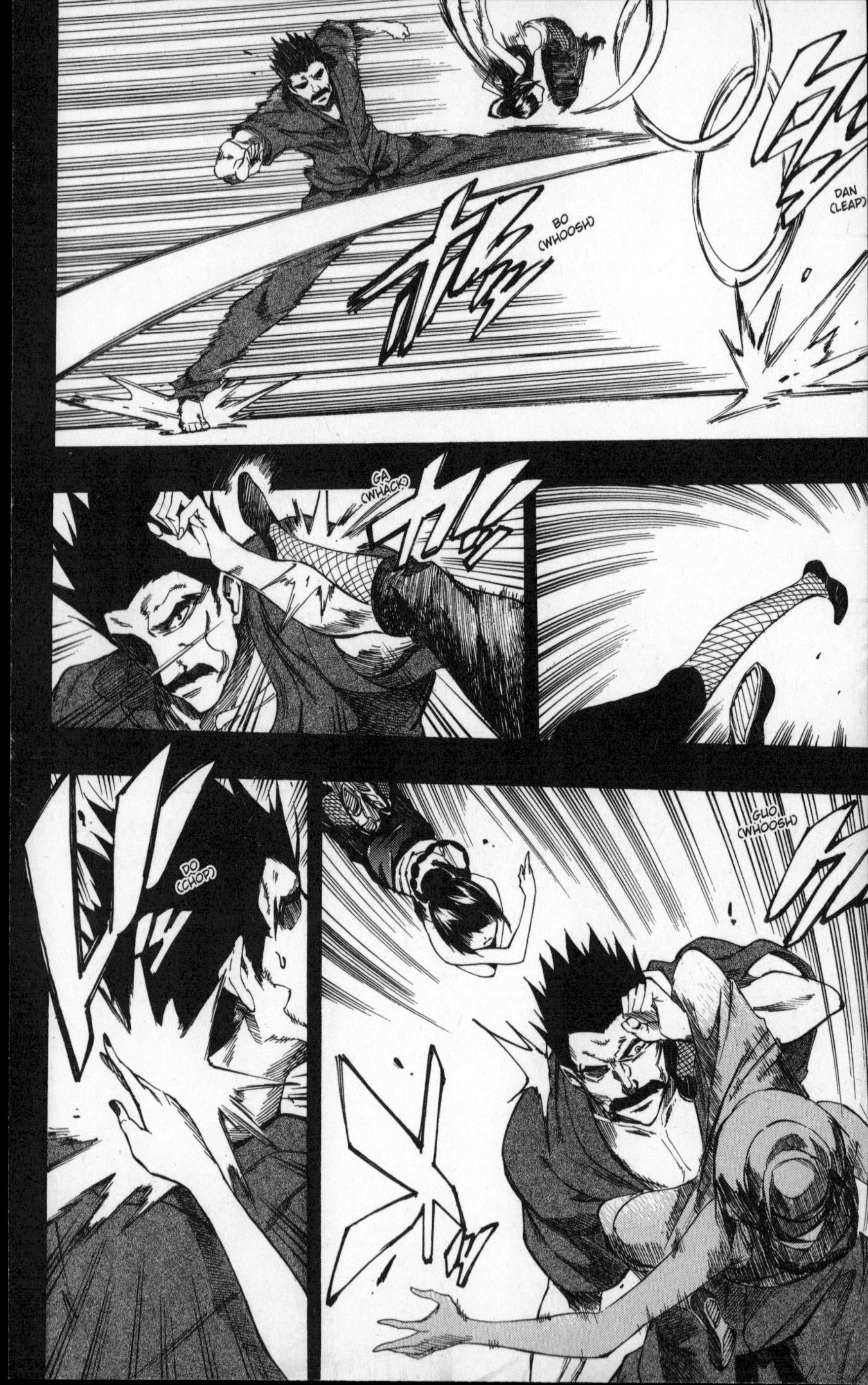
DAN
(LEAP)
BO
(WHOOSH)
GA
(WHACK)
GUO
(WHOOSH)
DO
(CHOP)

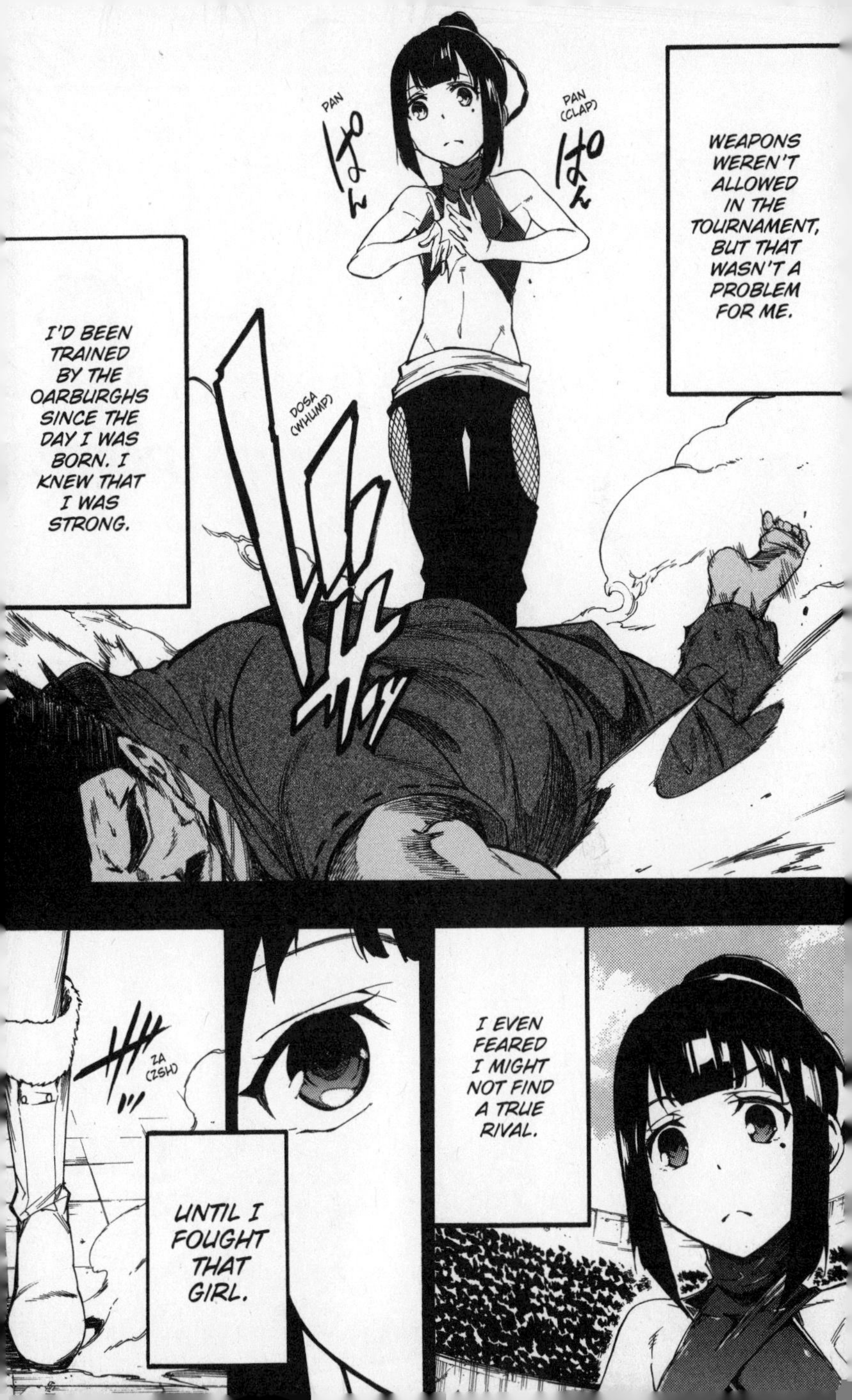
WEAPONS WEREN'T ALLOWED IN THE TOURNAMENT, BUT THAT WASN'T A PROBLEM FOR ME.
PAN (CLAP)
ぱん
PAN
ぱん
I'D BEEN TRAINED BY THE OARBURGHS SINCE THE DAY I WAS BORN. I KNEW THAT I WAS STRONG.
DOSA (WHUMP)
I EVEN FEARED I MIGHT NOT FIND A TRUE RIVAL.
UNTIL I FOUGHT THAT GIRL.
ZA (ZSH)

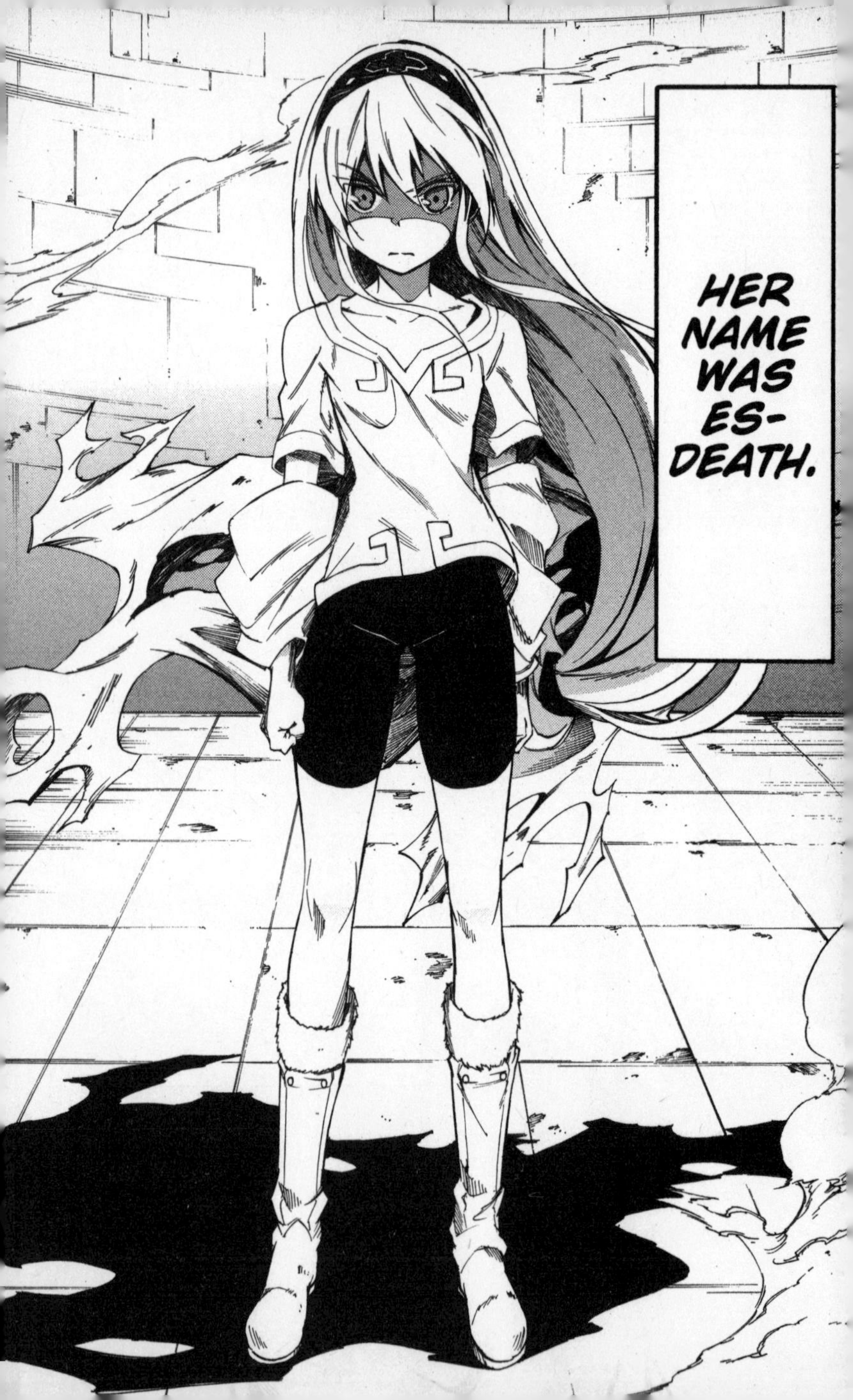
HER NAME WAS ES-DEATH.

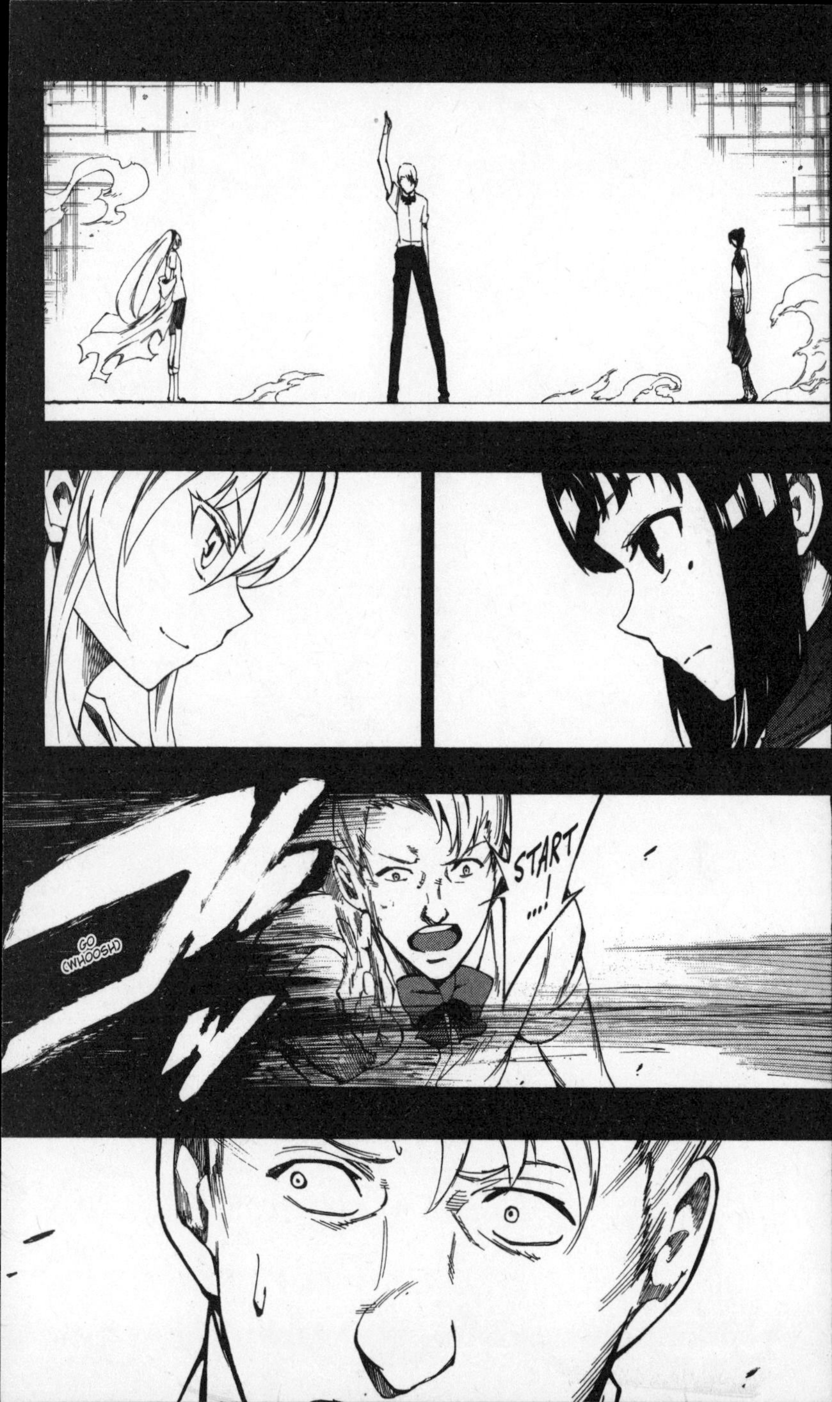
START ...!
GO (WHOOSH)

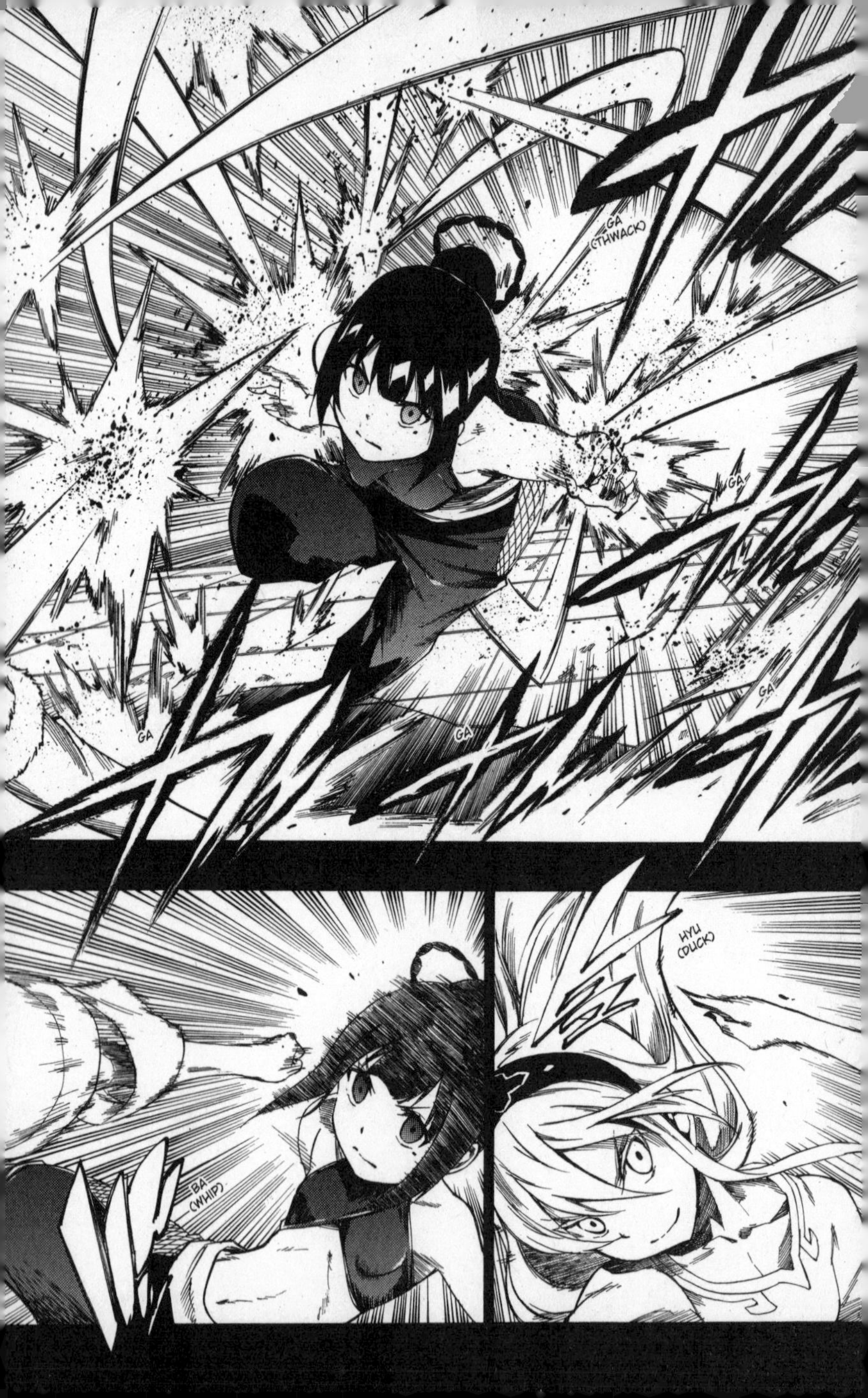
GA (THWACK)
GA
GA
GA
GA
HYU (DUCK)
BA (WHIP)

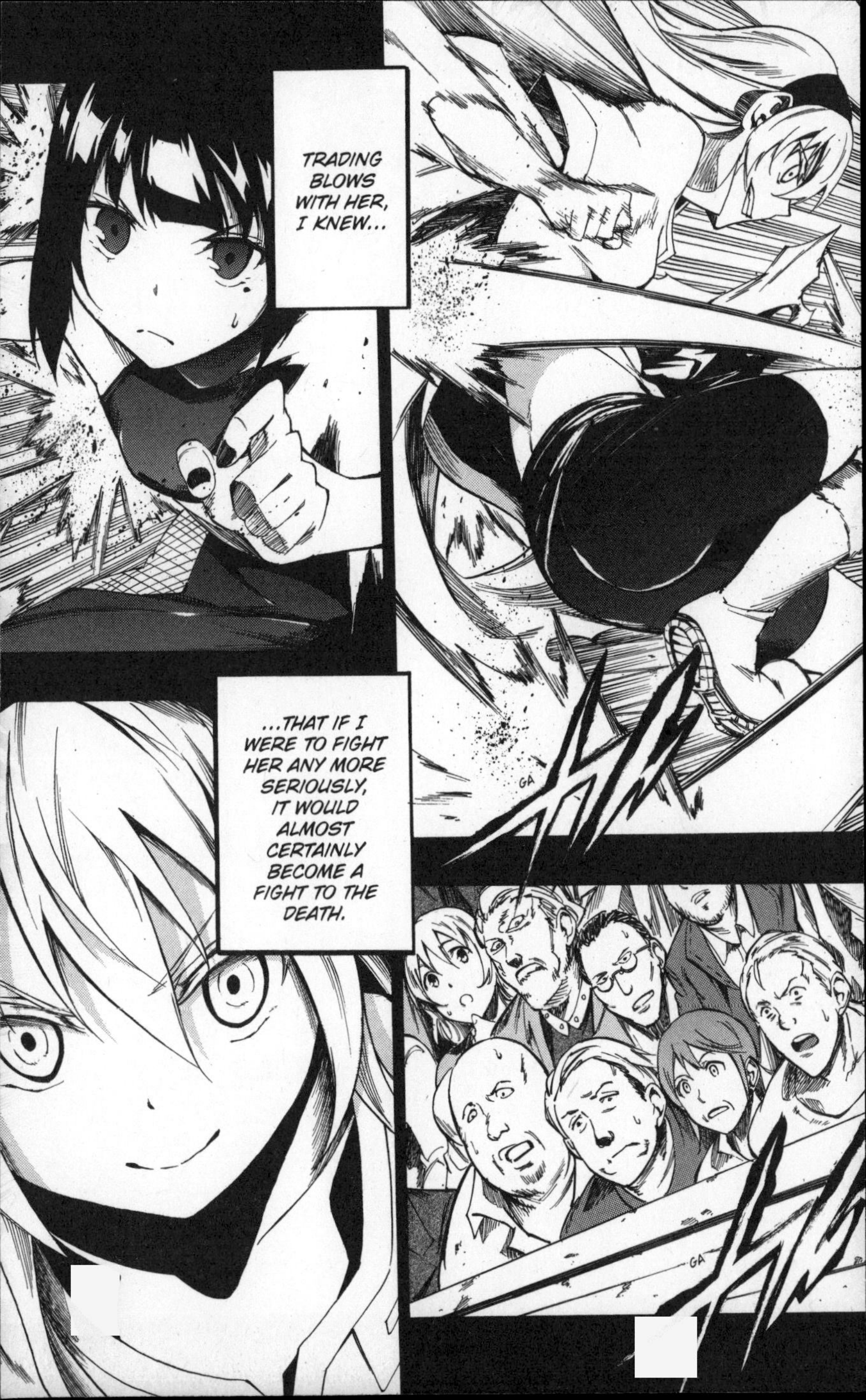
TRADING BLOWS WITH HER, I KNEW...
GA
...THAT IF I WERE TO FIGHT HER ANY MORE SERIOUSLY, IT WOULD ALMOST CERTAINLY BECOME A FIGHT TO THE DEATH.
GA

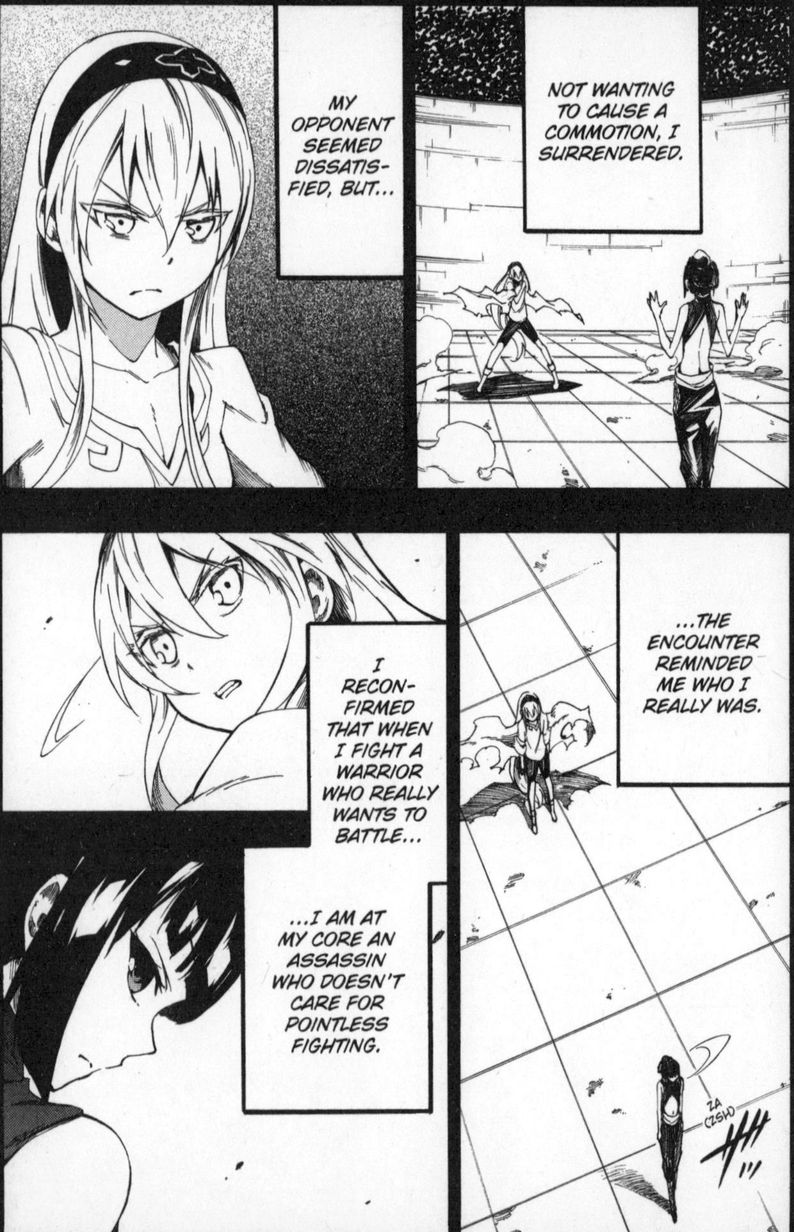
NOT WANTING TO CAUSE A COMMOTION, I SURRENDERED.
MY OPPONENT SEEMED DISSATIS-FIED, BUT...
...THE ENCOUNTER REMINDED ME WHO I REALLY WAS.
I RECON-FIRMED THAT WHEN I FIGHT A WARRIOR WHO REALLY WANTS TO BATTLE...
...I AM AT MY CORE AN ASSASSIN WHO DOESN'T CARE FOR POINTLESS FIGHTING.
ZA (ZSH)

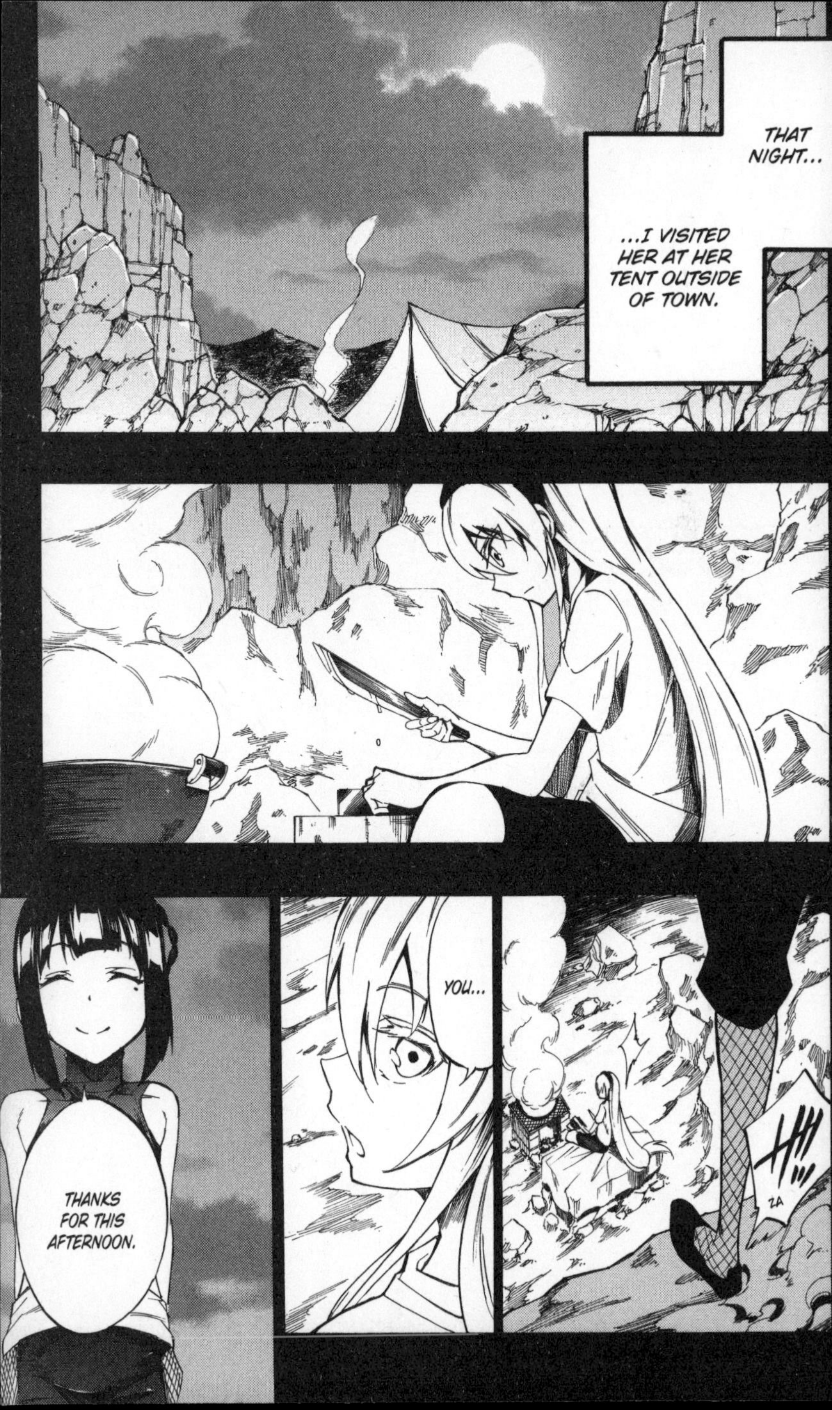
THAT NIGHT...
...I VISITED HER AT HER TENT OUTSIDE OF TOWN.
ZA
YOU...
THANKS FOR THIS AFTERNOON.

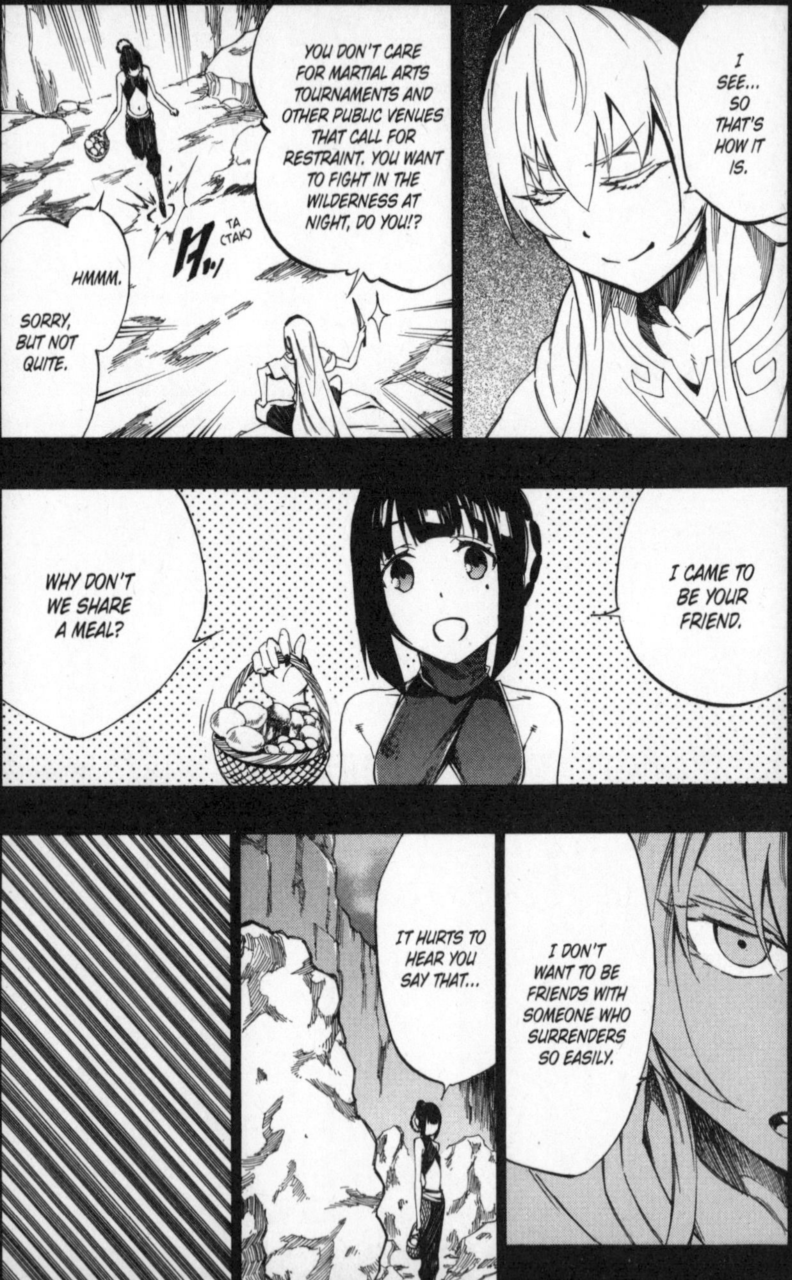

I SEE... SO THAT'S HOW IT IS.
YOU DON'T CARE FOR MARTIAL ARTS TOURNAMENTS AND OTHER PUBLIC VENUES THAT CALL FOR RESTRAINT. YOU WANT TO FIGHT IN THE WILDERNESS AT NIGHT, DO YOU!?
TA (TAK)
HMMM.
SORRY, BUT NOT QUITE.
I CAME TO BE YOUR FRIEND.
WHY DON'T WE SHARE A MEAL?
I DON'T WANT TO BE FRIENDS WITH SOMEONE WHO SURRENDERS SO EASILY.
IT HURTS TO HEAR YOU SAY THAT...

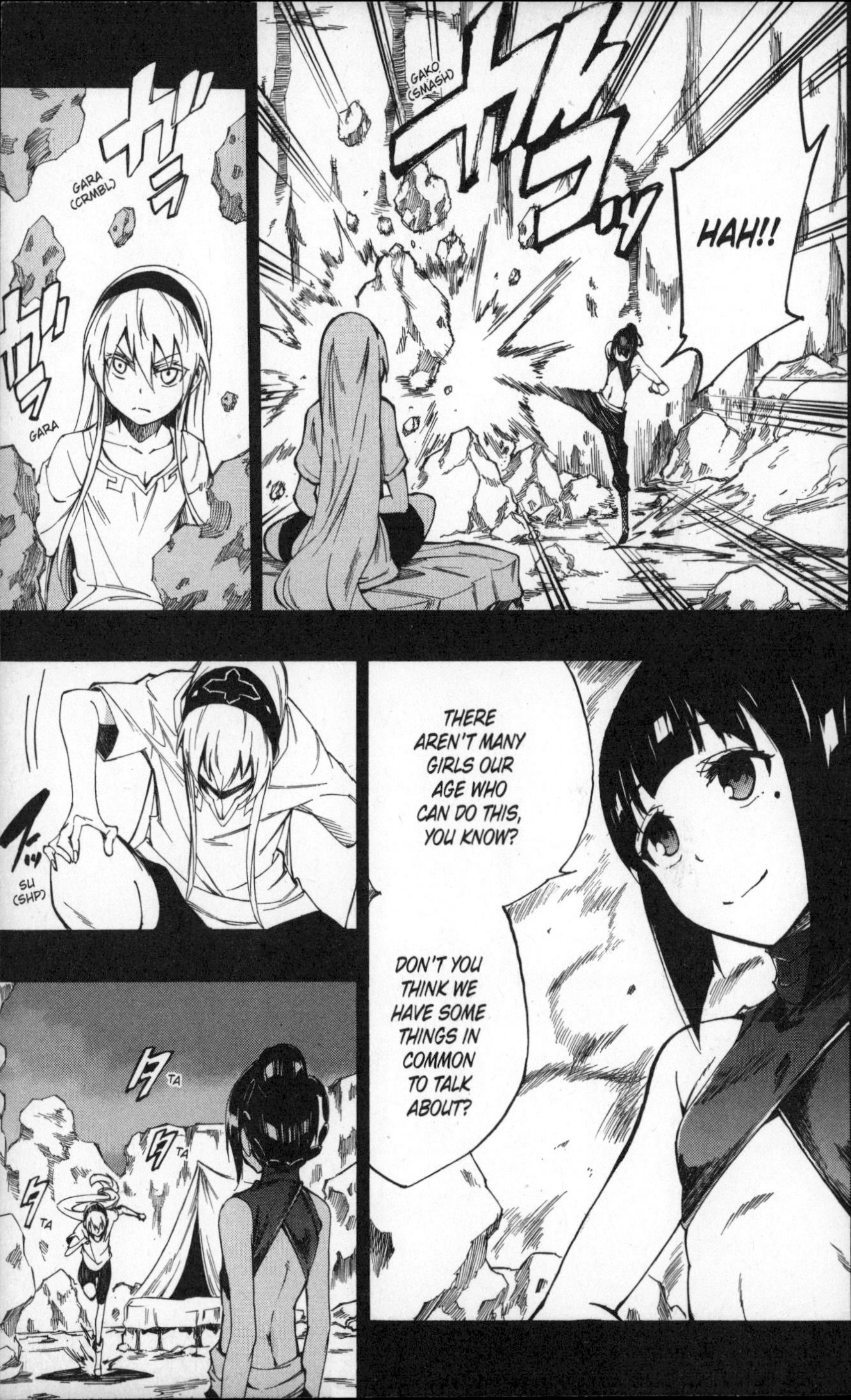

GAKO (SMASH)
HAH!!
GARA (CRMBL)
GARA
THERE AREN'T MANY GIRLS OUR AGE WHO CAN DO THIS, YOU KNOW?
DON'T YOU THINK WE HAVE SOME THINGS IN COMMON TO TALK ABOUT?
SU (SHP)
TA
TA
TA

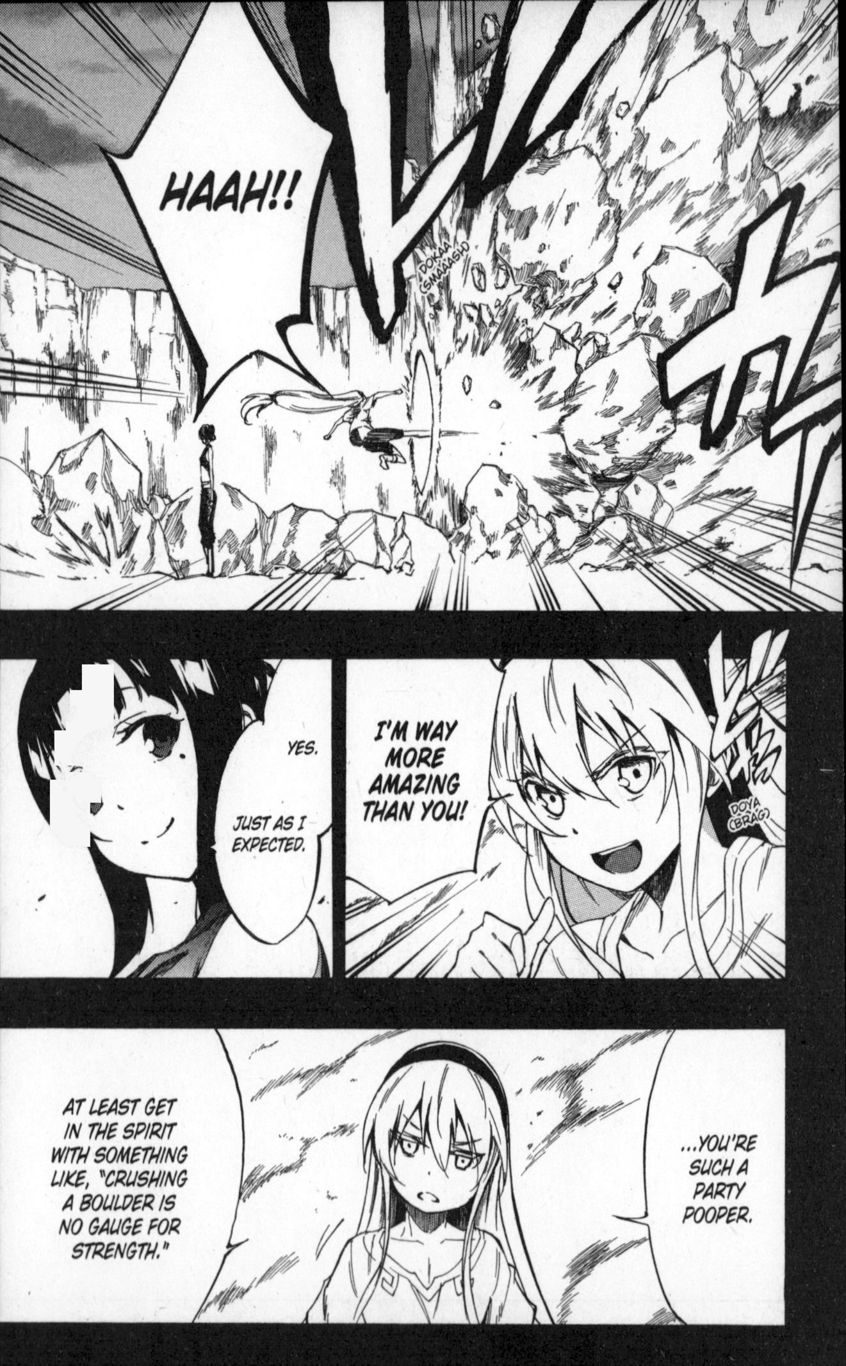
HAAH!!
DOKAA (SMAAASH)
I'M WAY MORE AMAZING THAN YOU!
DOYA (BRAG)
YES.
JUST AS I EXPECTED.
...YOU'RE SUCH A PARTY POOPER.
AT LEAST GET IN THE SPIRIT WITH SOMETHING LIKE, "CRUSHING A BOULDER IS NO GAUGE FOR STRENGTH."

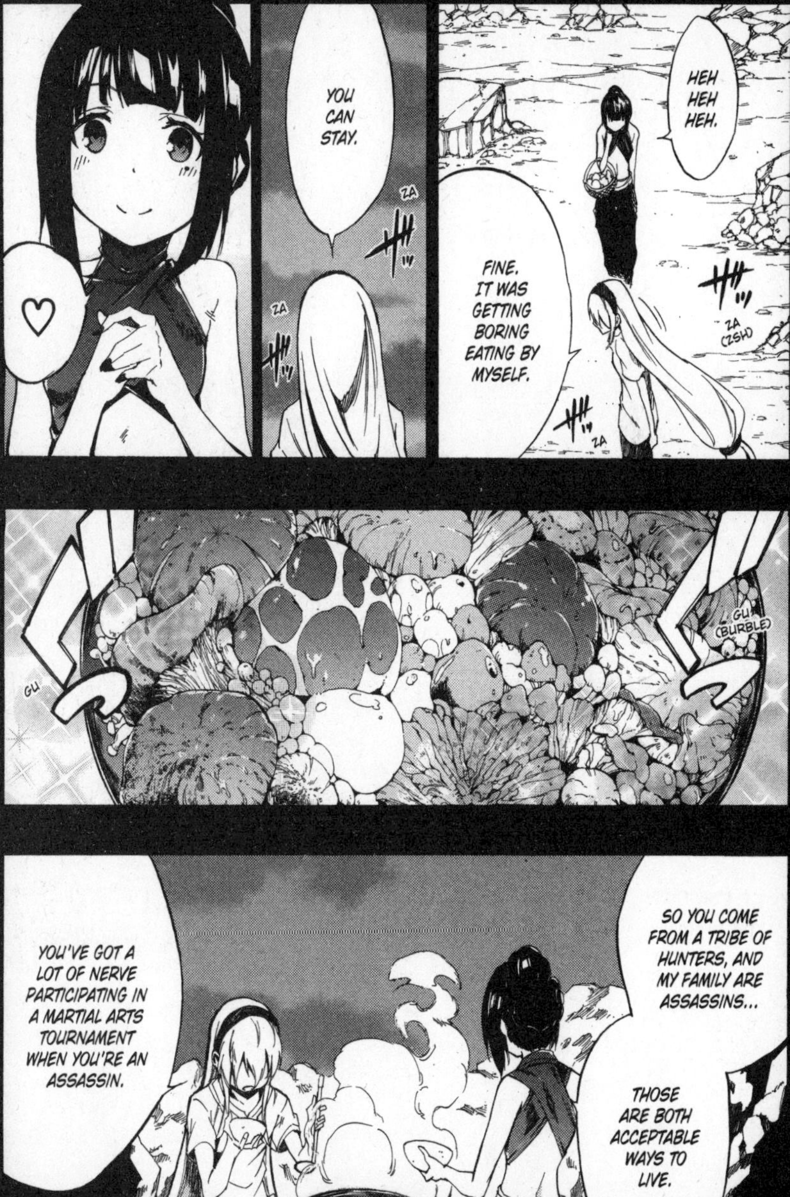
HEH HEH HEH.
FINE. IT WAS GETTING BORING EATING BY MYSELF.
ZA (ZSH)
ZA
YOU CAN STAY.
ZA
ZA
♡
GU (BURBLE)
GU
SO YOU COME FROM A TRIBE OF HUNTERS, AND MY FAMILY ARE ASSASSINS...
THOSE ARE BOTH ACCEPTABLE WAYS TO LIVE.
YOU'VE GOT A LOT OF NERVE PARTICIPATING IN A MARTIAL ARTS TOURNAMENT WHEN YOU'RE AN ASSASSIN.

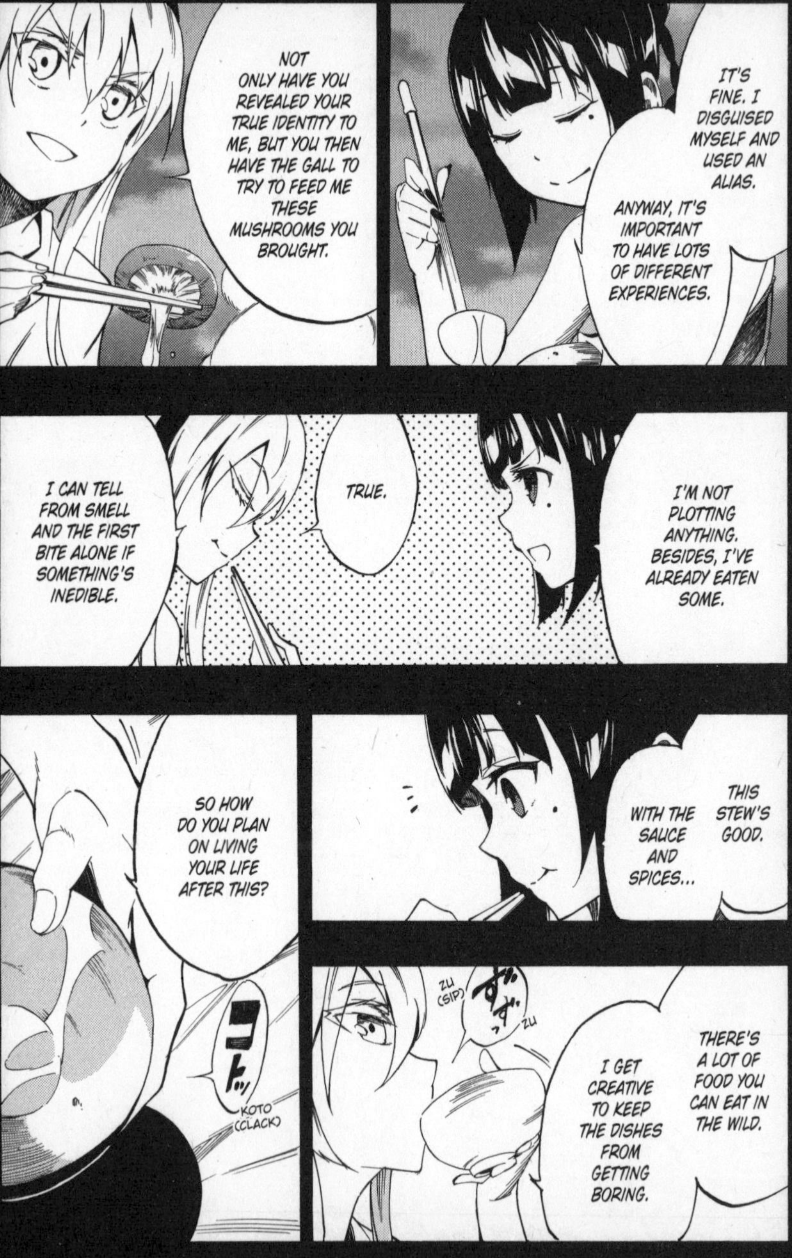

IT'S FINE. I DISGUISED MYSELF AND USED AN ALIAS.
ANYWAY, IT'S IMPORTANT TO HAVE LOTS OF DIFFERENT EXPERIENCES.
NOT ONLY HAVE YOU REVEALED YOUR TRUE IDENTITY TO ME, BUT YOU THEN HAVE THE GALL TO TRY TO FEED ME THESE MUSHROOMS YOU BROUGHT.
I'M NOT PLOTTING ANYTHING. BESIDES, I'VE ALREADY EATEN SOME.
TRUE.
I CAN TELL FROM SMELL AND THE FIRST BITE ALONE IF SOMETHING'S INEDIBLE.
THIS STEW'S GOOD.
WITH THE SAUCE AND SPICES...
SO HOW DO YOU PLAN ON LIVING YOUR LIFE AFTER THIS?
コトッ
KOTO (CLACK)
ずっ
ZU (SIP)
ずっ
ZU
THERE'S A LOT OF FOOD YOU CAN EAT IN THE WILD.
I GET CREATIVE TO KEEP THE DISHES FROM GETTING BORING.

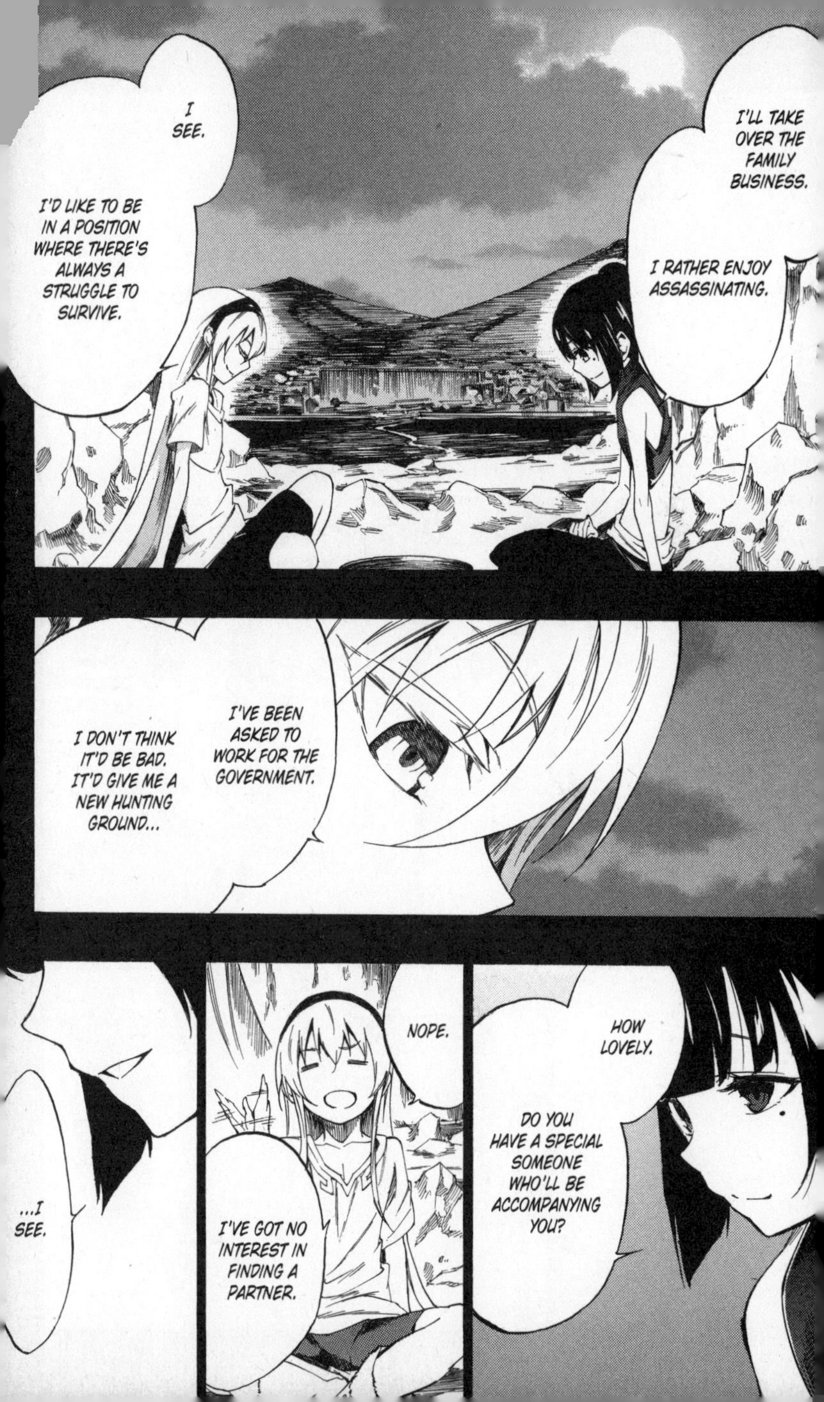
I'LL TAKE OVER THE FAMILY BUSINESS.
I RATHER ENJOY ASSASSINATING.
I SEE.
I'D LIKE TO BE IN A POSITION WHERE THERE'S ALWAYS A STRUGGLE TO SURVIVE.
I'VE BEEN ASKED TO WORK FOR THE GOVERNMENT.
I DON'T THINK IT'D BE BAD. IT'D GIVE ME A NEW HUNTING GROUND...
HOW LOVELY.
DO YOU HAVE A SPECIAL SOMEONE WHO'LL BE ACCOMPANYING YOU?
NOPE.
I'VE GOT NO INTEREST IN FINDING A PARTNER.
...I SEE.

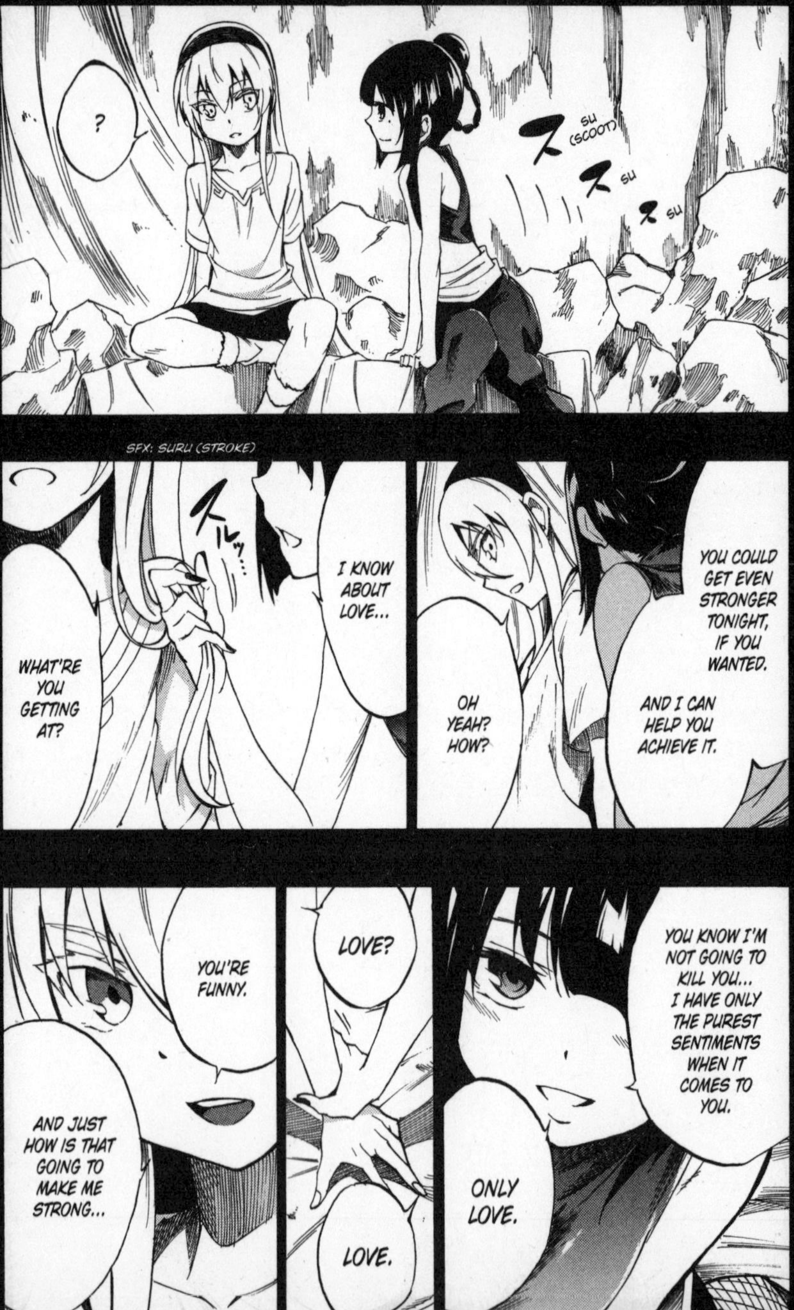
?
SU (SCOOT)
SU
SU
SFX: SURU (STROKE)
YOU COULD GET EVEN STRONGER TONIGHT, IF YOU WANTED.
AND I CAN HELP YOU ACHIEVE IT.
OH YEAH? HOW?
I KNOW ABOUT LOVE...
WHAT'RE YOU GETTING AT?
YOU KNOW I'M NOT GOING TO KILL YOU... I HAVE ONLY THE PUREST SENTIMENTS WHEN IT COMES TO YOU.
ONLY LOVE.
LOVE?
LOVE.
YOU'RE FUNNY.
AND JUST HOW IS THAT GOING TO MAKE ME STRONG...

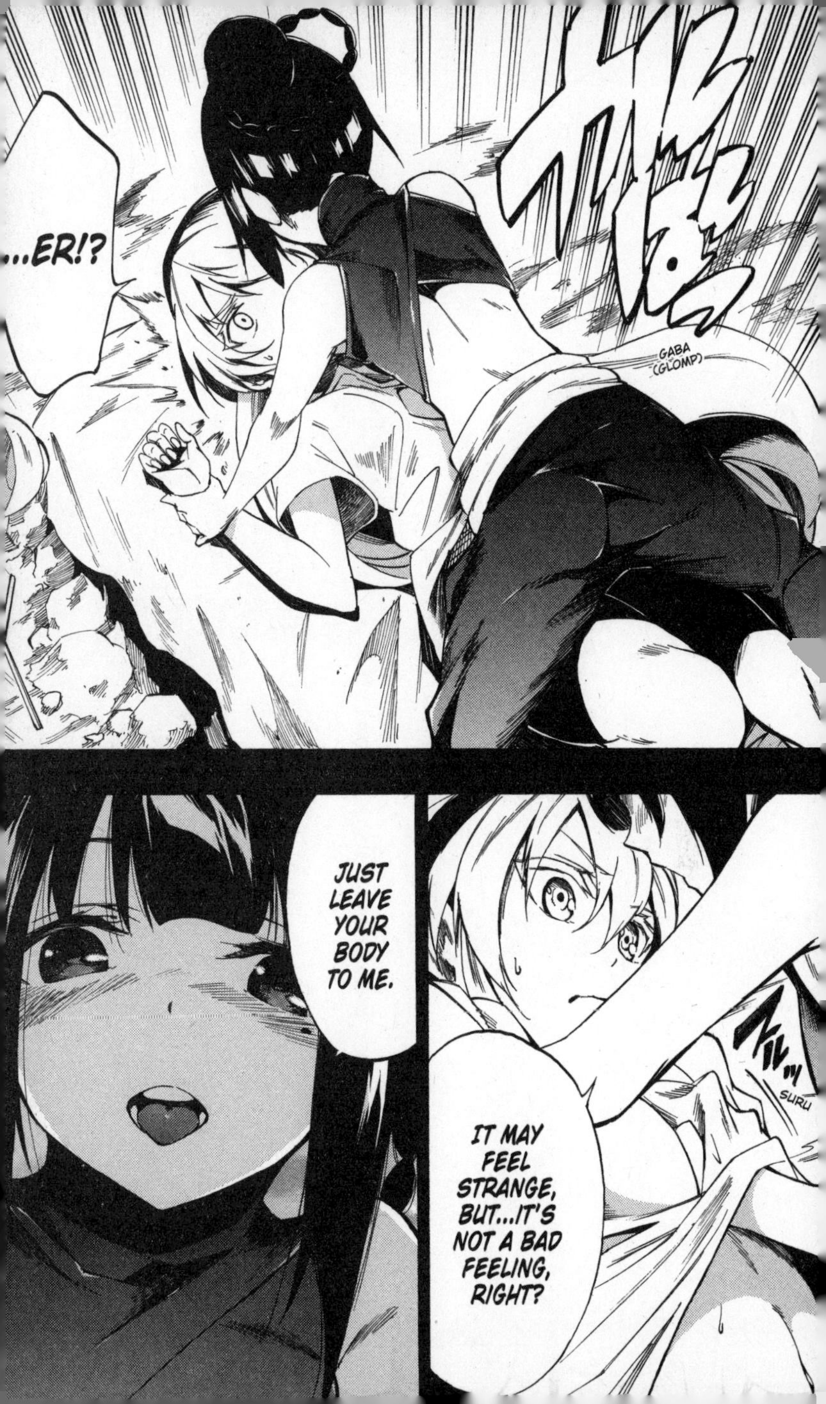
GABA
(GLOMP)
...ER!?
SURU
JUST LEAVE YOUR BODY TO ME.
IT MAY FEEL STRANGE, BUT...IT'S NOT A BAD FEELING, RIGHT?

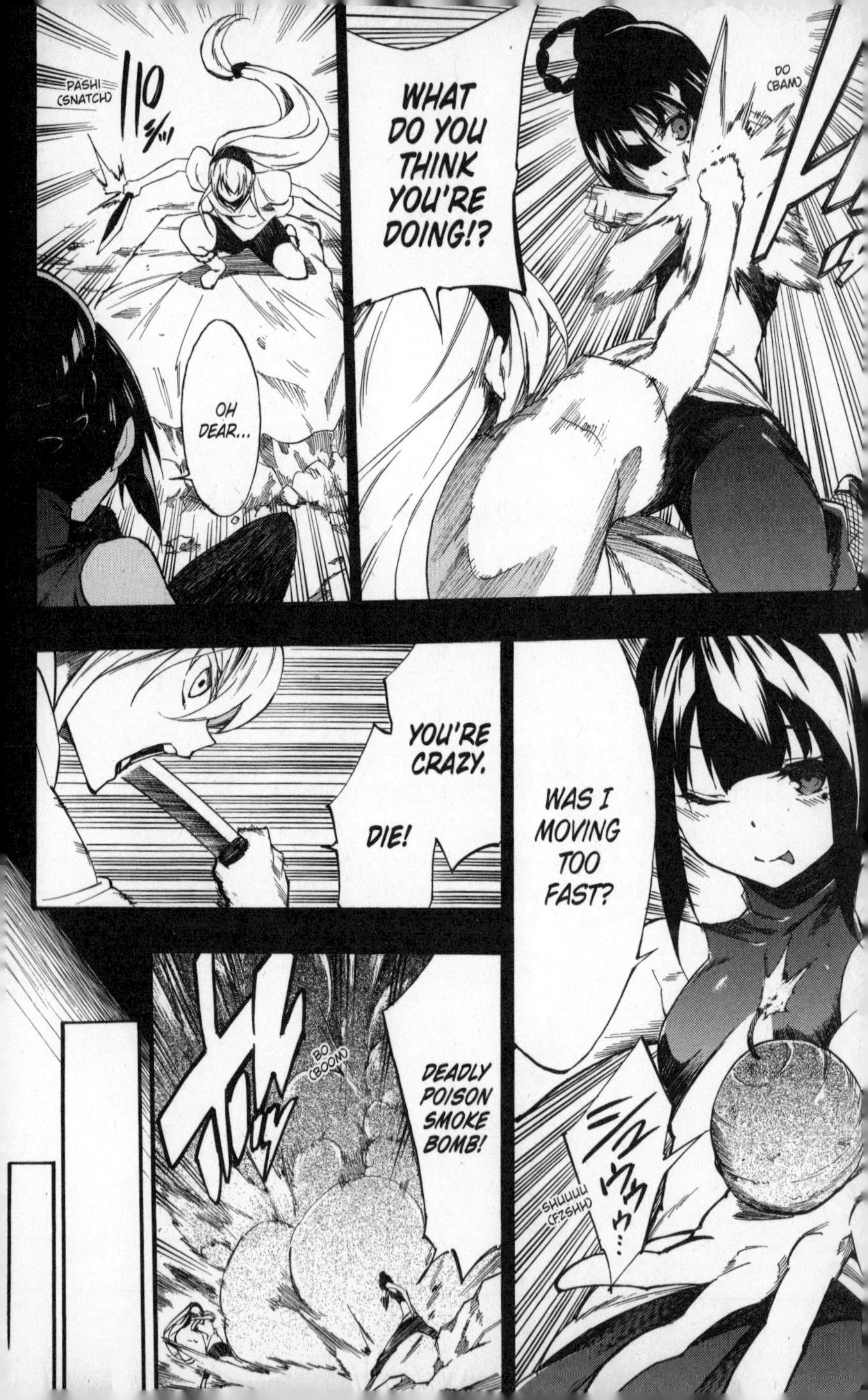

DO (BAM)
WHAT DO YOU THINK YOU'RE DOING!?
PASHI (SNATCH)
OH DEAR...
WAS I MOVING TOO FAST?
YOU'RE CRAZY.
DIE!
SHUUUU (FZSHH)
DEADLY POISON SMOKE BOMB!
BO (BOOM)

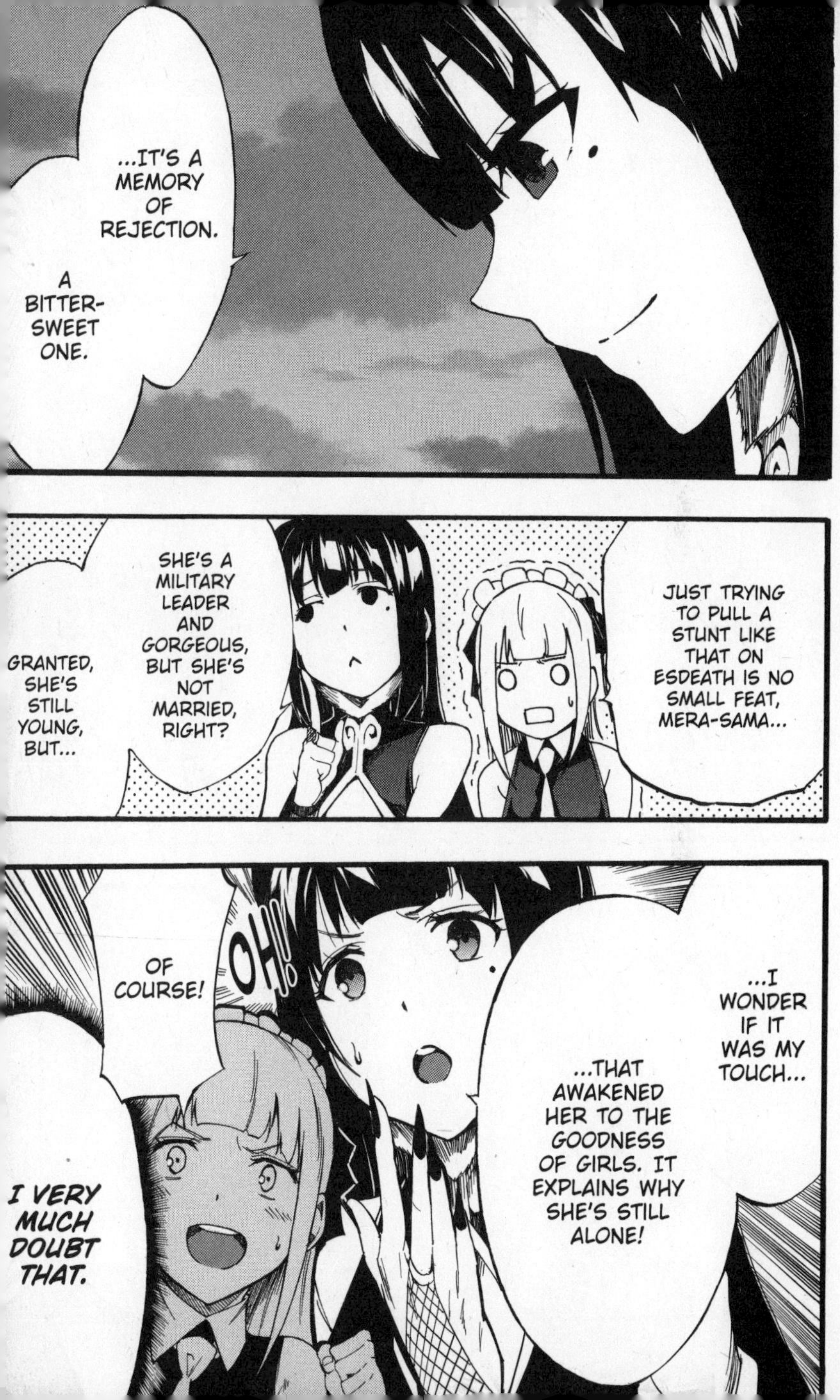
...IT'S A MEMORY OF REJECTION.
A BITTER-SWEET ONE.
JUST TRYING TO PULL A STUNT LIKE THAT ON ESDEATH IS NO SMALL FEAT, MERA-SAMA...
SHE'S A MILITARY LEADER AND GORGEOUS, BUT SHE'S NOT MARRIED, RIGHT?
GRANTED, SHE'S STILL YOUNG, BUT...
OH!!
OF COURSE!
...I WONDER IF IT WAS MY TOUCH...
...THAT AWAKENED HER TO THE GOODNESS OF GIRLS. IT EXPLAINS WHY SHE'S STILL ALONE!
I VERY MUCH DOUBT THAT.

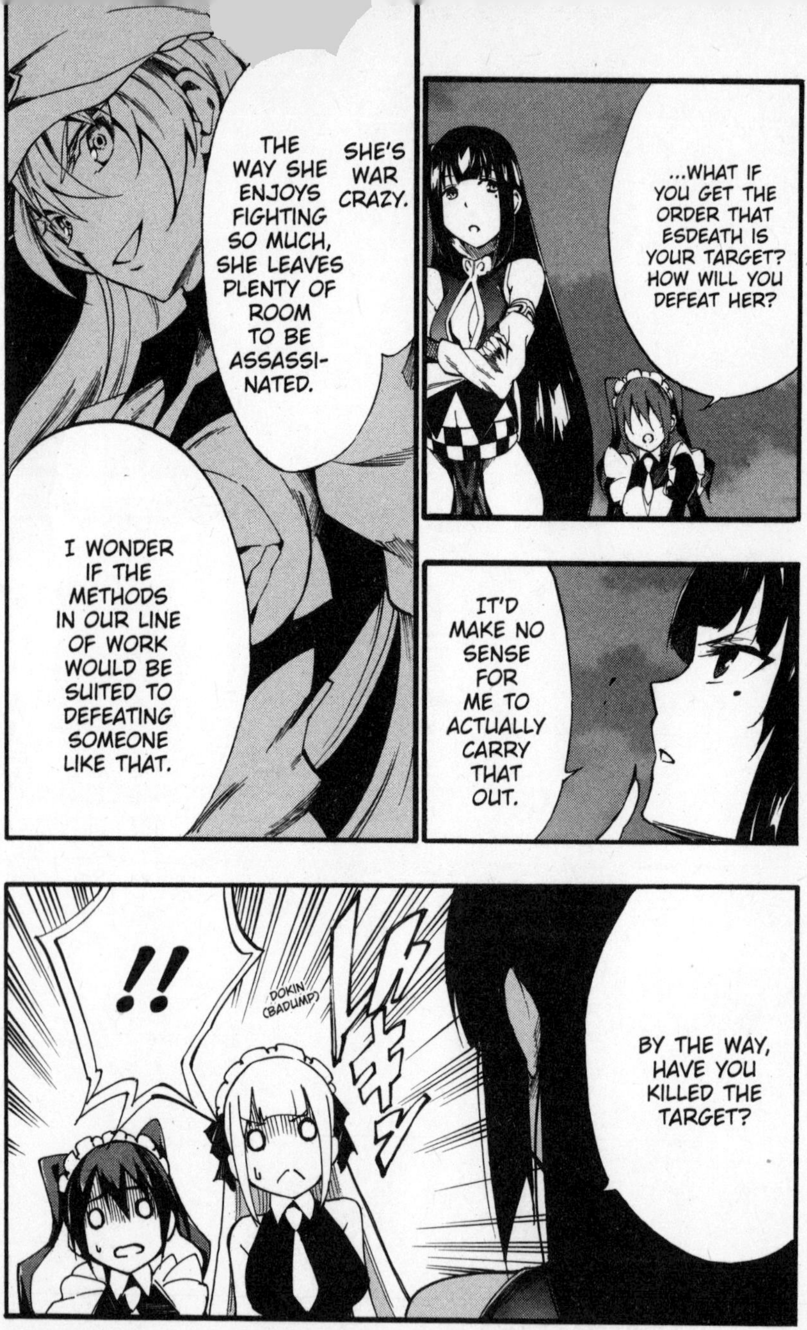
...WHAT IF YOU GET THE ORDER THAT ESDEATH IS YOUR TARGET? HOW WILL YOU DEFEAT HER?
IT'D MAKE NO SENSE FOR ME TO ACTUALLY CARRY THAT OUT.
SHE'S WAR CRAZY.
THE WAY SHE ENJOYS FIGHTING SO MUCH, SHE LEAVES PLENTY OF ROOM TO BE ASSASSI-NATED.
I WONDER IF THE METHODS IN OUR LINE OF WORK WOULD BE SUITED TO DEFEATING SOMEONE LIKE THAT.
BY THE WAY, HAVE YOU KILLED THE TARGET?
DOKIN (BADUMP)
!!

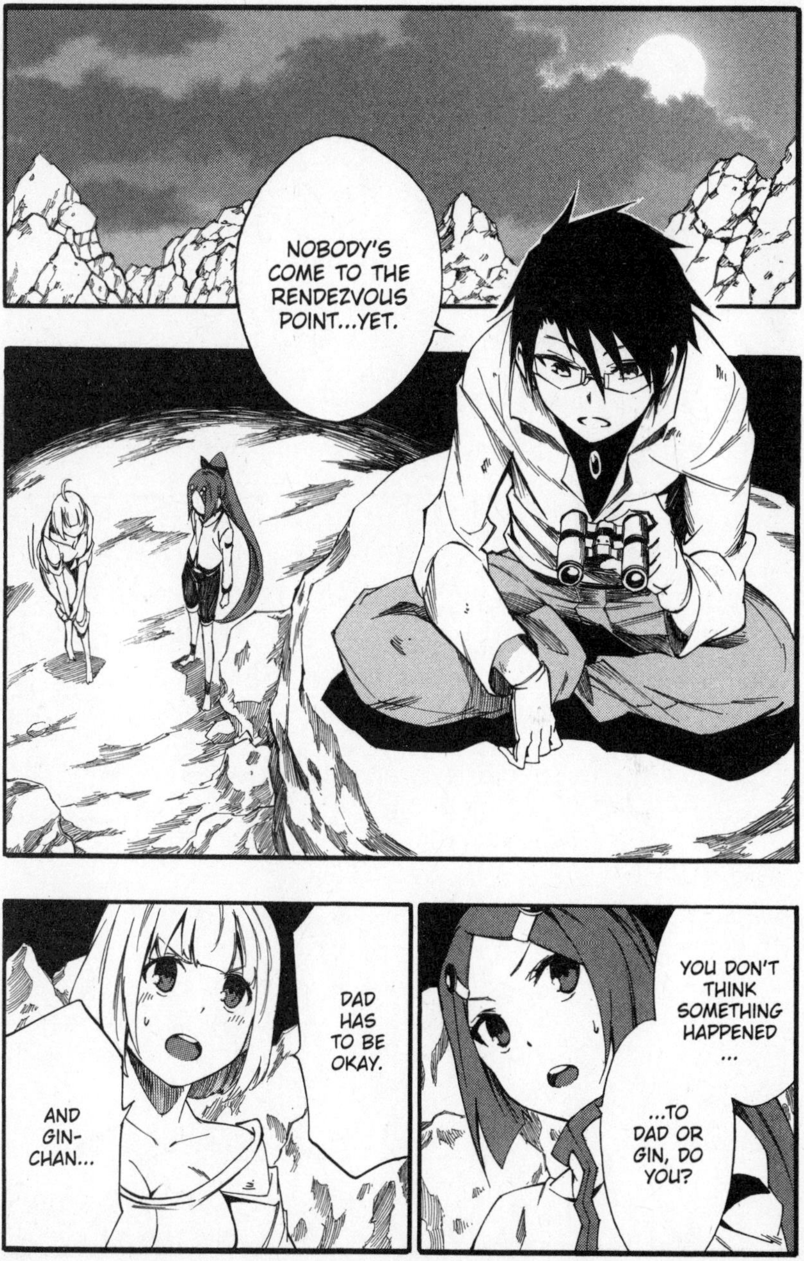
NOBODY'S COME TO THE RENDEZVOUS POINT...YET.
YOU DON'T THINK SOMETHING HAPPENED ...
...TO DAD OR GIN, DO YOU?
DAD HAS TO BE OKAY.
AND GIN-CHAN...

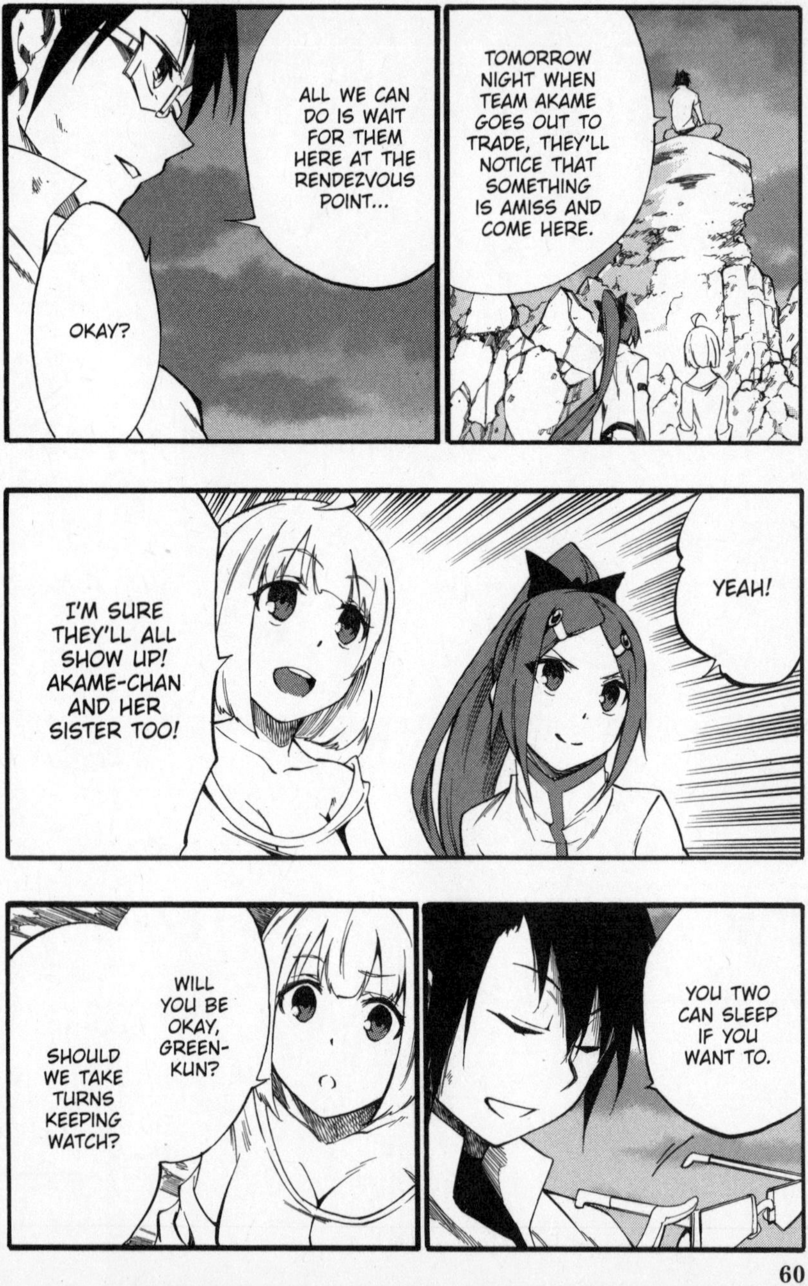
TOMORROW NIGHT WHEN TEAM AKAME GOES OUT TO TRADE, THEY'LL NOTICE THAT SOMETHING IS AMISS AND COME HERE.
ALL WE CAN DO IS WAIT FOR THEM HERE AT THE RENDEZVOUS POINT...
OKAY?
I'M SURE THEY'LL ALL SHOW UP! AKAME-CHAN AND HER SISTER TOO!
YEAH!
YOU TWO CAN SLEEP IF YOU WANT TO.
WILL YOU BE OKAY, GREEN-KUN?
SHOULD WE TAKE TURNS KEEPING WATCH?

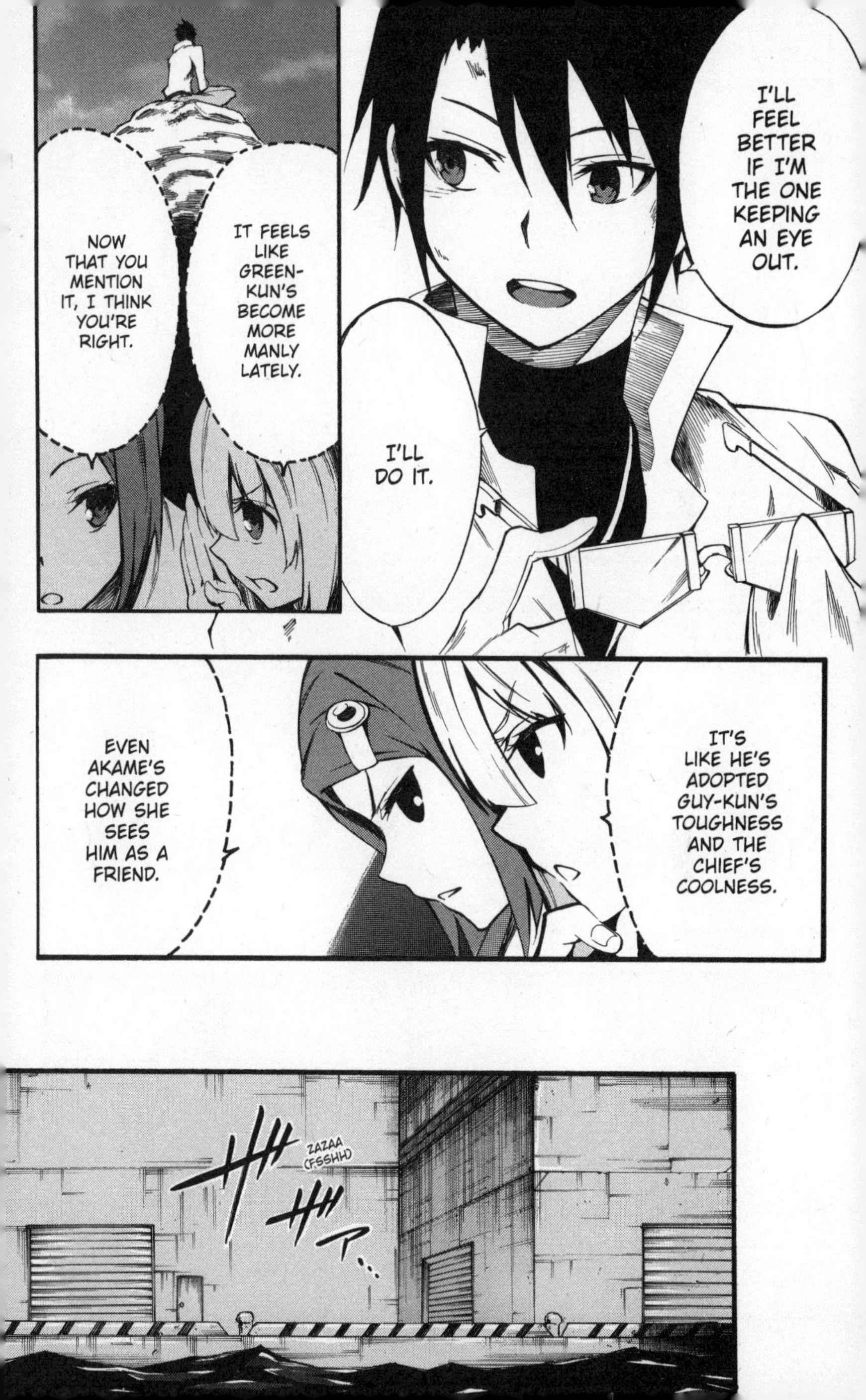
I'LL FEEL BETTER IF I'M THE ONE KEEPING AN EYE OUT.
I'LL DO IT.
IT FEELS LIKE GREEN-KUN'S BECOME MORE MANLY LATELY.
NOW THAT YOU MENTION IT, I THINK YOU'RE RIGHT.
IT'S LIKE HE'S ADOPTED GUY-KUN'S TOUGHNESS AND THE CHIEF'S COOLNESS.
EVEN AKAME'S CHANGED HOW SHE SEES HIM AS A FRIEND.
ZAZAA (FSSHH)

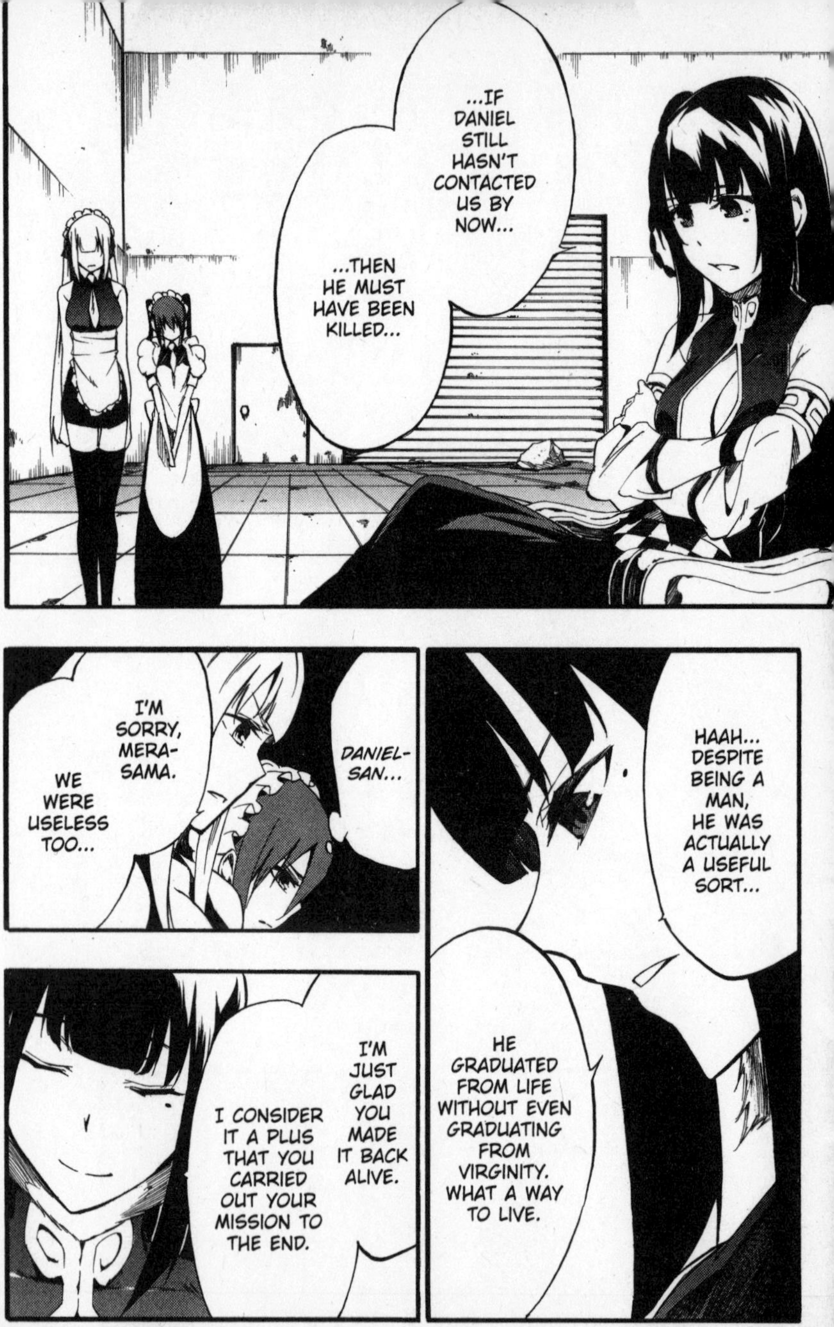
...IF DANIEL STILL HASN'T CONTACTED US BY NOW...
...THEN HE MUST HAVE BEEN KILLED...
HAAH... DESPITE BEING A MAN, HE WAS ACTUALLY A USEFUL SORT...
HE GRADUATED FROM LIFE WITHOUT EVEN GRADUATING FROM VIRGINITY. WHAT A WAY TO LIVE.
DANIEL-SAN...
I'M SORRY, MERA-SAMA.
WE WERE USELESS TOO...
I'M JUST GLAD YOU MADE IT BACK ALIVE.
I CONSIDER IT A PLUS THAT YOU CARRIED OUT YOUR MISSION TO THE END.

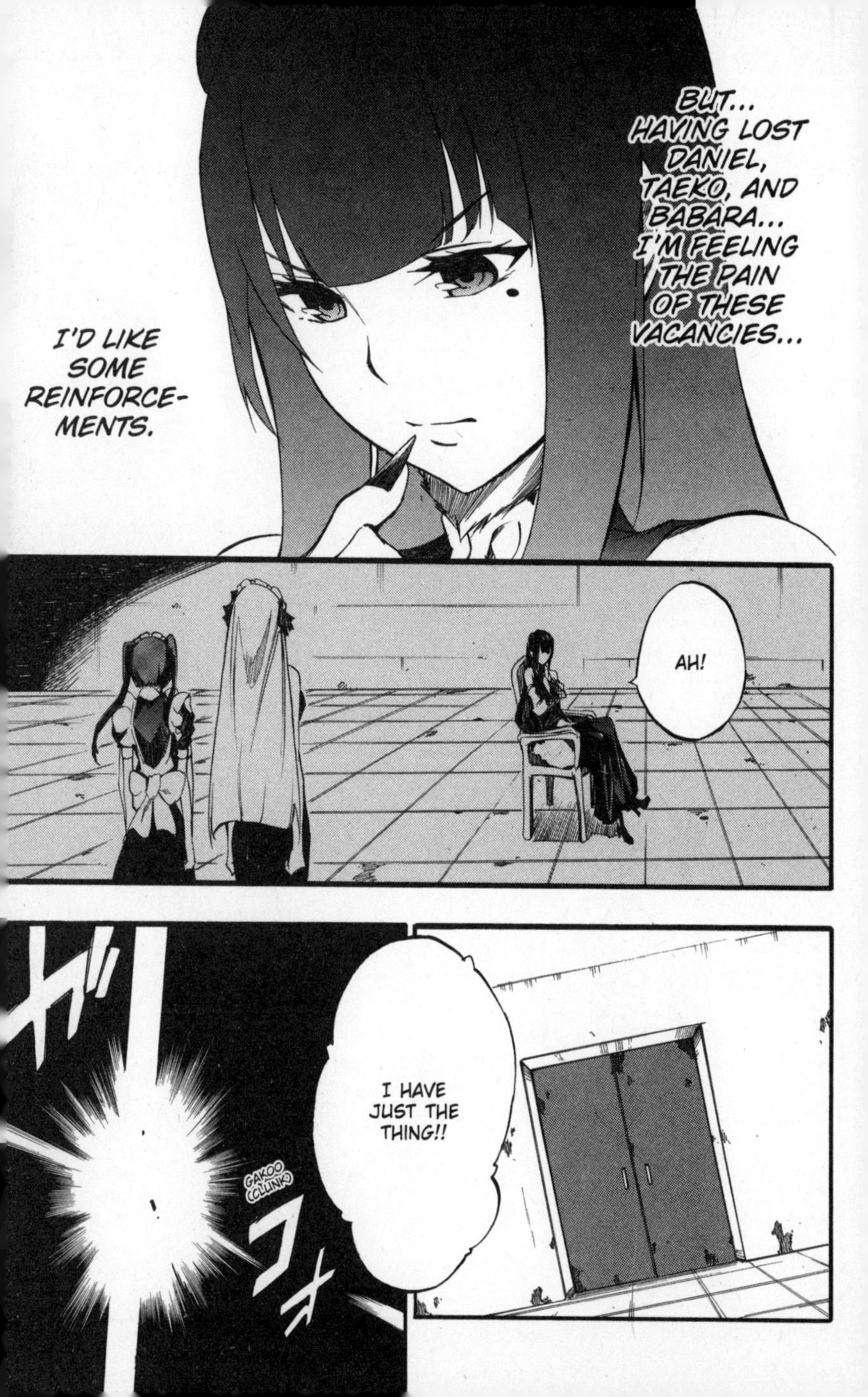
BUT... HAVING LOST DANIEL, TAEKO, AND BABARA... I'M FEELING THE PAIN OF THESE VACANCIES...
I'D LIKE SOME REINFORCE-MENTS.
AH!
I HAVE JUST THE THING!!
GAKOO (CLUNK)

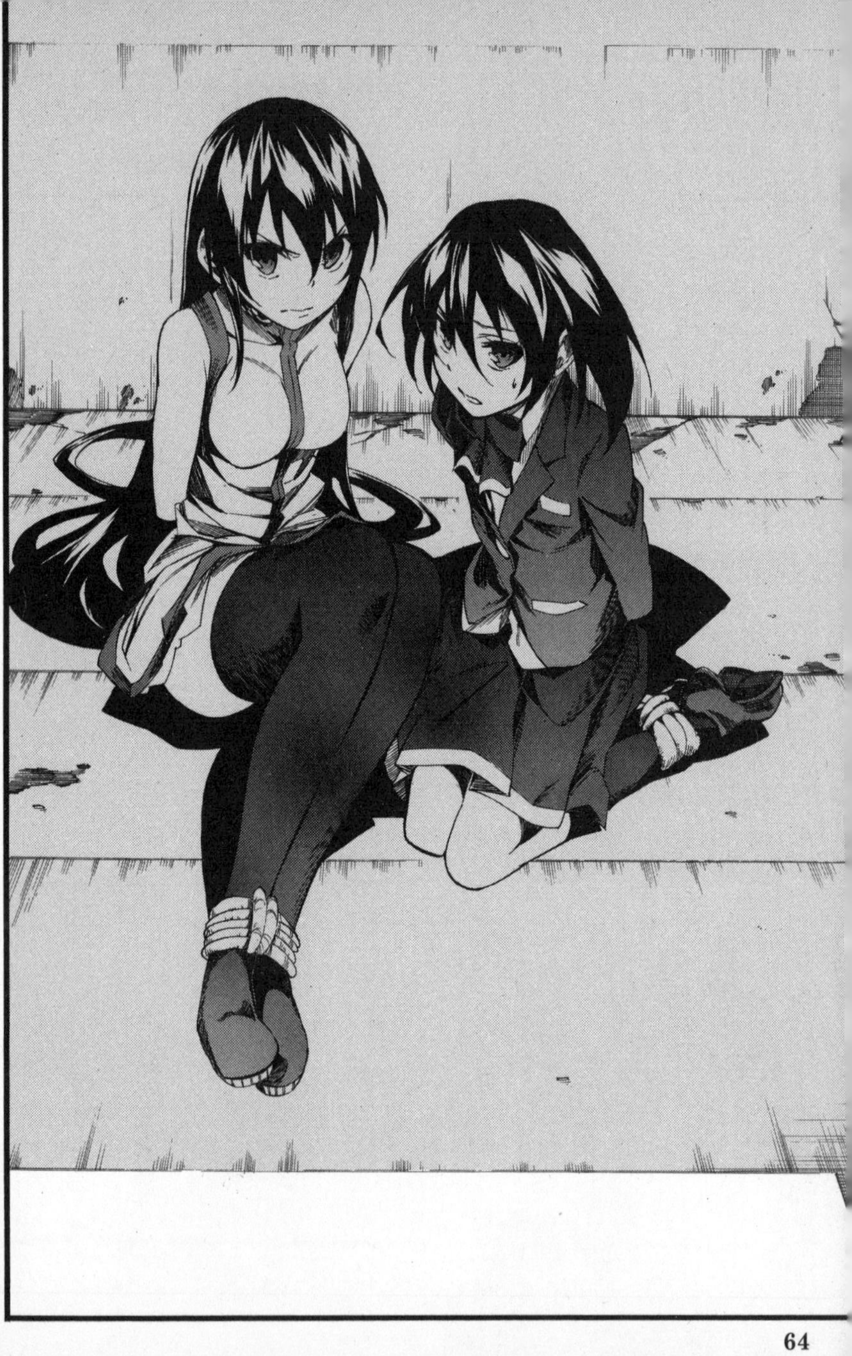

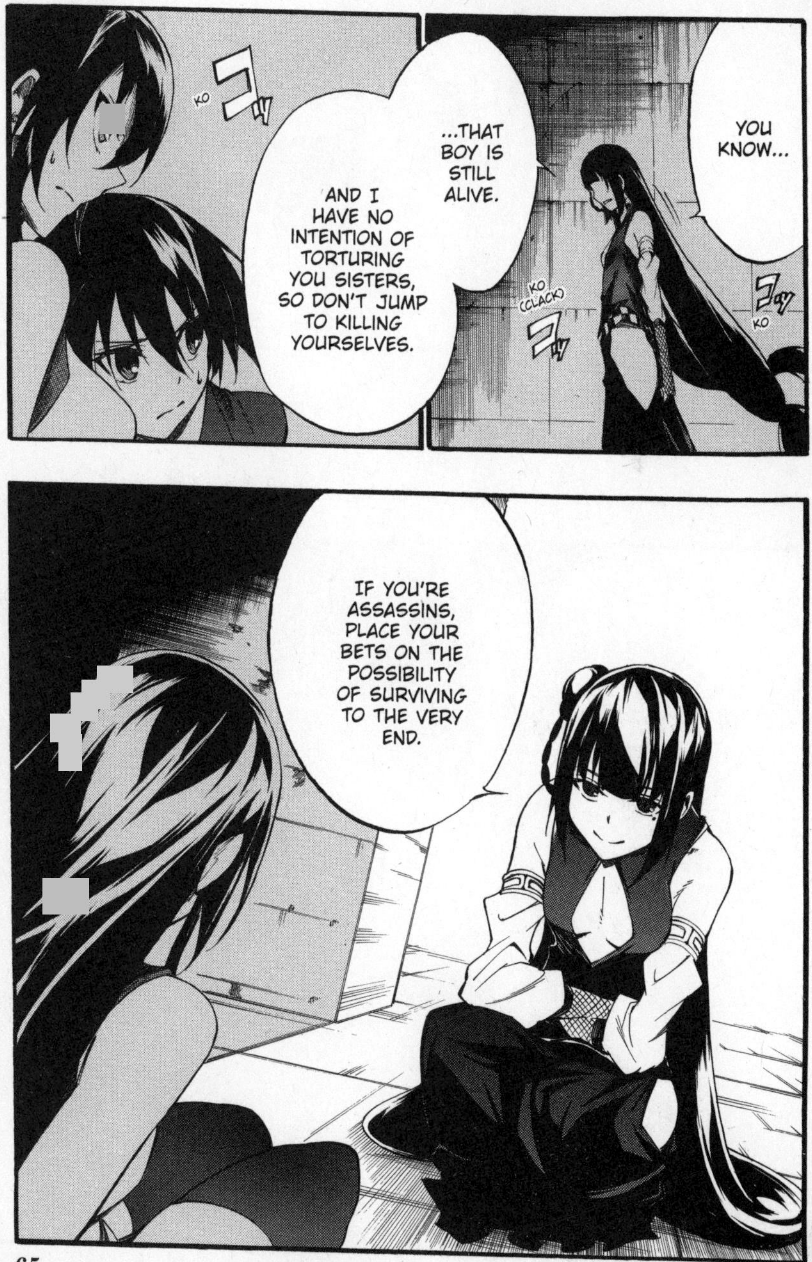
YOU KNOW...
KO
KO (CLACK)
...THAT BOY IS STILL ALIVE.
AND I HAVE NO INTENTION OF TORTURING YOU SISTERS, SO DON'T JUMP TO KILLING YOURSELVES.
KO
IF YOU'RE ASSASSINS, PLACE YOUR BETS ON THE POSSIBILITY OF SURVIVING TO THE VERY END.

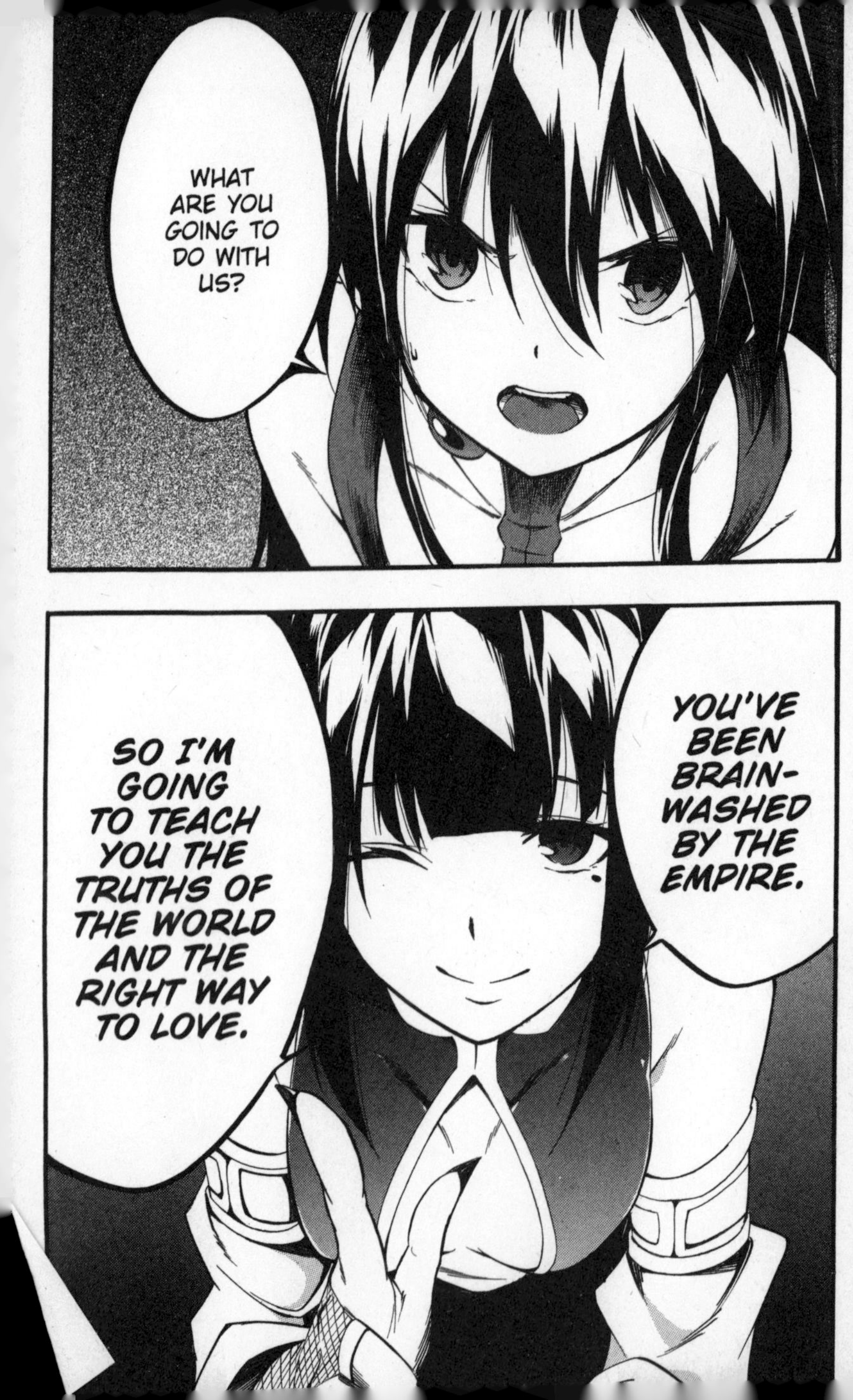
WHAT ARE YOU GOING TO DO WITH US?
YOU'VE BEEN BRAIN-WASHED BY THE EMPIRE.
SO I'M GOING TO TEACH YOU THE TRUTHS OF THE WORLD AND THE RIGHT WAY TO LOVE.

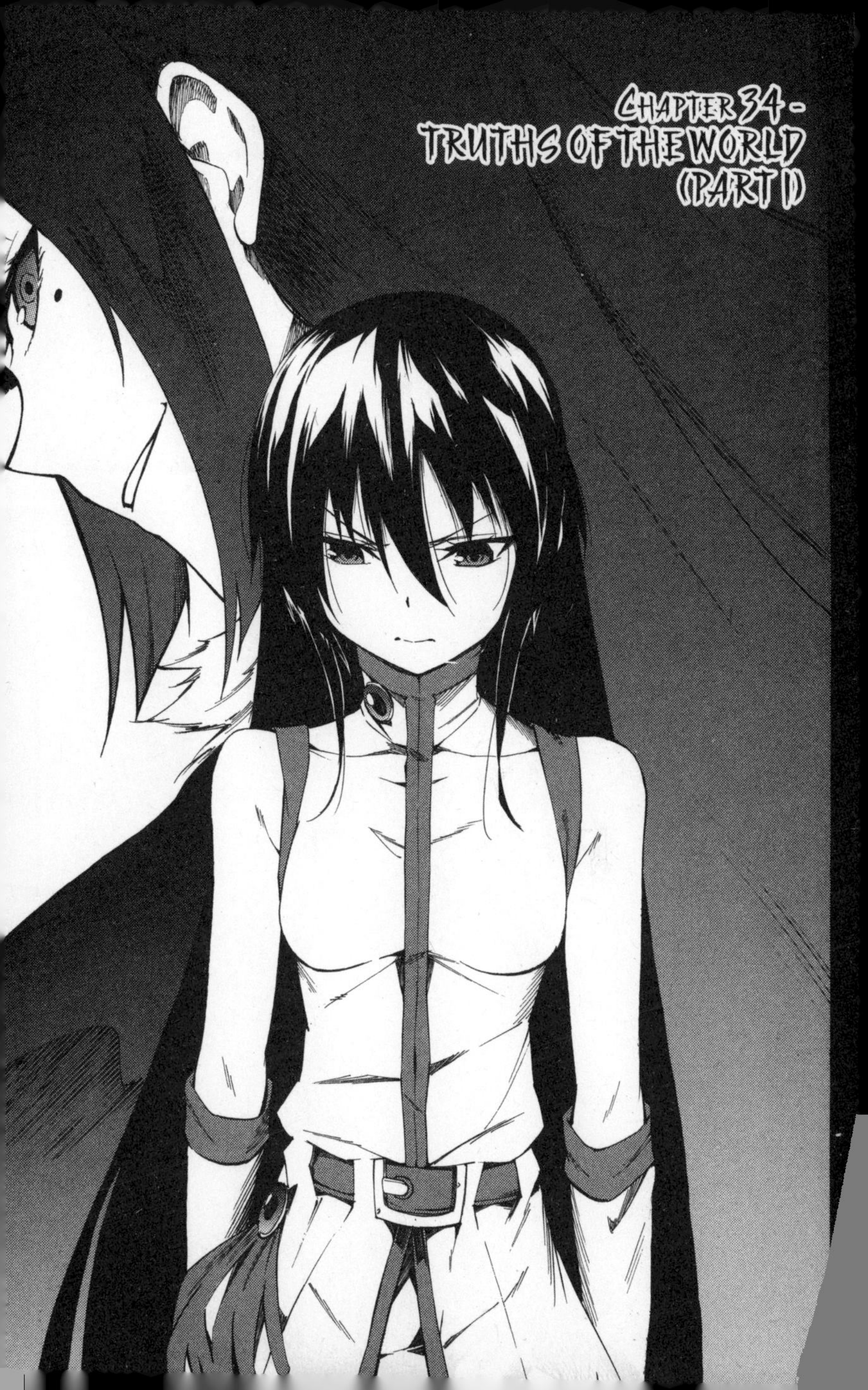
Chapter 34 - Truths of the World (Part 1)

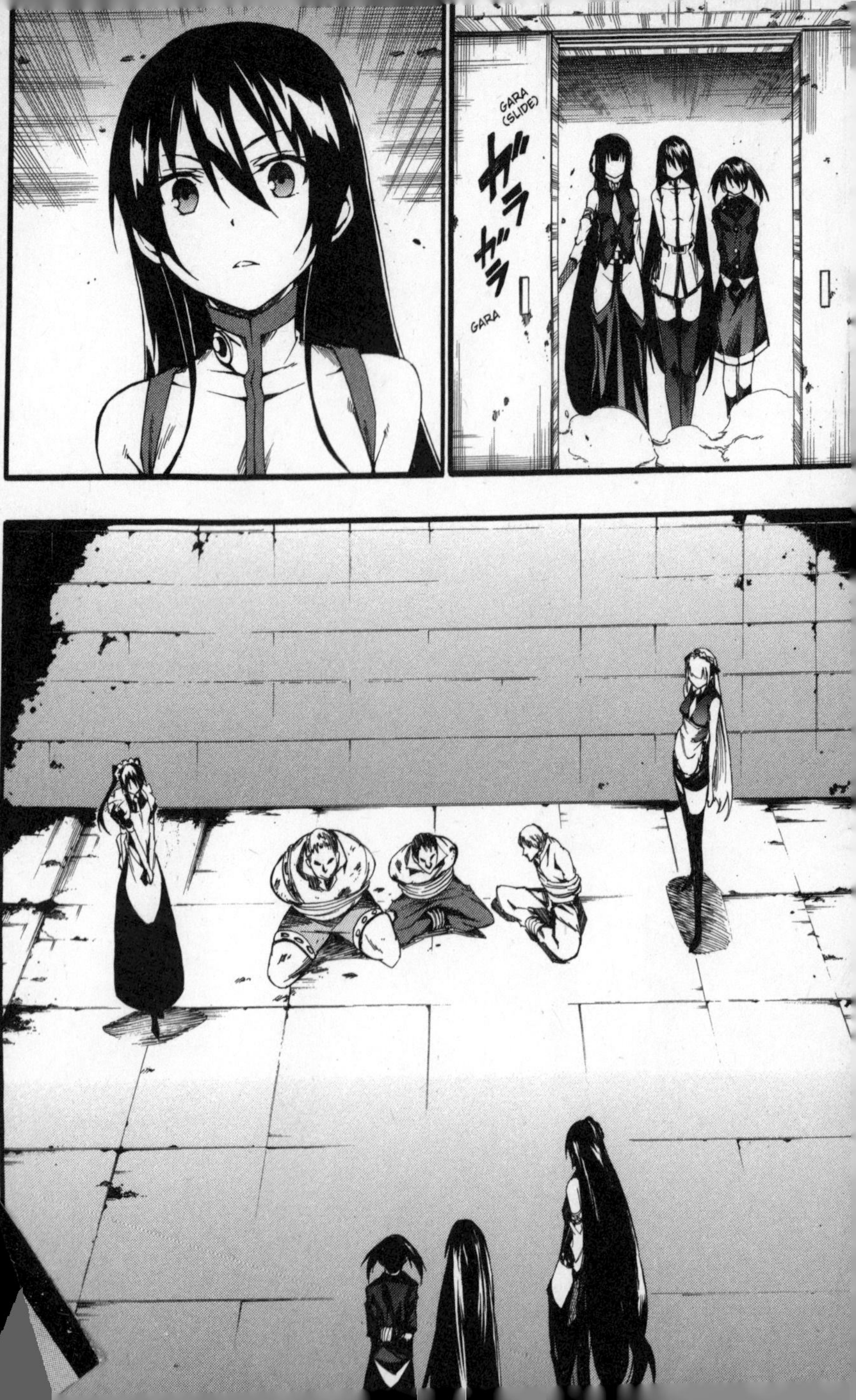
GARA (SLIDE)
ガラガラ
GARA

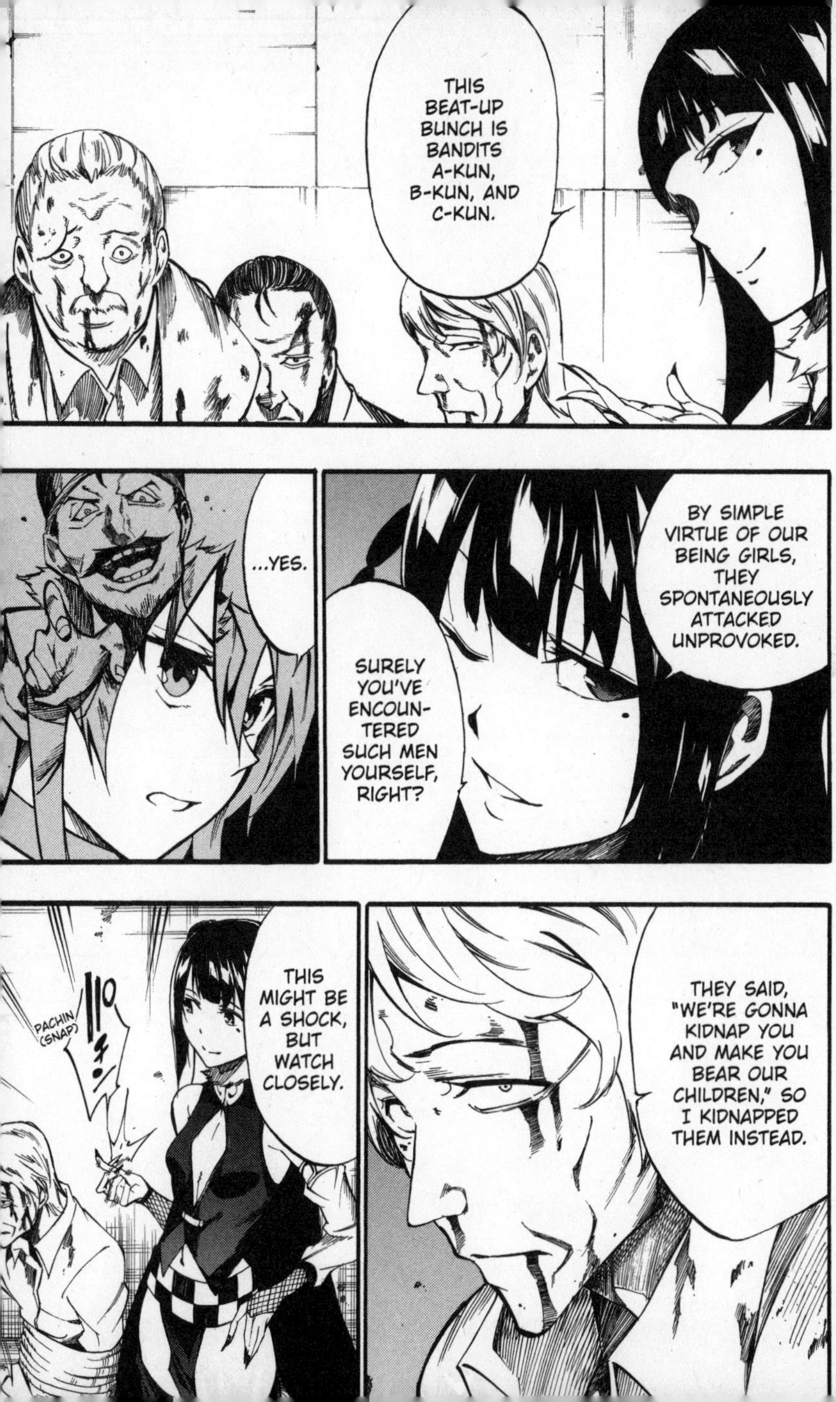
THIS BEAT-UP BUNCH IS BANDITS A-KUN, B-KUN, AND C-KUN.
BY SIMPLE VIRTUE OF OUR BEING GIRLS, THEY SPONTANEOUSLY ATTACKED UNPROVOKED.
SURELY YOU'VE ENCOUN-TERED SUCH MEN YOURSELF, RIGHT?
...YES.
THEY SAID, "WE'RE GONNA KIDNAP YOU AND MAKE YOU BEAR OUR CHILDREN," SO I KIDNAPPED THEM INSTEAD.
THIS MIGHT BE A SHOCK, BUT WATCH CLOSELY.
PACHIN (SNAP)

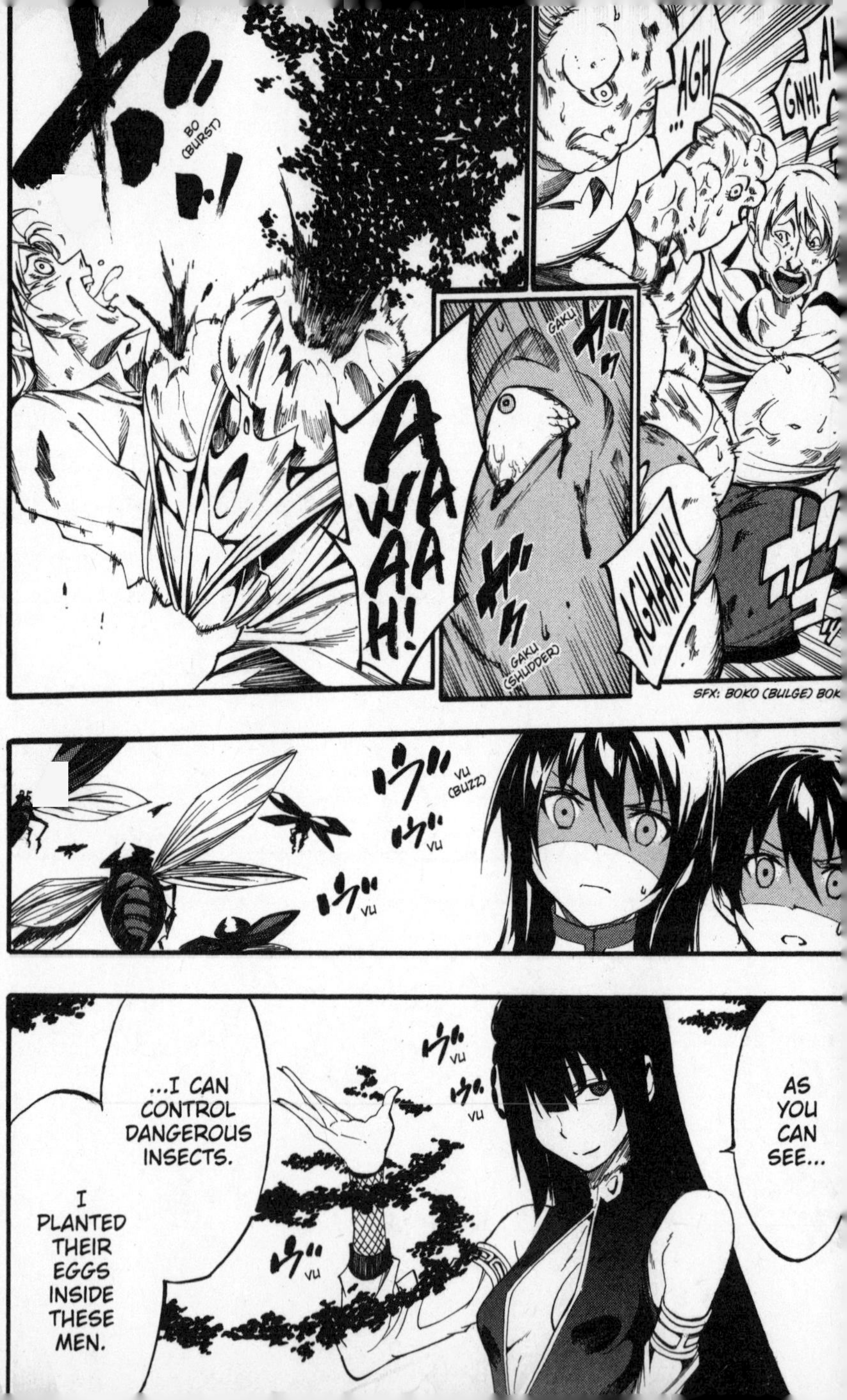
AGH...
GNH!
AGHAAH!
SFX: BOKO (BULGE) BOK
GAKU
GAKU (SHUDDER)
AWAAAH!
BO (BURST)
VU (BUZZ)
VU
VU
AS YOU CAN SEE...
VU
VU
...I CAN CONTROL DANGEROUS INSECTS.
I PLANTED THEIR EGGS INSIDE THESE MEN.
VU

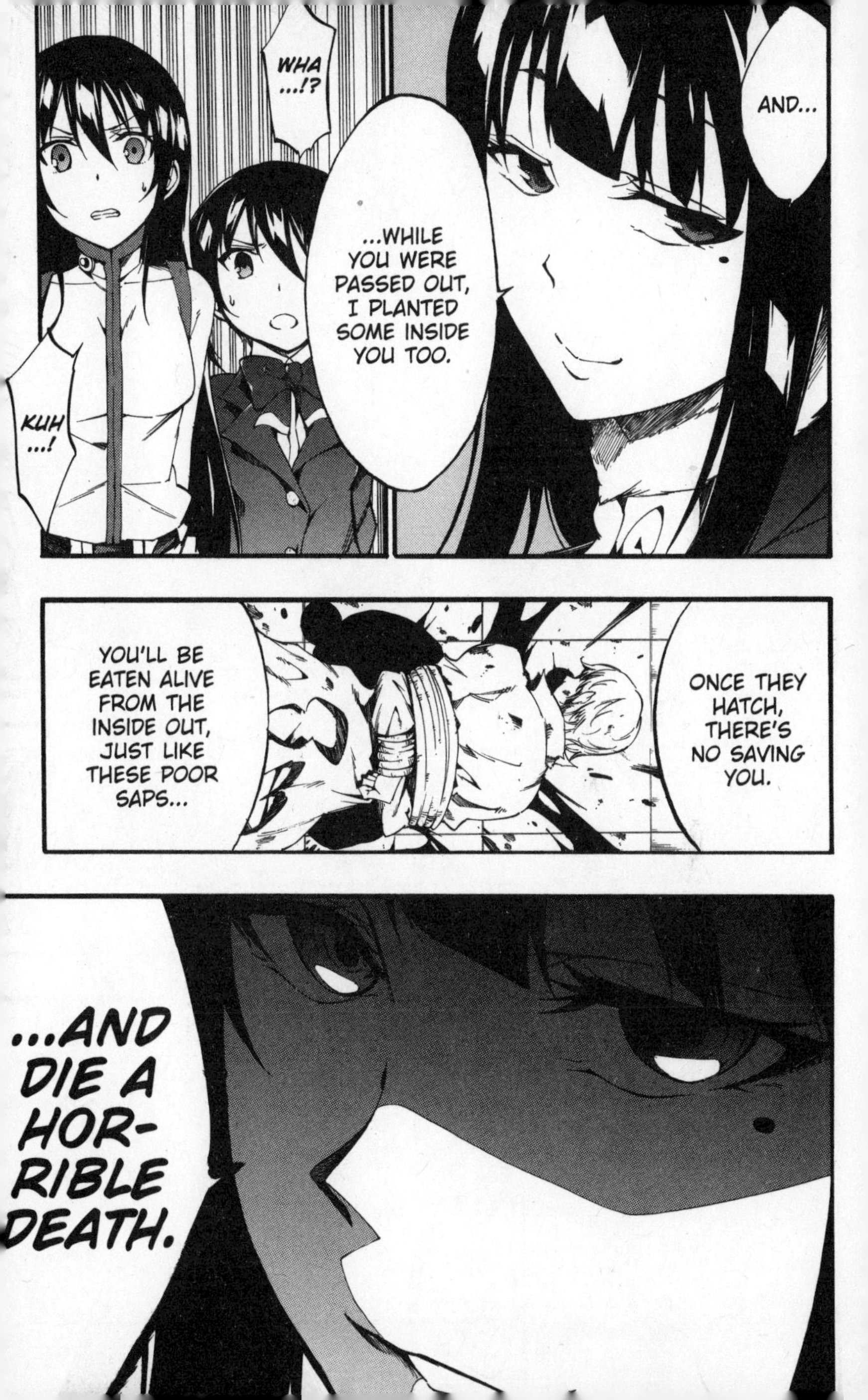
AND...
...WHILE YOU WERE PASSED OUT, I PLANTED SOME INSIDE YOU TOO.
WHA ...!?
KUH ...!
ONCE THEY HATCH, THERE'S NO SAVING YOU.
YOU'LL BE EATEN ALIVE FROM THE INSIDE OUT, JUST LIKE THESE POOR SAPS...
...AND DIE A HOR-RIBLE DEATH.

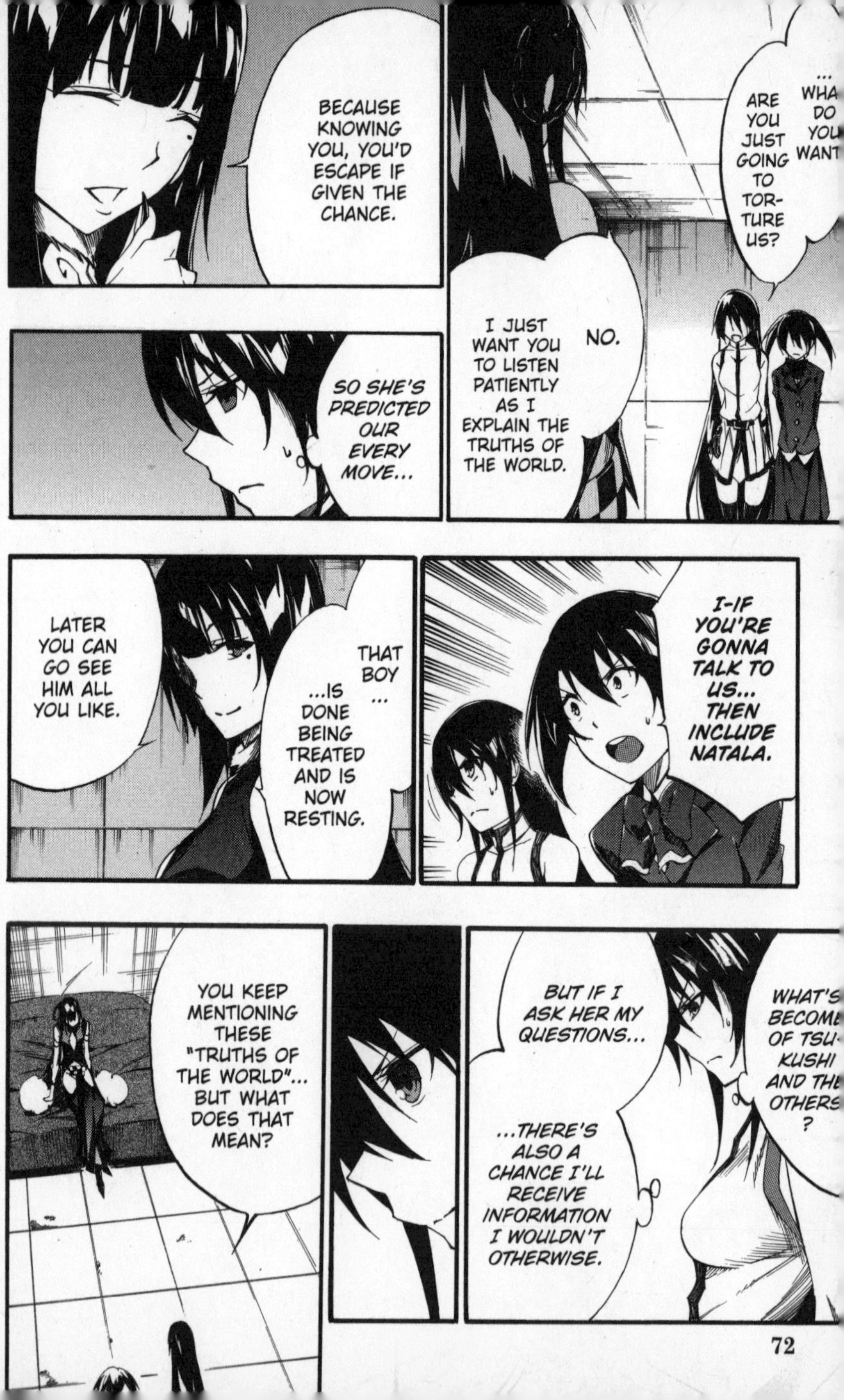
...WHA DO YOU WANT
ARE YOU JUST GOING TO TOR-TURE US?
BECAUSE KNOWING YOU, YOU'D ESCAPE IF GIVEN THE CHANCE.
NO.
I JUST WANT YOU TO LISTEN PATIENTLY AS I EXPLAIN THE TRUTHS OF THE WORLD.
SO SHE'S PREDICTED OUR EVERY MOVE...
I-IF YOU'RE GONNA TALK TO US... THEN INCLUDE NATALA.
THAT BOY ...
...IS DONE BEING TREATED AND IS NOW RESTING.
LATER YOU CAN GO SEE HIM ALL YOU LIKE.
WHAT'S BECOME OF TSU-KUSHI AND THE OTHERS ?
BUT IF I ASK HER MY QUESTIONS...
...THERE'S ALSO A CHANCE I'LL RECEIVE INFORMATION I WOULDN'T OTHERWISE.
YOU KEEP MENTIONING THESE "TRUTHS OF THE WORLD"... BUT WHAT DOES THAT MEAN?

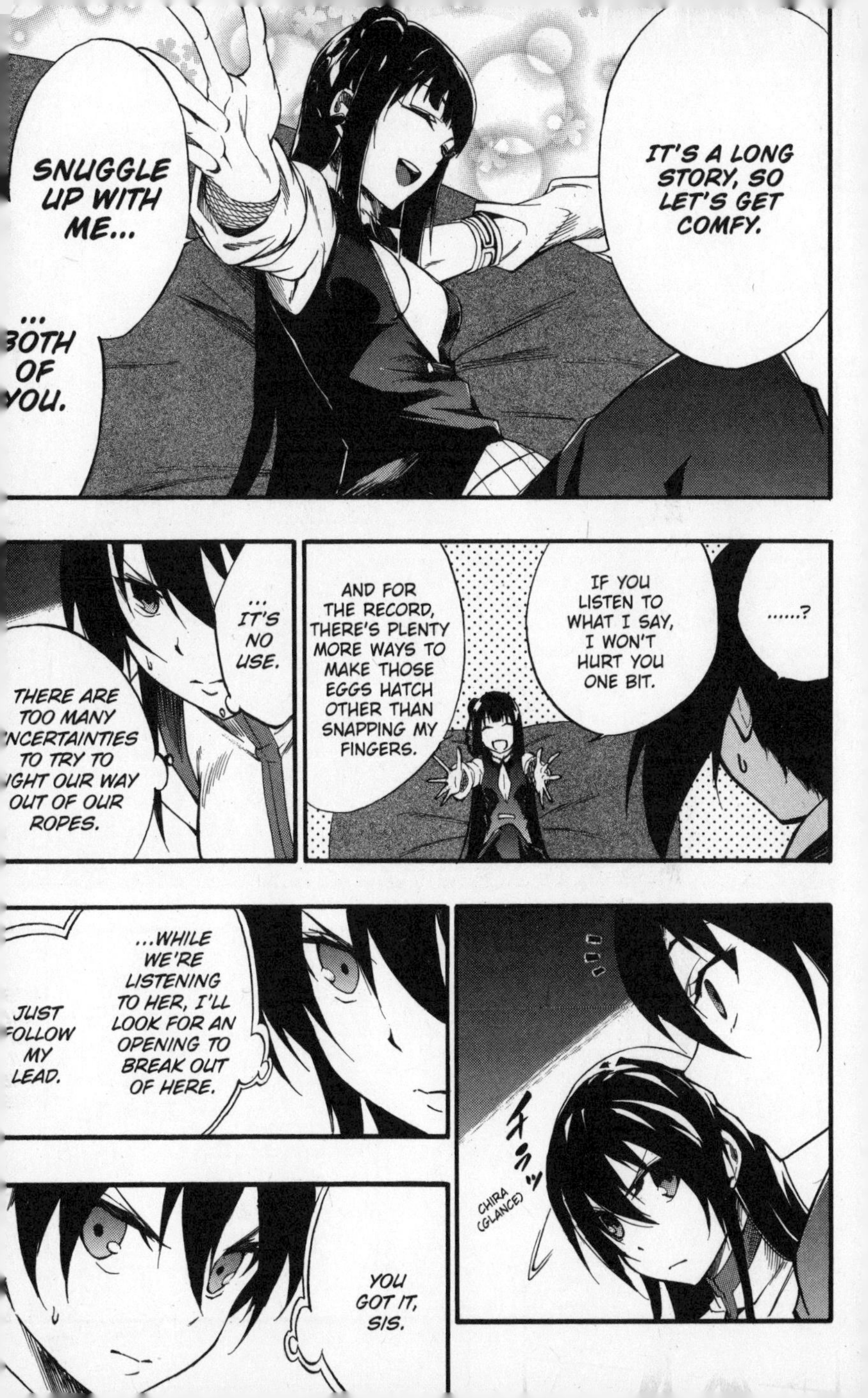
IT'S A LONG STORY, SO LET'S GET COMFY.
SNUGGLE UP WITH ME...
... BOTH OF YOU.
......?
IF YOU LISTEN TO WHAT I SAY, I WON'T HURT YOU ONE BIT.
AND FOR THE RECORD, THERE'S PLENTY MORE WAYS TO MAKE THOSE EGGS HATCH OTHER THAN SNAPPING MY FINGERS.
... IT'S NO USE.
THERE ARE TOO MANY UNCERTAINTIES TO TRY TO FIGHT OUR WAY OUT OF OUR ROPES.
チラッ
CHIRA (GLANCE)
...WHILE WE'RE LISTENING TO HER, I'LL LOOK FOR AN OPENING TO BREAK OUT OF HERE.
JUST FOLLOW MY LEAD.
YOU GOT IT, SIS.

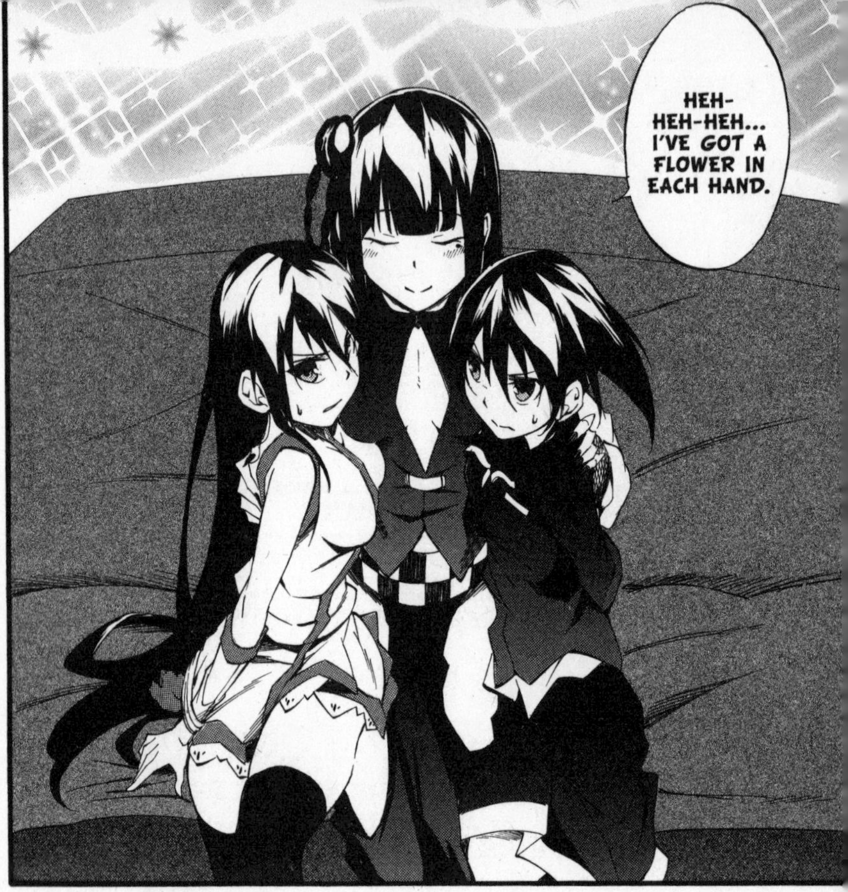
HEH-HEH-HEH... I'VE GOT A FLOWER IN EACH HAND.

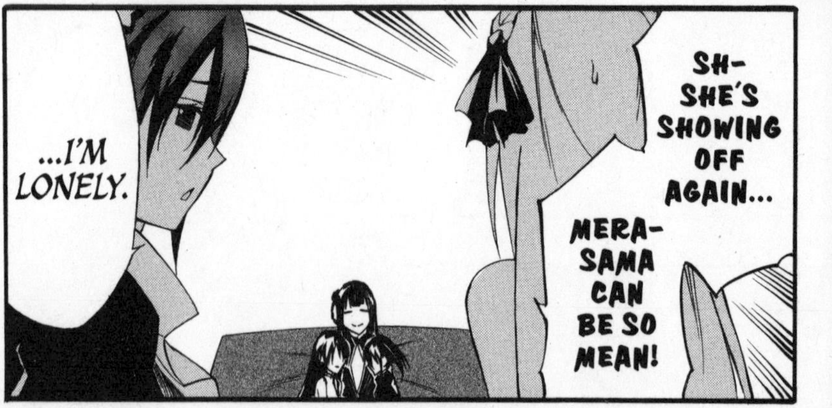
SH-SHE'S SHOWING OFF AGAIN...
MERA-SAMA CAN BE SO MEAN!
...I'M LONELY.

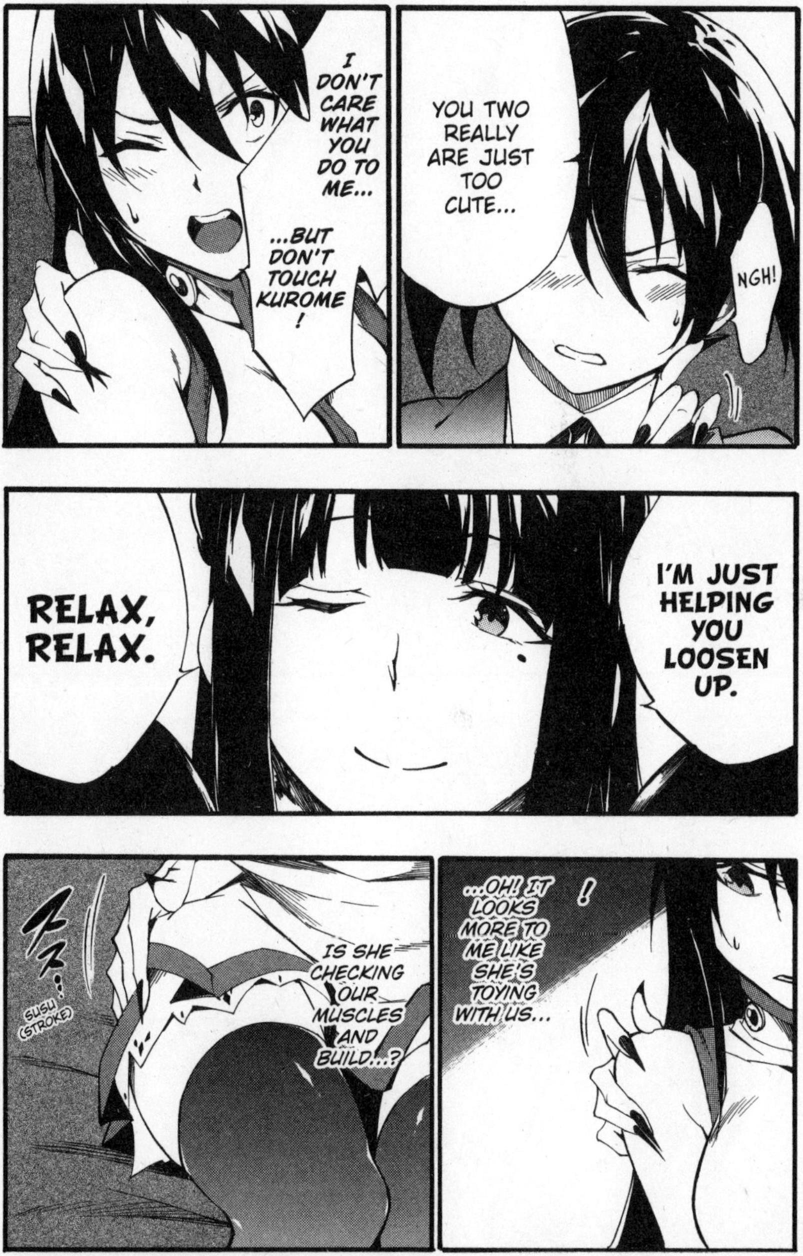
YOU TWO REALLY ARE JUST TOO CUTE...
NGH!
I DON'T CARE WHAT YOU DO TO ME...
...BUT DON'T TOUCH KUROME!
I'M JUST HELPING YOU LOOSEN UP.
RELAX, RELAX.
!
...OH! IT LOOKS MORE TO ME LIKE SHE'S TOYING WITH US...
IS SHE CHECKING OUR MUSCLES AND BUILD...?
SUSU (STROKE)

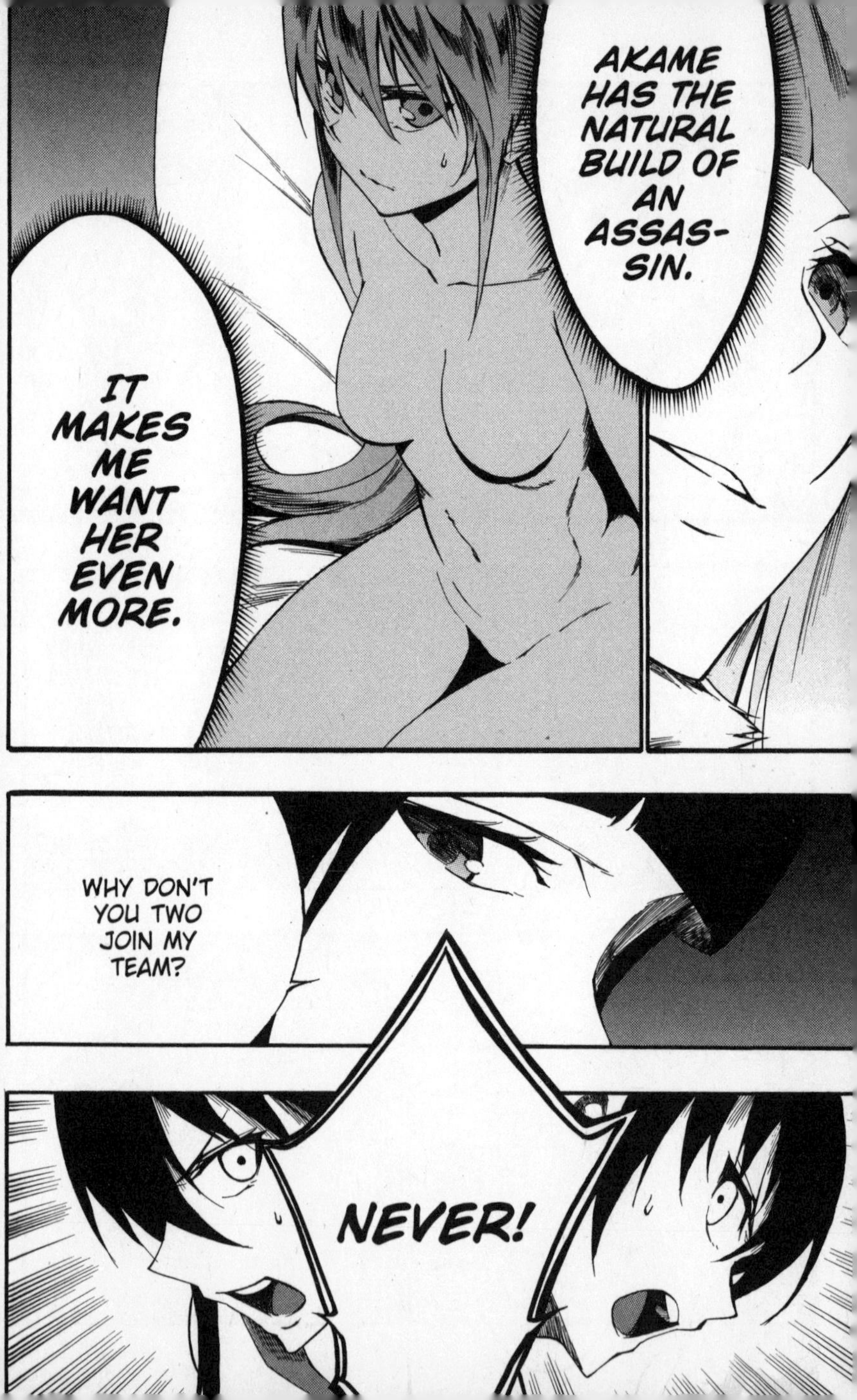
AKAME HAS THE NATURAL BUILD OF AN ASSAS-SIN.
IT MAKES ME WANT HER EVEN MORE.
WHY DON'T YOU TWO JOIN MY TEAM?
NEVER!

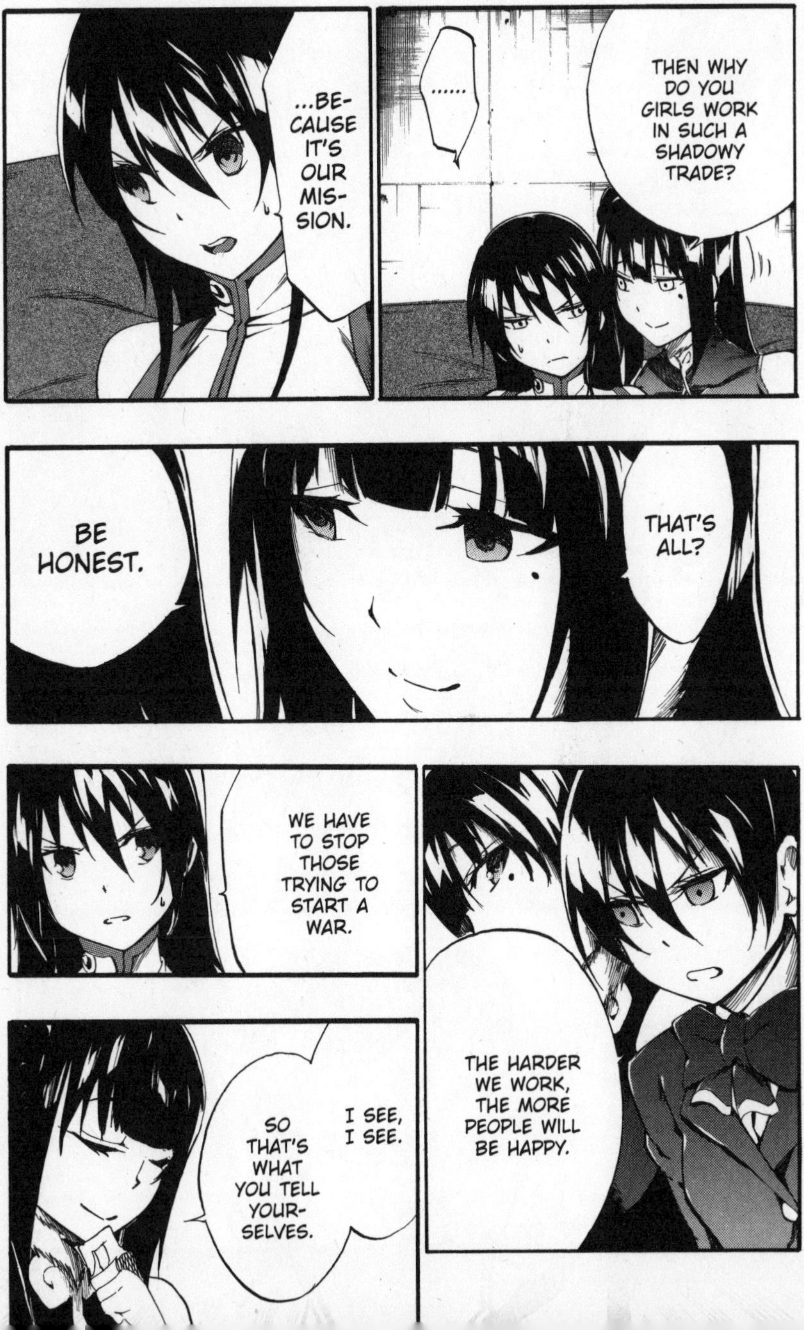
THEN WHY DO YOU GIRLS WORK IN SUCH A SHADOWY TRADE?
......
...BE-CAUSE IT'S OUR MIS-SION.
THAT'S ALL?
BE HONEST.
WE HAVE TO STOP THOSE TRYING TO START A WAR.
THE HARDER WE WORK, THE MORE PEOPLE WILL BE HAPPY.
I SEE, I SEE.
SO THAT'S WHAT YOU TELL YOUR-SELVES.

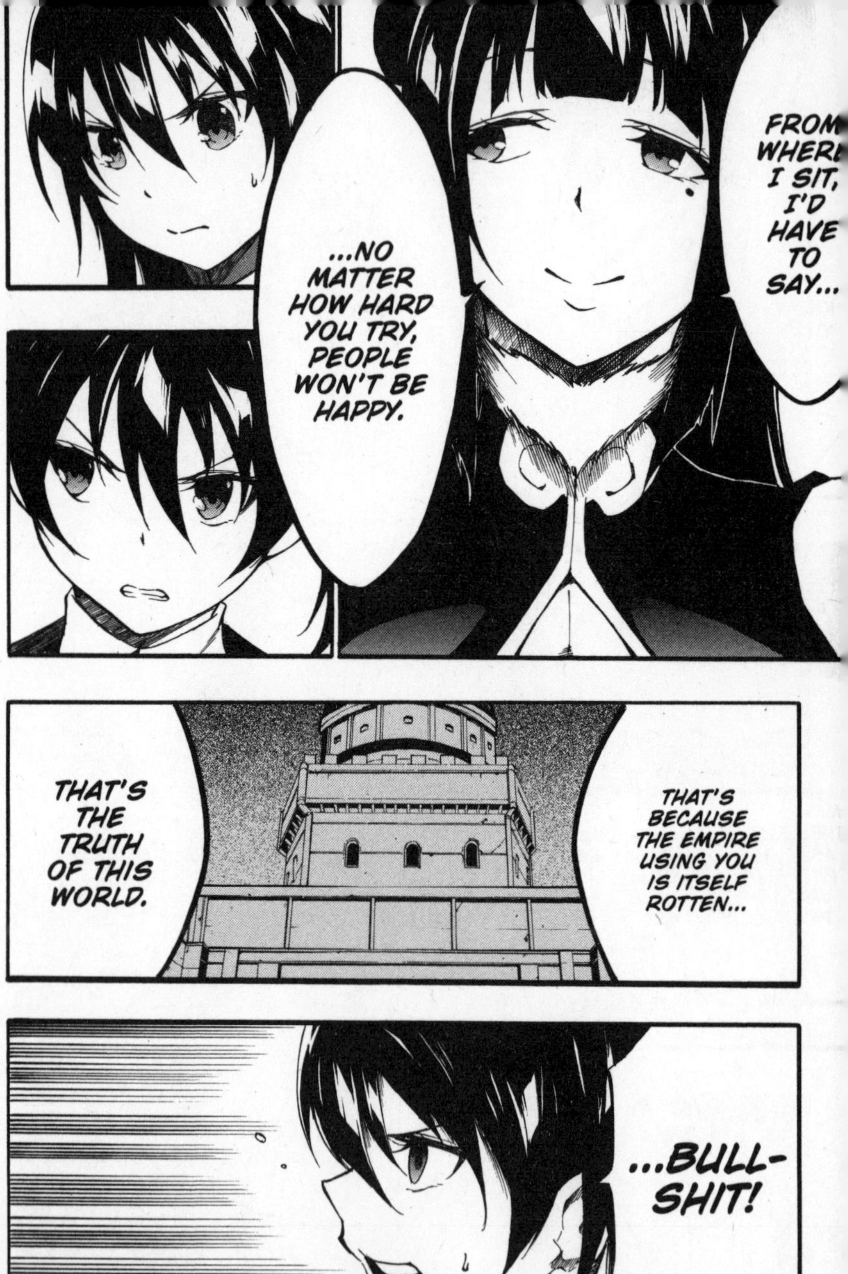
FROM WHERE I SIT, I'D HAVE TO SAY...
...NO MATTER HOW HARD YOU TRY, PEOPLE WON'T BE HAPPY.
THAT'S BECAUSE THE EMPIRE USING YOU IS ITSELF ROTTEN...
THAT'S THE TRUTH OF THIS WORLD.
...BULL-SHIT!

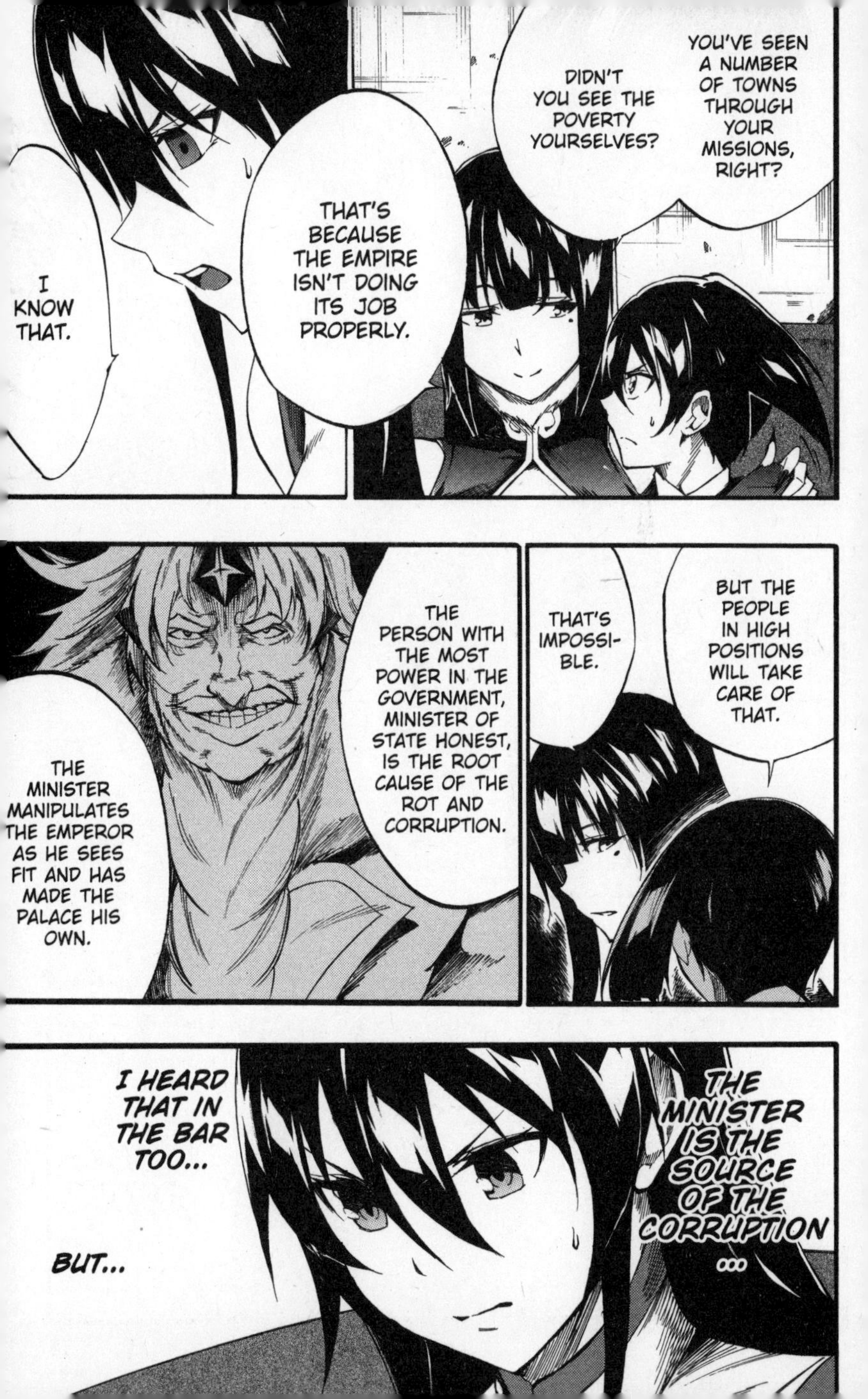
YOU'VE SEEN A NUMBER OF TOWNS THROUGH YOUR MISSIONS, RIGHT?
DIDN'T YOU SEE THE POVERTY YOURSELVES?
THAT'S BECAUSE THE EMPIRE ISN'T DOING ITS JOB PROPERLY.
I KNOW THAT.
BUT THE PEOPLE IN HIGH POSITIONS WILL TAKE CARE OF THAT.
THAT'S IMPOSSI-BLE.
THE PERSON WITH THE MOST POWER IN THE GOVERNMENT, MINISTER OF STATE HONEST, IS THE ROOT CAUSE OF THE ROT AND CORRUPTION.
THE MINISTER MANIPULATES THE EMPEROR AS HE SEES FIT AND HAS MADE THE PALACE HIS OWN.
THE MINISTER IS THE SOURCE OF THE CORRUPTION...
I HEARD THAT IN THE BAR TOO...
BUT...

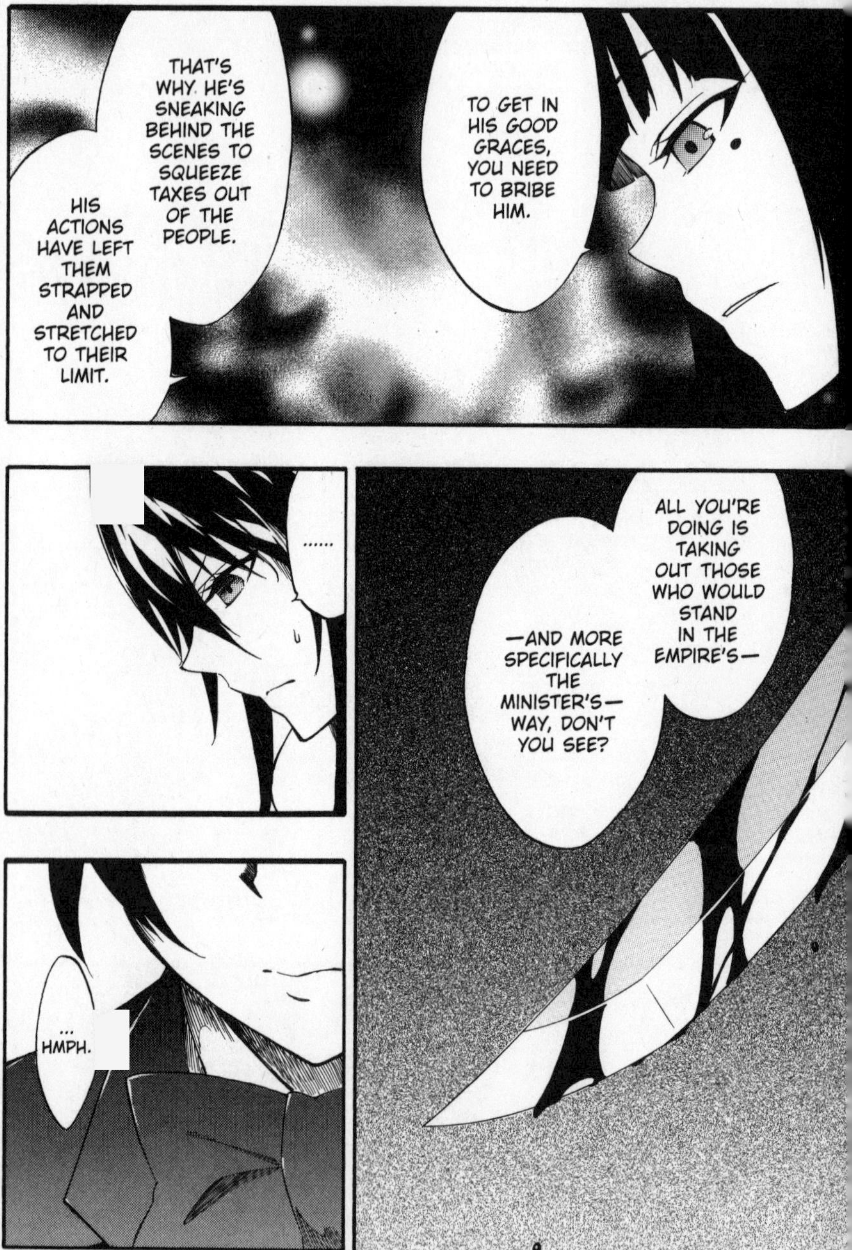
TO GET IN HIS GOOD GRACES, YOU NEED TO BRIBE HIM.
THAT'S WHY HE'S SNEAKING BEHIND THE SCENES TO SQUEEZE TAXES OUT OF THE PEOPLE.
HIS ACTIONS HAVE LEFT THEM STRAPPED AND STRETCHED TO THEIR LIMIT.
ALL YOU'RE DOING IS TAKING OUT THOSE WHO WOULD STAND IN THE EMPIRE'S—
—AND MORE SPECIFICALLY THE MINISTER'S—WAY, DON'T YOU SEE?
......
... HMPH.

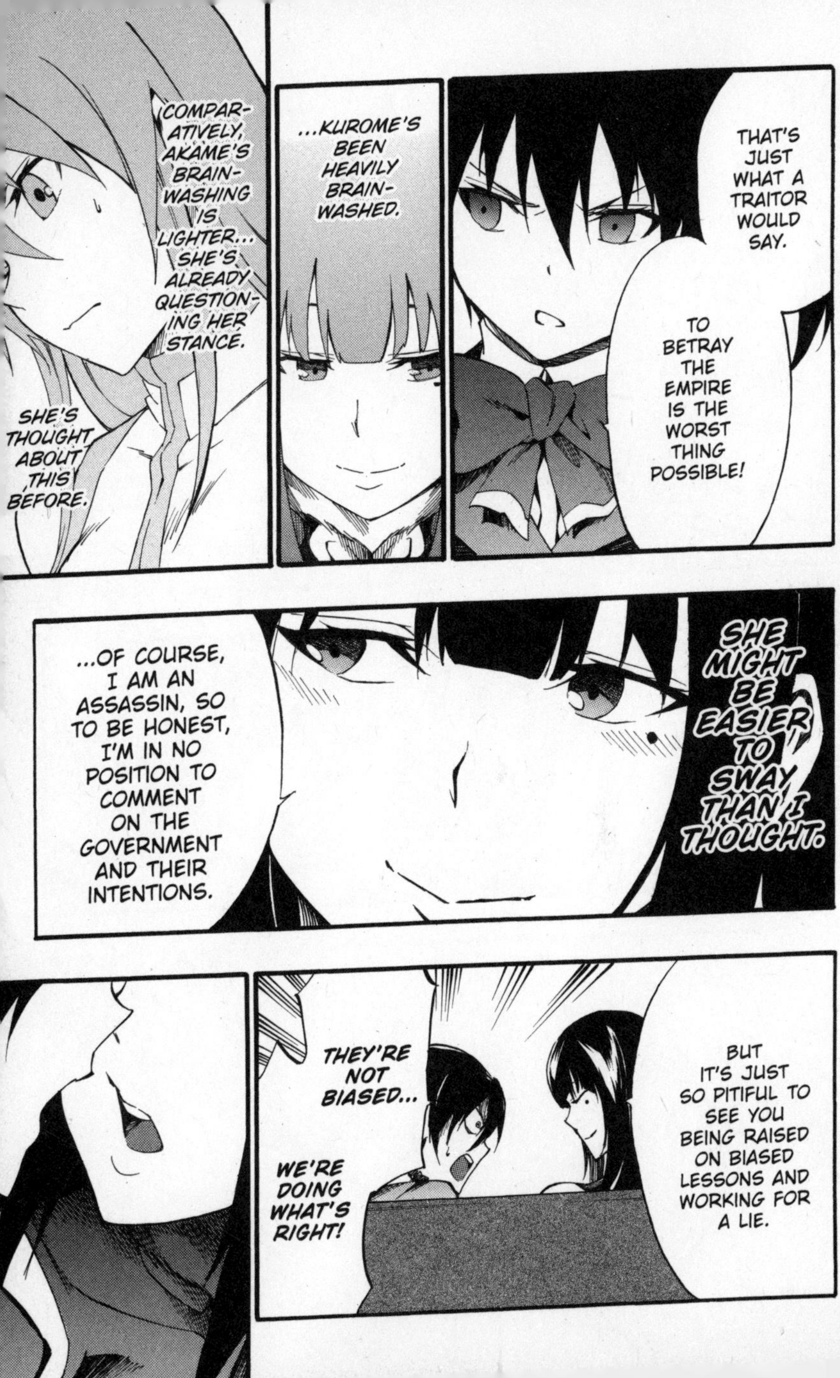
THAT'S JUST WHAT A TRAITOR WOULD SAY.
TO BETRAY THE EMPIRE IS THE WORST THING POSSIBLE!
...KUROME'S BEEN HEAVILY BRAIN-WASHED.
COMPAR-ATIVELY, AKAME'S BRAIN-WASHING IS LIGHTER... SHE'S ALREADY QUESTION-ING HER STANCE.
SHE'S THOUGHT ABOUT THIS BEFORE.
SHE MIGHT BE EASIER TO SWAY THAN I THOUGHT.
...OF COURSE, I AM AN ASSASSIN, SO TO BE HONEST, I'M IN NO POSITION TO COMMENT ON THE GOVERNMENT AND THEIR INTENTIONS.
BUT IT'S JUST SO PITIFUL TO SEE YOU BEING RAISED ON BIASED LESSONS AND WORKING FOR A LIE.
THEY'RE NOT BIASED...
WE'RE DOING WHAT'S RIGHT!

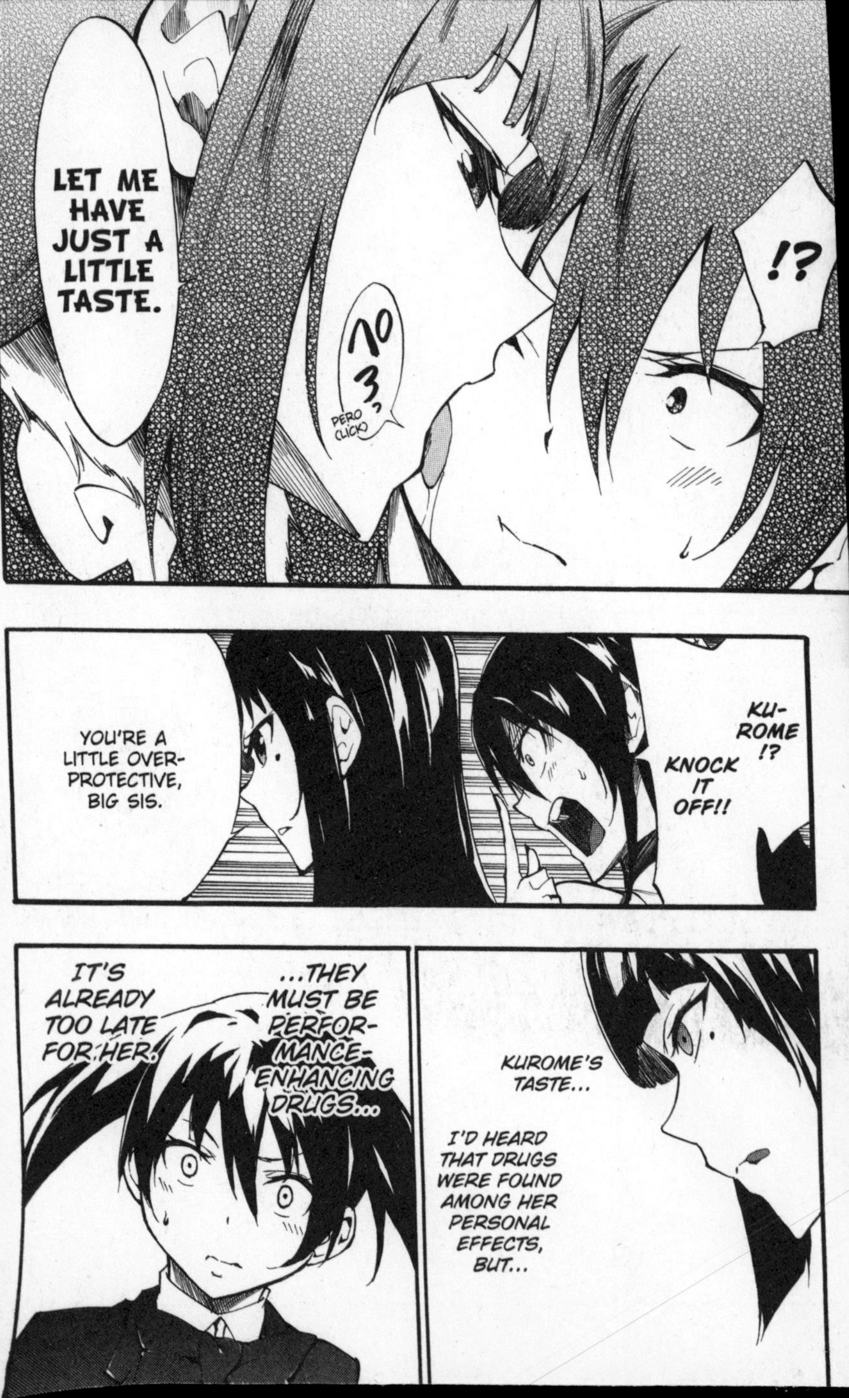
!?
PERO (LICK)
LET ME HAVE JUST A LITTLE TASTE.
KU-ROME !?
KNOCK IT OFF!!
YOU'RE A LITTLE OVER-PROTECTIVE, BIG SIS.
KUROME'S TASTE...
I'D HEARD THAT DRUGS WERE FOUND AMONG HER PERSONAL EFFECTS, BUT...
...THEY MUST BE PERFORMANCE-ENHANCING DRUGS...
IT'S ALREADY TOO LATE FOR HER.

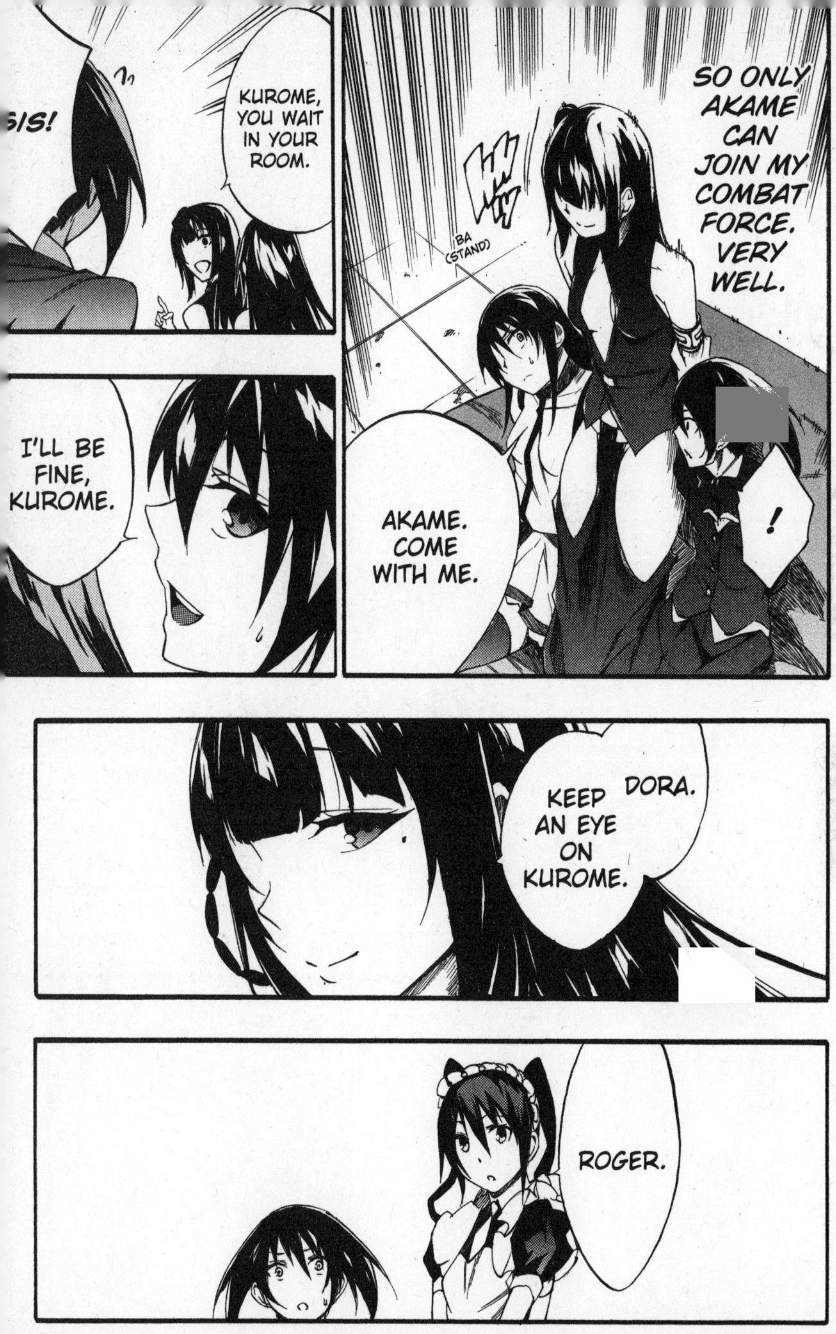
SO ONLY AKAME CAN JOIN MY COMBAT FORCE. VERY WELL.
BA (STAND)
AKAME. COME WITH ME.
!
SIS!
KUROME, YOU WAIT IN YOUR ROOM.
I'LL BE FINE, KUROME.
DORA.
KEEP AN EYE ON KUROME.
ROGER.

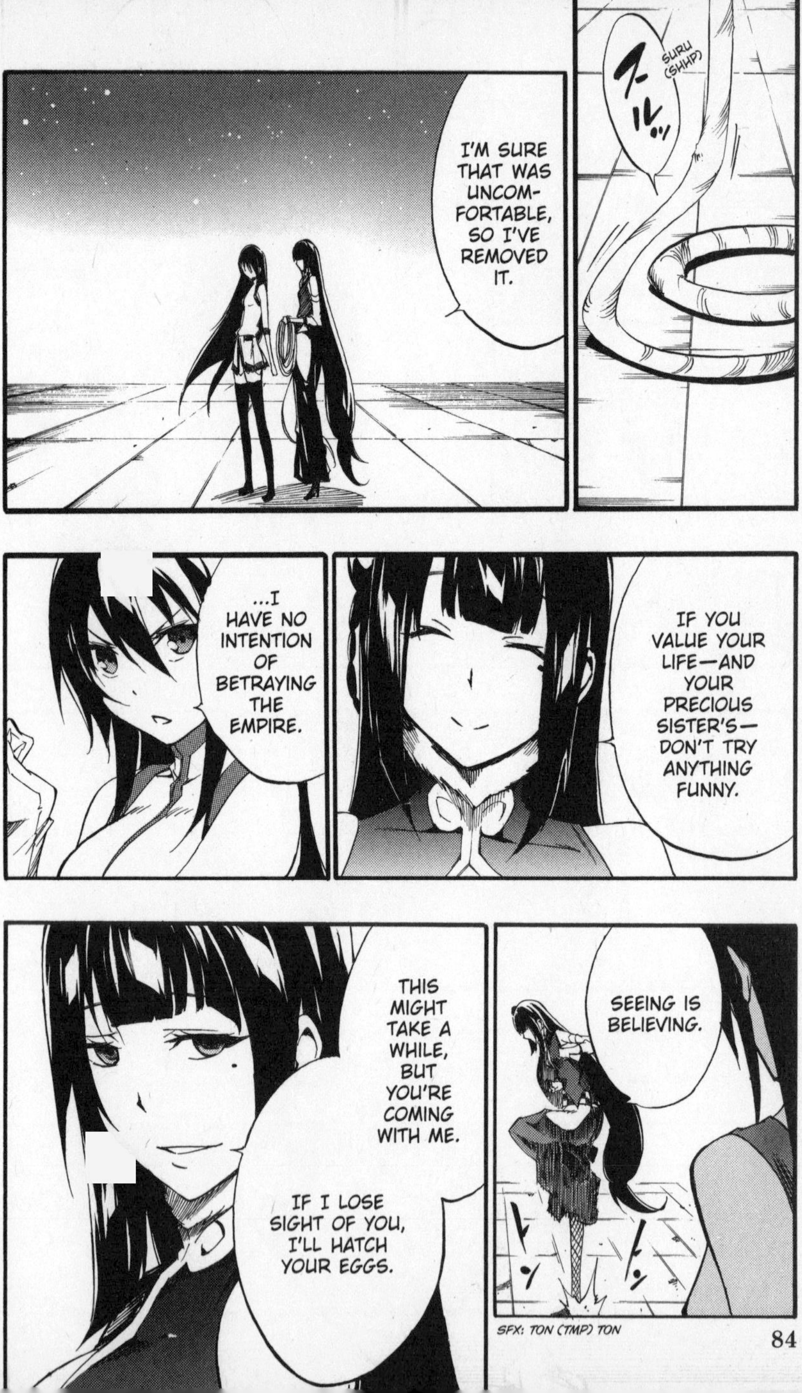
SURU (SHHP)
I'M SURE THAT WAS UNCOM-FORTABLE, SO I'VE REMOVED IT.
IF YOU VALUE YOUR LIFE—AND YOUR PRECIOUS SISTER'S—DON'T TRY ANYTHING FUNNY.
...I HAVE NO INTENTION OF BETRAYING THE EMPIRE.
SEEING IS BELIEVING.
THIS MIGHT TAKE A WHILE, BUT YOU'RE COMING WITH ME.
IF I LOSE SIGHT OF YOU, I'LL HATCH YOUR EGGS.
SFX: TON (TMP) TON

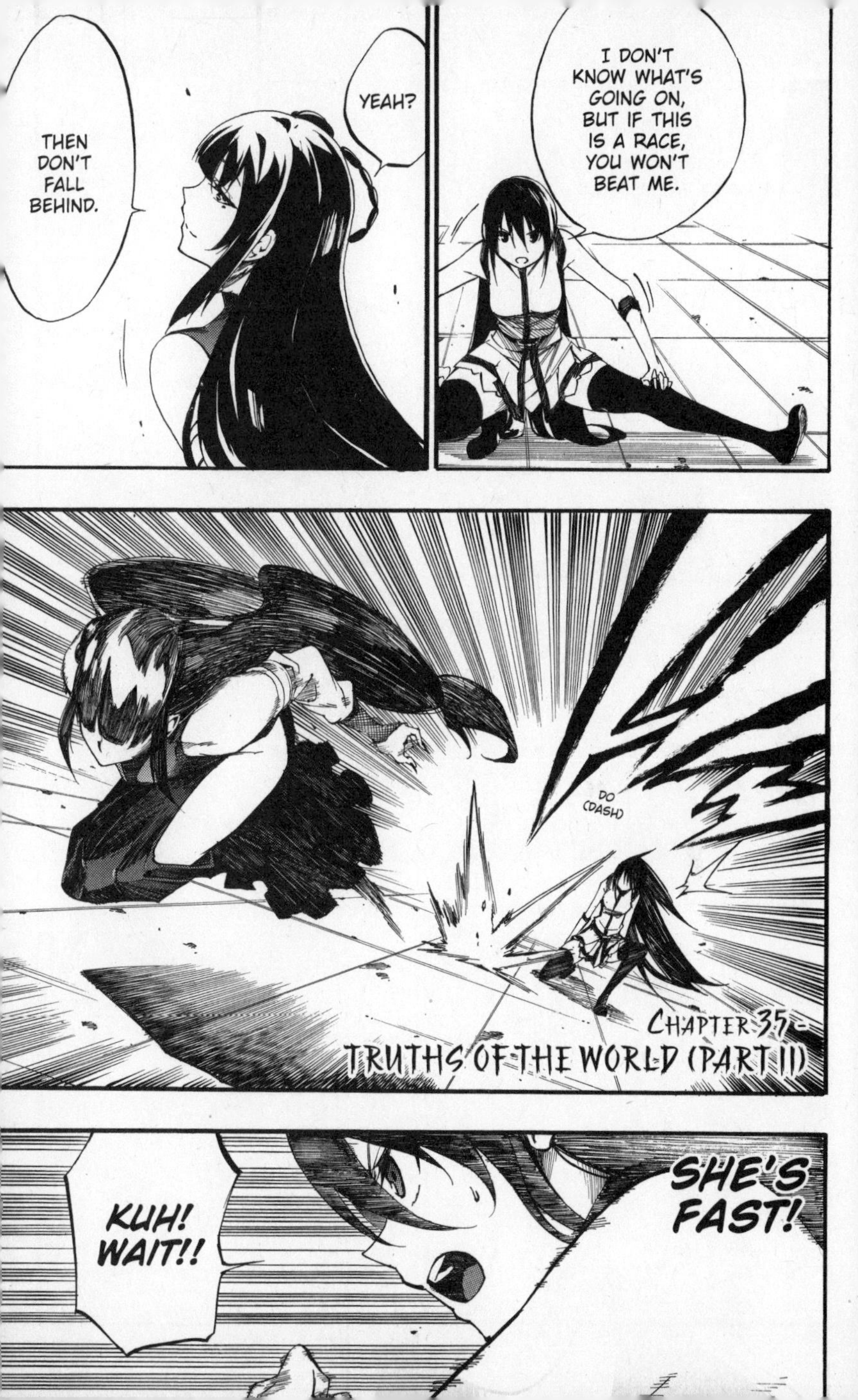
I DON'T KNOW WHAT'S GOING ON, BUT IF THIS IS A RACE, YOU WON'T BEAT ME.
YEAH?
THEN DON'T FALL BEHIND.
DO (DASH)
CHAPTER 35 - TRUTHS OF THE WORLD (PART II)
SHE'S FAST!
KUH! WAIT!!

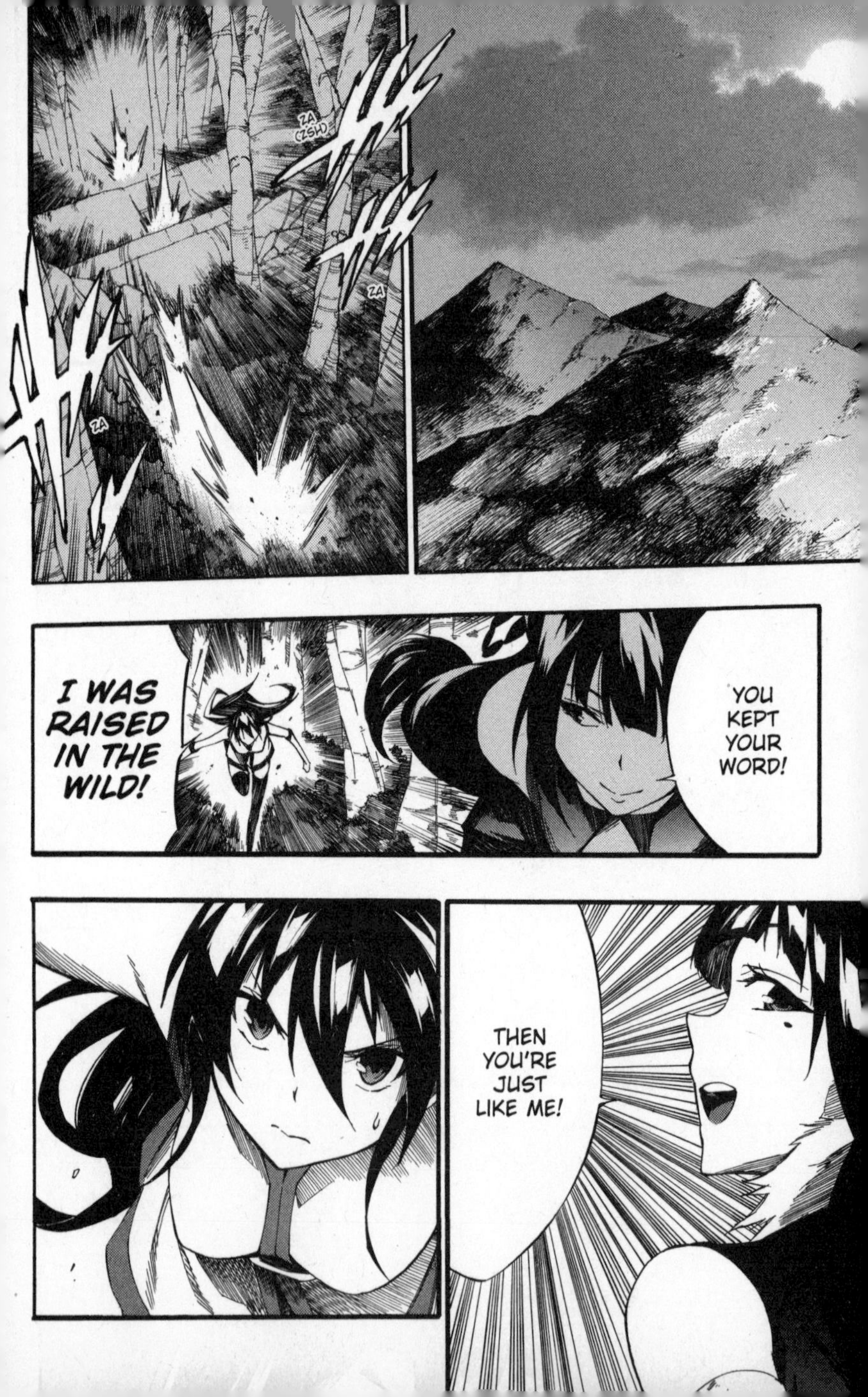
ZA (ZSH)
ZA
ZA
YOU KEPT YOUR WORD!
I WAS RAISED IN THE WILD!
THEN YOU'RE JUST LIKE ME!

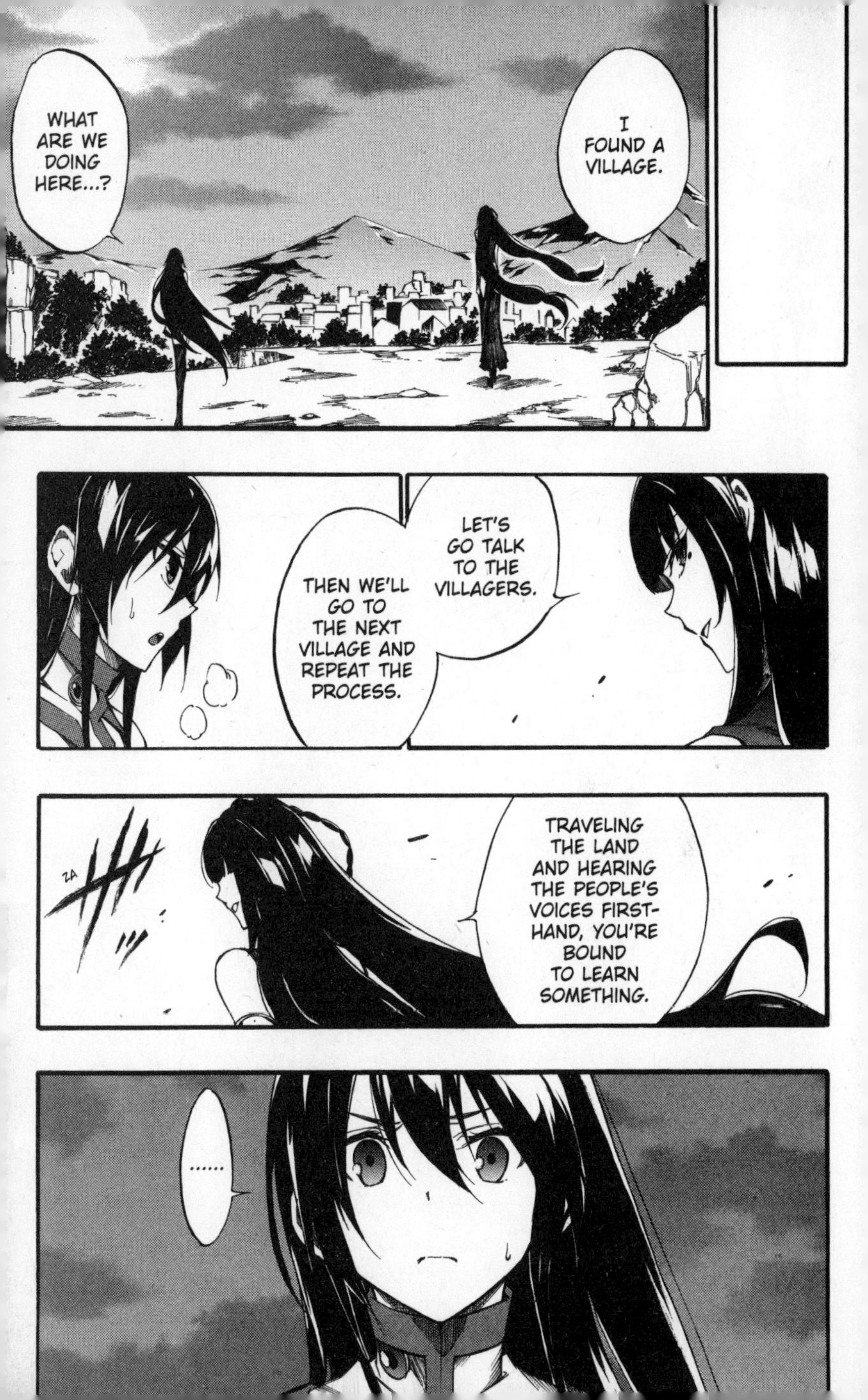
I FOUND A VILLAGE.
WHAT ARE WE DOING HERE...?
LET'S GO TALK TO THE VILLAGERS.
THEN WE'LL GO TO THE NEXT VILLAGE AND REPEAT THE PROCESS.
TRAVELING THE LAND AND HEARING THE PEOPLE'S VOICES FIRST-HAND, YOU'RE BOUND TO LEARN SOMETHING.
ZA
......

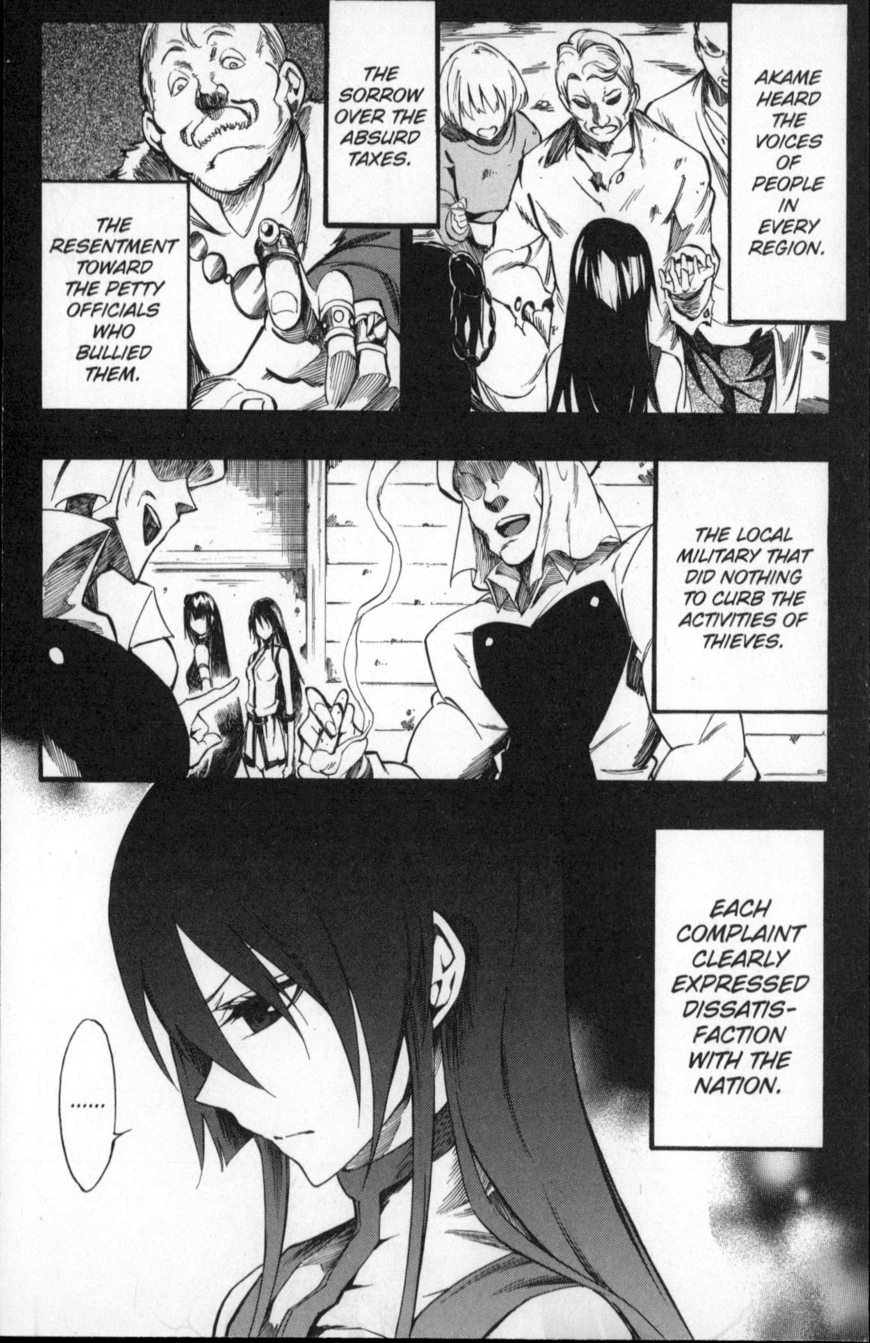
AKAME HEARD THE VOICES OF PEOPLE IN EVERY REGION.
THE SORROW OVER THE ABSURD TAXES.
THE RESENTMENT TOWARD THE PETTY OFFICIALS WHO BULLIED THEM.
THE LOCAL MILITARY THAT DID NOTHING TO CURB THE ACTIVITIES OF THIEVES.
EACH COMPLAINT CLEARLY EXPRESSED DISSATIS-FACTION WITH THE NATION.
......

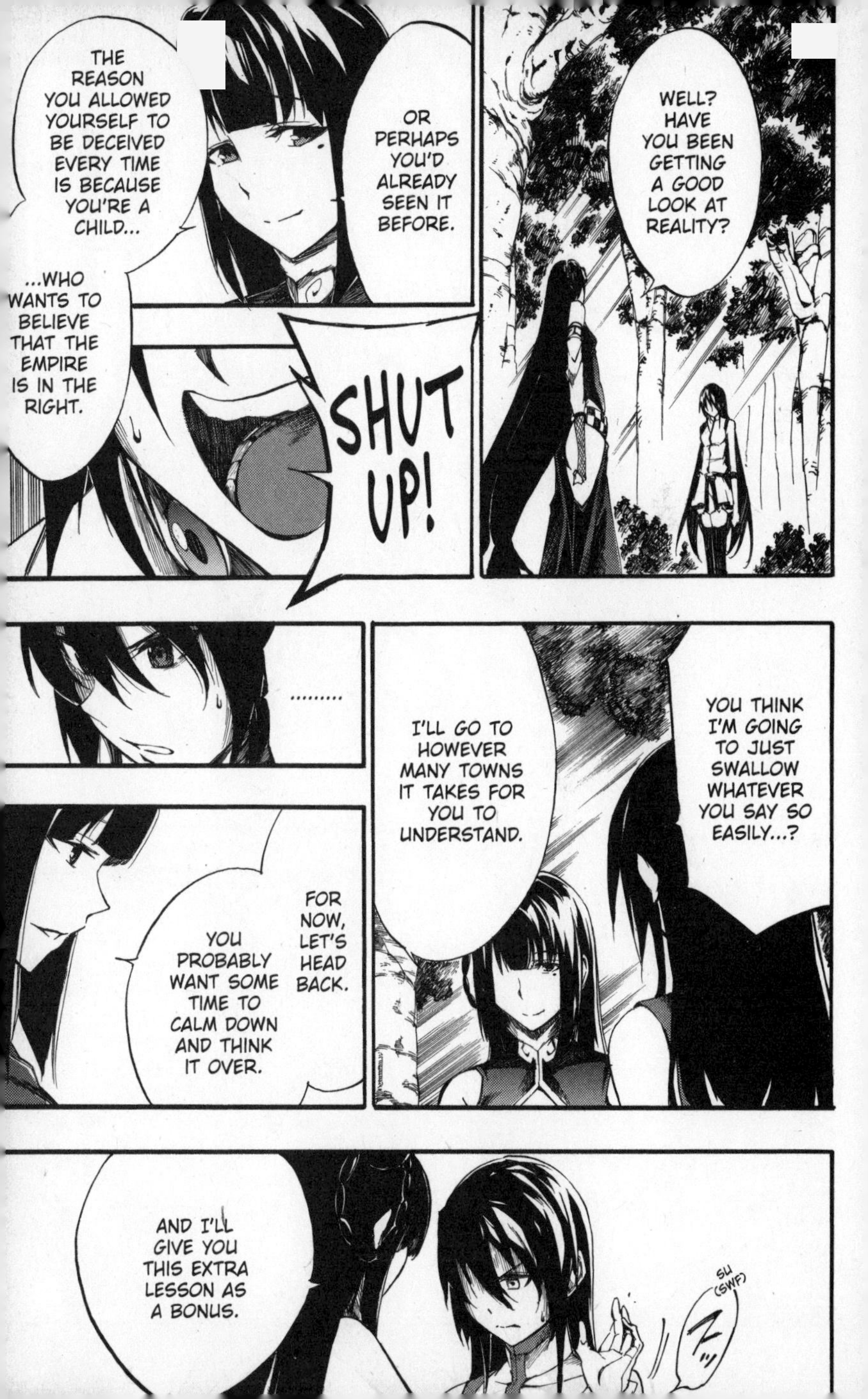
WELL? HAVE YOU BEEN GETTING A GOOD LOOK AT REALITY?
OR PERHAPS YOU'D ALREADY SEEN IT BEFORE.
THE REASON YOU ALLOWED YOURSELF TO BE DECEIVED EVERY TIME IS BECAUSE YOU'RE A CHILD...
...WHO WANTS TO BELIEVE THAT THE EMPIRE IS IN THE RIGHT.
SHUT UP!
YOU THINK I'M GOING TO JUST SWALLOW WHATEVER YOU SAY SO EASILY...?
I'LL GO TO HOWEVER MANY TOWNS IT TAKES FOR YOU TO UNDERSTAND.
....
FOR NOW, LET'S HEAD BACK.
YOU PROBABLY WANT SOME TIME TO CALM DOWN AND THINK IT OVER.
AND I'LL GIVE YOU THIS EXTRA LESSON AS A BONUS.
SU (SWF)

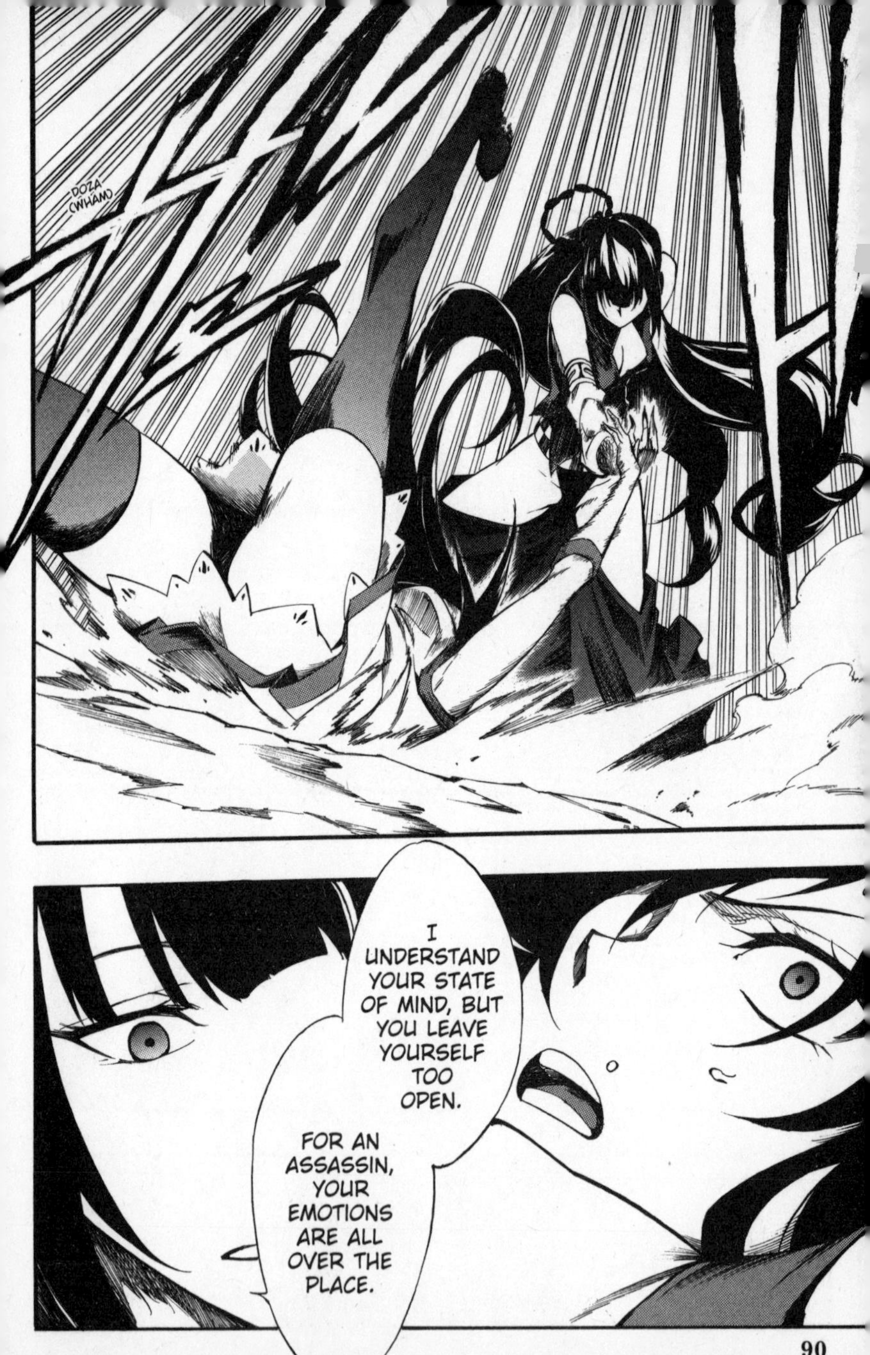
DOZA (WHAM)
I UNDERSTAND YOUR STATE OF MIND, BUT YOU LEAVE YOURSELF TOO OPEN.
FOR AN ASSASSIN, YOUR EMOTIONS ARE ALL OVER THE PLACE.

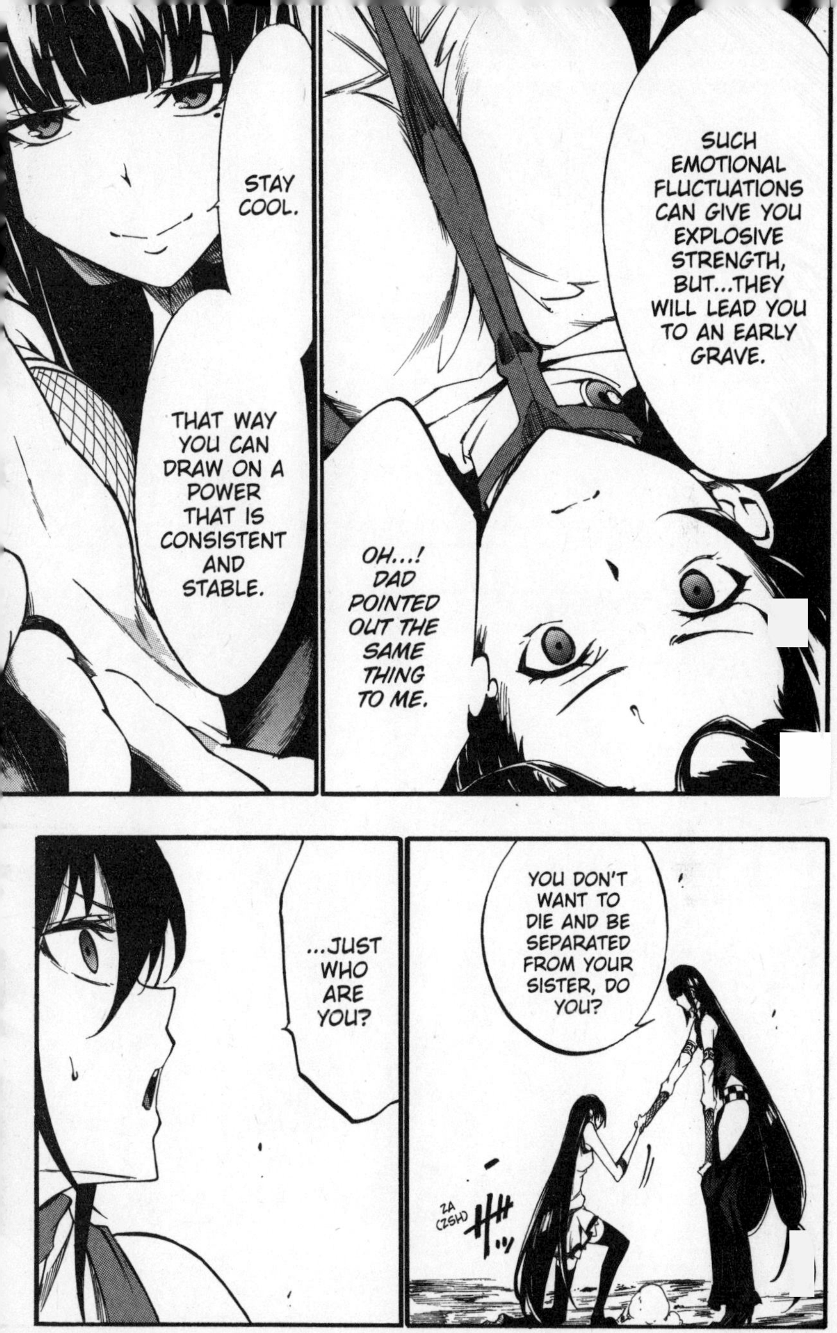
SUCH EMOTIONAL FLUCTUATIONS CAN GIVE YOU EXPLOSIVE STRENGTH, BUT...THEY WILL LEAD YOU TO AN EARLY GRAVE.
OH...! DAD POINTED OUT THE SAME THING TO ME.
STAY COOL.
THAT WAY YOU CAN DRAW ON A POWER THAT IS CONSISTENT AND STABLE.
YOU DON'T WANT TO DIE AND BE SEPARATED FROM YOUR SISTER, DO YOU?
ZA (ZSH)
...JUST WHO ARE YOU?

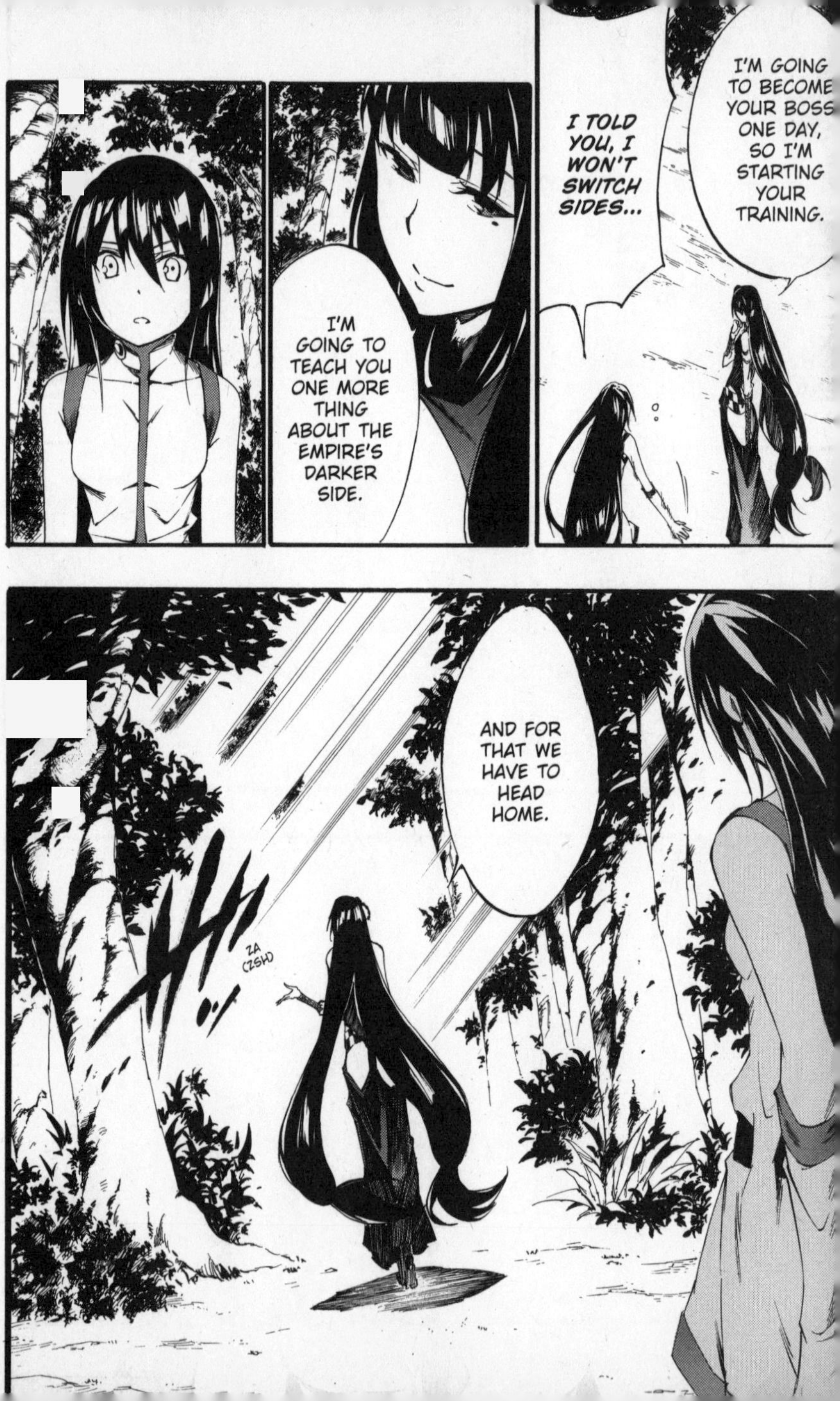
I'M GOING TO BECOME YOUR BOSS ONE DAY, SO I'M STARTING YOUR TRAINING.
I TOLD YOU, I WON'T SWITCH SIDES...
I'M GOING TO TEACH YOU ONE MORE THING ABOUT THE EMPIRE'S DARKER SIDE.
AND FOR THAT WE HAVE TO HEAD HOME.
ZA (ZSH)

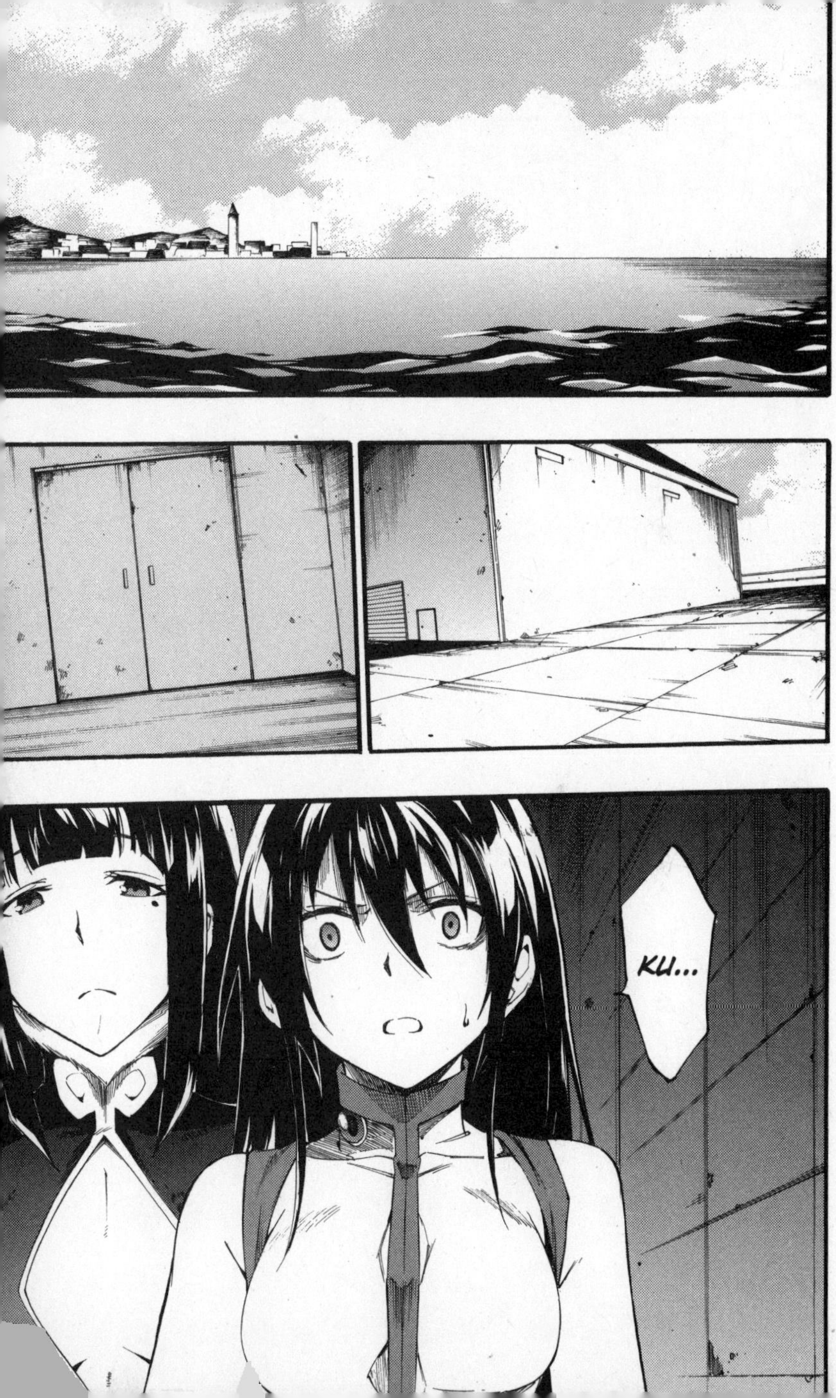
KU...

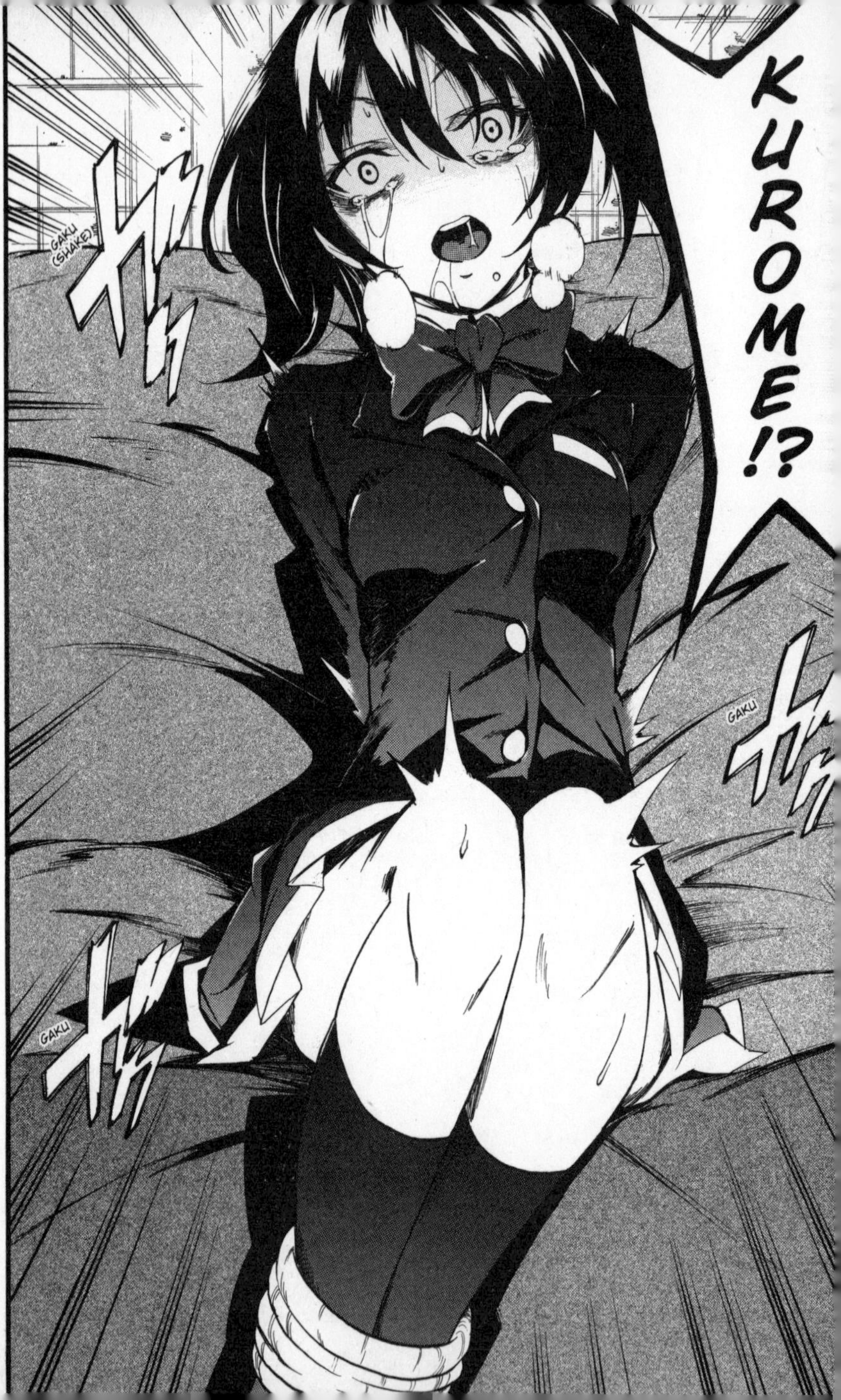
KUROME!?
GAKU (SHAKE)
GAKU
GAKU

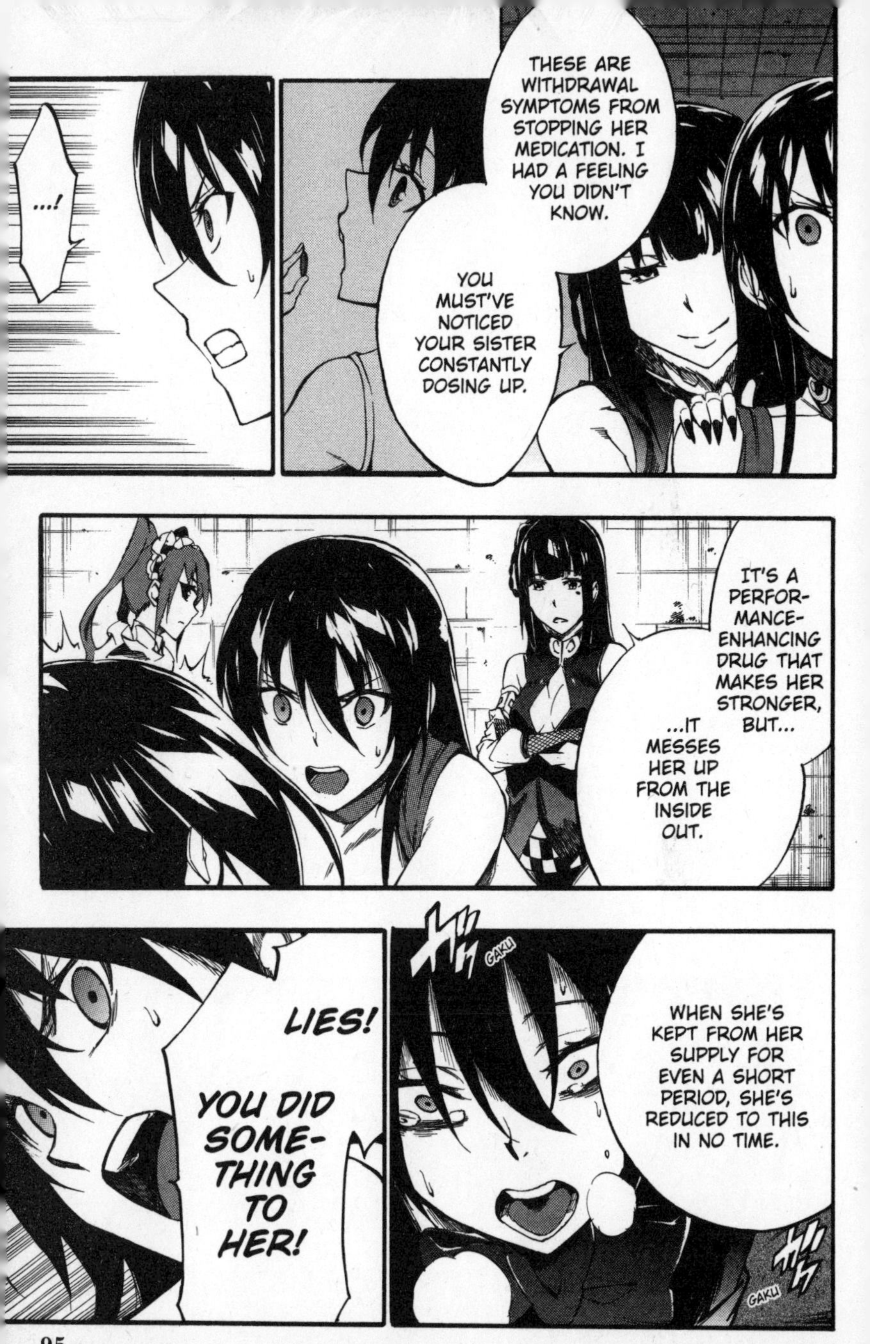
THESE ARE WITHDRAWAL SYMPTOMS FROM STOPPING HER MEDICATION. I HAD A FEELING YOU DIDN'T KNOW.
YOU MUST'VE NOTICED YOUR SISTER CONSTANTLY DOSING UP.
...!
IT'S A PERFORMANCE-ENHANCING DRUG THAT MAKES HER STRONGER, BUT...
...IT MESSES HER UP FROM THE INSIDE OUT.
GAKU
WHEN SHE'S KEPT FROM HER SUPPLY FOR EVEN A SHORT PERIOD, SHE'S REDUCED TO THIS IN NO TIME.
GAKU
LIES!
YOU DID SOMETHING TO HER!

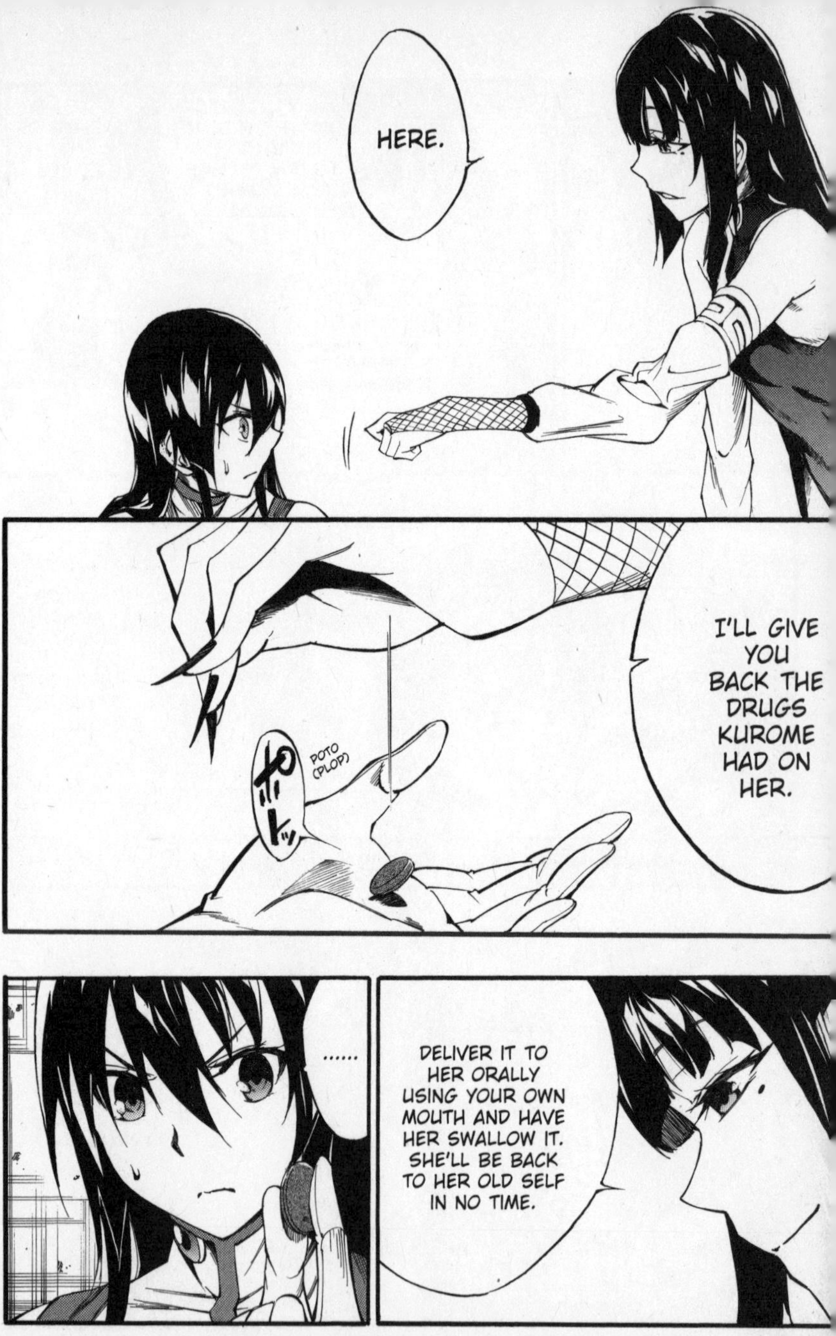
HERE.
I'LL GIVE YOU BACK THE DRUGS KUROME HAD ON HER.
ポトッ
POTO (PLOP)
DELIVER IT TO HER ORALLY USING YOUR OWN MOUTH AND HAVE HER SWALLOW IT. SHE'LL BE BACK TO HER OLD SELF IN NO TIME.
......

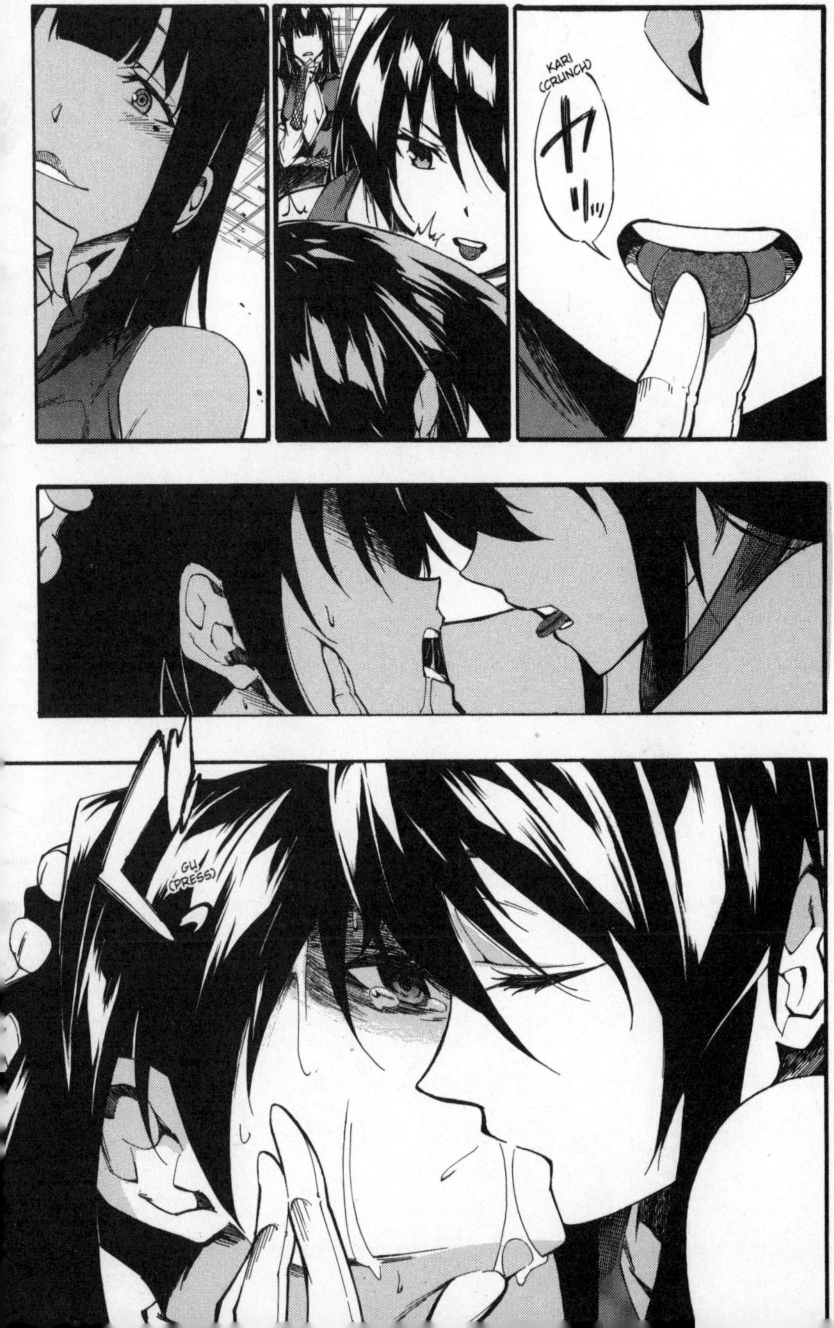

KARI (CRUNCH)
カリッ
GU (PRESS)

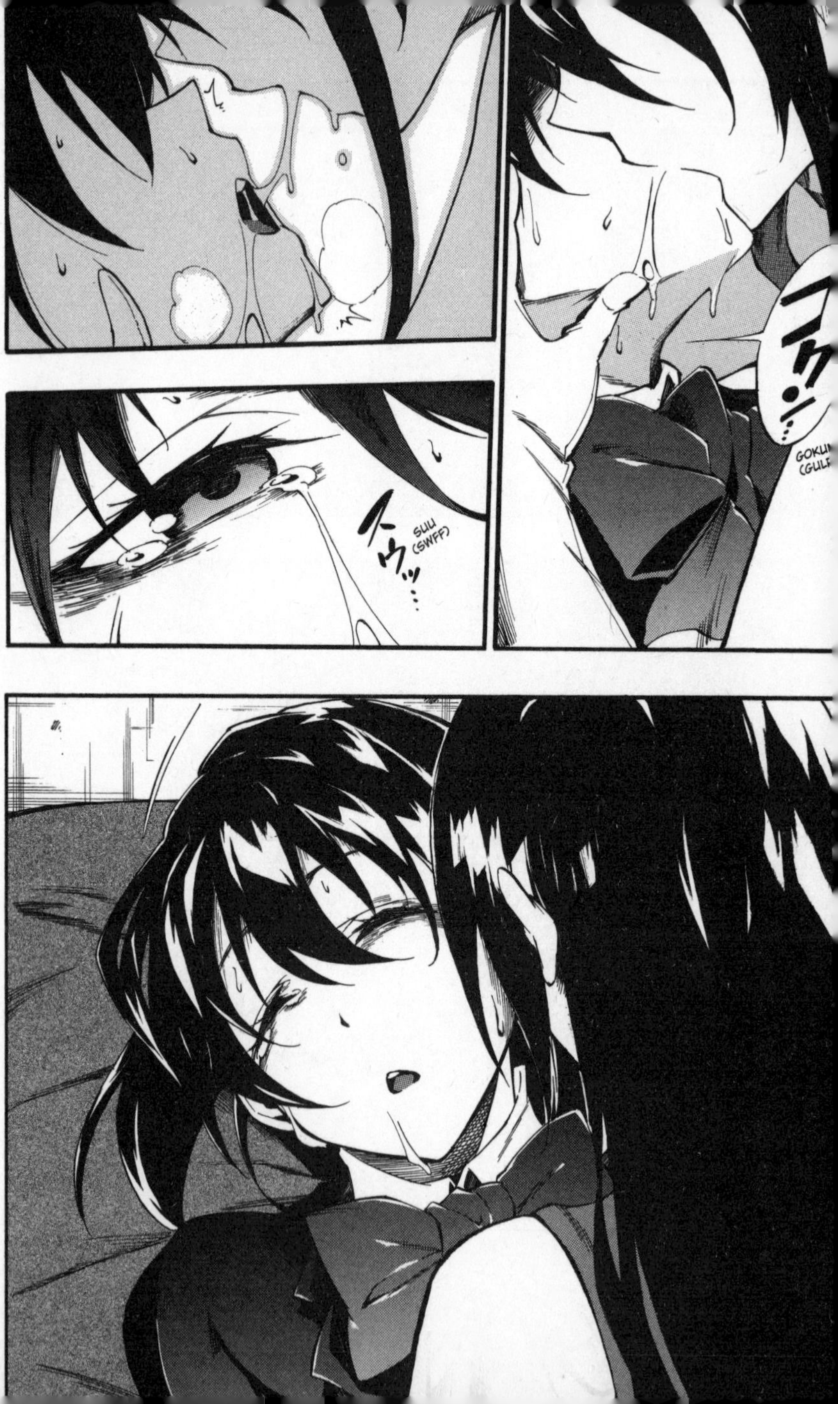
GOKU
(GUL
スゥッ…
SUU
(SWFF)

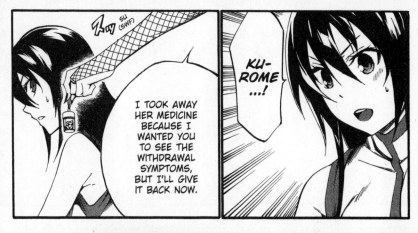

SH
(SWF)

I TOOK AWAY HER MEDICINE BECAUSE I WANTED YOU TO SEE THE WITHDRAWAL SYMPTOMS, BUT I'LL GIVE IT BACK NOW.

KU-ROME...!

THINK IT OVER, AKAME.

GYU
(GRIP)

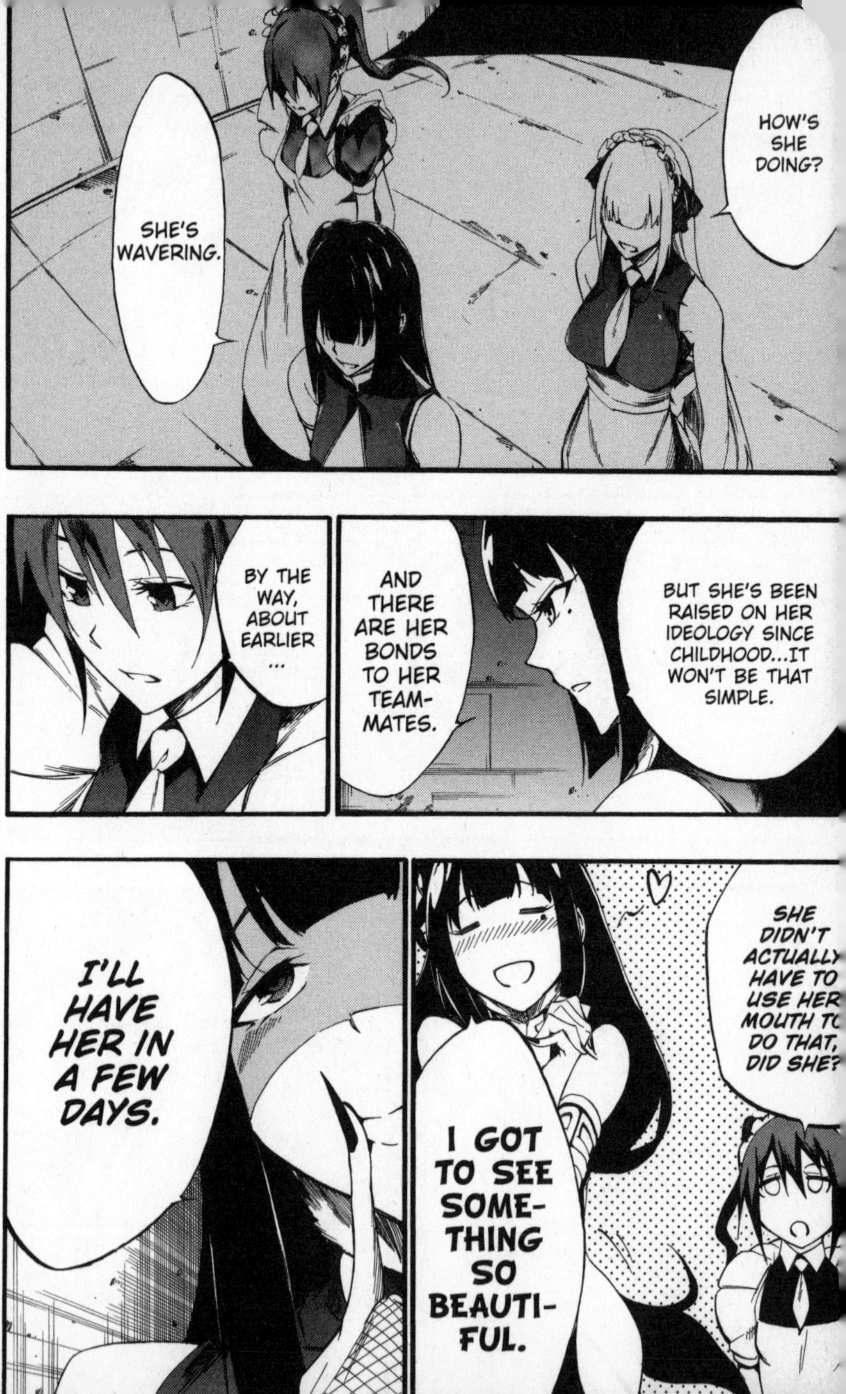
HOW'S SHE DOING?
SHE'S WAVERING.
BUT SHE'S BEEN RAISED ON HER IDEOLOGY SINCE CHILDHOOD...IT WON'T BE THAT SIMPLE.
AND THERE ARE HER BONDS TO HER TEAM-MATES.
BY THE WAY, ABOUT EARLIER ...
SHE DIDN'T ACTUALLY HAVE TO USE HER MOUTH T DO THAT, DID SHE?
I GOT TO SEE SOME-THING SO BEAUTI-FUL.
I'LL HAVE HER IN A FEW DAYS.

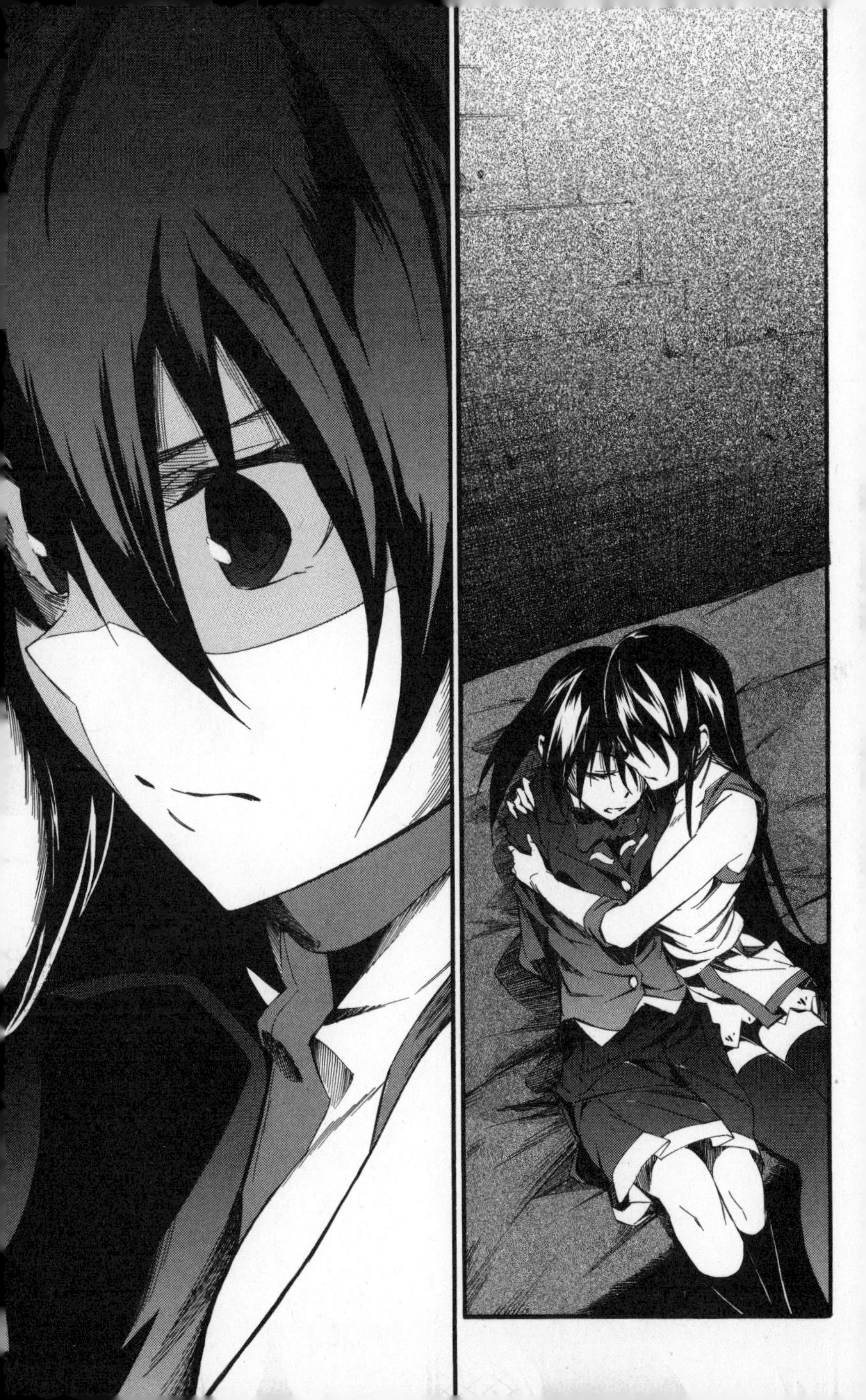

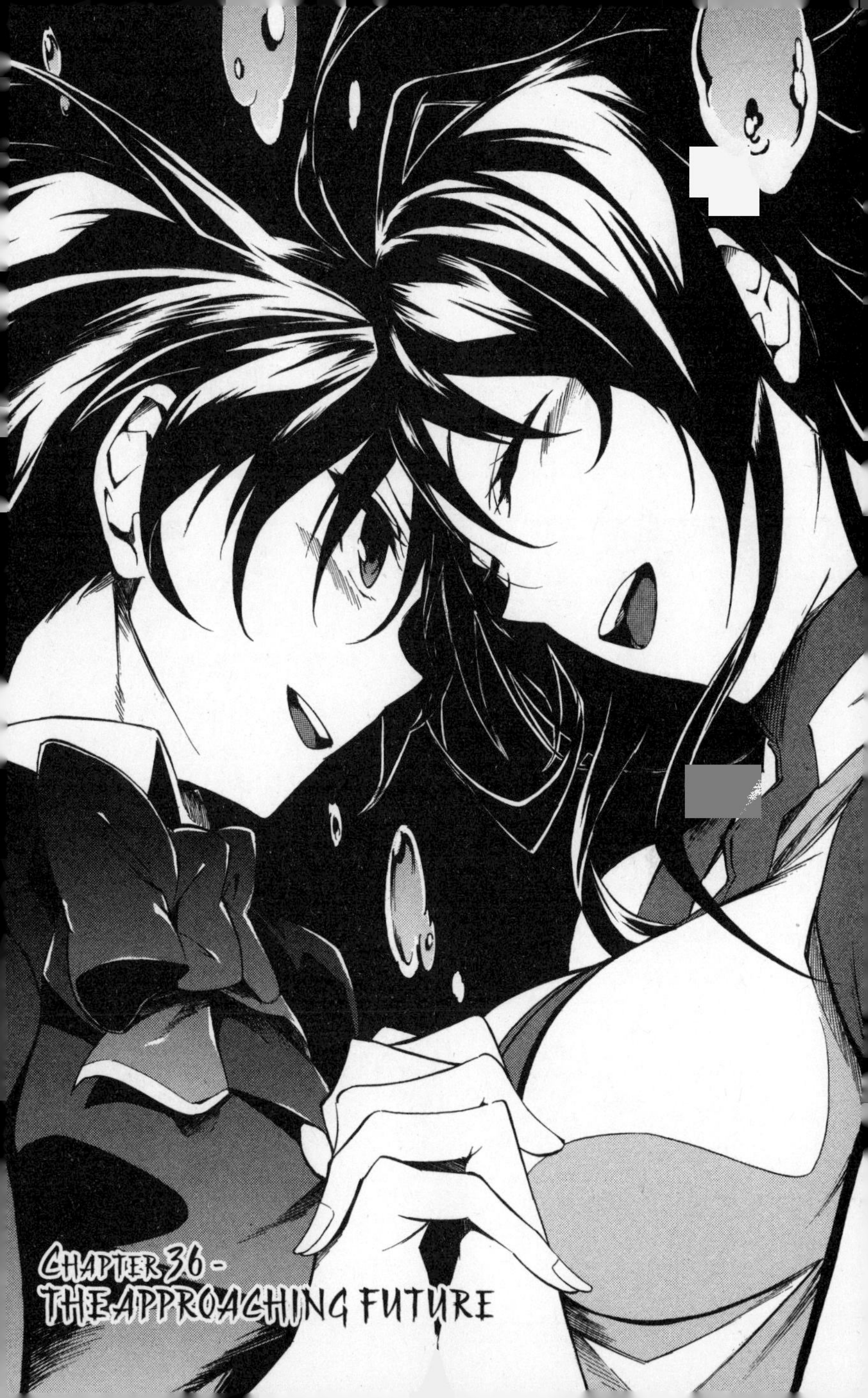
Chapter 36 -
The Approaching Future

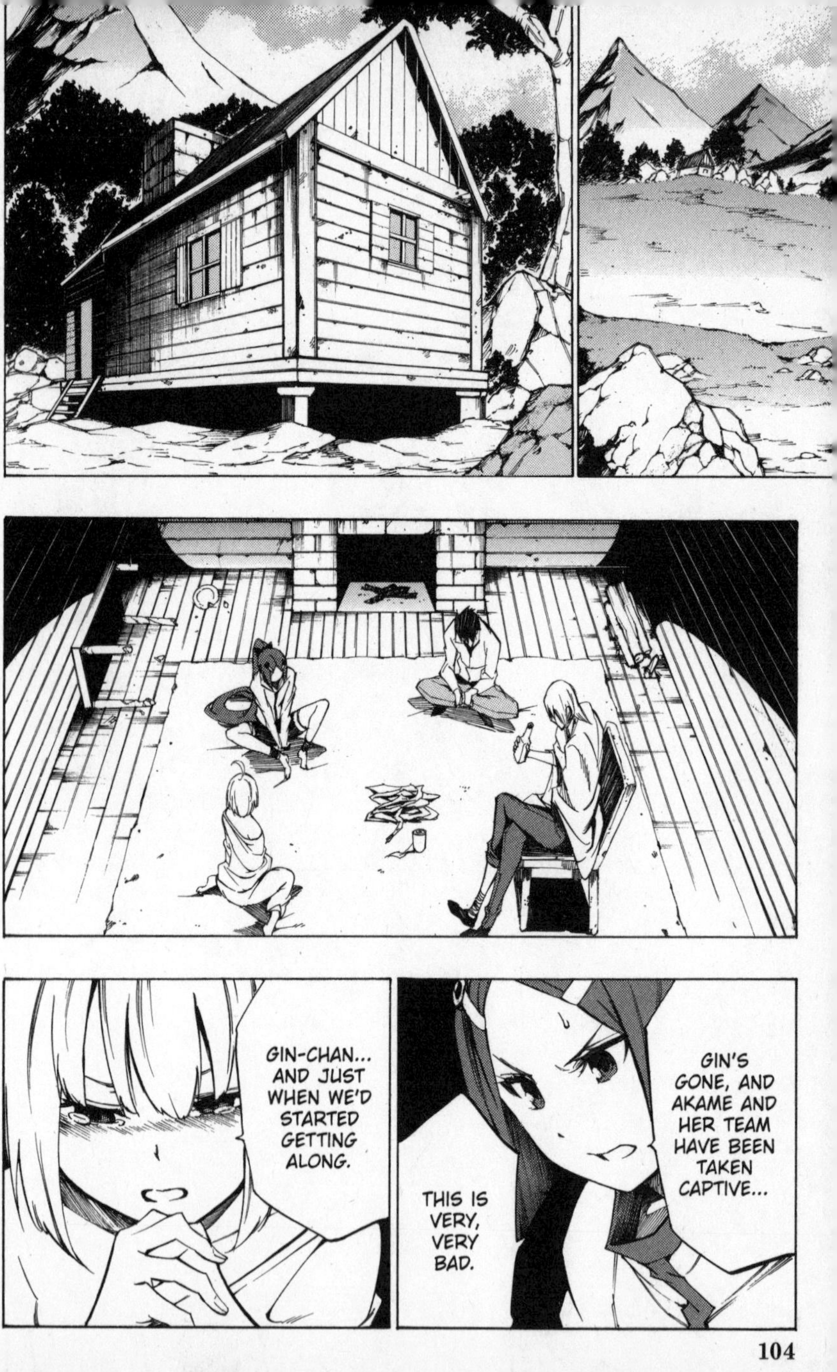
GIN'S GONE, AND AKAME AND HER TEAM HAVE BEEN TAKEN CAPTIVE...
THIS IS VERY, VERY BAD.
GIN-CHAN... AND JUST WHEN WE'D STARTED GETTING ALONG.

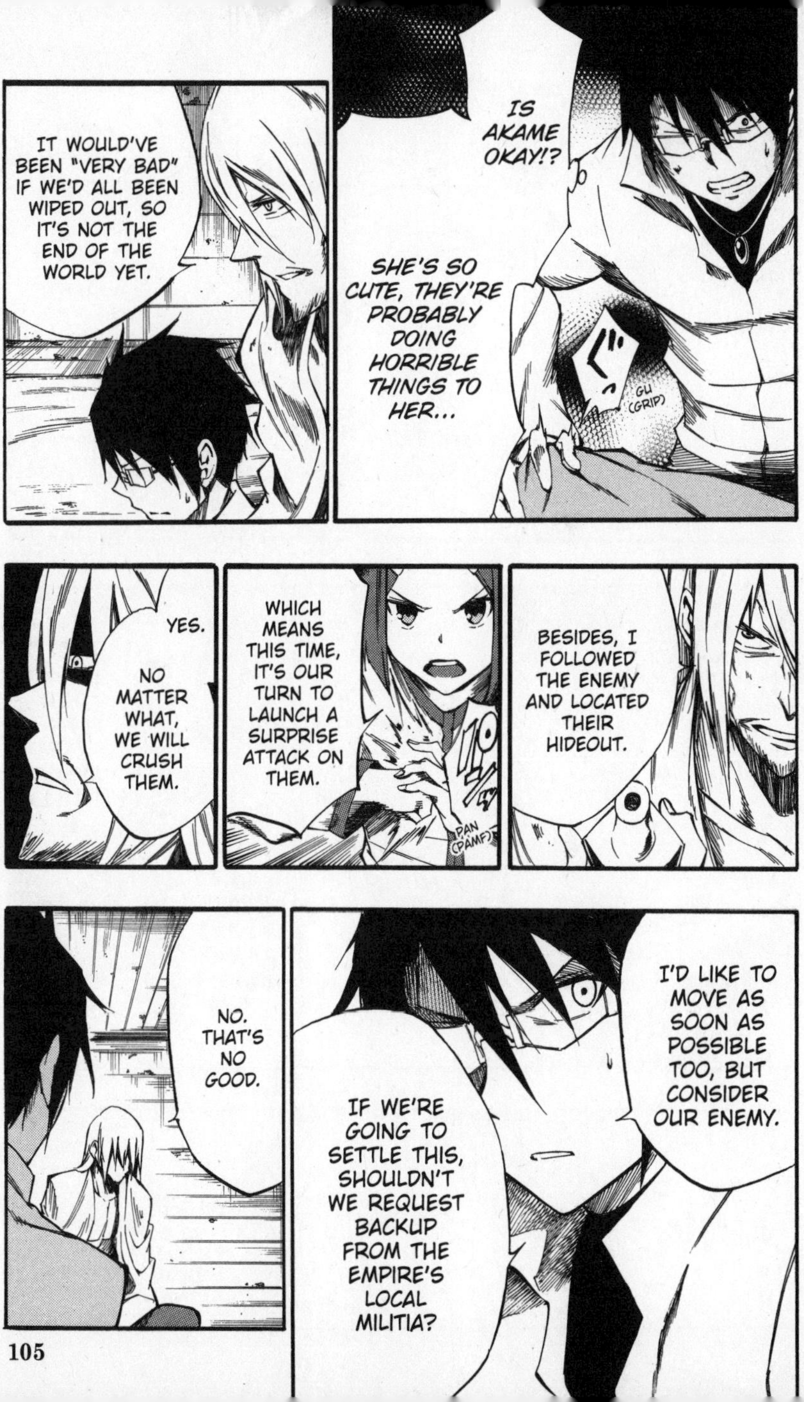
IS AKAME OKAY!?
SHE'S SO CUTE, THEY'RE PROBABLY DOING HORRIBLE THINGS TO HER...
GU (GRIP)
IT WOULD'VE BEEN "VERY BAD" IF WE'D ALL BEEN WIPED OUT, SO IT'S NOT THE END OF THE WORLD YET.
BESIDES, I FOLLOWED THE ENEMY AND LOCATED THEIR HIDEOUT.
WHICH MEANS THIS TIME, IT'S OUR TURN TO LAUNCH A SURPRISE ATTACK ON THEM.
PAN (PAMF)
YES.
NO MATTER WHAT, WE WILL CRUSH THEM.
I'D LIKE TO MOVE AS SOON AS POSSIBLE TOO, BUT CONSIDER OUR ENEMY.
IF WE'RE GOING TO SETTLE THIS, SHOULDN'T WE REQUEST BACKUP FROM THE EMPIRE'S LOCAL MILITIA?
NO. THAT'S NO GOOD.

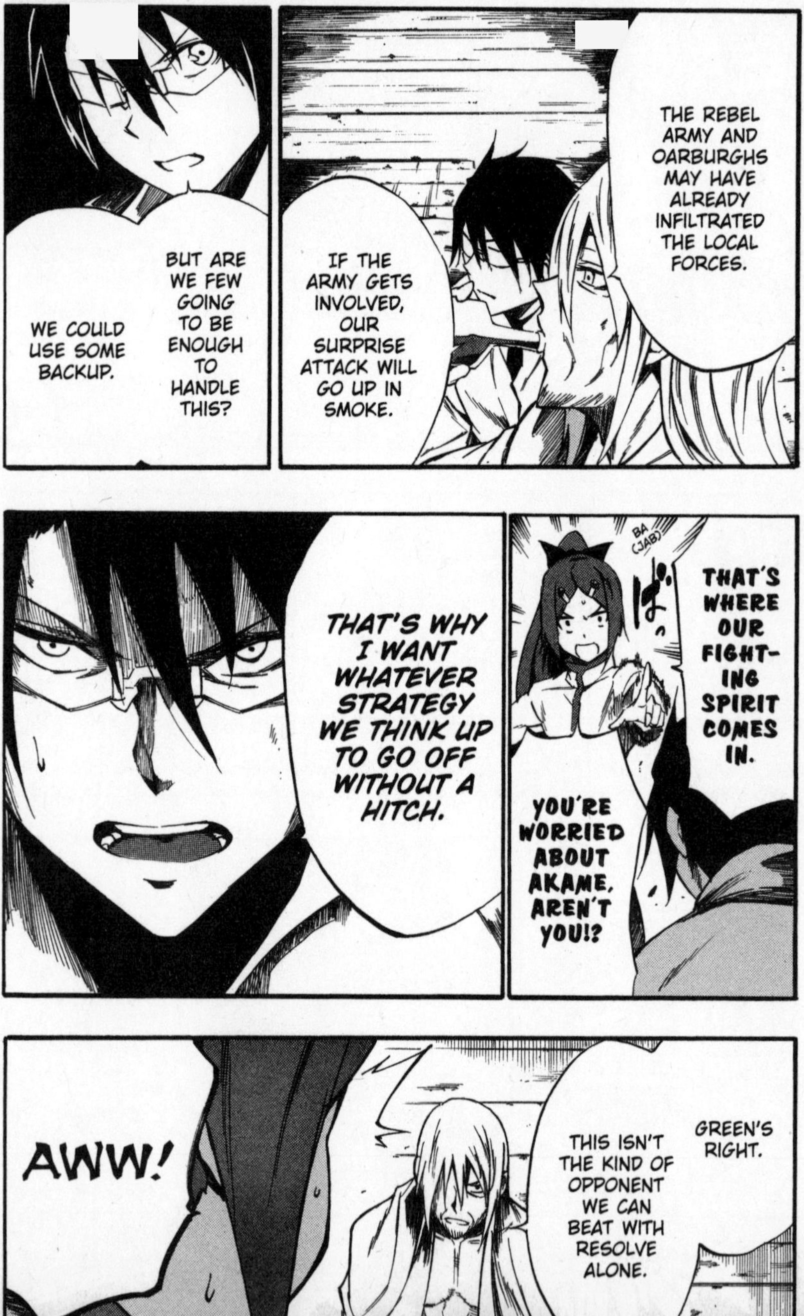
THE REBEL ARMY AND OARBURGHS MAY HAVE ALREADY INFILTRATED THE LOCAL FORCES.
IF THE ARMY GETS INVOLVED, OUR SURPRISE ATTACK WILL GO UP IN SMOKE.
BUT ARE WE FEW GOING TO BE ENOUGH TO HANDLE THIS?
WE COULD USE SOME BACKUP.
BA (JAB)
THAT'S WHERE OUR FIGHTING SPIRIT COMES IN.
YOU'RE WORRIED ABOUT AKAME, AREN'T YOU!?
THAT'S WHY I WANT WHATEVER STRATEGY WE THINK UP TO GO OFF WITHOUT A HITCH.
GREEN'S RIGHT.
THIS ISN'T THE KIND OF OPPONENT WE CAN BEAT WITH RESOLVE ALONE.
AWW!

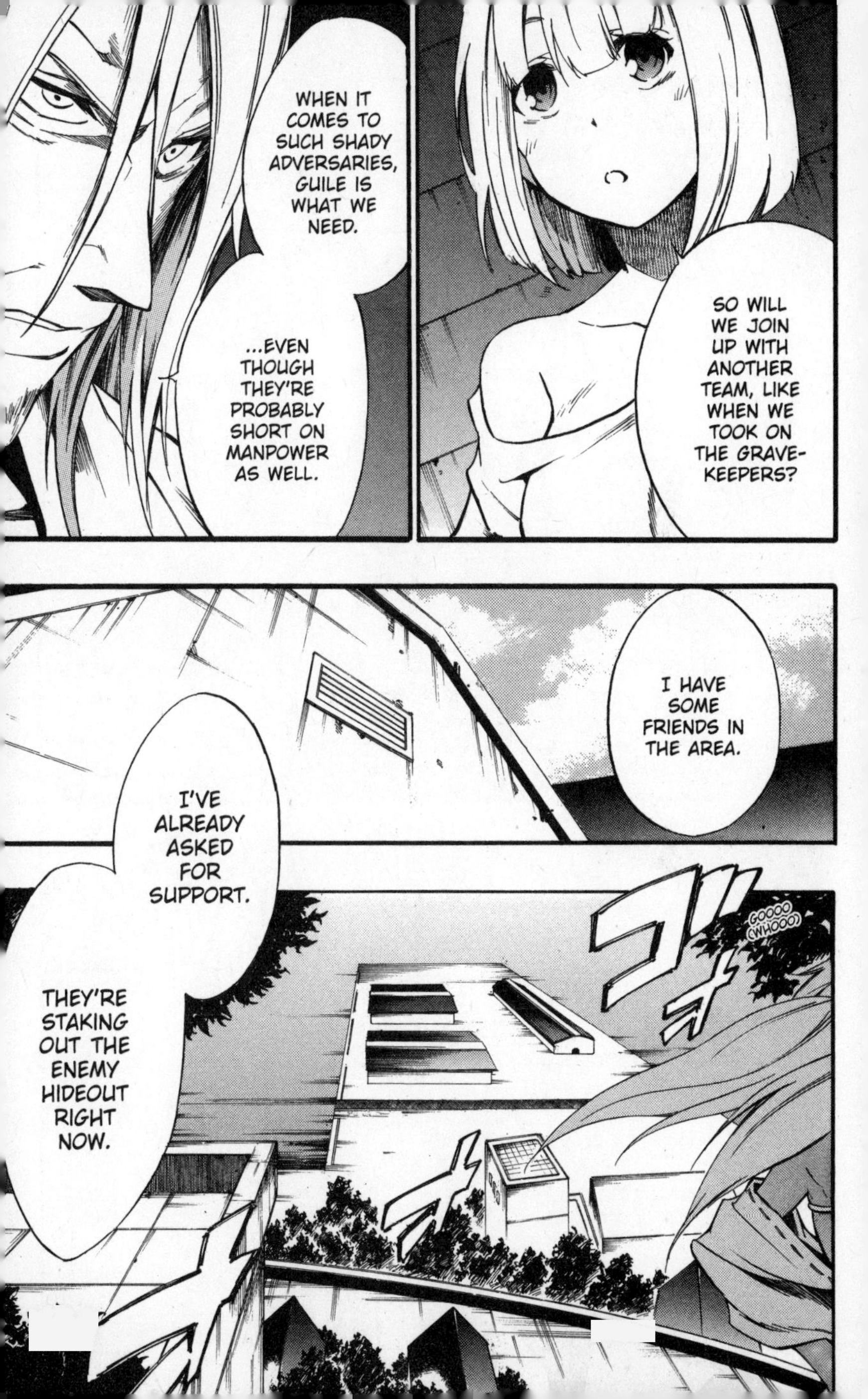

SO WILL WE JOIN UP WITH ANOTHER TEAM, LIKE WHEN WE TOOK ON THE GRAVE-KEEPERS?
WHEN IT COMES TO SUCH SHADY ADVERSARIES, GUILE IS WHAT WE NEED.
...EVEN THOUGH THEY'RE PROBABLY SHORT ON MANPOWER AS WELL.
I HAVE SOME FRIENDS IN THE AREA.
I'VE ALREADY ASKED FOR SUPPORT.
GOOOO (WHOOO)
THEY'RE STAKING OUT THE ENEMY HIDEOUT RIGHT NOW.

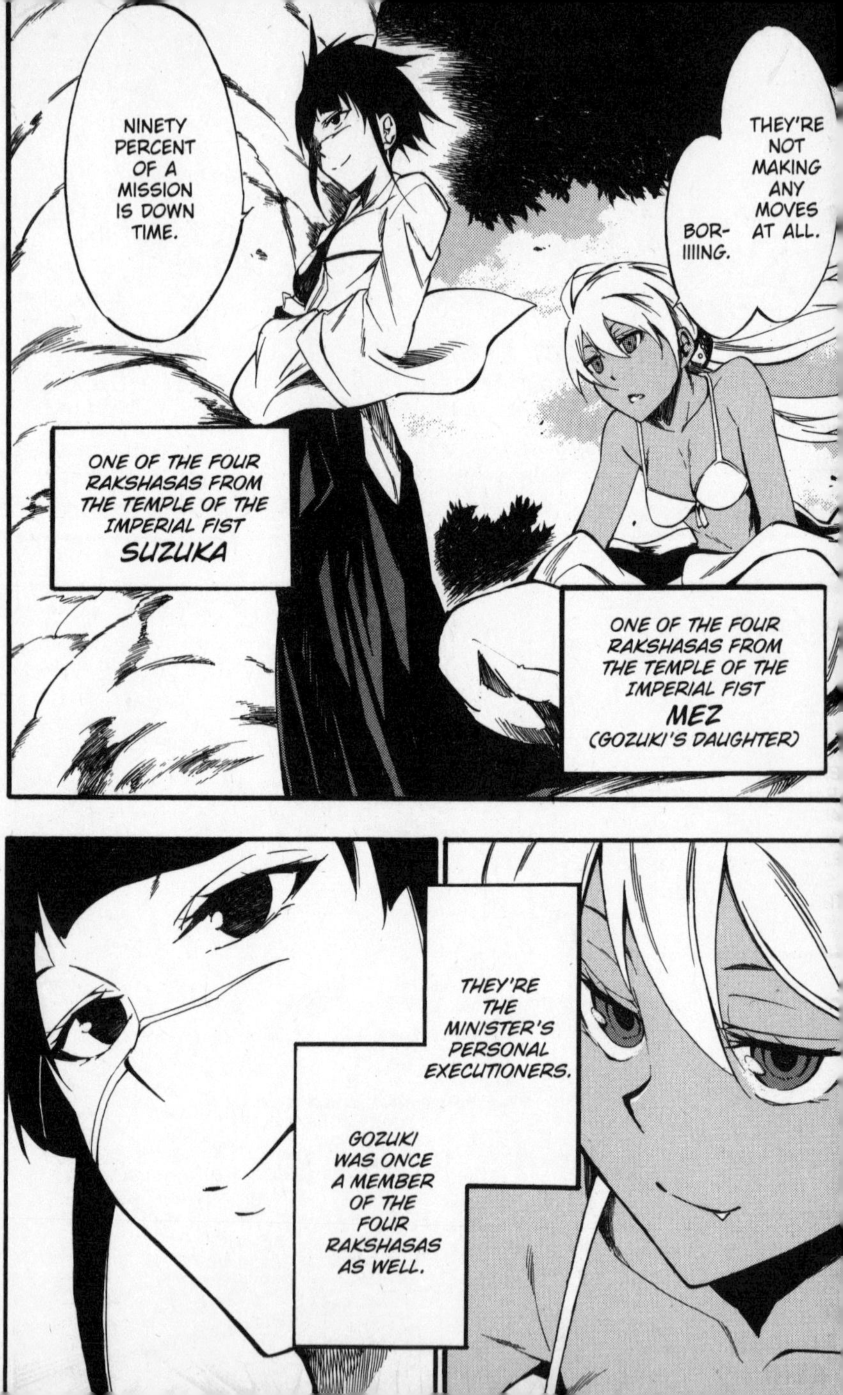
THEY'RE NOT MAKING ANY MOVES AT ALL.
BOR-IIIING.
NINETY PERCENT OF A MISSION IS DOWN TIME.
ONE OF THE FOUR RAKSHASAS FROM THE TEMPLE OF THE IMPERIAL FIST MEZ (GOZUKI'S DAUGHTER)
ONE OF THE FOUR RAKSHASAS FROM THE TEMPLE OF THE IMPERIAL FIST SUZUKA
THEY'RE THE MINISTER'S PERSONAL EXECUTIONERS.
GOZUKI WAS ONCE A MEMBER OF THE FOUR RAKSHASAS AS WELL.

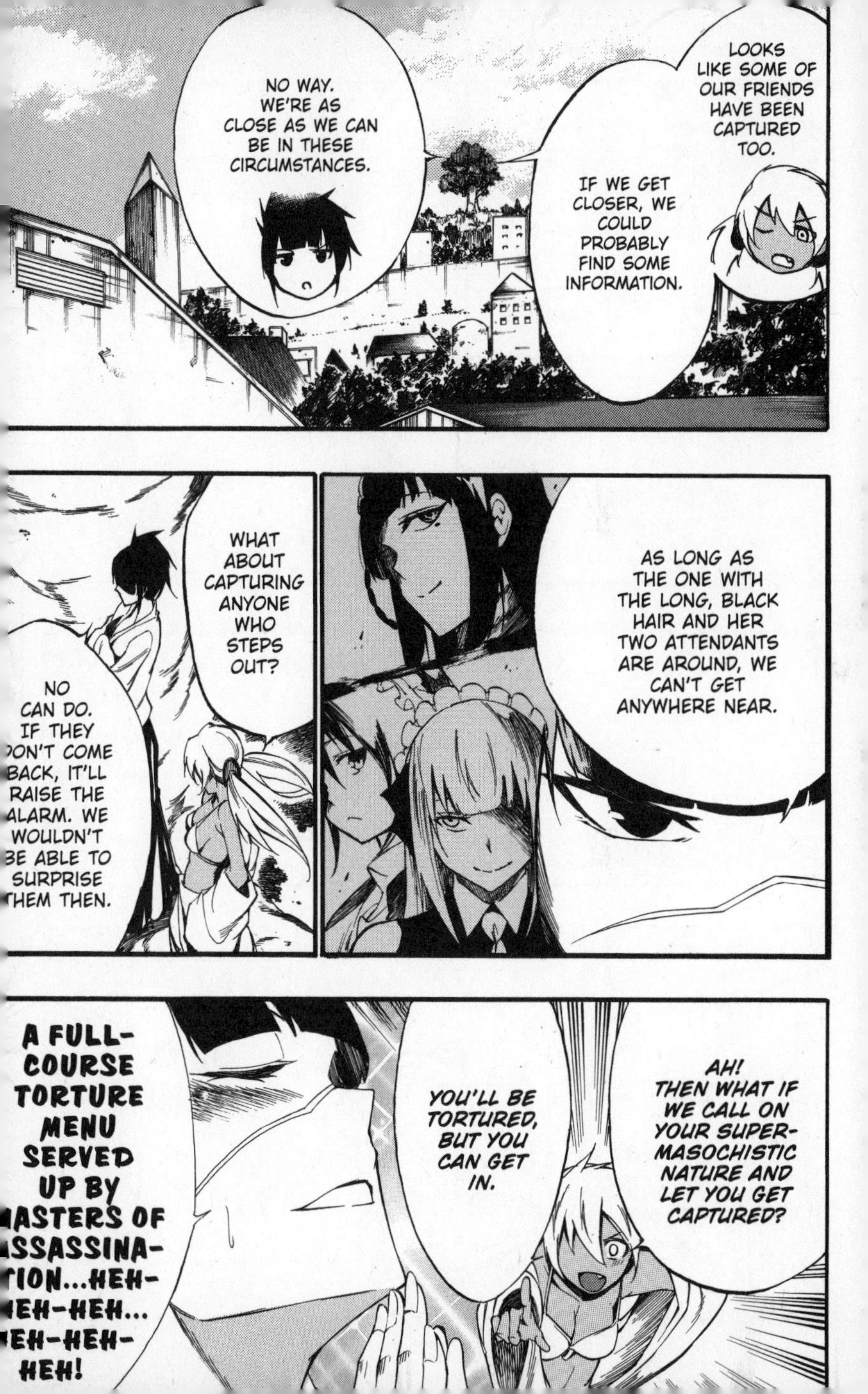
LOOKS LIKE SOME OF OUR FRIENDS HAVE BEEN CAPTURED TOO.
IF WE GET CLOSER, WE COULD PROBABLY FIND SOME INFORMATION.
NO WAY. WE'RE AS CLOSE AS WE CAN BE IN THESE CIRCUMSTANCES.
AS LONG AS THE ONE WITH THE LONG, BLACK HAIR AND HER TWO ATTENDANTS ARE AROUND, WE CAN'T GET ANYWHERE NEAR.
WHAT ABOUT CAPTURING ANYONE WHO STEPS OUT?
NO CAN DO. IF THEY DON'T COME BACK, IT'LL RAISE THE ALARM. WE WOULDN'T BE ABLE TO SURPRISE THEM THEN.
AH! THEN WHAT IF WE CALL ON YOUR SUPER-MASOCHISTIC NATURE AND LET YOU GET CAPTURED?
YOU'LL BE TORTURED, BUT YOU CAN GET IN.
A FULL-COURSE TORTURE MENU SERVED UP BY MASTERS OF ASSASSINATION...HEH-HEH-HEH...HEH-HEH-HEH!

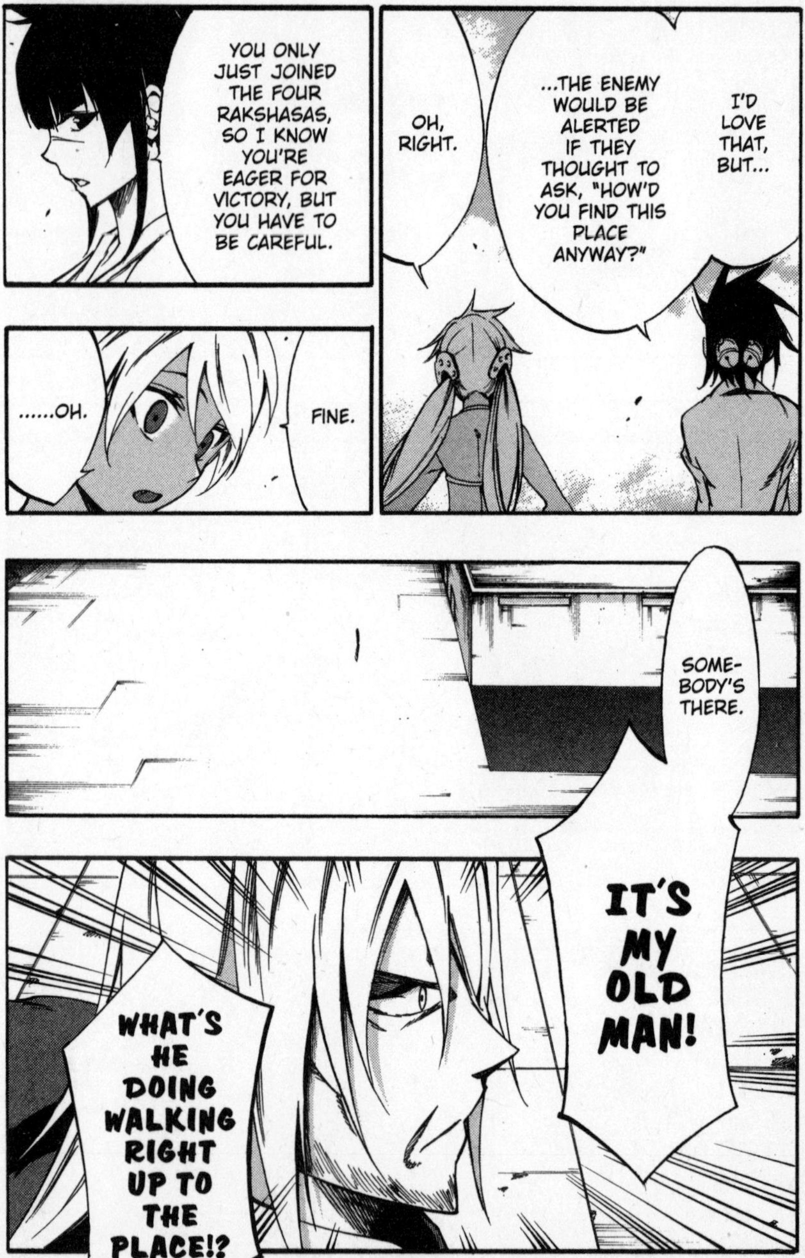
I'D LOVE THAT, BUT...
...THE ENEMY WOULD BE ALERTED IF THEY THOUGHT TO ASK, "HOW'D YOU FIND THIS PLACE ANYWAY?"
OH, RIGHT.
YOU ONLY JUST JOINED THE FOUR RAKSHASAS, SO I KNOW YOU'RE EAGER FOR VICTORY, BUT YOU HAVE TO BE CAREFUL.
......OH.
FINE.
SOME-BODY'S THERE.
IT'S MY OLD MAN!
WHAT'S HE DOING WALKING RIGHT UP TO THE PLACE!?

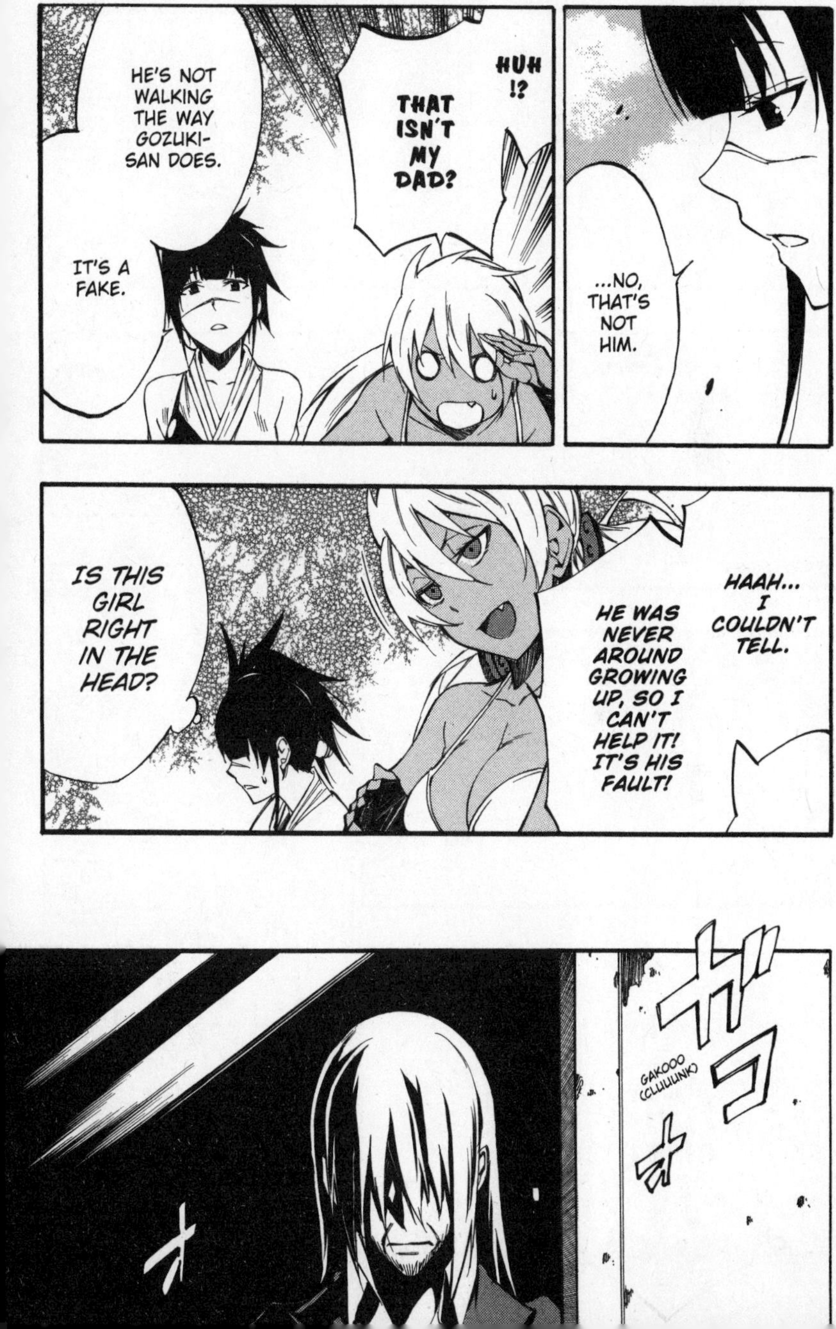
...NO, THAT'S NOT HIM.
HUH !?
THAT ISN'T MY DAD?
HE'S NOT WALKING THE WAY GOZUKI-SAN DOES.
IT'S A FAKE.
HAAH... I COULDN'T TELL.
HE WAS NEVER AROUND GROWING UP, SO I CAN'T HELP IT! IT'S HIS FAULT!
IS THIS GIRL RIGHT IN THE HEAD?
GAKOOO (CLUUUNK)

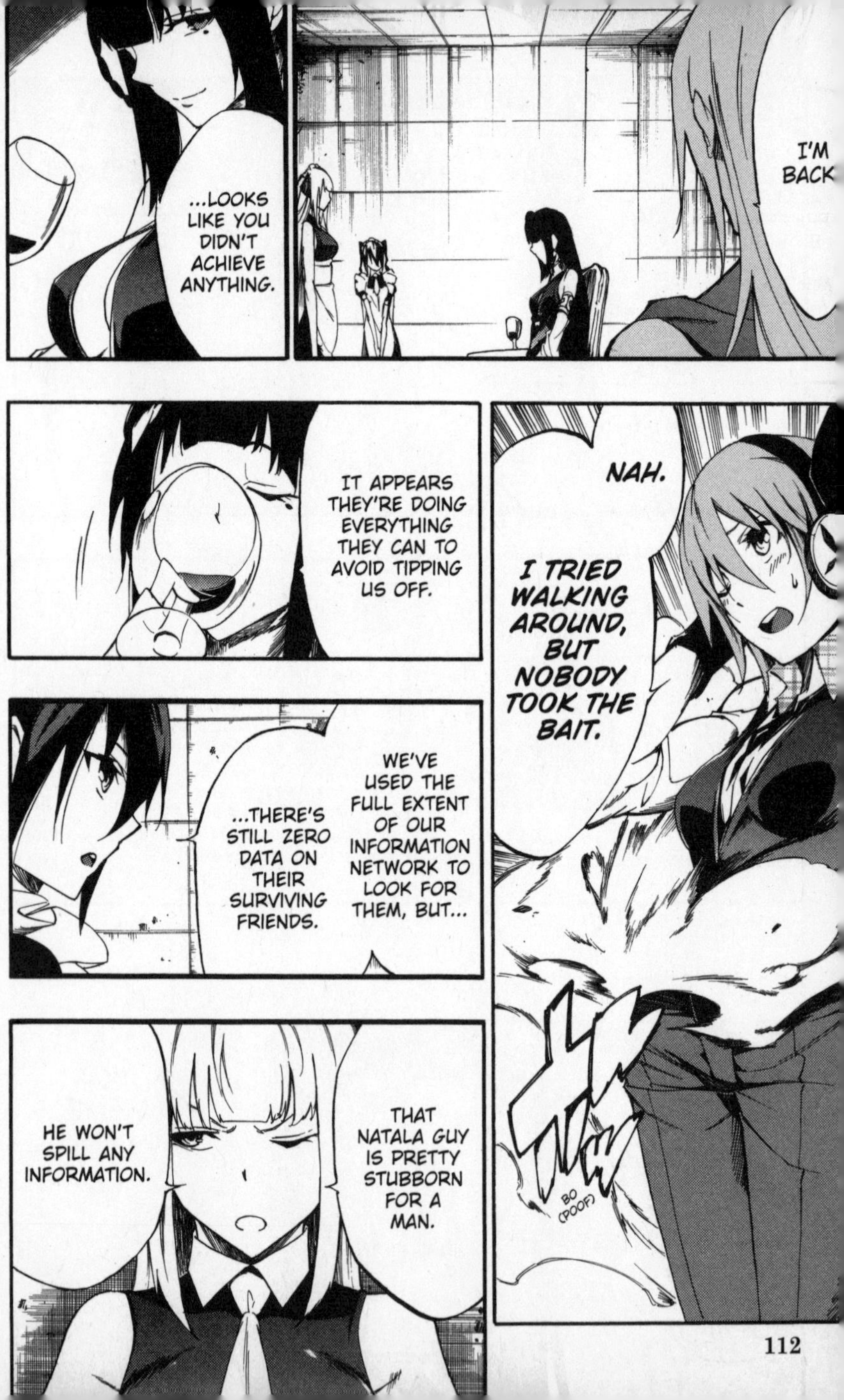
I'M BACK
...LOOKS LIKE YOU DIDN'T ACHIEVE ANYTHING.
NAH.
I TRIED WALKING AROUND, BUT NOBODY TOOK THE BAIT.
BO (POOF)
IT APPEARS THEY'RE DOING EVERYTHING THEY CAN TO AVOID TIPPING US OFF.
WE'VE USED THE FULL EXTENT OF OUR INFORMATION NETWORK TO LOOK FOR THEM, BUT...
...THERE'S STILL ZERO DATA ON THEIR SURVIVING FRIENDS.
THAT NATALA GUY IS PRETTY STUBBORN FOR A MAN.
HE WON'T SPILL ANY INFORMATION.

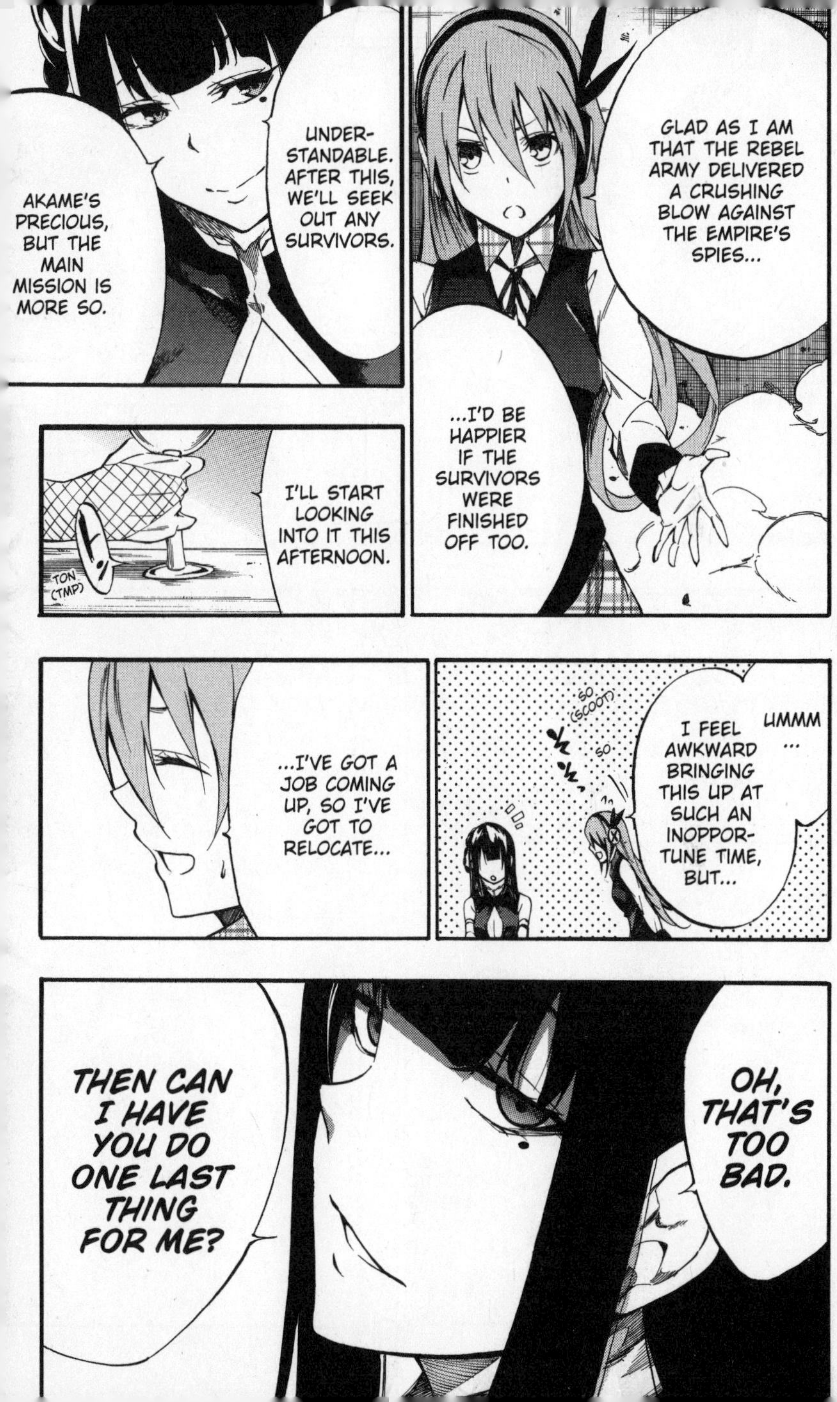
GLAD AS I AM THAT THE REBEL ARMY DELIVERED A CRUSHING BLOW AGAINST THE EMPIRE'S SPIES...
...I'D BE HAPPIER IF THE SURVIVORS WERE FINISHED OFF TOO.
UNDER-STANDABLE. AFTER THIS, WE'LL SEEK OUT ANY SURVIVORS.
AKAME'S PRECIOUS, BUT THE MAIN MISSION IS MORE SO.
I'LL START LOOKING INTO IT THIS AFTERNOON.
TON (TMP)
UMMM...
I FEEL AWKWARD BRINGING THIS UP AT SUCH AN INOPPOR-TUNE TIME, BUT...
SO (SCOOT)
SO
...I'VE GOT A JOB COMING UP, SO I'VE GOT TO RELOCATE...
OH, THAT'S TOO BAD.
THEN CAN I HAVE YOU DO ONE LAST THING FOR ME?

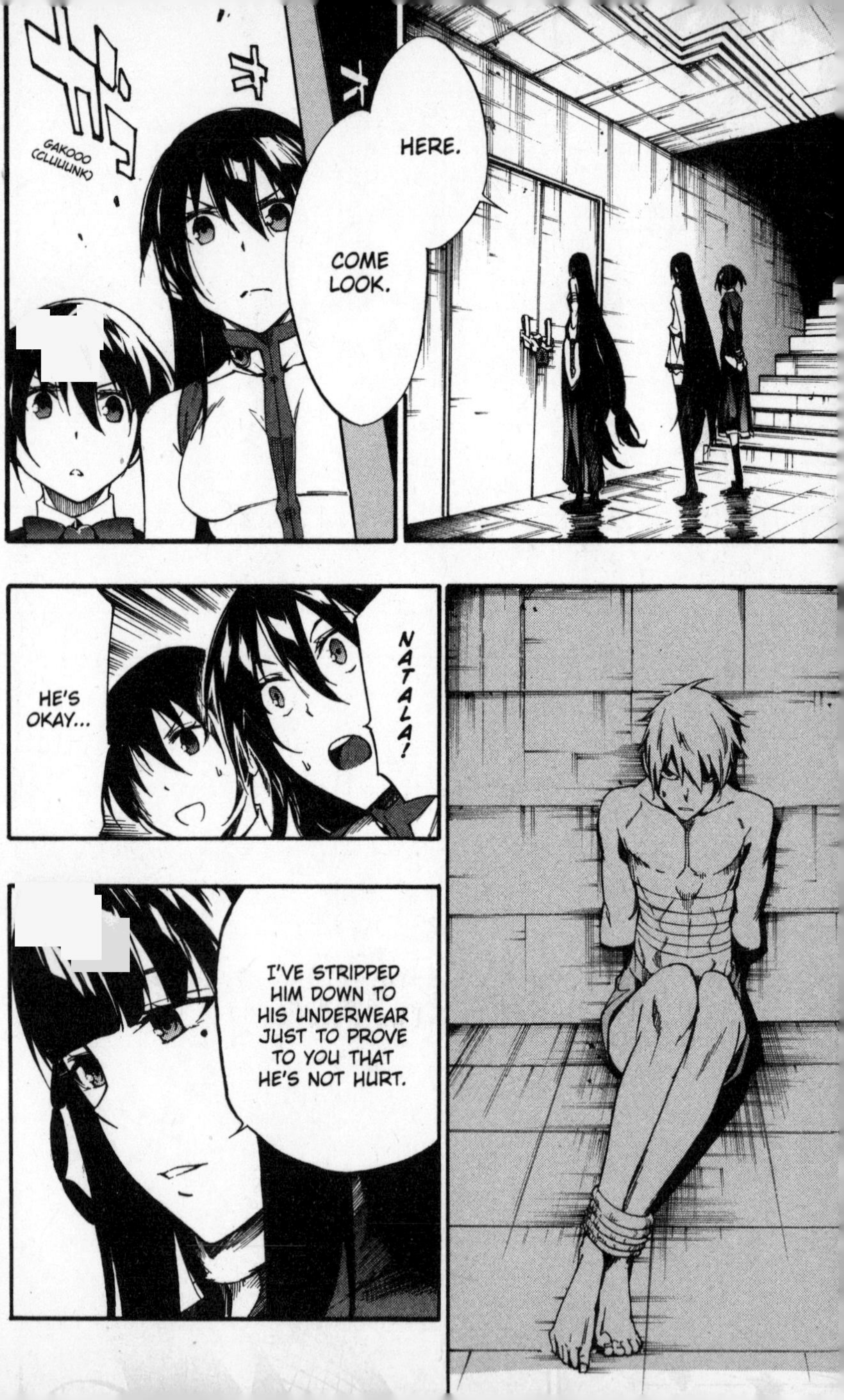
HERE.
COME LOOK.
GAKOOO (CLUUUNK)
NATALA!
HE'S OKAY...
I'VE STRIPPED HIM DOWN TO HIS UNDERWEAR JUST TO PROVE TO YOU THAT HE'S NOT HURT.

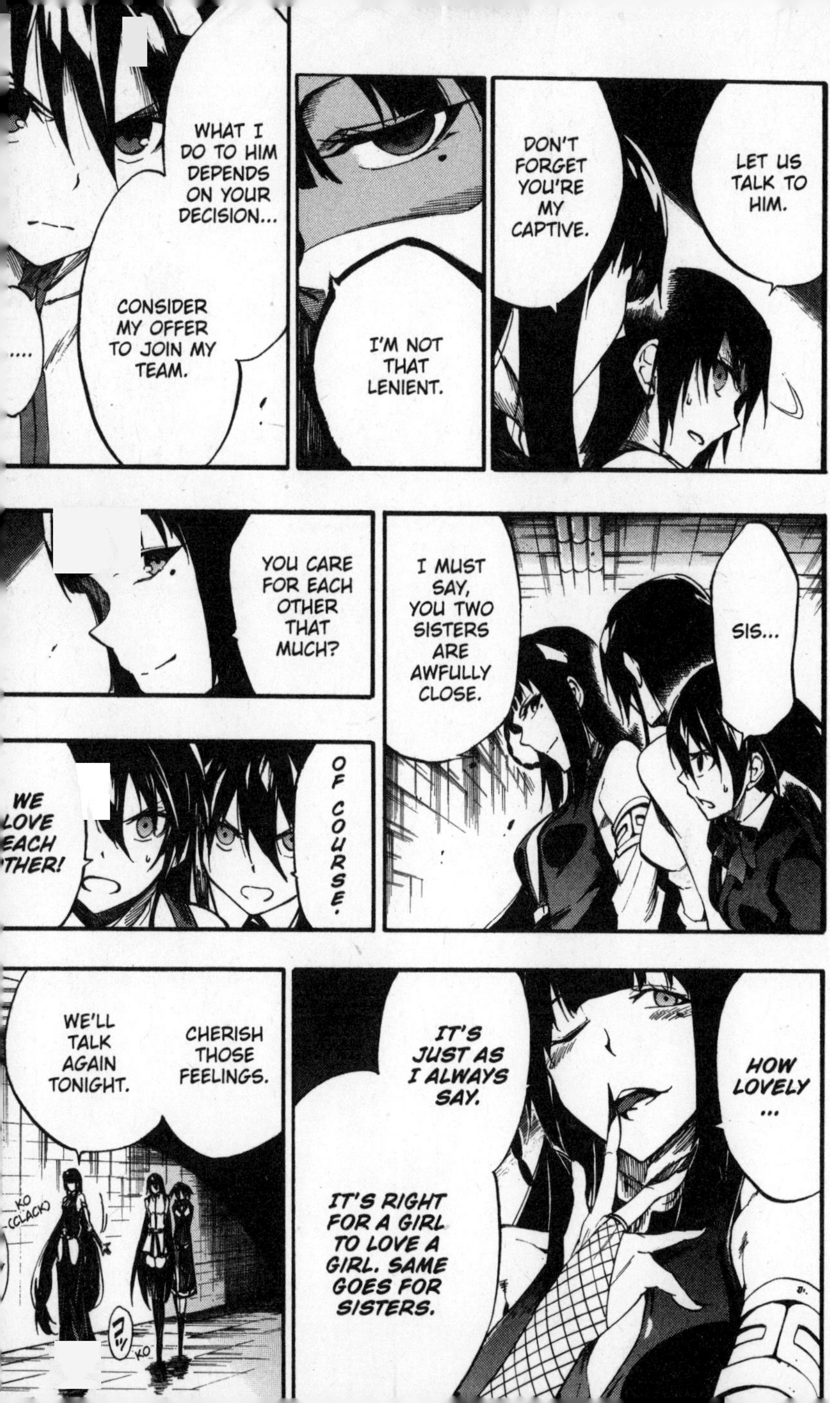
LET US TALK TO HIM.
DON'T FORGET YOU'RE MY CAPTIVE.
I'M NOT THAT LENIENT.
WHAT I DO TO HIM DEPENDS ON YOUR DECISION...
CONSIDER MY OFFER TO JOIN MY TEAM.
....
SIS...
I MUST SAY, YOU TWO SISTERS ARE AWFULLY CLOSE.
YOU CARE FOR EACH OTHER THAT MUCH?
OF COURSE.
WE LOVE EACH OTHER!
HOW LOVELY...
IT'S JUST AS I ALWAYS SAY.
IT'S RIGHT FOR A GIRL TO LOVE A GIRL. SAME GOES FOR SISTERS.
CHERISH THOSE FEELINGS.
WE'LL TALK AGAIN TONIGHT.
KO (CLACK)
KO

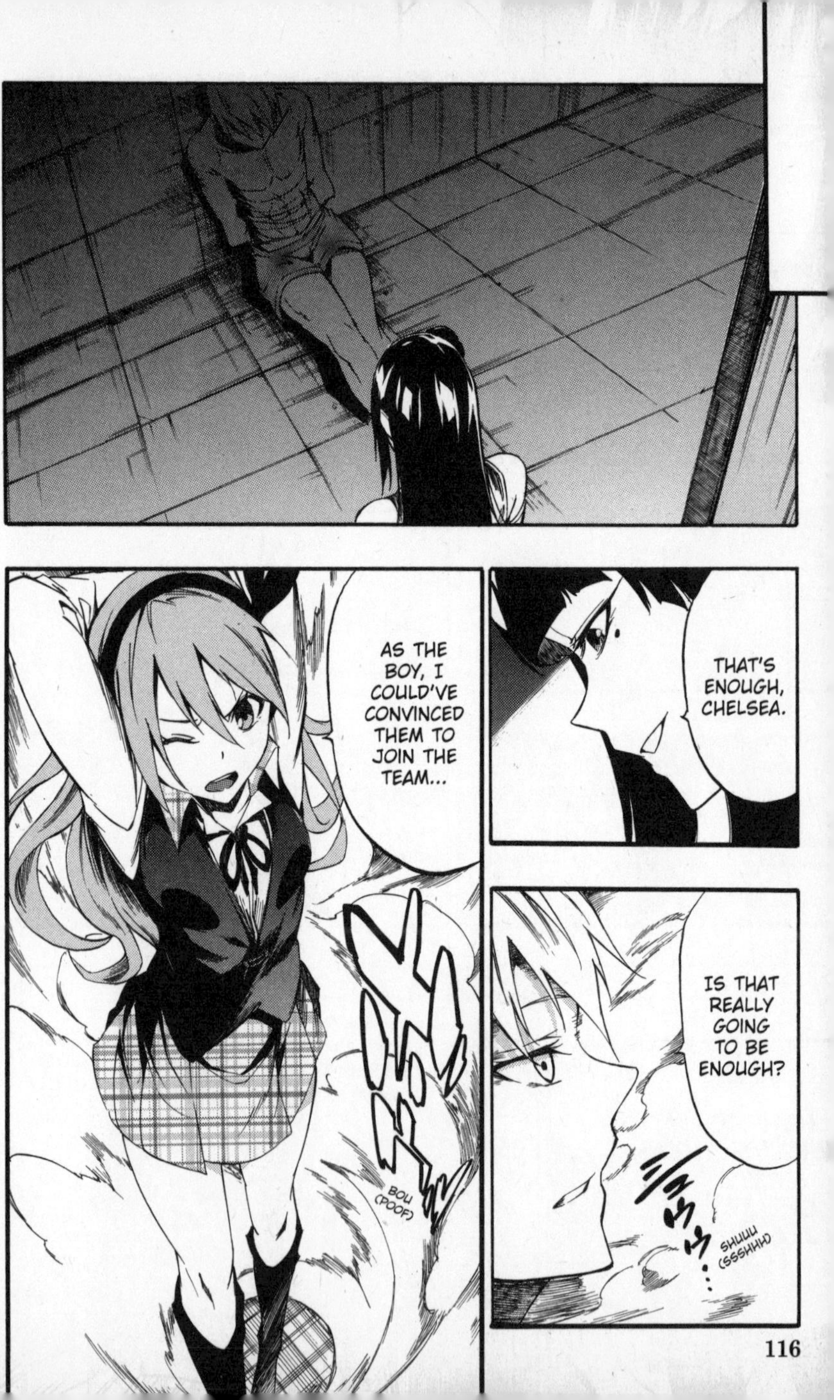
THAT'S ENOUGH, CHELSEA.
IS THAT REALLY GOING TO BE ENOUGH?
SHUUU (SSSHHH)
AS THE BOY, I COULD'VE CONVINCED THEM TO JOIN THE TEAM...
BOU (POOF)

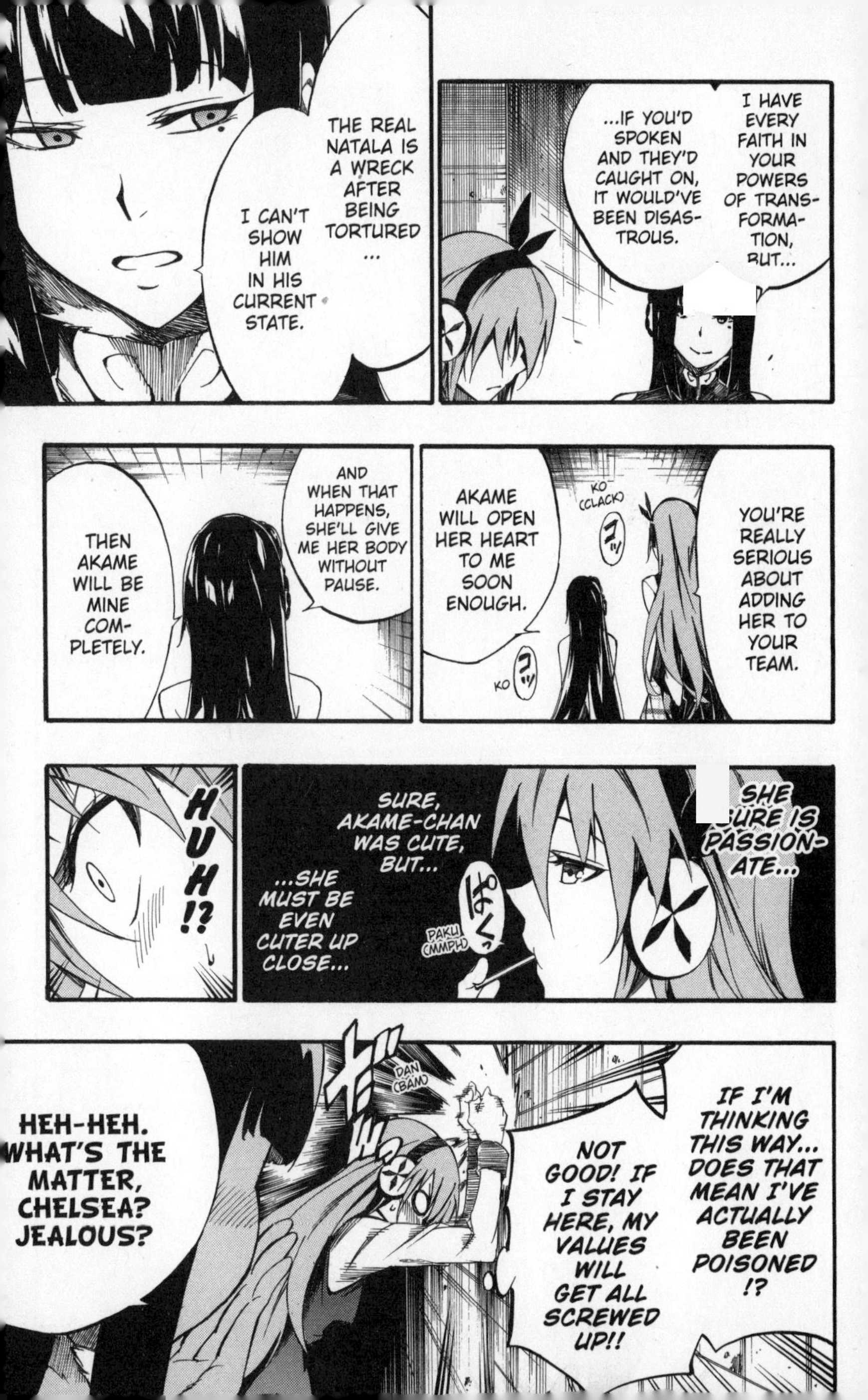
I HAVE EVERY FAITH IN YOUR POWERS OF TRANS-FORMATION, BUT...
...IF YOU'D SPOKEN AND THEY'D CAUGHT ON, IT WOULD'VE BEEN DISAS-TROUS.
THE REAL NATALA IS A WRECK AFTER BEING TORTURED...
I CAN'T SHOW HIM IN HIS CURRENT STATE.
YOU'RE REALLY SERIOUS ABOUT ADDING HER TO YOUR TEAM.
KO (CLACK)
AKAME WILL OPEN HER HEART TO ME SOON ENOUGH.
KO
AND WHEN THAT HAPPENS, SHE'LL GIVE ME HER BODY WITHOUT PAUSE.
THEN AKAME WILL BE MINE COM-PLETELY.
SHE SURE IS PASSION-ATE...
PAKU (MMPH)
SURE, AKAME-CHAN WAS CUTE, BUT...
...SHE MUST BE EVEN CUTER UP CLOSE...
HUH!?
IF I'M THINKING THIS WAY... DOES THAT MEAN I'VE ACTUALLY BEEN POISONED!?
NOT GOOD! IF I STAY HERE, MY VALUES WILL GET ALL SCREWED UP!!
DAN (BAM)
HEH-HEH. WHAT'S THE MATTER, CHELSEA? JEALOUS?

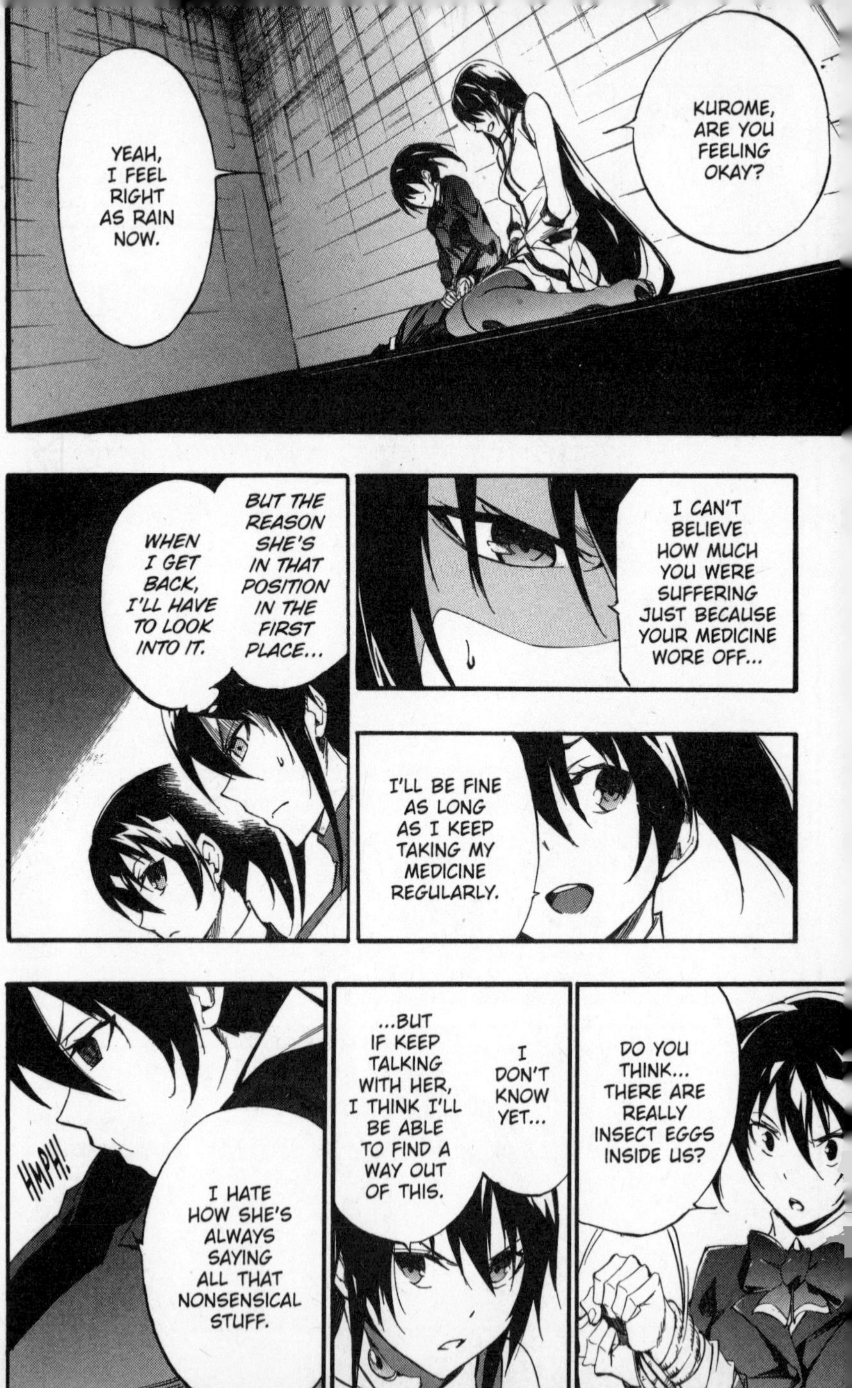
KUROME, ARE YOU FEELING OKAY?
YEAH, I FEEL RIGHT AS RAIN NOW.
I CAN'T BELIEVE HOW MUCH YOU WERE SUFFERING JUST BECAUSE YOUR MEDICINE WORE OFF...
I'LL BE FINE AS LONG AS I KEEP TAKING MY MEDICINE REGULARLY.
BUT THE REASON SHE'S IN THAT POSITION IN THE FIRST PLACE...
WHEN I GET BACK, I'LL HAVE TO LOOK INTO IT.
DO YOU THINK... THERE ARE REALLY INSECT EGGS INSIDE US?
I DON'T KNOW YET...
...BUT IF KEEP TALKING WITH HER, I THINK I'LL BE ABLE TO FIND A WAY OUT OF THIS.
HMPH!
I HATE HOW SHE'S ALWAYS SAYING ALL THAT NONSENSICAL STUFF.

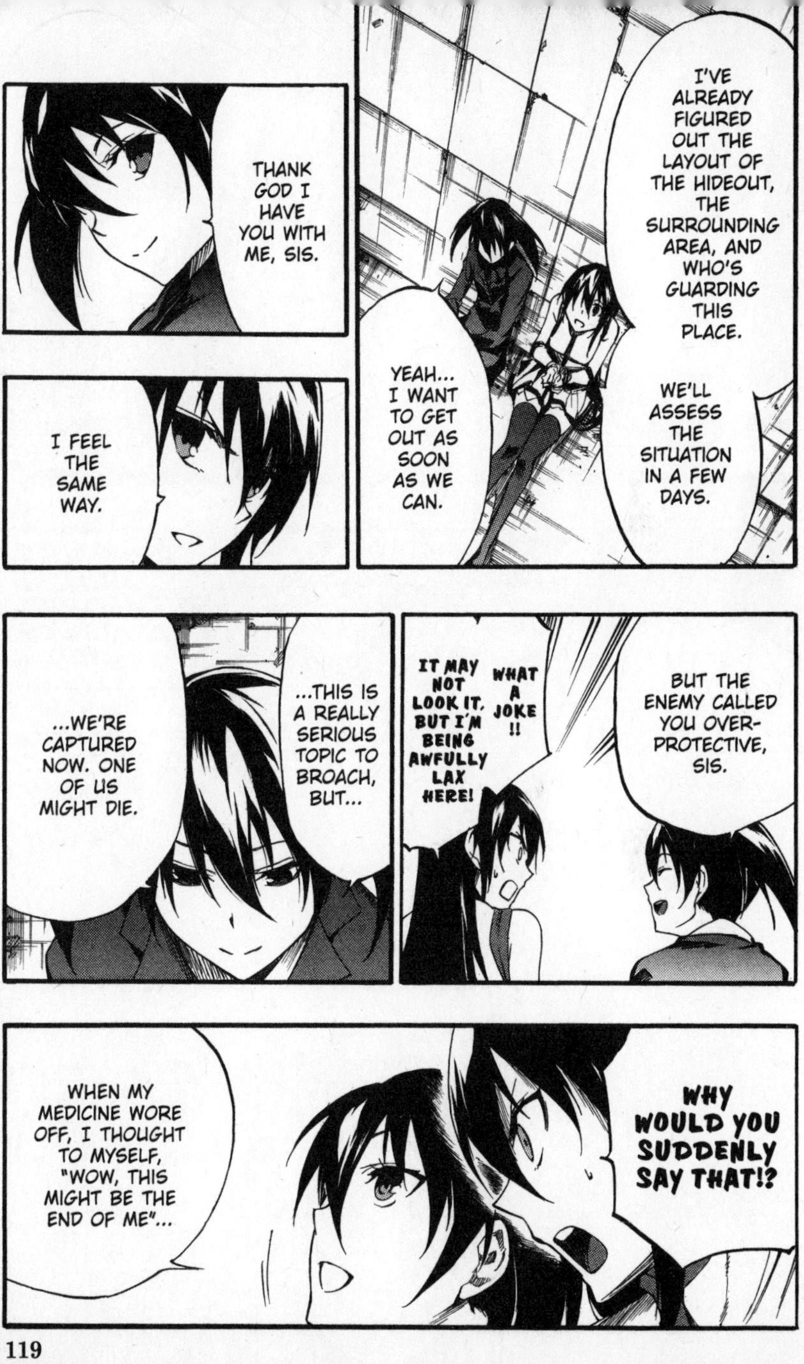

I'VE ALREADY FIGURED OUT THE LAYOUT OF THE HIDEOUT, THE SURROUNDING AREA, AND WHO'S GUARDING THIS PLACE.
WE'LL ASSESS THE SITUATION IN A FEW DAYS.
YEAH... I WANT TO GET OUT AS SOON AS WE CAN.
THANK GOD I HAVE YOU WITH ME, SIS.
I FEEL THE SAME WAY.
BUT THE ENEMY CALLED YOU OVER-PROTECTIVE, SIS.
WHAT A JOKE !!
IT MAY NOT LOOK IT, BUT I'M BEING AWFULLY LAX HERE!
...THIS IS A REALLY SERIOUS TOPIC TO BROACH, BUT...
...WE'RE CAPTURED NOW. ONE OF US MIGHT DIE.
WHY WOULD YOU SUDDENLY SAY THAT!?
WHEN MY MEDICINE WORE OFF, I THOUGHT TO MYSELF, "WOW, THIS MIGHT BE THE END OF ME"...

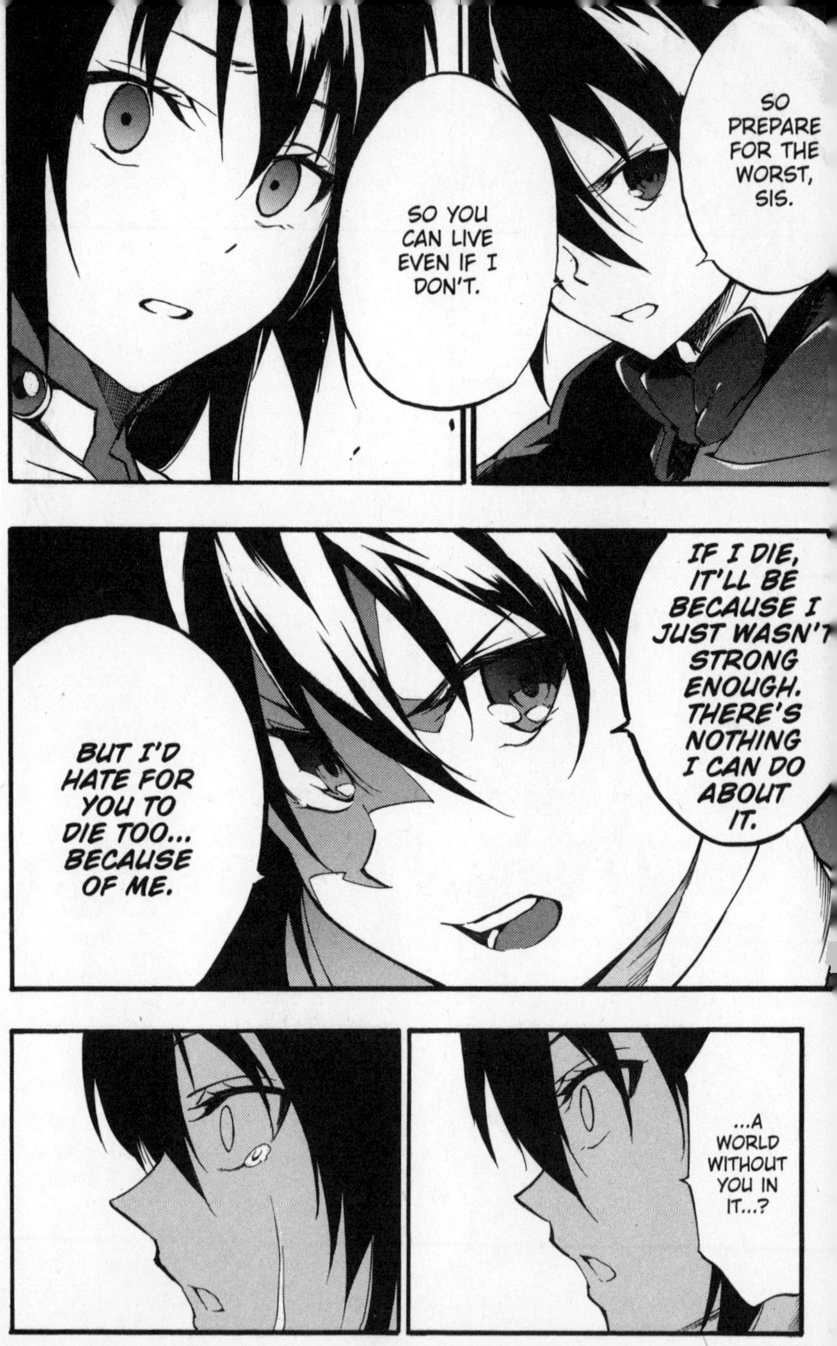
SO PREPARE FOR THE WORST, SIS.
SO YOU CAN LIVE EVEN IF I DON'T.
IF I DIE, IT'LL BE BECAUSE I JUST WASN'T STRONG ENOUGH. THERE'S NOTHING I CAN DO ABOUT IT.
BUT I'D HATE FOR YOU TO DIE TOO... BECAUSE OF ME.
...A WORLD WITHOUT YOU IN IT...?

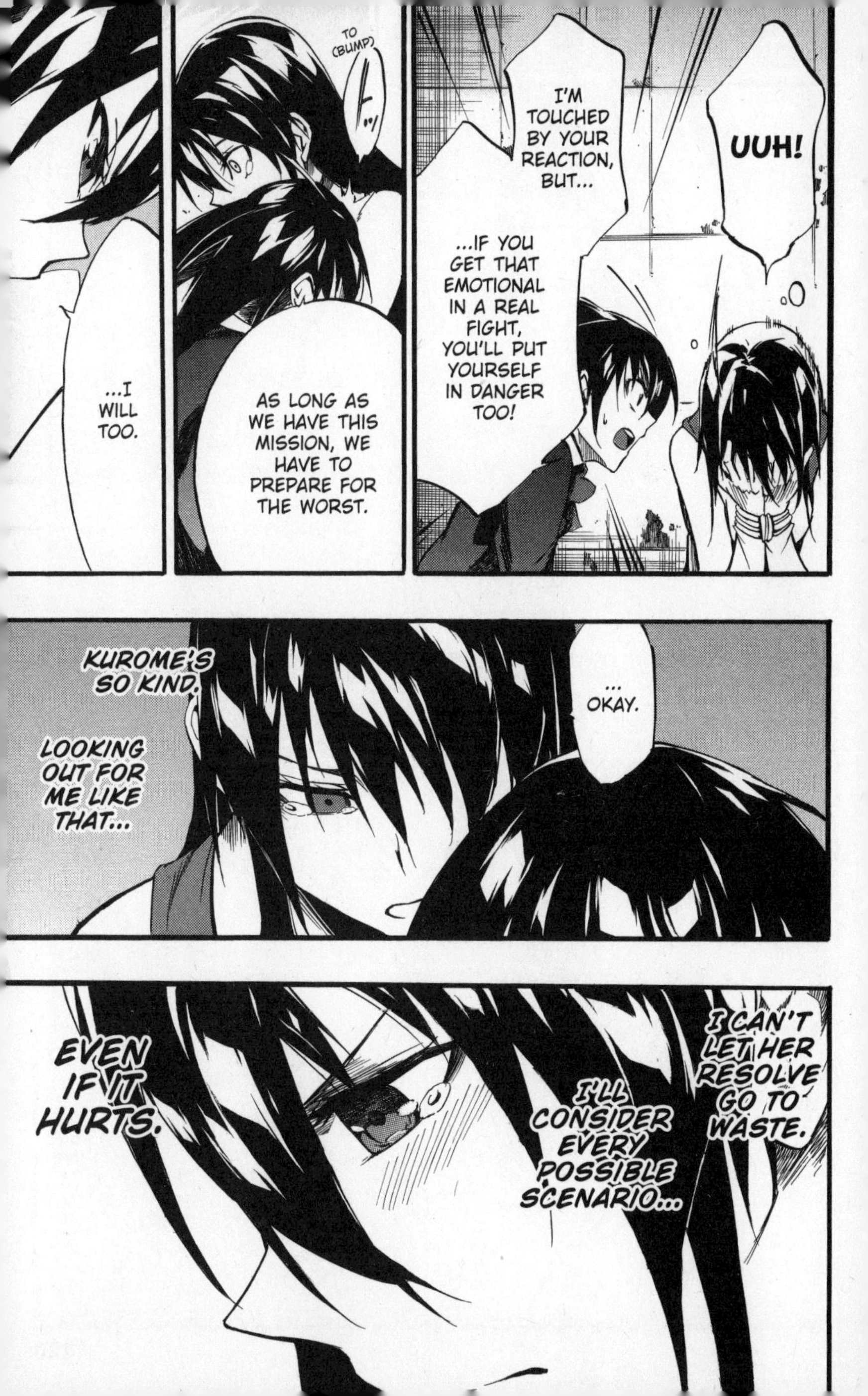
UUH!
I'M TOUCHED BY YOUR REACTION, BUT...
...IF YOU GET THAT EMOTIONAL IN A REAL FIGHT, YOU'LL PUT YOURSELF IN DANGER TOO!
TO (BUMP)
AS LONG AS WE HAVE THIS MISSION, WE HAVE TO PREPARE FOR THE WORST.
...I WILL TOO.
...OKAY.
KUROME'S SO KIND.
LOOKING OUT FOR ME LIKE THAT...
I CAN'T LET HER RESOLVE GO TO WASTE.
I'LL CONSIDER EVERY POSSIBLE SCENARIO...
EVEN IF IT HURTS.

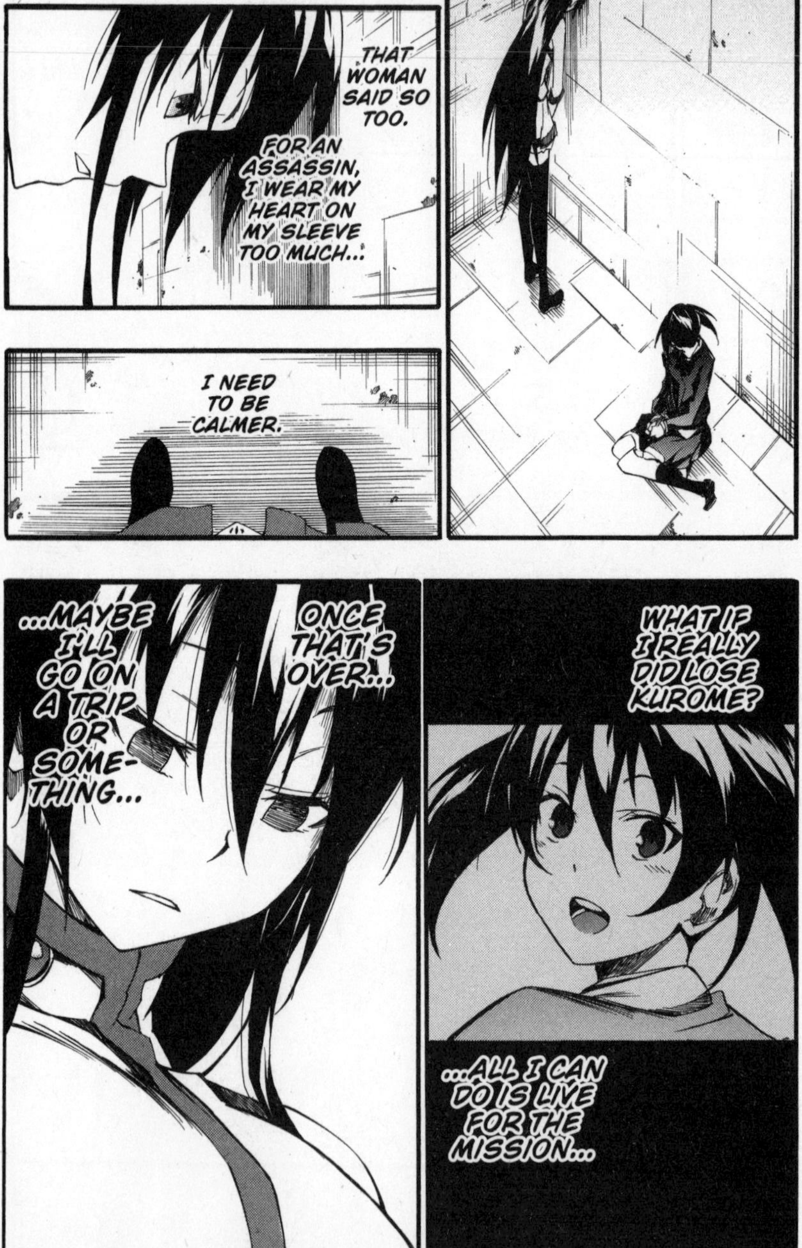
THAT WOMAN SAID SO TOO.
FOR AN ASSASSIN, I WEAR MY HEART ON MY SLEEVE TOO MUCH...
I NEED TO BE CALMER.
WHAT IF I REALLY DID LOSE KUROME?
...ALL I CAN DO IS LIVE FOR THE MISSION...
ONCE THAT'S OVER...
...MAYBE I'LL GO ON A TRIP OR SOME-THING...

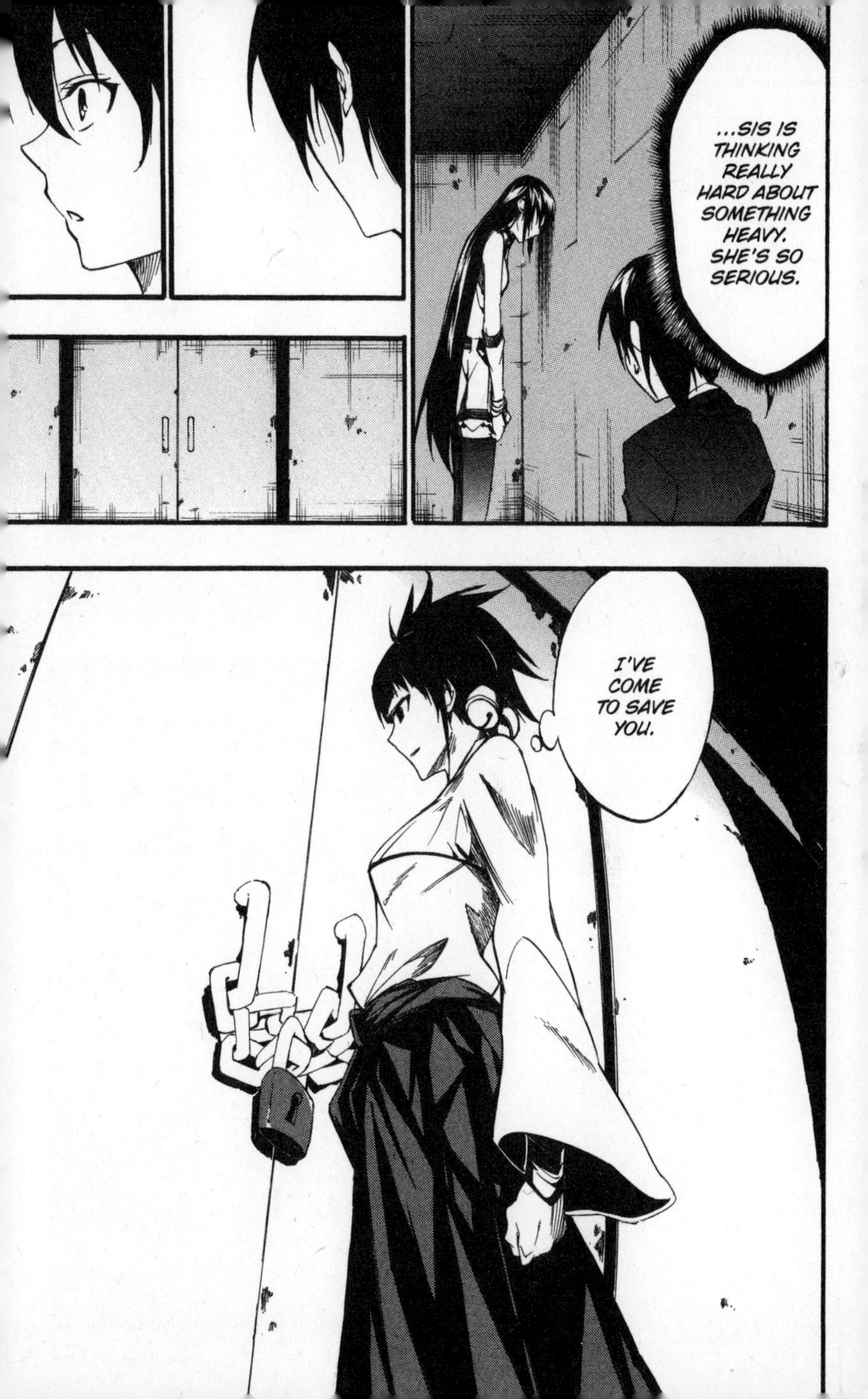
...SIS IS THINKING REALLY HARD ABOUT SOMETHING HEAVY. SHE'S SO SERIOUS.
I'VE COME TO SAVE YOU.

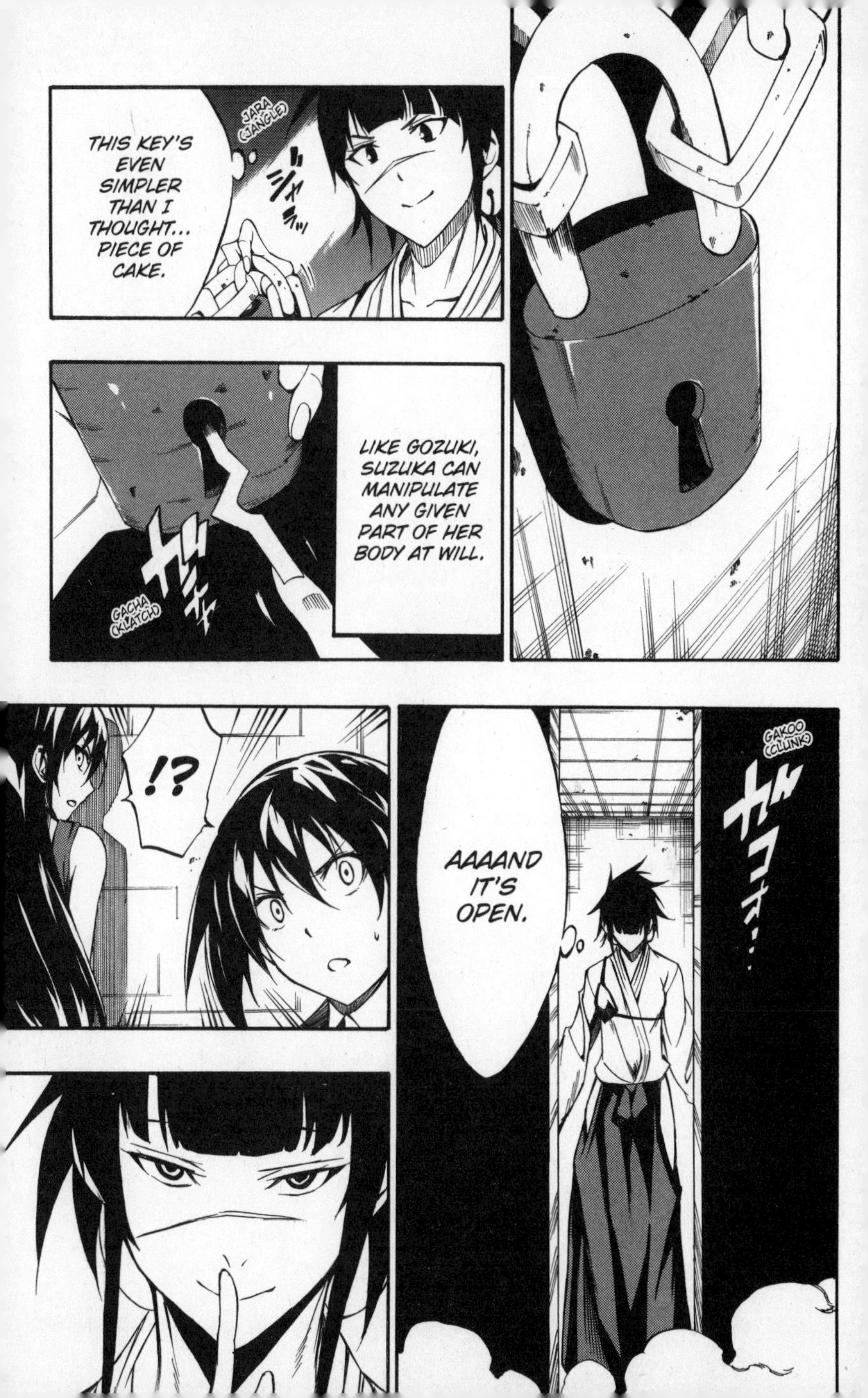
JARA (JANGLE)
THIS KEY'S EVEN SIMPLER THAN I THOUGHT... PIECE OF CAKE.
LIKE GOZUKI, SUZUKA CAN MANIPULATE ANY GIVEN PART OF HER BODY AT WILL.
GACHA (KLATCH)
GAKOO (CLUNK)
AAAAND IT'S OPEN.
!?

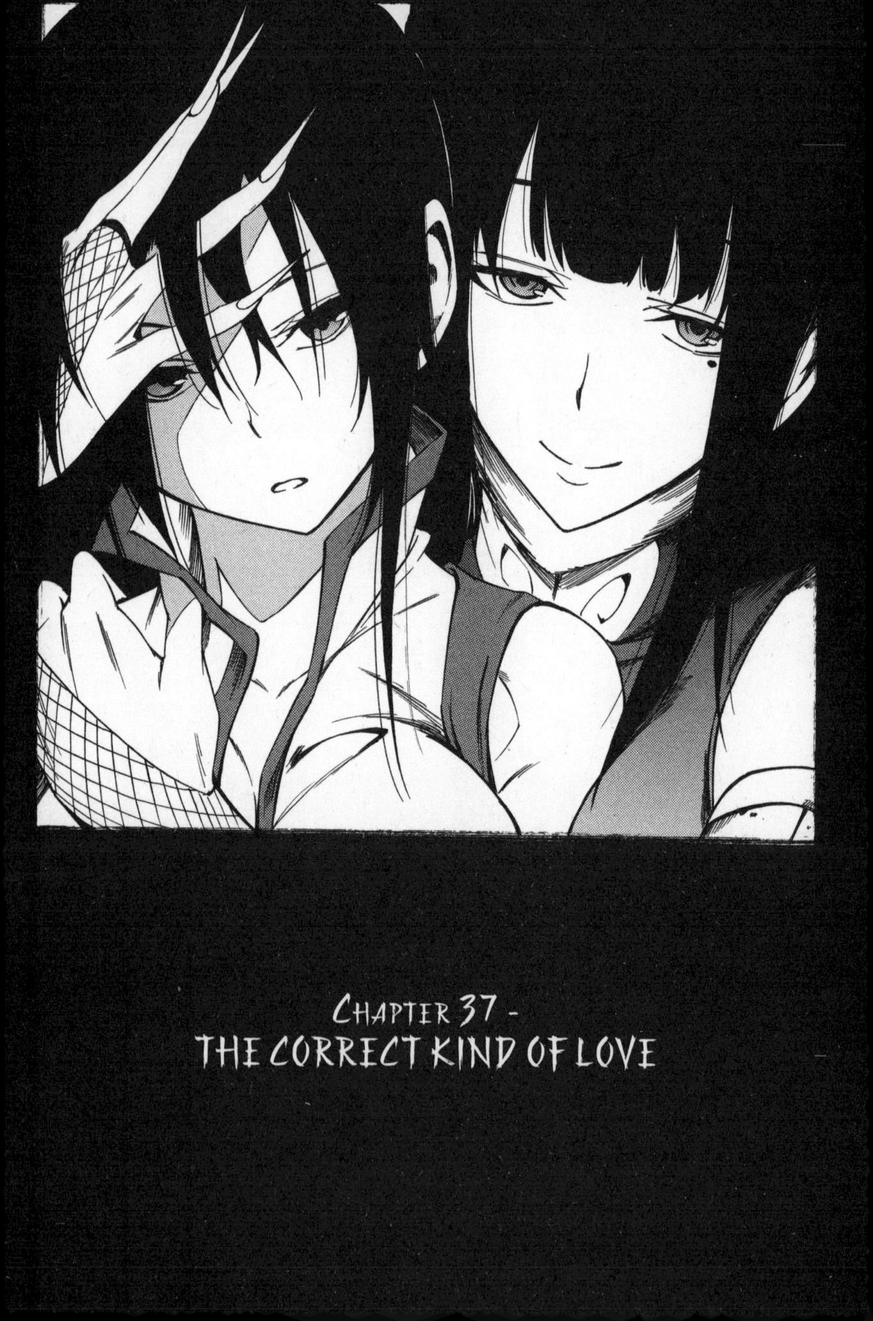

Chapter 37 -
THE CORRECT KIND OF LOVE

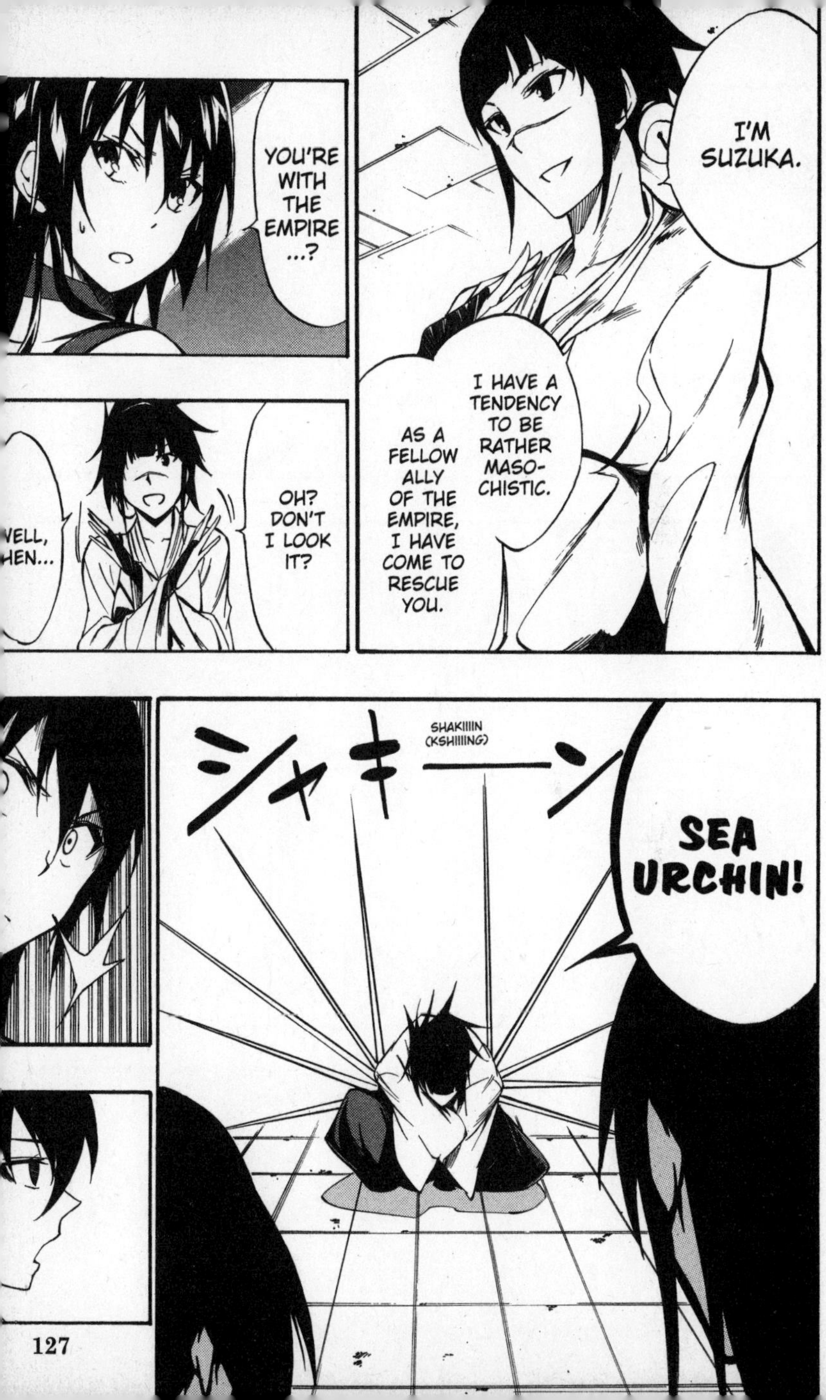
I'M SUZUKA.
I HAVE A TENDENCY TO BE RATHER MASO-CHISTIC.
AS A FELLOW ALLY OF THE EMPIRE, I HAVE COME TO RESCUE YOU.
YOU'RE WITH THE EMPIRE ...?
OH? DON'T I LOOK IT?
VELL, HEN...
SEA URCHIN!
シャキーーン
SHAKIIIIN (KSHIIIING)

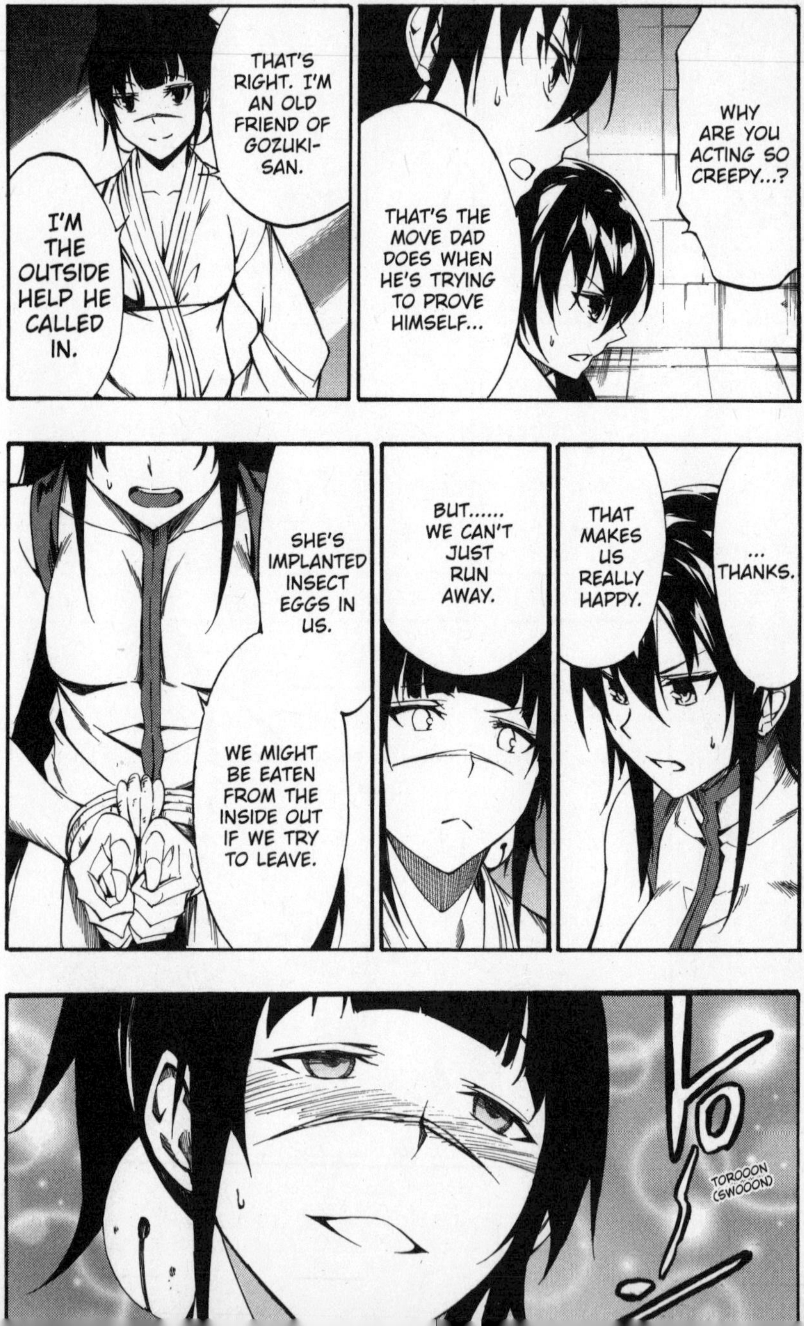
WHY ARE YOU ACTING SO CREEPY...?
THAT'S THE MOVE DAD DOES WHEN HE'S TRYING TO PROVE HIMSELF...
THAT'S RIGHT. I'M AN OLD FRIEND OF GOZUKI-SAN.
I'M THE OUTSIDE HELP HE CALLED IN.
... THANKS.
THAT MAKES US REALLY HAPPY.
BUT...... WE CAN'T JUST RUN AWAY.
SHE'S IMPLANTED INSECT EGGS IN US.
WE MIGHT BE EATEN FROM THE INSIDE OUT IF WE TRY TO LEAVE.
TOROOON (SWOOON)

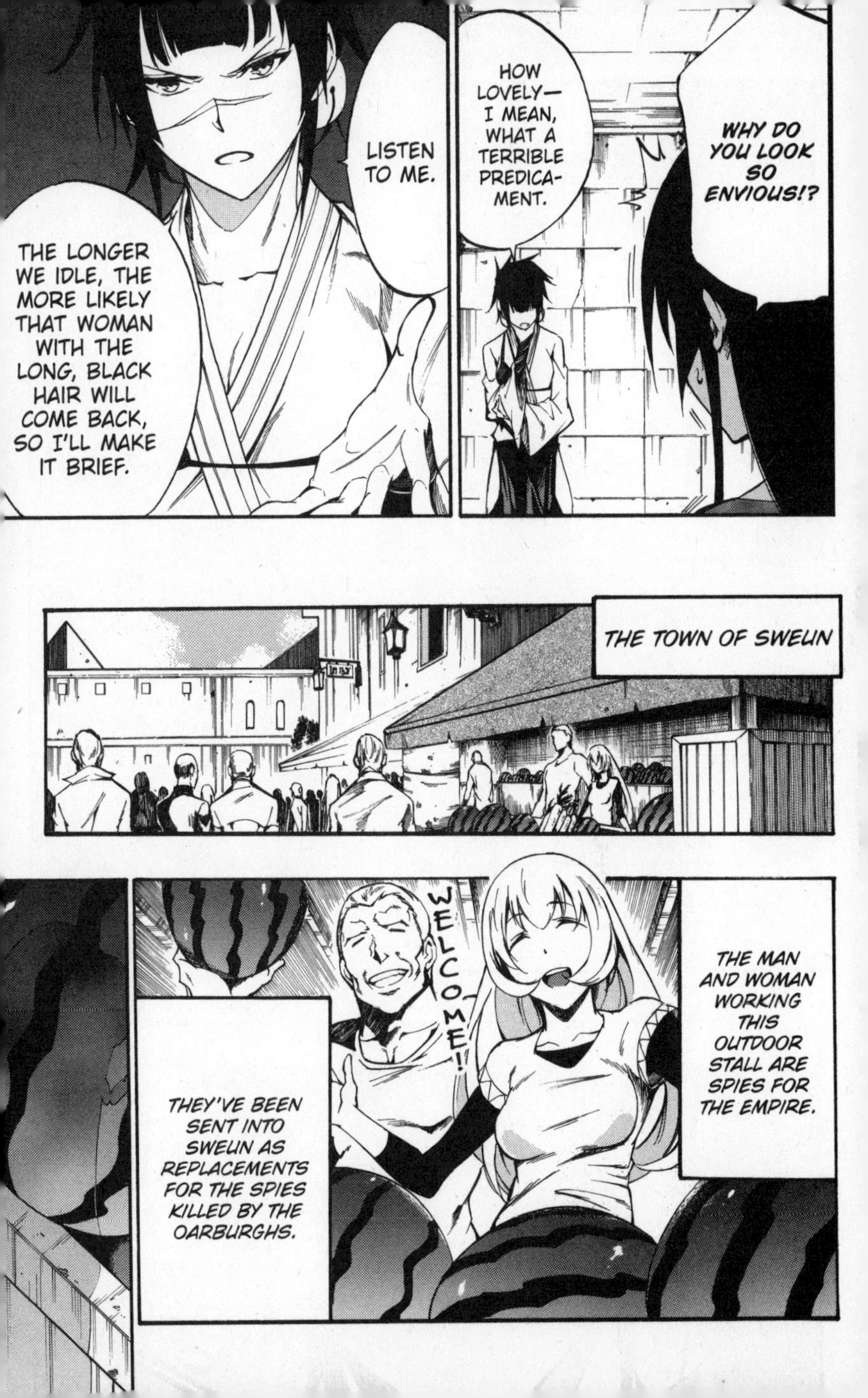
WHY DO YOU LOOK SO ENVIOUS!?
HOW LOVELY—I MEAN, WHAT A TERRIBLE PREDICAMENT.
LISTEN TO ME.
THE LONGER WE IDLE, THE MORE LIKELY THAT WOMAN WITH THE LONG, BLACK HAIR WILL COME BACK, SO I'LL MAKE IT BRIEF.
THE TOWN OF SWEUN
THE MAN AND WOMAN WORKING THIS OUTDOOR STALL ARE SPIES FOR THE EMPIRE.
WELCOME!!
THEY'VE BEEN SENT INTO SWEUN AS REPLACEMENTS FOR THE SPIES KILLED BY THE OARBURGHS.

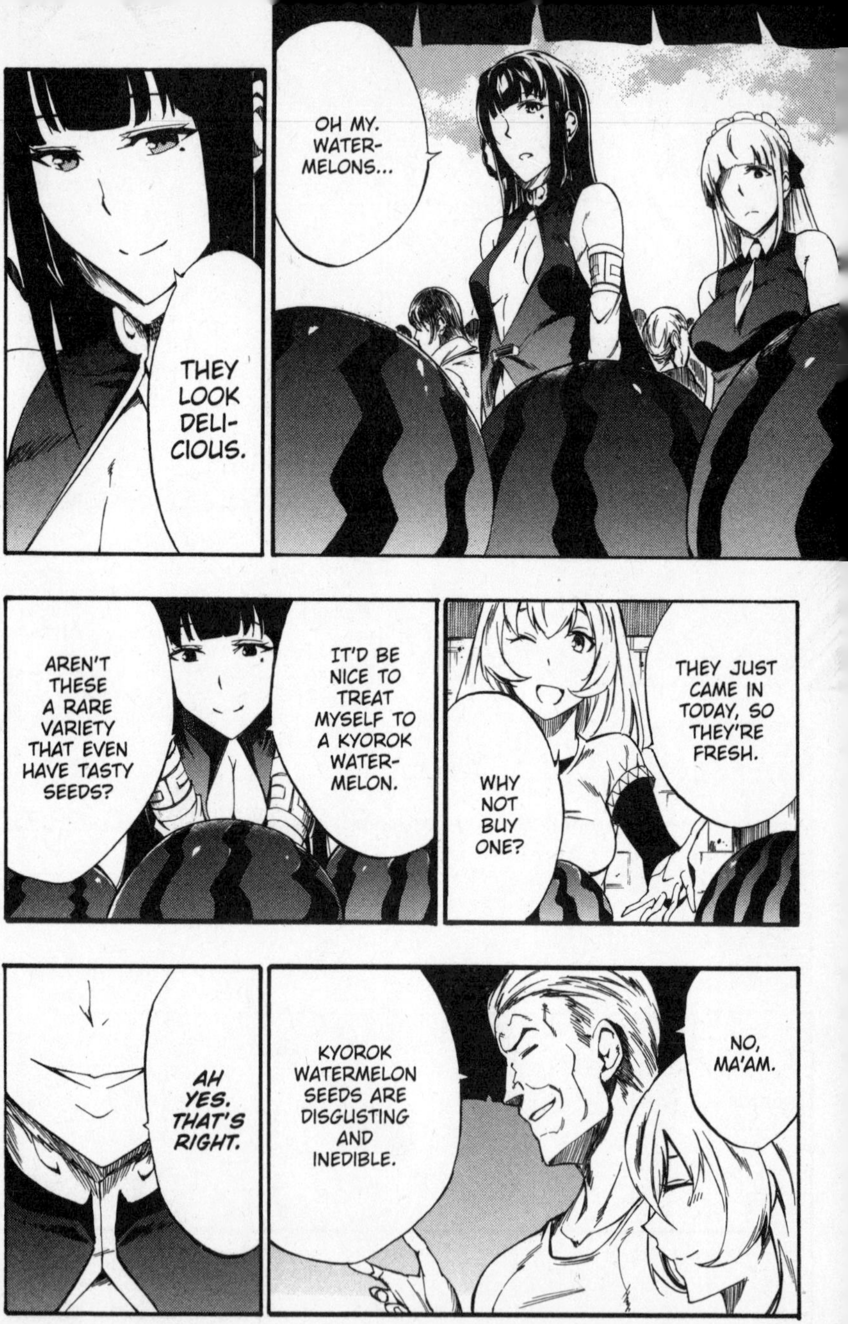
OH MY. WATER-MELONS...
THEY LOOK DELI-CIOUS.
THEY JUST CAME IN TODAY, SO THEY'RE FRESH.
WHY NOT BUY ONE?
IT'D BE NICE TO TREAT MYSELF TO A KYOROK WATER-MELON.
AREN'T THESE A RARE VARIETY THAT EVEN HAVE TASTY SEEDS?
NO, MA'AM.
KYOROK WATERMELON SEEDS ARE DISGUSTING AND INEDIBLE.
AH YES. THAT'S RIGHT.

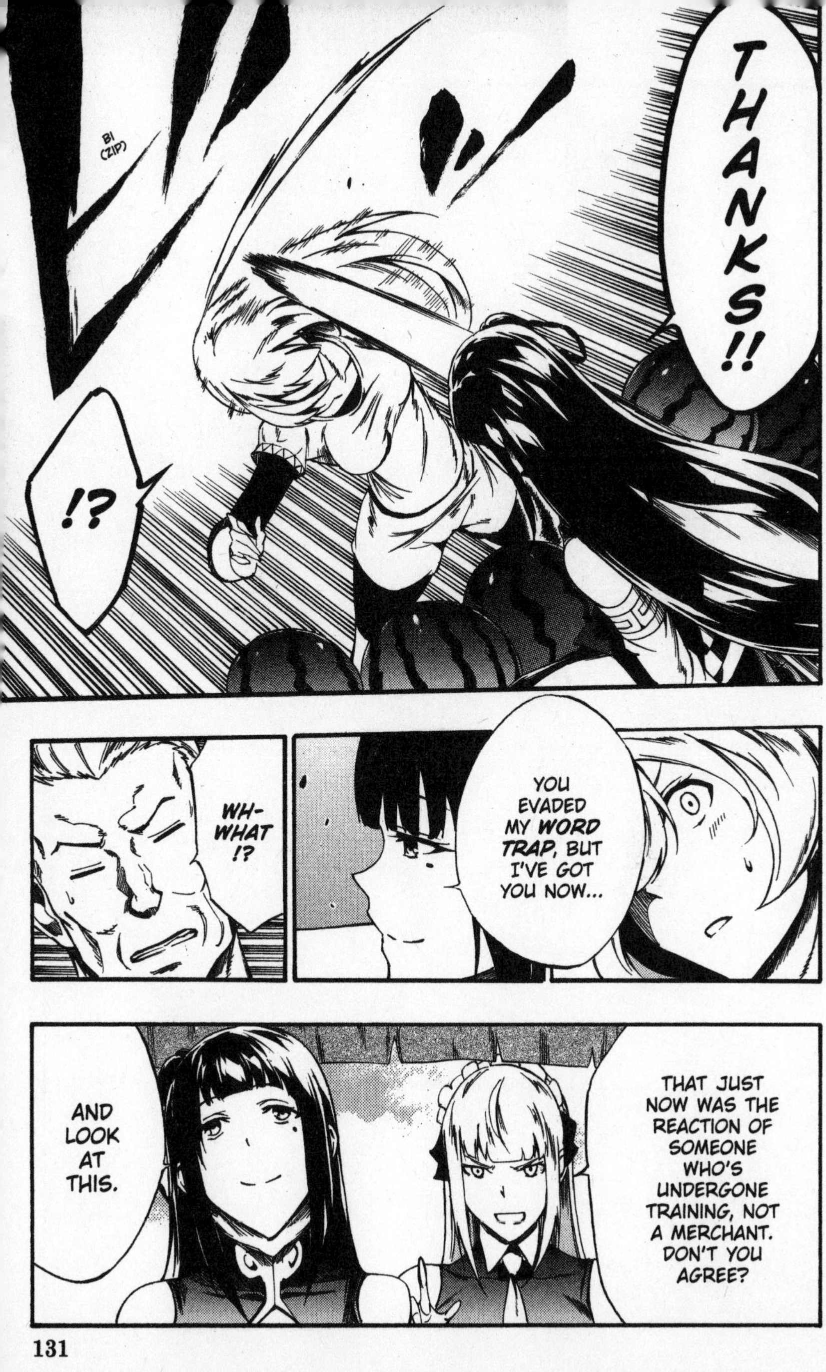
THANKS!!
BI (ZIP)
!?
YOU EVADED MY WORD TRAP, BUT I'VE GOT YOU NOW...
WH-WHAT!?
THAT JUST NOW WAS THE REACTION OF SOMEONE WHO'S UNDERGONE TRAINING, NOT A MERCHANT. DON'T YOU AGREE?
AND LOOK AT THIS.

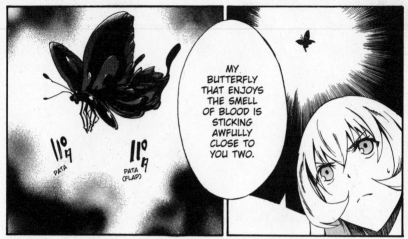

MY BUTTERFLY THAT ENJOYS THE SMELL OF BLOOD IS STICKING AWFULLY CLOSE TO YOU TWO.

PATA

PATA (FLAP)

BA

BA (FWD)

KUH!!

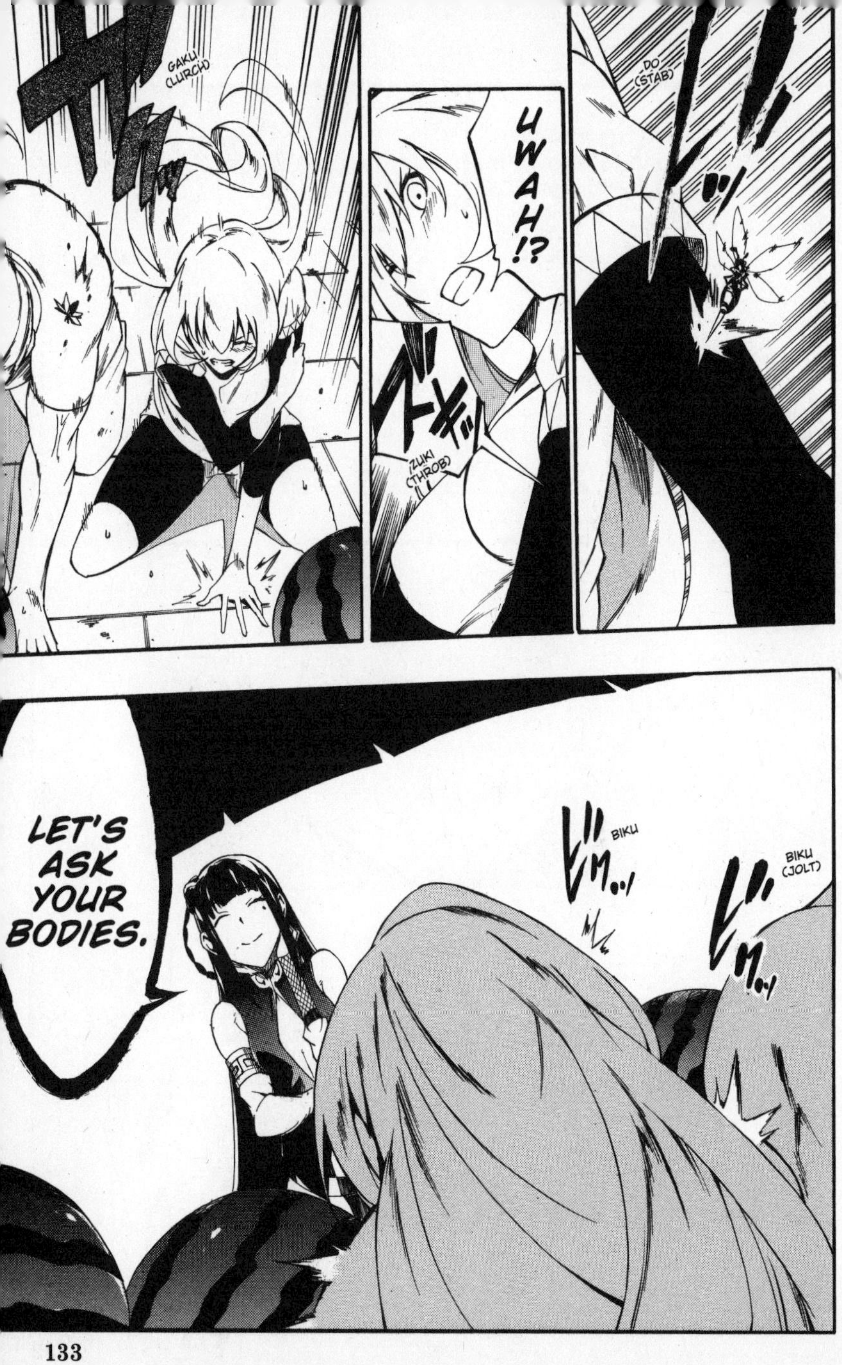

DO (STAB)
UWAH!?
IZUKI (THROB)
GAKU (LURCH)
BIKU
BIKU (JOLT)
LET'S ASK YOUR BODIES.

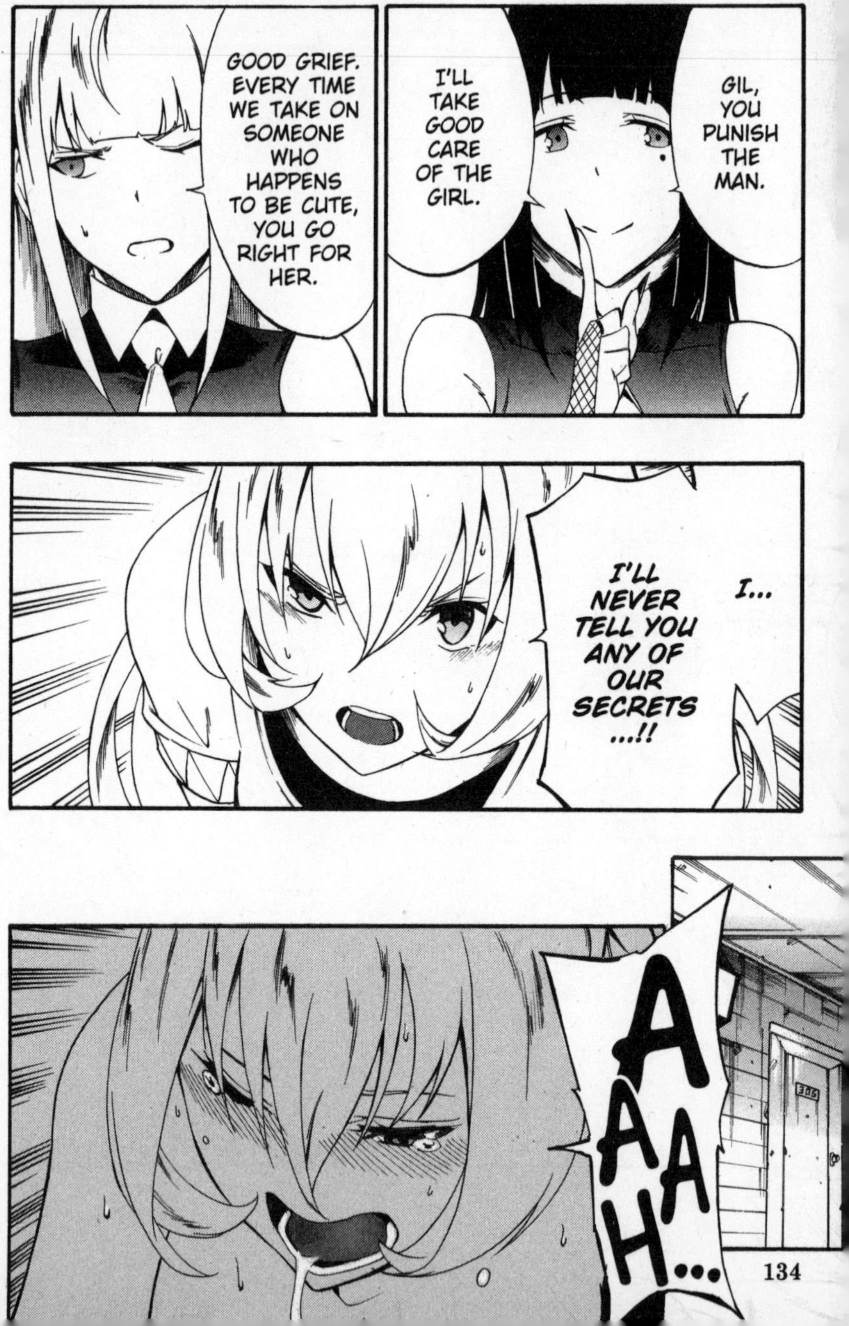
GIL, YOU PUNISH THE MAN.
I'LL TAKE GOOD CARE OF THE GIRL.
GOOD GRIEF. EVERY TIME WE TAKE ON SOMEONE WHO HAPPENS TO BE CUTE, YOU GO RIGHT FOR HER.
I...
I'LL NEVER TELL YOU ANY OF OUR SECRETS ...!!
AAAAH...

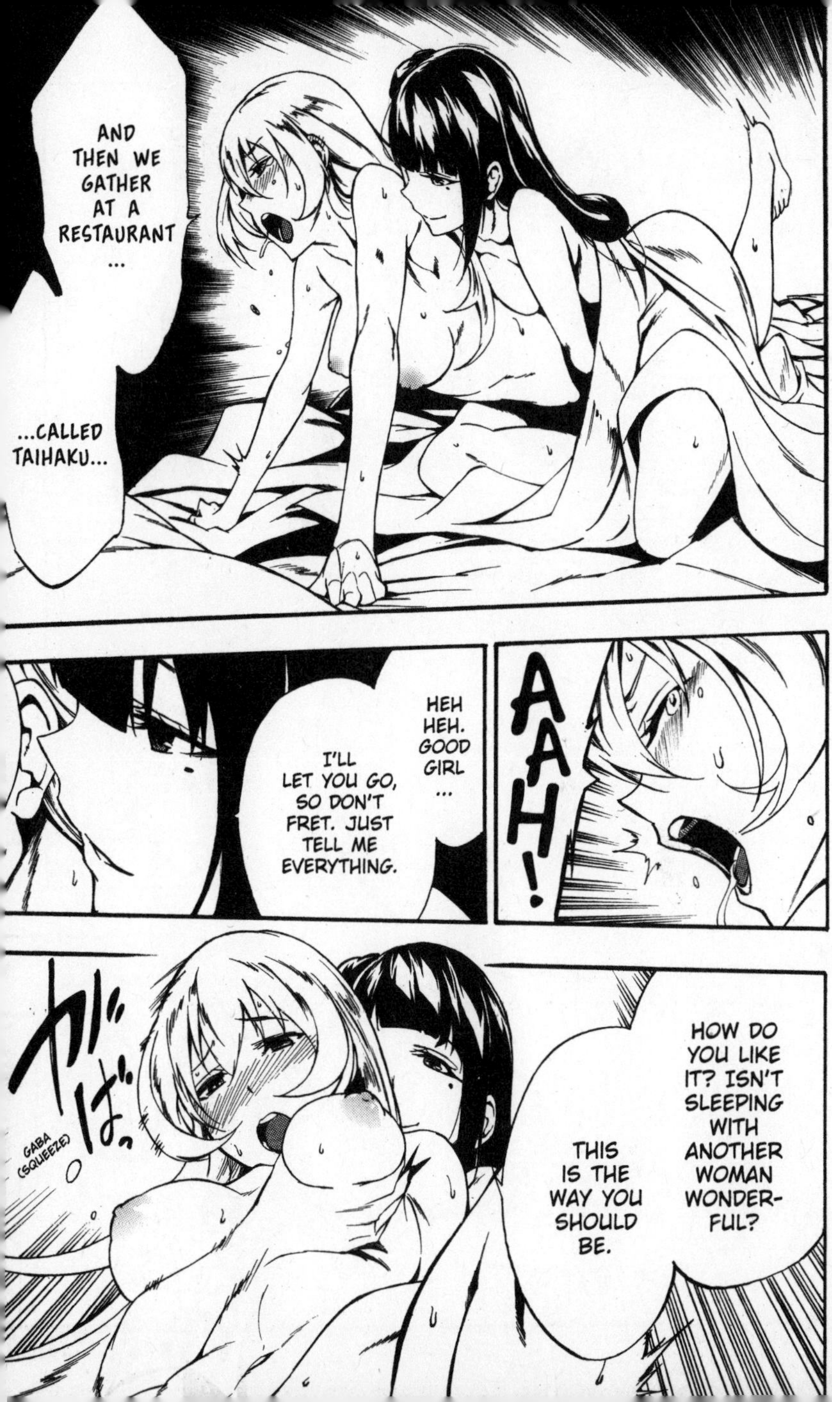
AND THEN WE GATHER AT A RESTAURANT ...
...CALLED TAIHAKU...
AAH!
HEH HEH. GOOD GIRL ...
I'LL LET YOU GO, SO DON'T FRET. JUST TELL ME EVERYTHING.
HOW DO YOU LIKE IT? ISN'T SLEEPING WITH ANOTHER WOMAN WONDERFUL?
THIS IS THE WAY YOU SHOULD BE.
GABA (SQUEEZE)

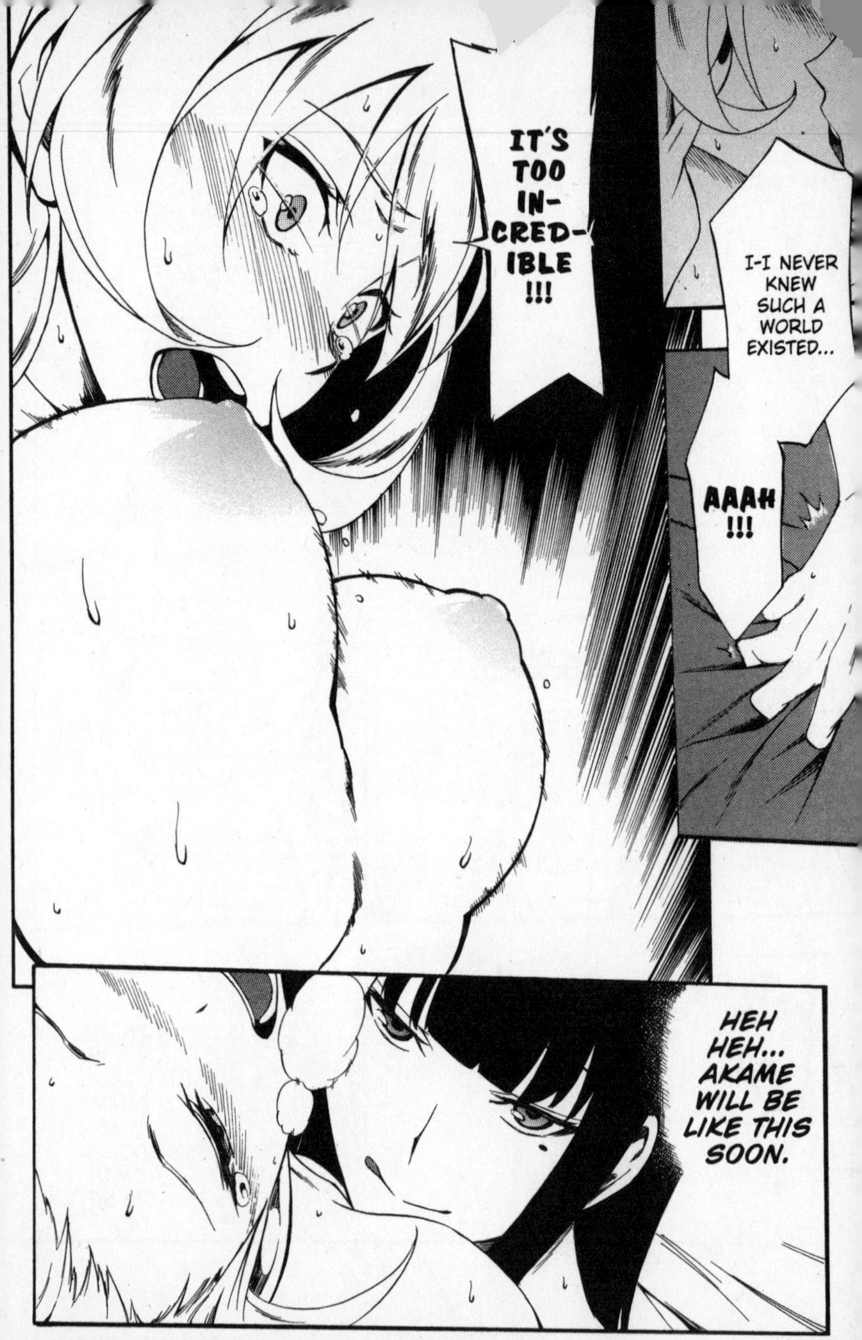
I-I NEVER KNEW SUCH A WORLD EXISTED...
AAAH!!!
IT'S TOO IN-CRED-IBLE!!!
HEH HEH... AKAME WILL BE LIKE THIS SOON.

SORRY!

?

SU
(SWP)

OH.
IT'S RUDE
TO THINK
THINGS LIKE
THAT WHILE
YOU'RE
STILL HERE.

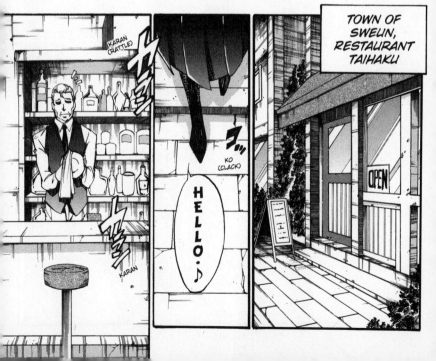

KARAN
(RATTLE)

KARAN

KO
(CLACK)

HELLO. ♪

TOWN OF
SWELIN,
RESTAURANT
TAIHAKU

OPEN

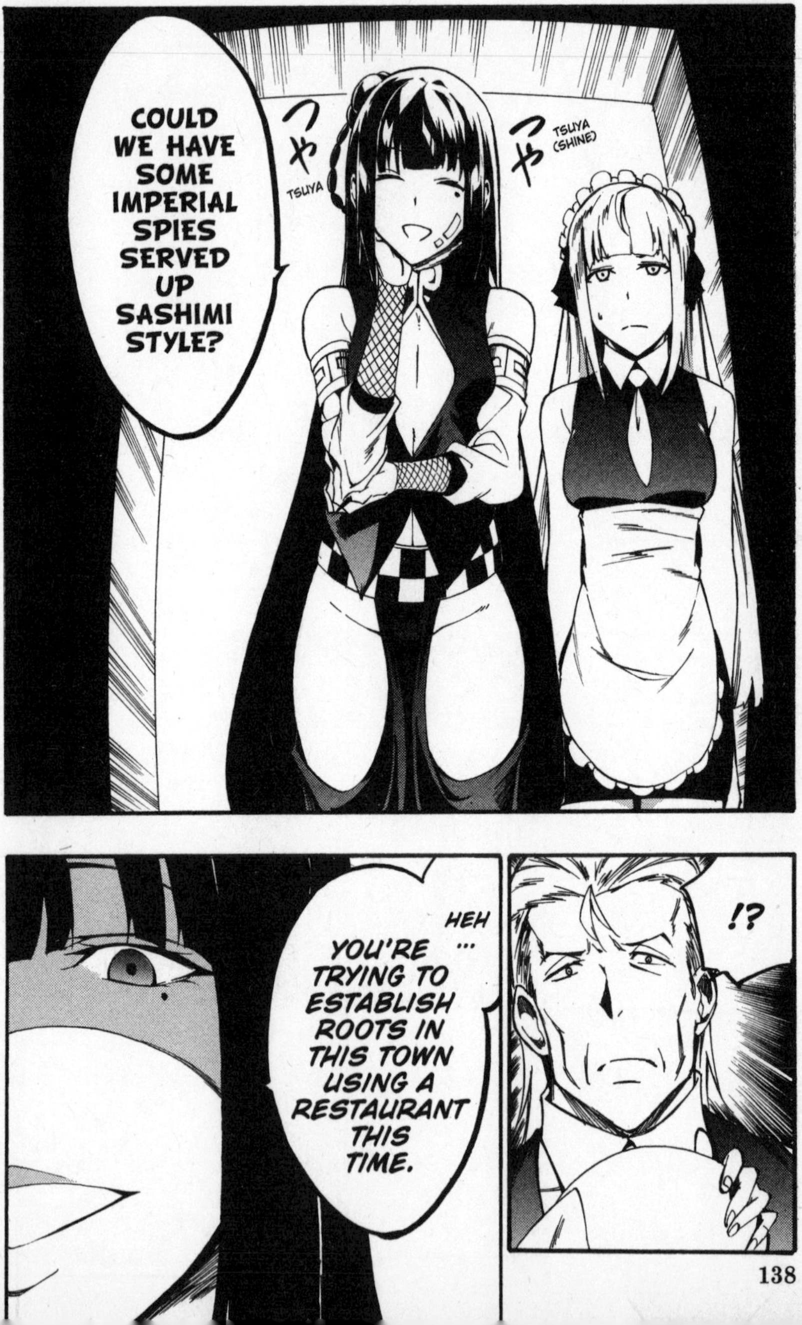
つや TSUYA (SHINE)
つや TSUYA
COULD WE HAVE SOME IMPERIAL SPIES SERVED UP SASHIMI STYLE?
!?
HEH...
YOU'RE TRYING TO ESTABLISH ROOTS IN THIS TOWN USING A RESTAURANT THIS TIME.

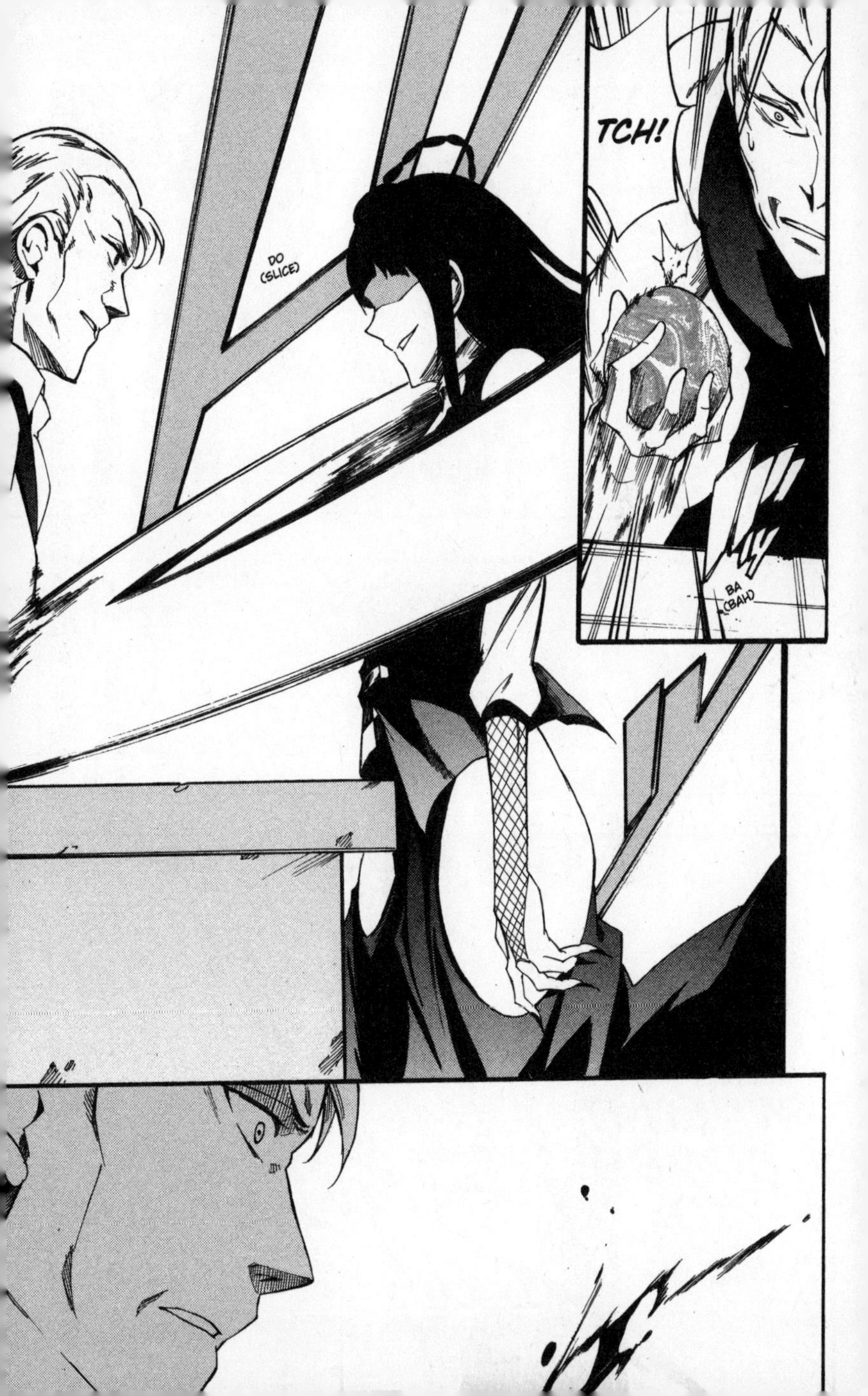
TCH!
BA
(BAH)
DO
(SLICE)

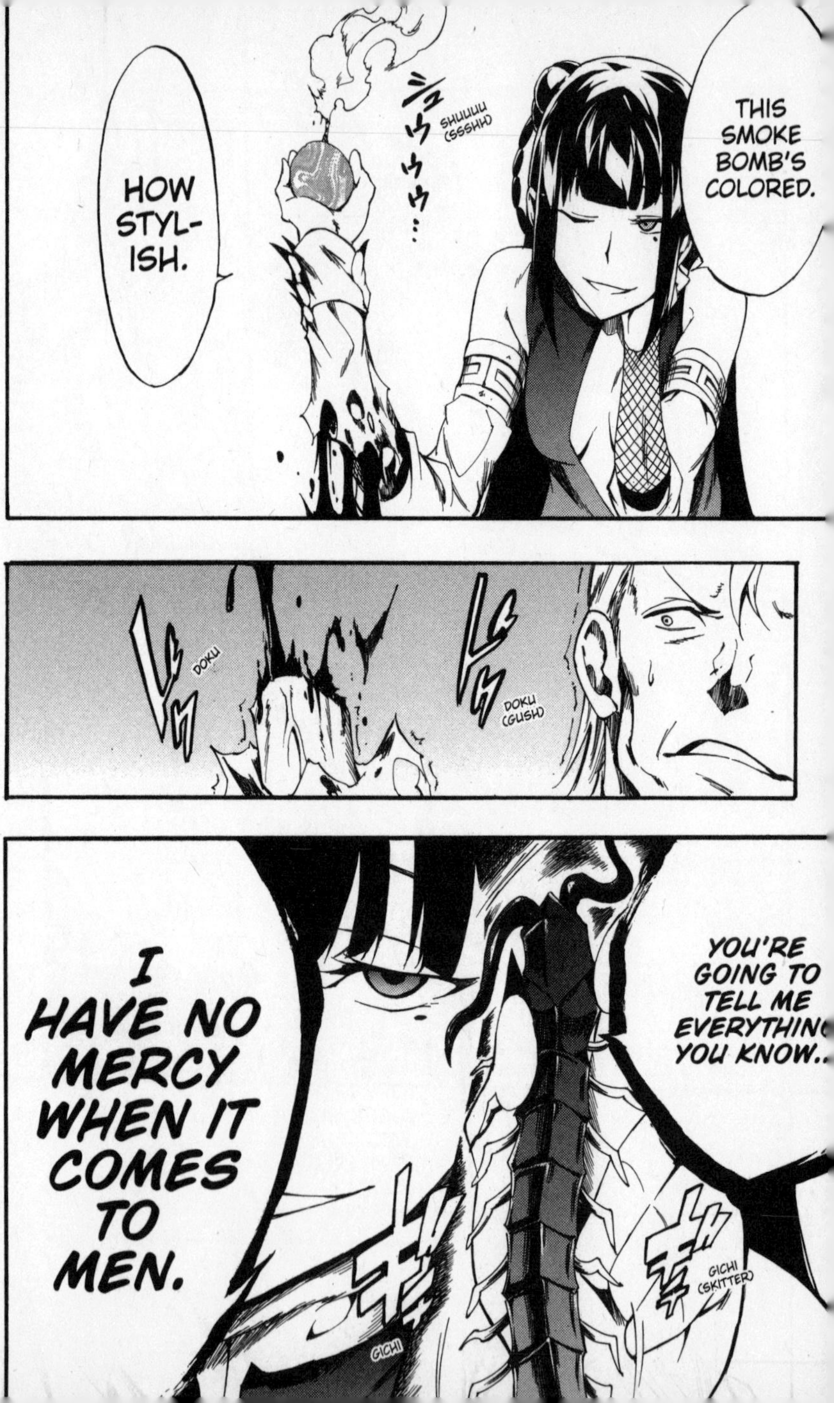
THIS SMOKE BOMB'S COLORED.
SHUUUUU (SSSHH)
HOW STYL-ISH.
DOKU (GUSH)
DOKU
YOU'RE GOING TO TELL ME EVERYTHIN YOU KNOW..
I HAVE NO MERCY WHEN IT COMES TO MEN.
GICHI (SKITTER)
GICHI

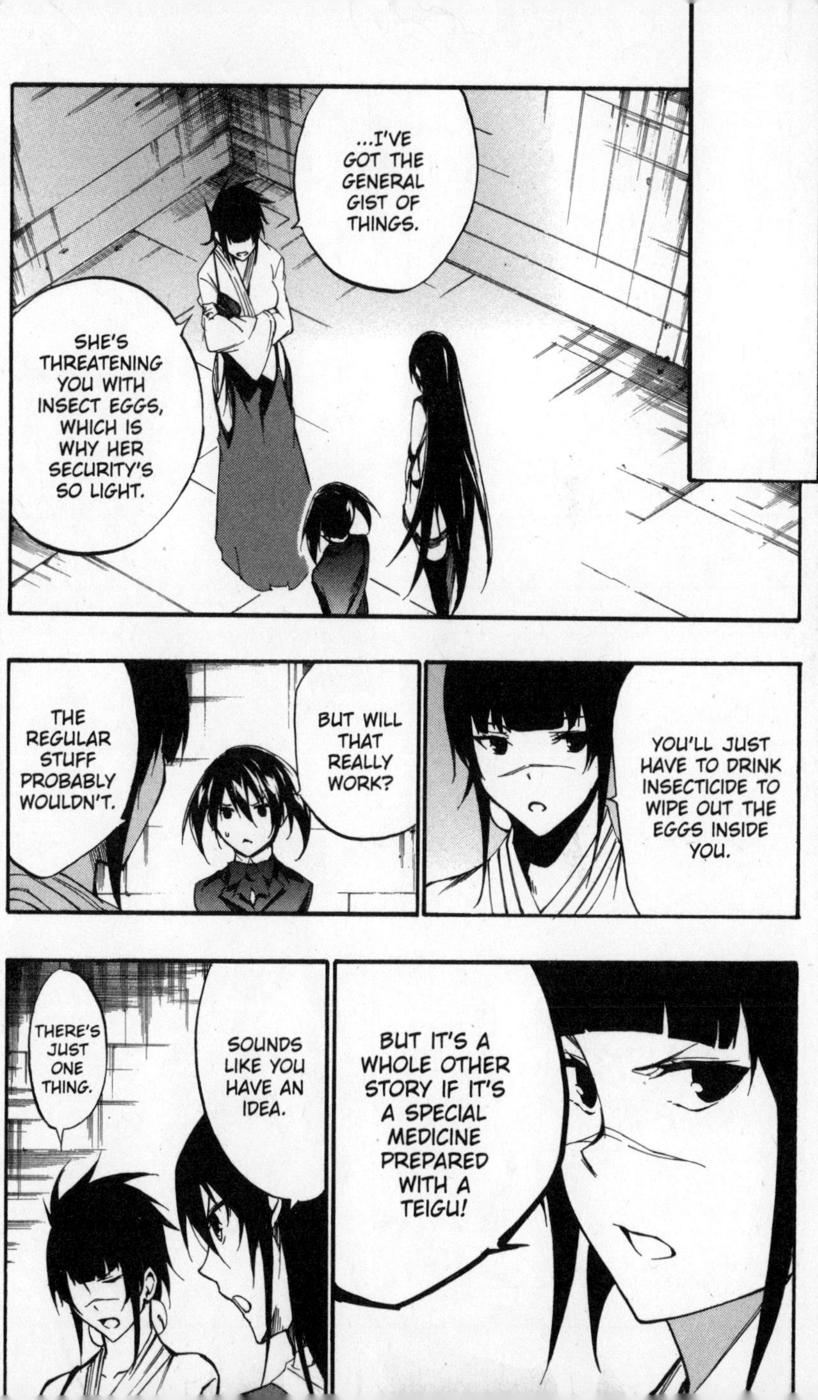
...I'VE GOT THE GENERAL GIST OF THINGS.
SHE'S THREATENING YOU WITH INSECT EGGS, WHICH IS WHY HER SECURITY'S SO LIGHT.
YOU'LL JUST HAVE TO DRINK INSECTICIDE TO WIPE OUT THE EGGS INSIDE YOU.
BUT WILL THAT REALLY WORK?
THE REGULAR STUFF PROBABLY WOULDN'T.
BUT IT'S A WHOLE OTHER STORY IF IT'S A SPECIAL MEDICINE PREPARED WITH A TEIGU!
SOUNDS LIKE YOU HAVE AN IDEA.
THERE'S JUST ONE THING.

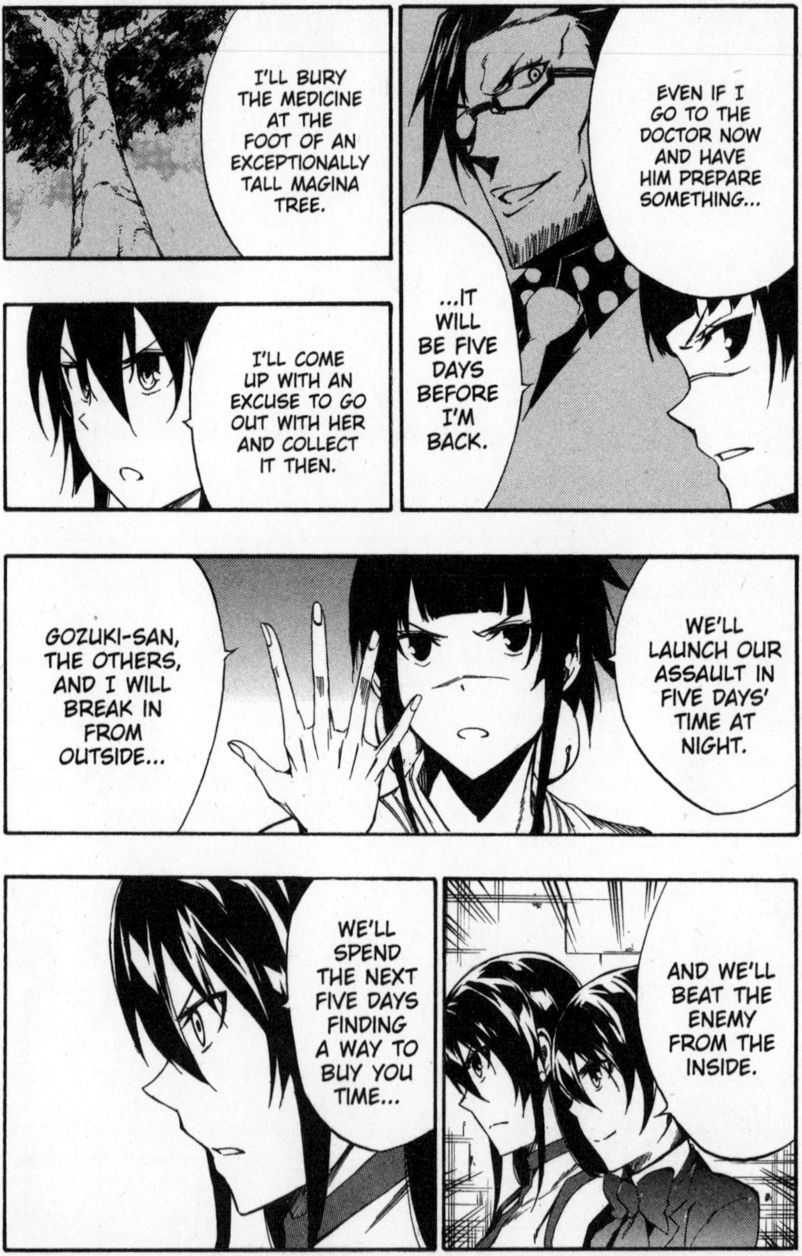
EVEN IF I GO TO THE DOCTOR NOW AND HAVE HIM PREPARE SOMETHING...
...IT WILL BE FIVE DAYS BEFORE I'M BACK.
I'LL BURY THE MEDICINE AT THE FOOT OF AN EXCEPTIONALLY TALL MAGINA TREE.
I'LL COME UP WITH AN EXCUSE TO GO OUT WITH HER AND COLLECT IT THEN.
WE'LL LAUNCH OUR ASSAULT IN FIVE DAYS' TIME AT NIGHT.
GOZUKI-SAN, THE OTHERS, AND I WILL BREAK IN FROM OUTSIDE...
AND WE'LL BEAT THE ENEMY FROM THE INSIDE.
WE'LL SPEND THE NEXT FIVE DAYS FINDING A WAY TO BUY YOU TIME...

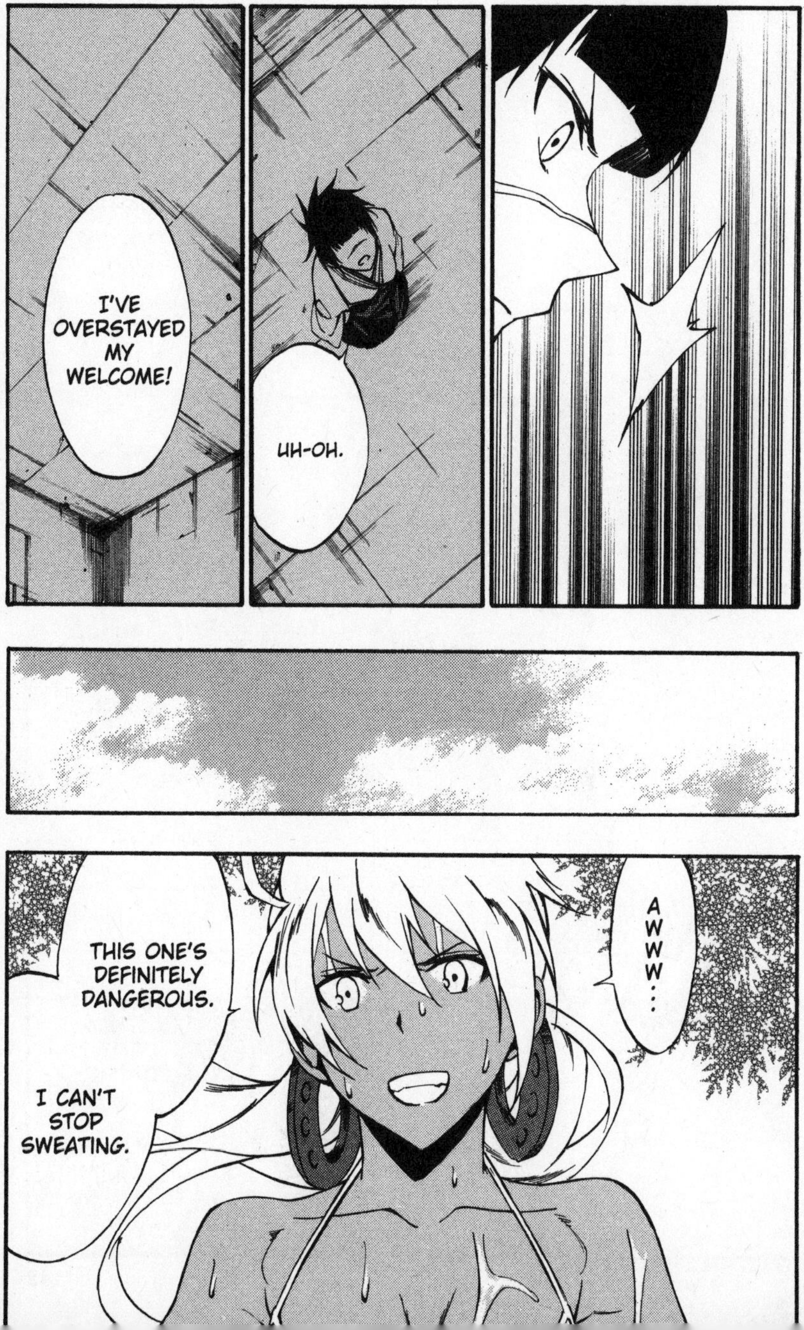
UH-OH.
I'VE OVERSTAYED MY WELCOME!
AWWW...
THIS ONE'S DEFINITELY DANGEROUS.
I CAN'T STOP SWEATING.

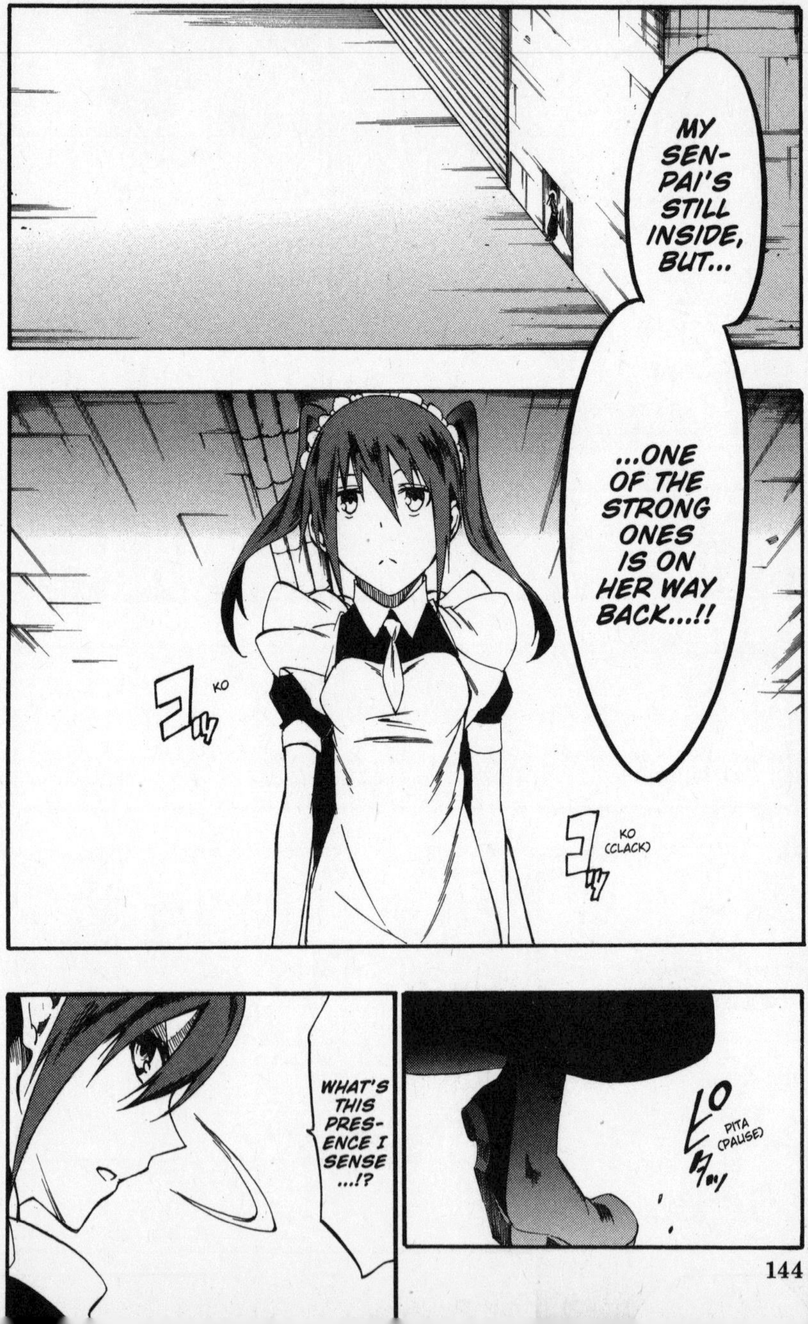
MY SEN-PAI'S STILL INSIDE, BUT...
...ONE OF THE STRONG ONES IS ON HER WAY BACK...!!
KO
KO (CLACK)
PITA (PAUSE)
WHAT'S THIS PRES-ENCE I SENSE ...!?

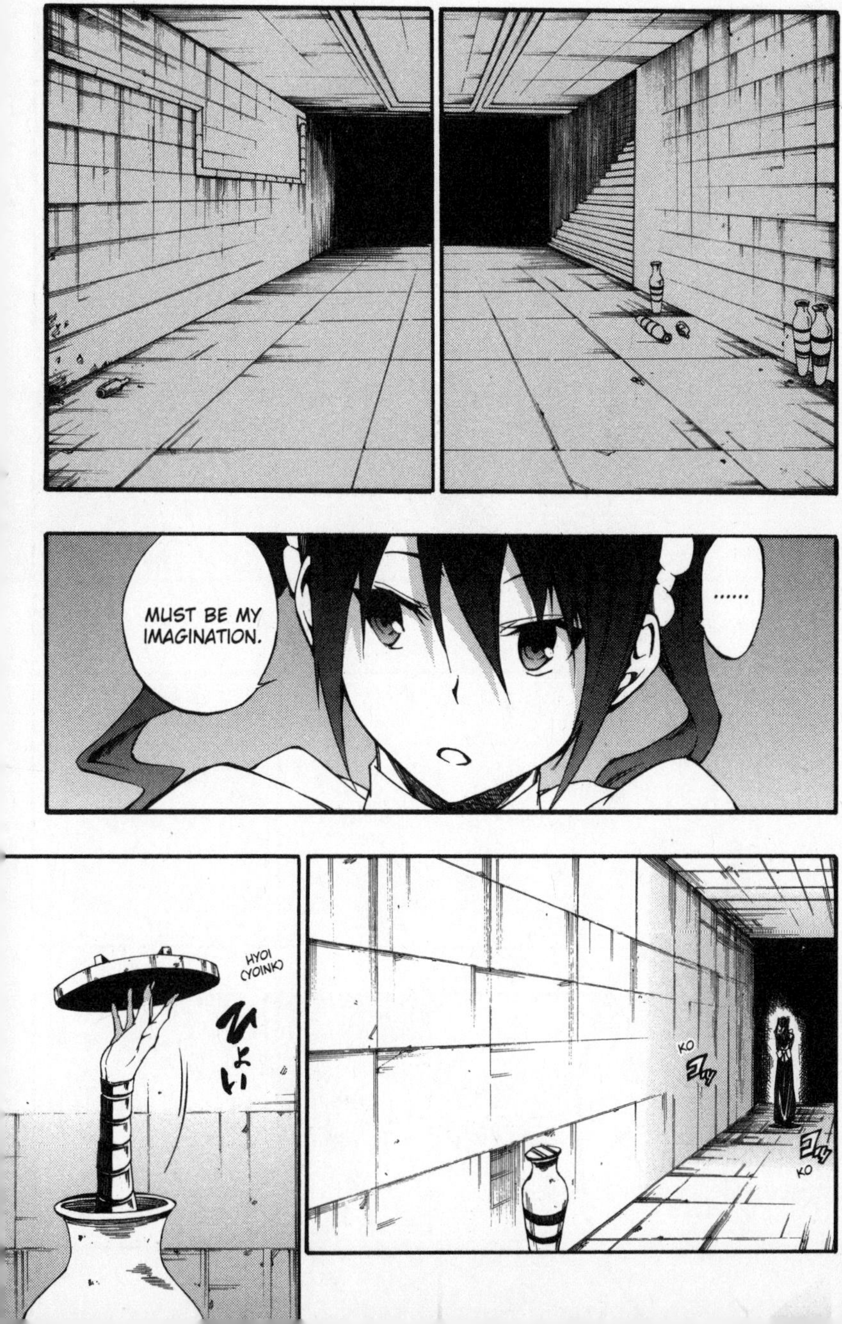
......
MUST BE MY IMAGINATION.
HYOI (YOINK)
ひょい
KO
コツ
KO
コツ

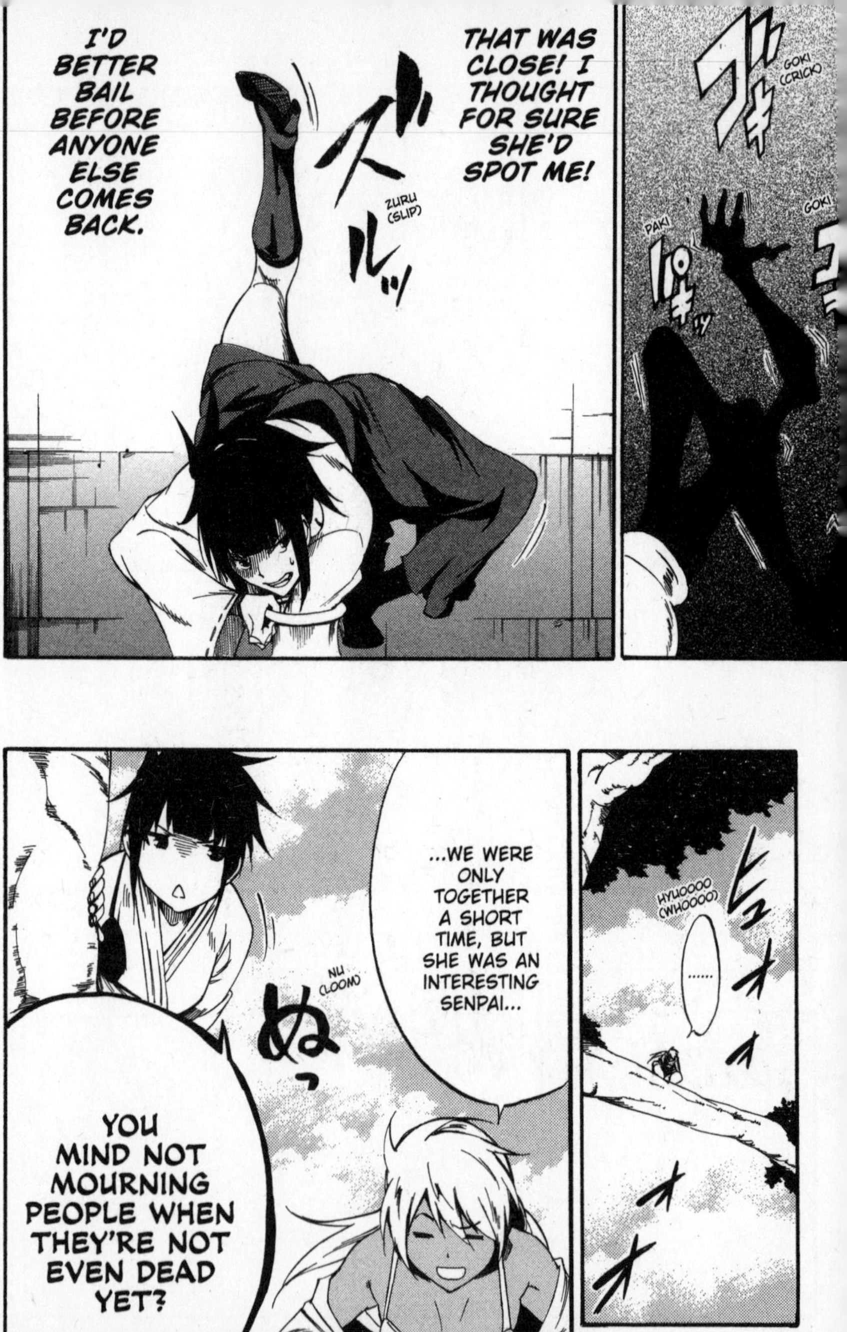
GOKI (CRICK)
PAKI
GOKI
THAT WAS CLOSE! I THOUGHT FOR SURE SHE'D SPOT ME!
I'D BETTER BAIL BEFORE ANYONE ELSE COMES BACK.
ZURU (SLIP)
HYUOOOO (WHOOOO)
......
...WE WERE ONLY TOGETHER A SHORT TIME, BUT SHE WAS AN INTERESTING SENPAI...
NU (LOOM)
YOU MIND NOT MOURNING PEOPLE WHEN THEY'RE NOT EVEN DEAD YET?

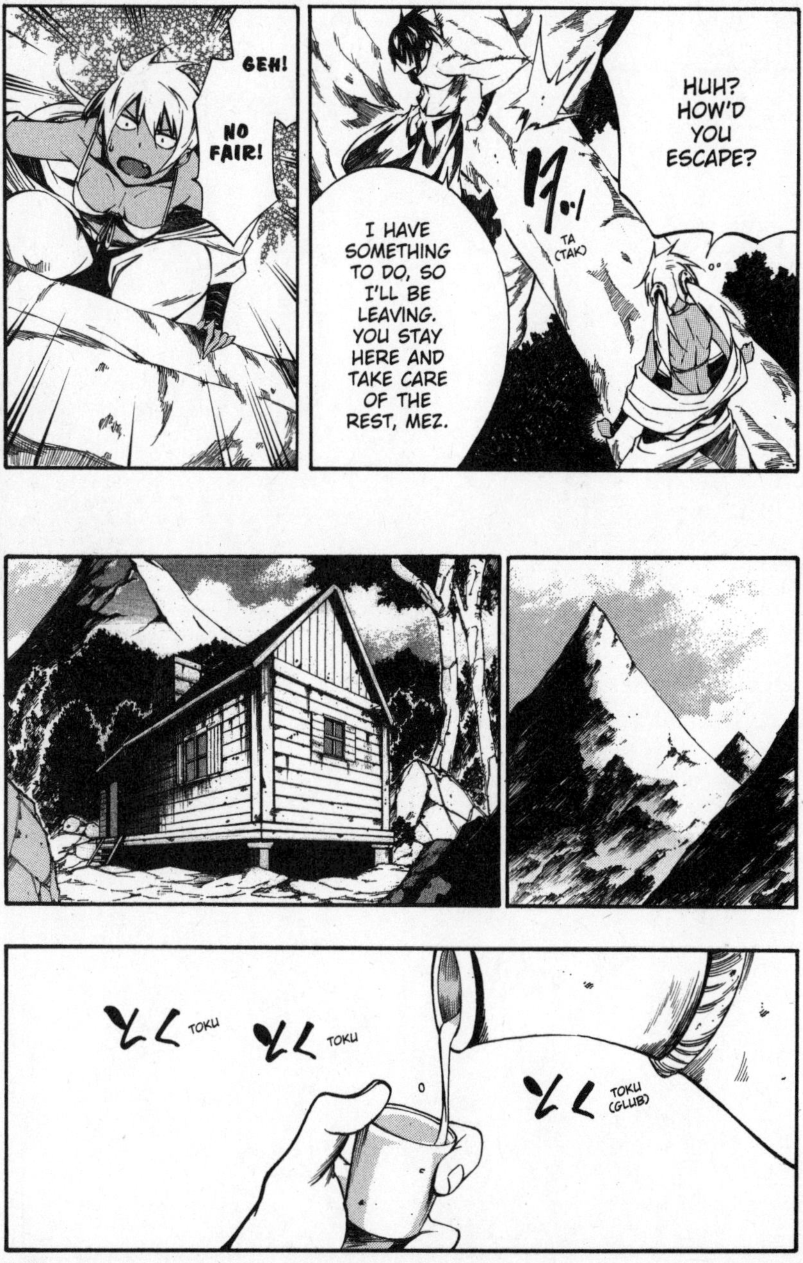

HUH? HOW'D YOU ESCAPE?
TA (TAK)
I HAVE SOMETHING TO DO, SO I'LL BE LEAVING. YOU STAY HERE AND TAKE CARE OF THE REST, MEZ.
GEH!
NO FAIR!
TOKU
TOKU
TOKU (GLUB)

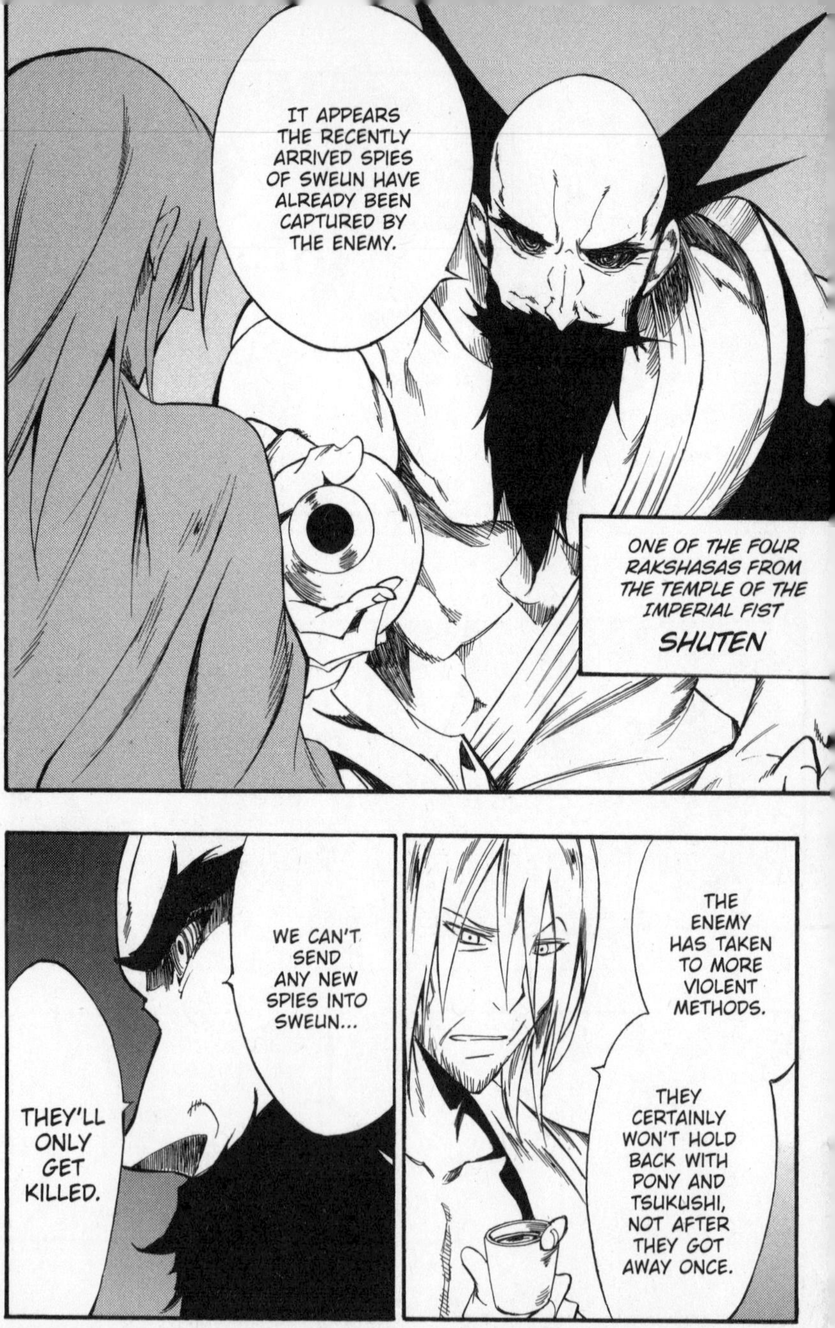
IT APPEARS THE RECENTLY ARRIVED SPIES OF SWEUN HAVE ALREADY BEEN CAPTURED BY THE ENEMY.
ONE OF THE FOUR RAKSHASAS FROM THE TEMPLE OF THE IMPERIAL FIST
SHUTEN
THE ENEMY HAS TAKEN TO MORE VIOLENT METHODS.
THEY CERTAINLY WON'T HOLD BACK WITH PONY AND TSUKUSHI, NOT AFTER THEY GOT AWAY ONCE.
WE CAN'T SEND ANY NEW SPIES INTO SWEUN...
THEY'LL ONLY GET KILLED.

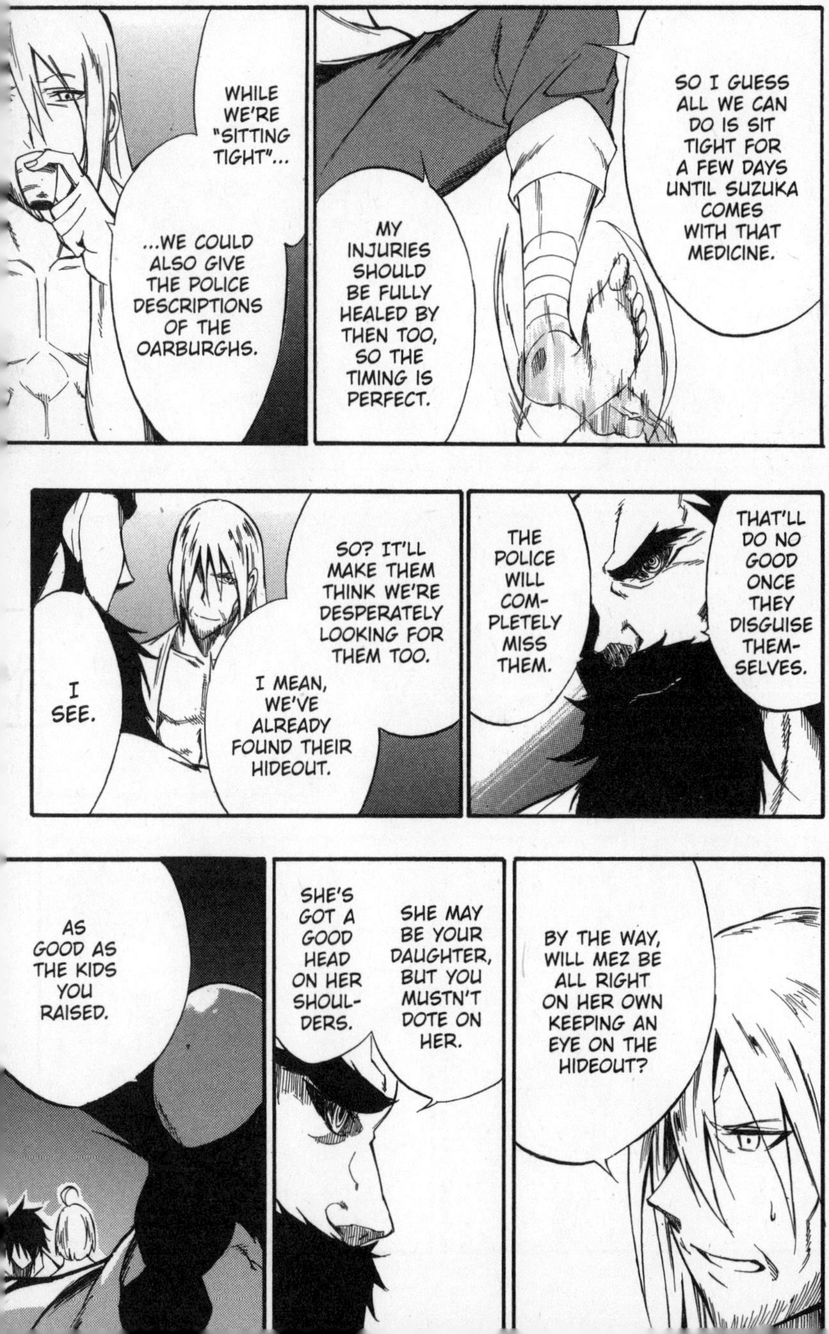
SO I GUESS ALL WE CAN DO IS SIT TIGHT FOR A FEW DAYS UNTIL SUZUKA COMES WITH THAT MEDICINE.
MY INJURIES SHOULD BE FULLY HEALED BY THEN TOO, SO THE TIMING IS PERFECT.
WHILE WE'RE "SITTING TIGHT"...
...WE COULD ALSO GIVE THE POLICE DESCRIPTIONS OF THE OARBURGHS.
THAT'LL DO NO GOOD ONCE THEY DISGUISE THEM-SELVES.
THE POLICE WILL COM-PLETELY MISS THEM.
SO? IT'LL MAKE THEM THINK WE'RE DESPERATELY LOOKING FOR THEM TOO.
I MEAN, WE'VE ALREADY FOUND THEIR HIDEOUT.
I SEE.
BY THE WAY, WILL MEZ BE ALL RIGHT ON HER OWN KEEPING AN EYE ON THE HIDEOUT?
SHE MAY BE YOUR DAUGHTER, BUT YOU MUSTN'T DOTE ON HER.
SHE'S GOT A GOOD HEAD ON HER SHOUL-DERS.
AS GOOD AS THE KIDS YOU RAISED.

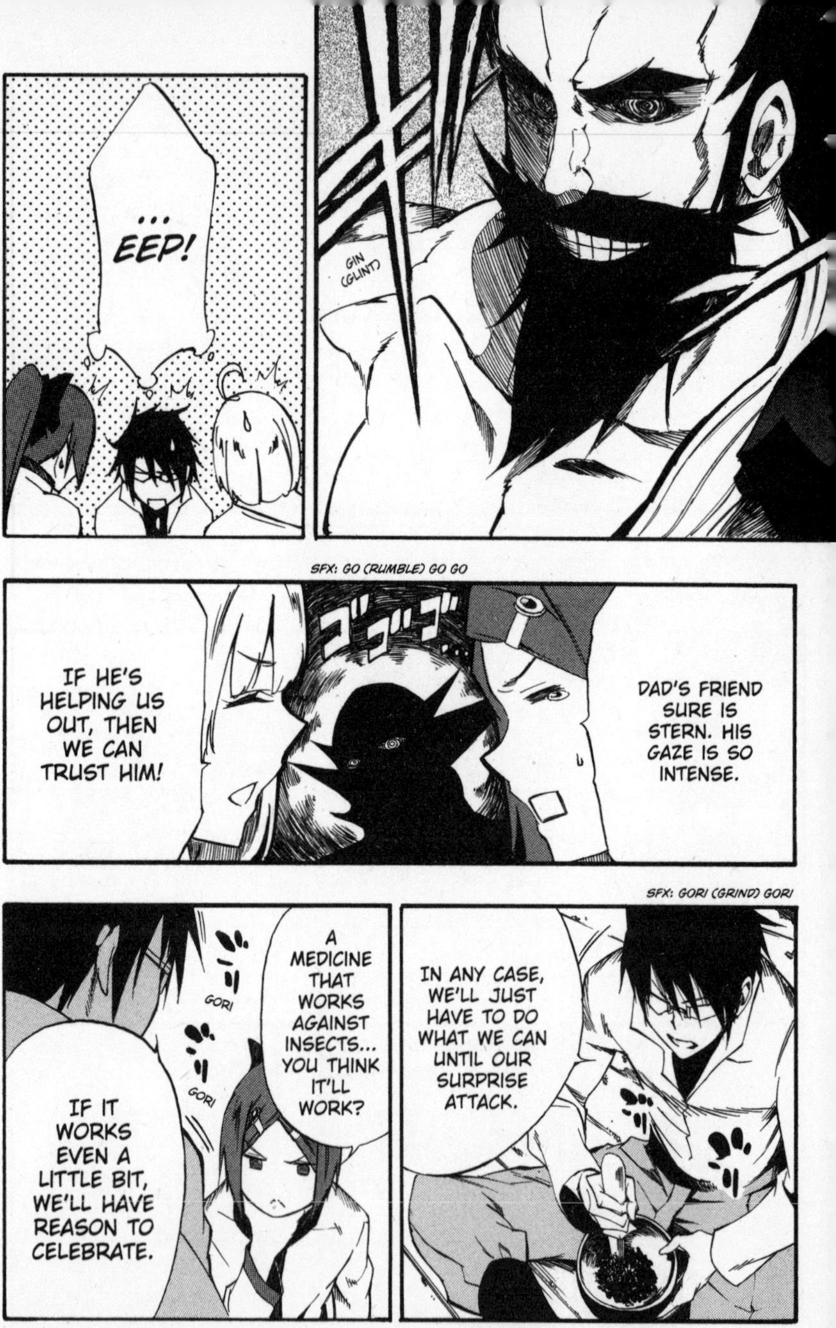
GIN (GLINT)
... EEP!
SFX: GO (RUMBLE) GO GO
DAD'S FRIEND SURE IS STERN. HIS GAZE IS SO INTENSE.
IF HE'S HELPING US OUT, THEN WE CAN TRUST HIM!
SFX: GORI (GRIND) GORI
IN ANY CASE, WE'LL JUST HAVE TO DO WHAT WE CAN UNTIL OUR SURPRISE ATTACK.
A MEDICINE THAT WORKS AGAINST INSECTS... YOU THINK IT'LL WORK?
GORI
GORI
IF IT WORKS EVEN A LITTLE BIT, WE'LL HAVE REASON TO CELEBRATE.

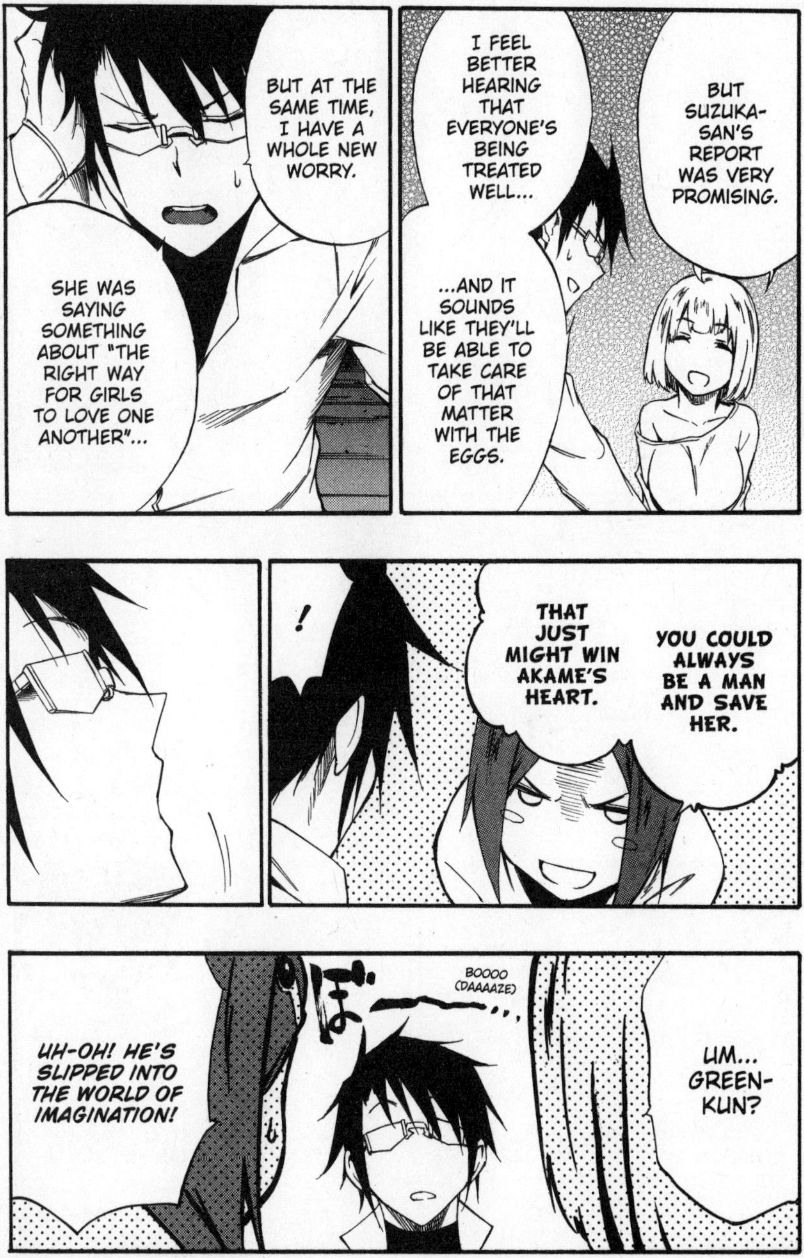
BUT SUZUKA-SAN'S REPORT WAS VERY PROMISING.
I FEEL BETTER HEARING THAT EVERYONE'S BEING TREATED WELL...
...AND IT SOUNDS LIKE THEY'LL BE ABLE TO TAKE CARE OF THAT MATTER WITH THE EGGS.
BUT AT THE SAME TIME, I HAVE A WHOLE NEW WORRY.
SHE WAS SAYING SOMETHING ABOUT "THE RIGHT WAY FOR GIRLS TO LOVE ONE ANOTHER"...
YOU COULD ALWAYS BE A MAN AND SAVE HER.
THAT JUST MIGHT WIN AKAME'S HEART.
!
UM... GREEN-KUN?
BOOOO (DAAAAZE)
UH-OH! HE'S SLIPPED INTO THE WORLD OF IMAGINATION!

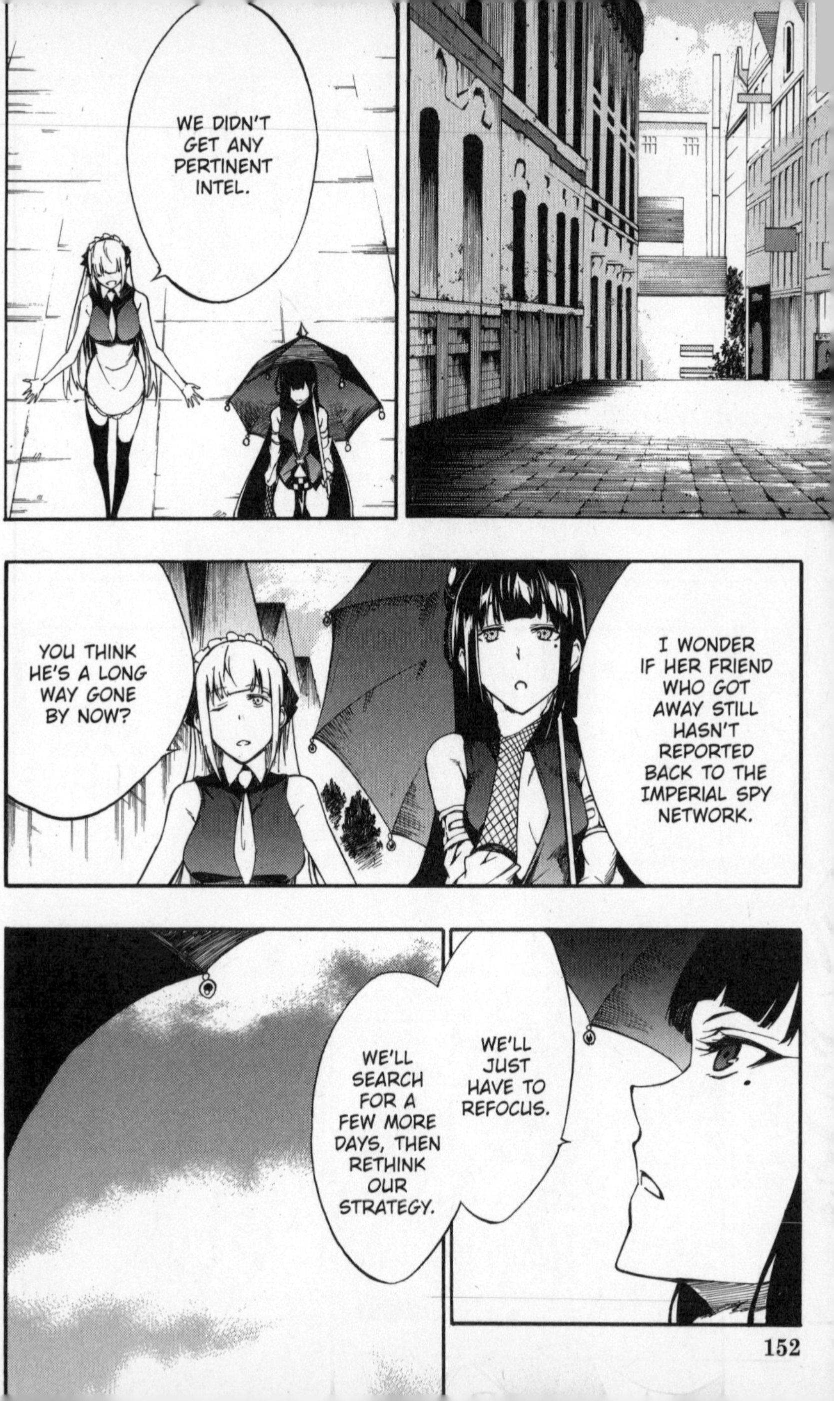

WE DIDN'T GET ANY PERTINENT INTEL.
I WONDER IF HER FRIEND WHO GOT AWAY STILL HASN'T REPORTED BACK TO THE IMPERIAL SPY NETWORK.
YOU THINK HE'S A LONG WAY GONE BY NOW?
WE'LL JUST HAVE TO REFOCUS.
WE'LL SEARCH FOR A FEW MORE DAYS, THEN RETHINK OUR STRATEGY.

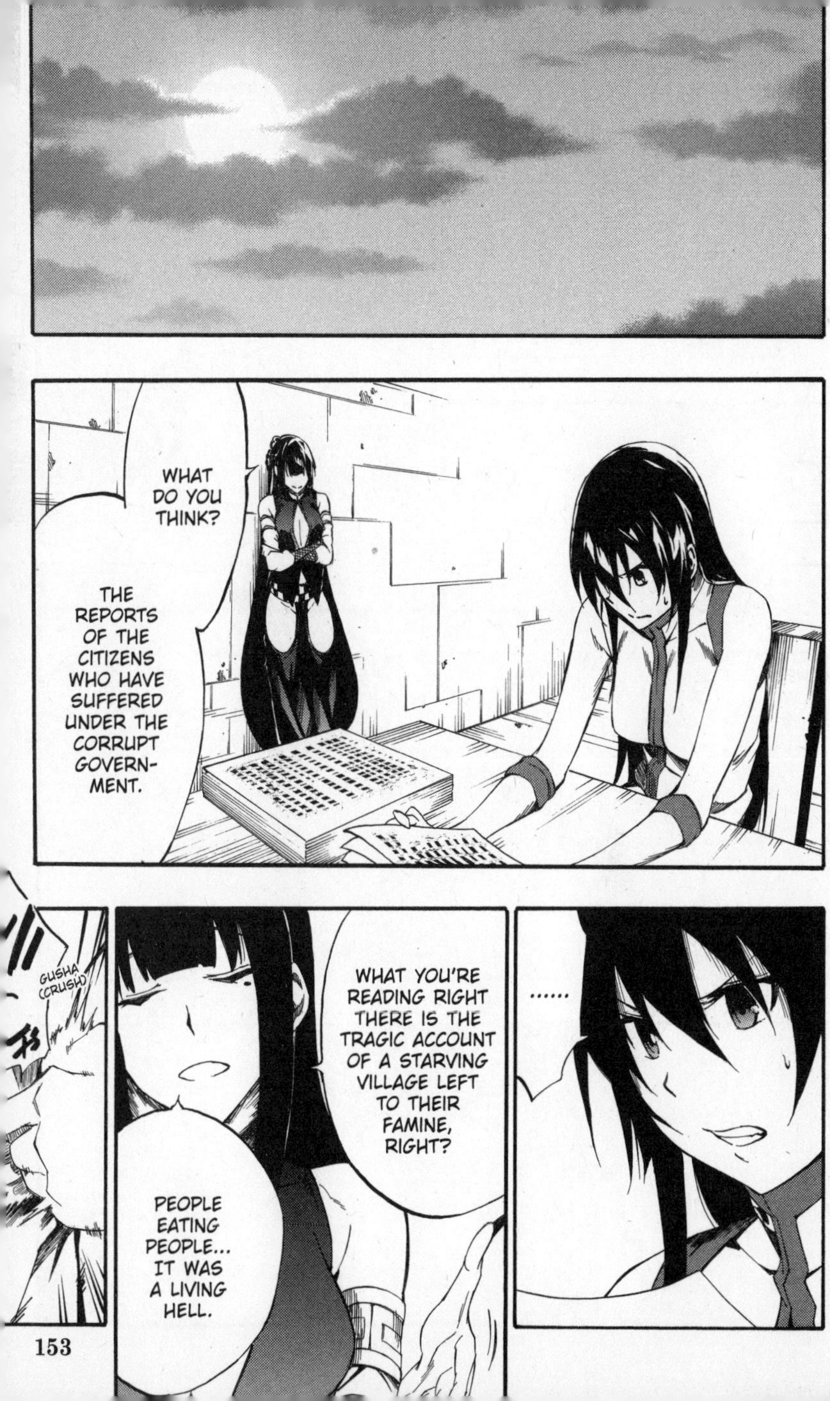
WHAT DO YOU THINK?
THE REPORTS OF THE CITIZENS WHO HAVE SUFFERED UNDER THE CORRUPT GOVERN-MENT.
......
WHAT YOU'RE READING RIGHT THERE IS THE TRAGIC ACCOUNT OF A STARVING VILLAGE LEFT TO THEIR FAMINE, RIGHT?
PEOPLE EATING PEOPLE... IT WAS A LIVING HELL.
GUSHA (CRUSH)

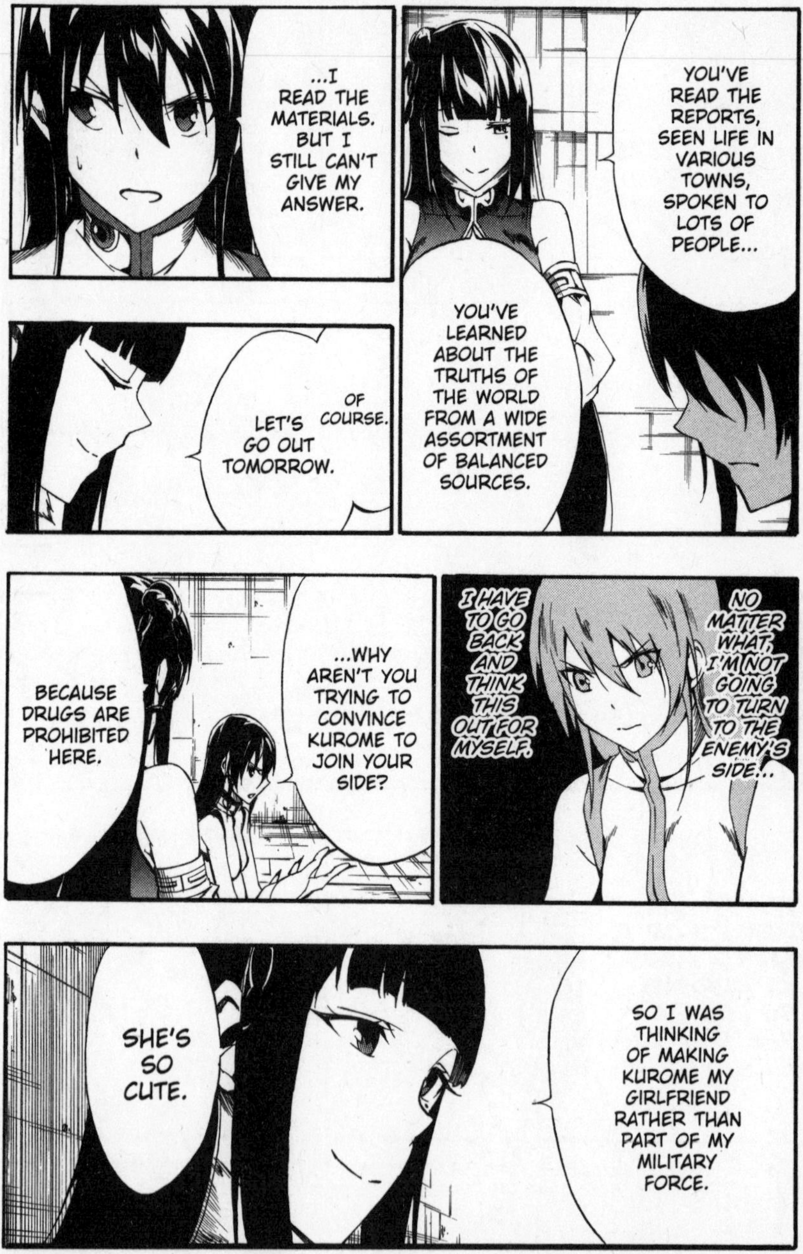
YOU'VE READ THE REPORTS, SEEN LIFE IN VARIOUS TOWNS, SPOKEN TO LOTS OF PEOPLE...
YOU'VE LEARNED ABOUT THE TRUTHS OF THE WORLD FROM A WIDE ASSORTMENT OF BALANCED SOURCES.
...I READ THE MATERIALS. BUT I STILL CAN'T GIVE MY ANSWER.
OF COURSE. LET'S GO OUT TOMORROW.
NO MATTER WHAT, I'M NOT GOING TO TURN TO THE ENEMY'S SIDE...
I HAVE TO GO BACK AND THINK THIS OUT FOR MYSELF.
...WHY AREN'T YOU TRYING TO CONVINCE KUROME TO JOIN YOUR SIDE?
BECAUSE DRUGS ARE PROHIBITED HERE.
SO I WAS THINKING OF MAKING KUROME MY GIRLFRIEND RATHER THAN PART OF MY MILITARY FORCE.
SHE'S SO CUTE.

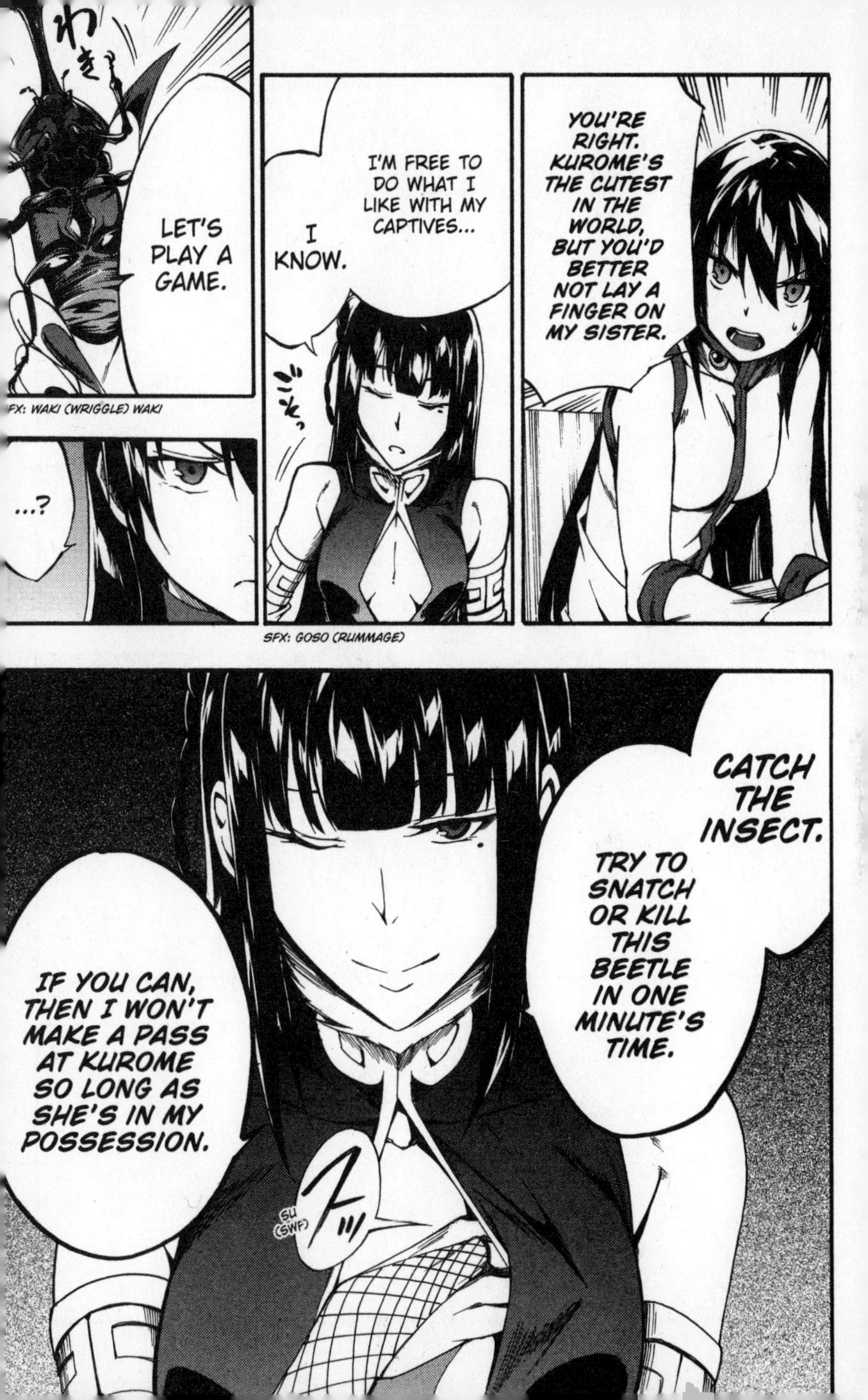
YOU'RE RIGHT. KUROME'S THE CUTEST IN THE WORLD, BUT YOU'D BETTER NOT LAY A FINGER ON MY SISTER.
I'M FREE TO DO WHAT I LIKE WITH MY CAPTIVES...
I KNOW.
SFX: GOSO (RUMMAGE)
わき
LET'S PLAY A GAME.
SFX: WAKI (WRIGGLE) WAKI
...?
CATCH THE INSECT.
TRY TO SNATCH OR KILL THIS BEETLE IN ONE MINUTE'S TIME.
IF YOU CAN, THEN I WON'T MAKE A PASS AT KUROME SO LONG AS SHE'S IN MY POSSESSION.
SU (SWF)

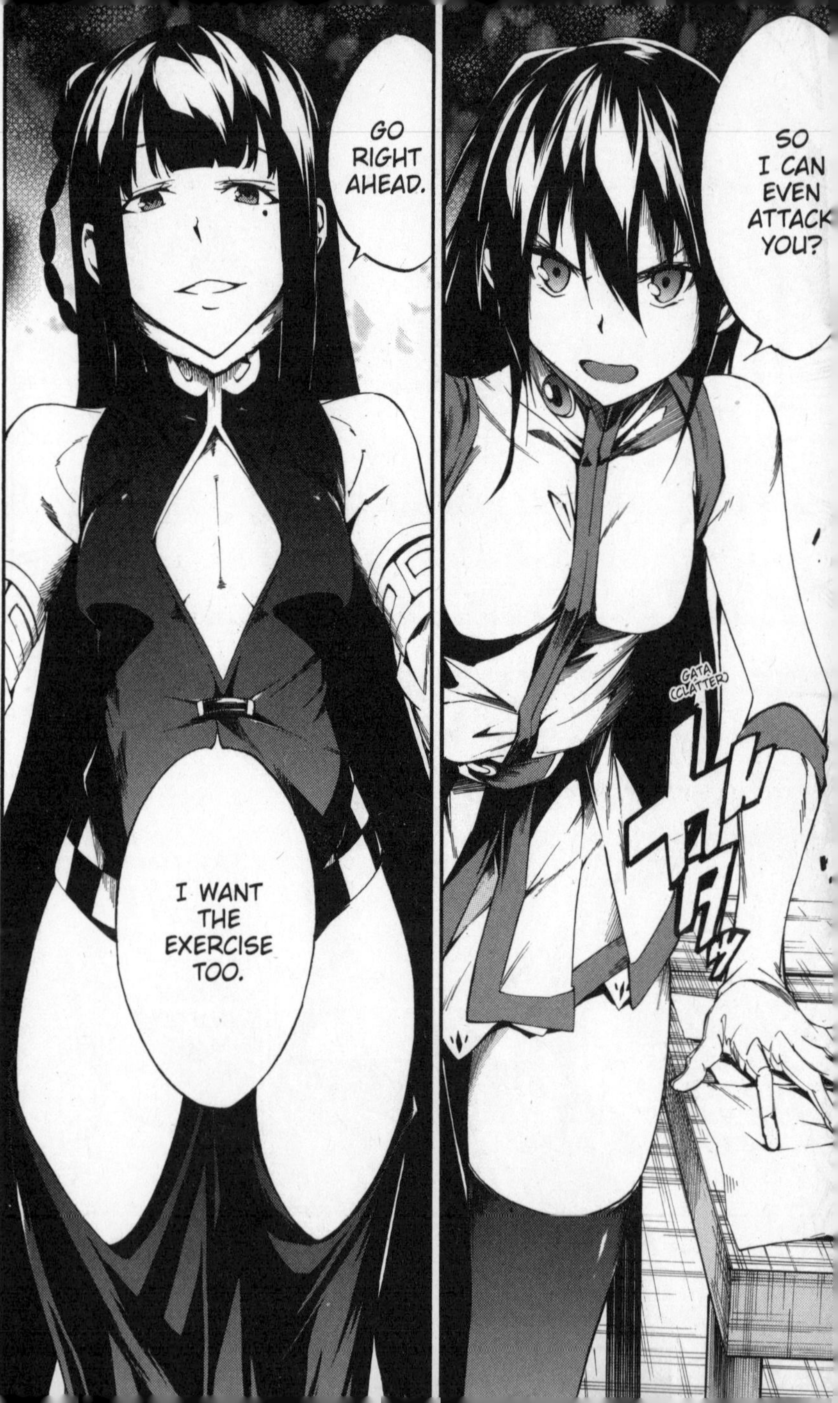
SO I CAN EVEN ATTACK YOU?
GATA (CLATTER)
GO RIGHT AHEAD.
I WANT THE EXERCISE TOO.

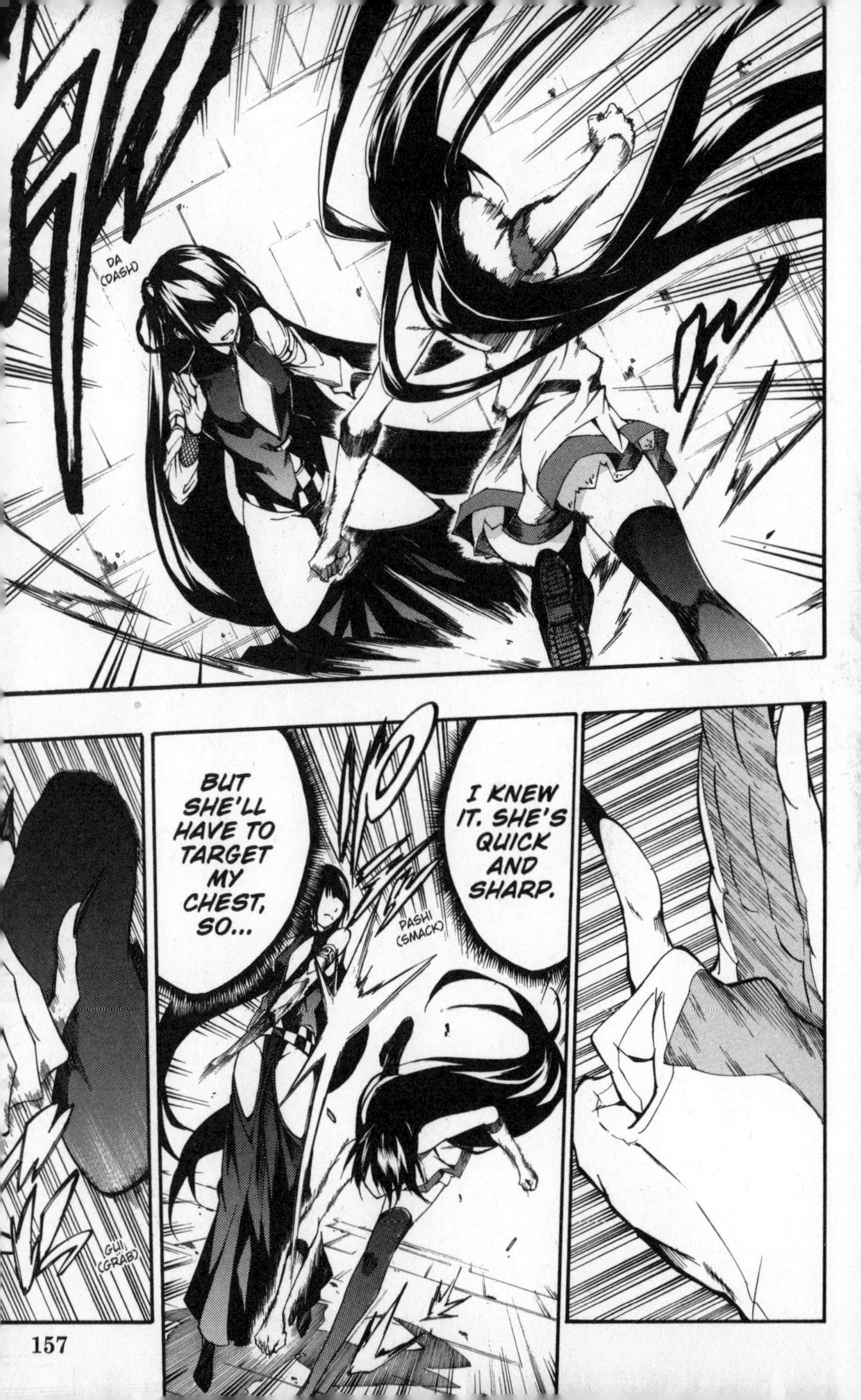
DA (DASH)
I KNEW IT. SHE'S QUICK AND SHARP.
BUT SHE'LL HAVE TO TARGET MY CHEST, SO...
PASHI (SMACK)
GUI (GRAB)

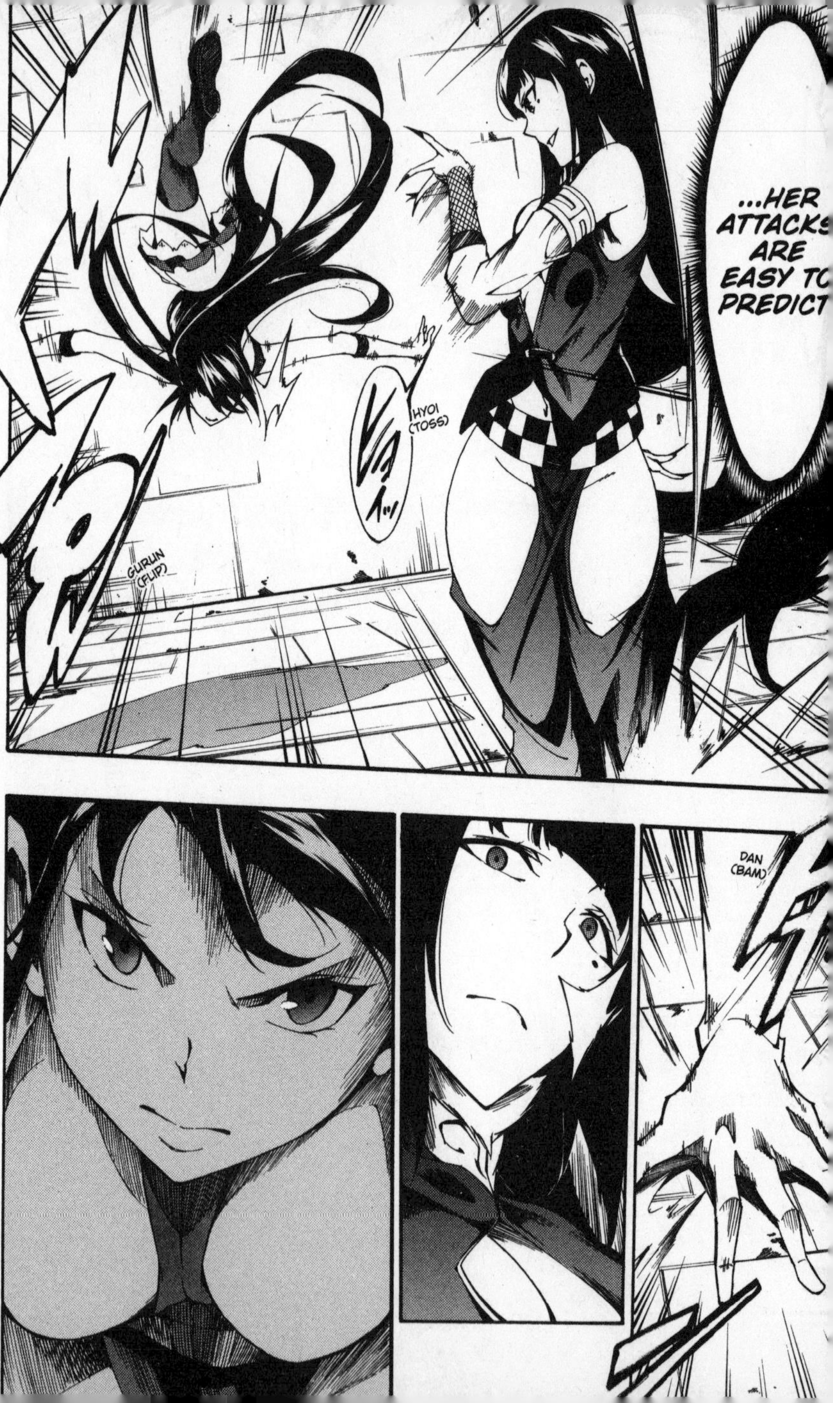
...HER ATTACKS ARE EASY TO PREDICT
HYOI (TOSS)
GURUN (FLIP)
DAN (BAM)

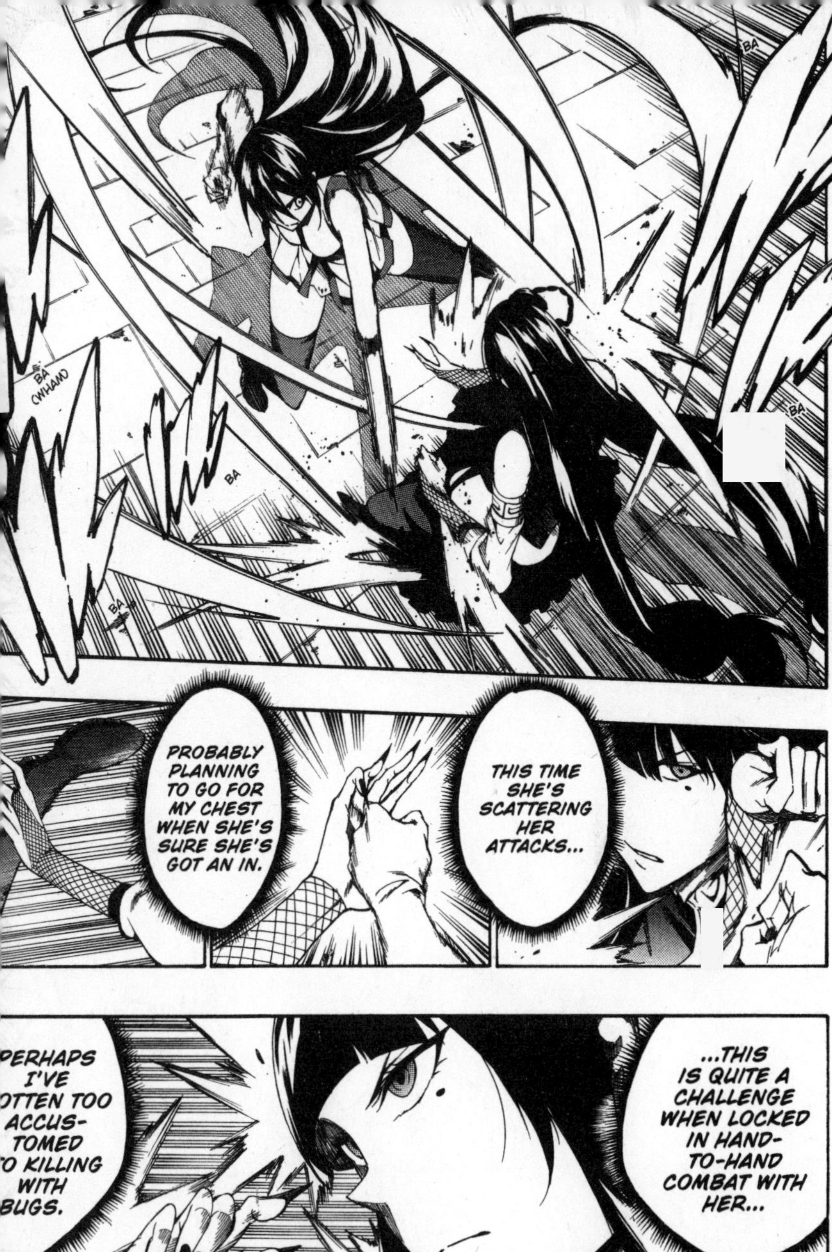

BA
BA
BA
BA (WHAM)
BA
THIS TIME SHE'S SCATTERING HER ATTACKS...
PROBABLY PLANNING TO GO FOR MY CHEST WHEN SHE'S SURE SHE'S GOT AN IN.
...THIS IS QUITE A CHALLENGE WHEN LOCKED IN HAND-TO-HAND COMBAT WITH HER...
PERHAPS I'VE OTTEN TOO ACCUS-TOMED O KILLING WITH BUGS.

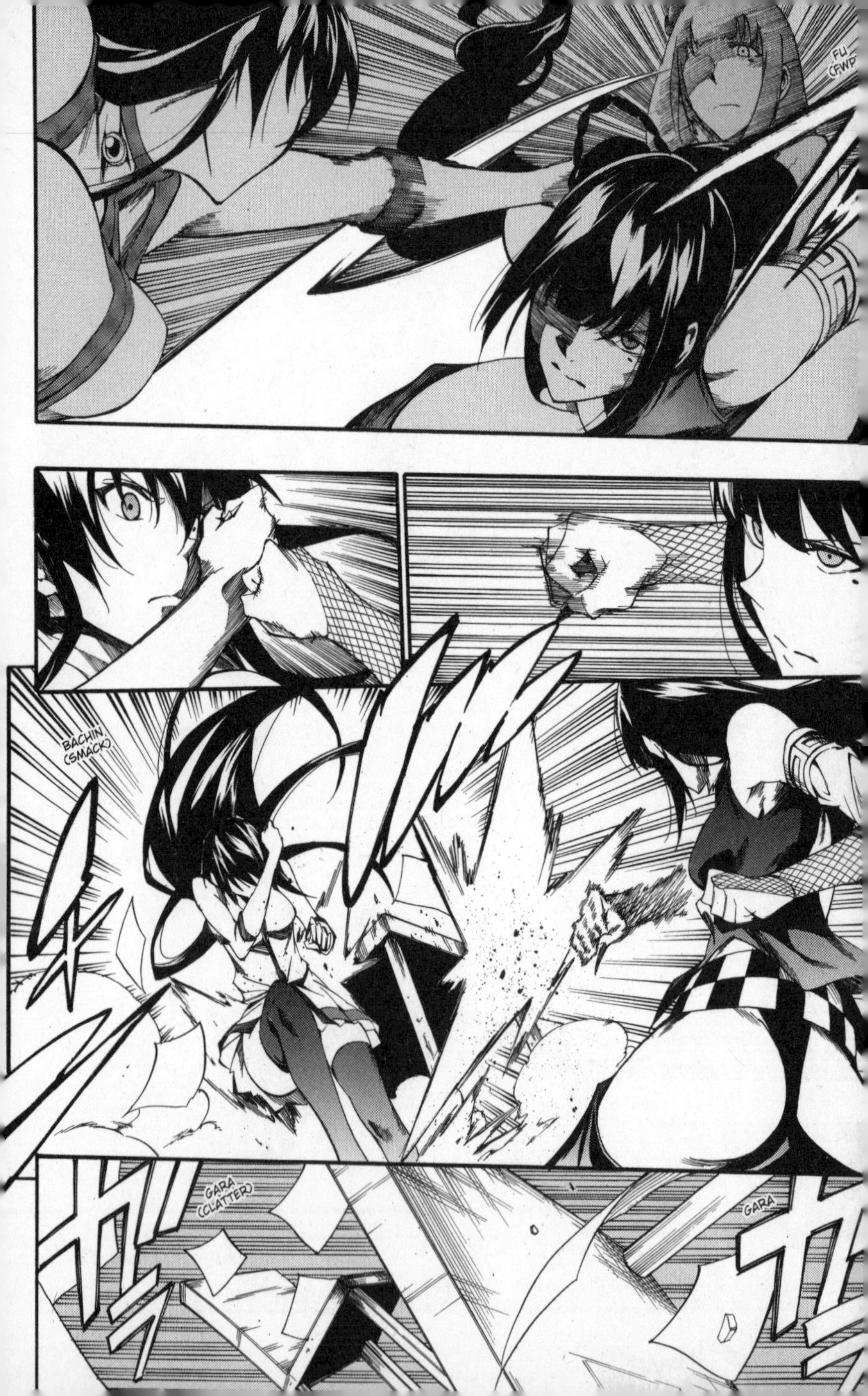
FU (FWP)
BACHIN (SMACK)
GARA (CLATTER)
GARA

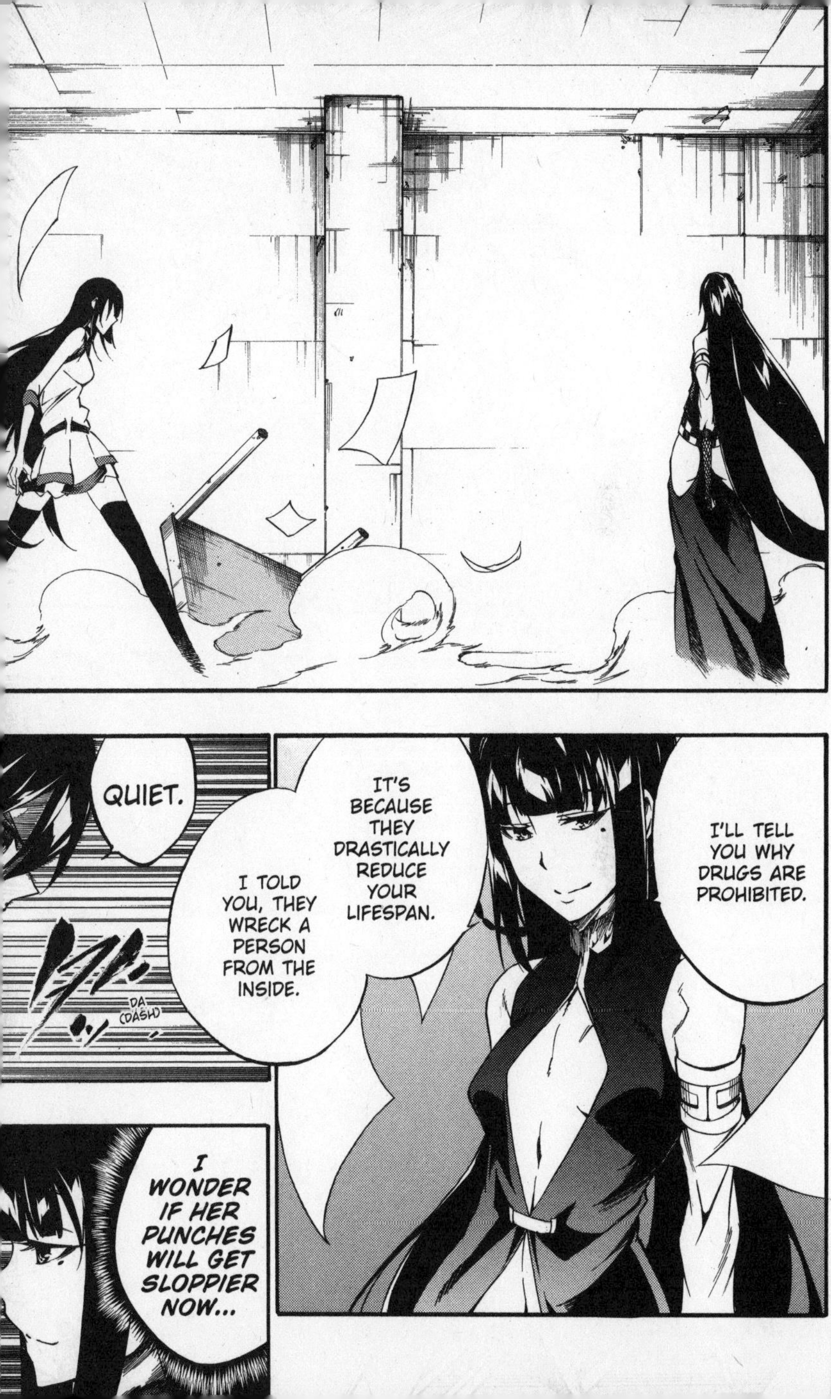
I'LL TELL YOU WHY DRUGS ARE PROHIBITED.
IT'S BECAUSE THEY DRASTICALLY REDUCE YOUR LIFESPAN.
I TOLD YOU, THEY WRECK A PERSON FROM THE INSIDE.
QUIET.
DA (DASH)
I WONDER IF HER PUNCHES WILL GET SLOPPIER NOW...

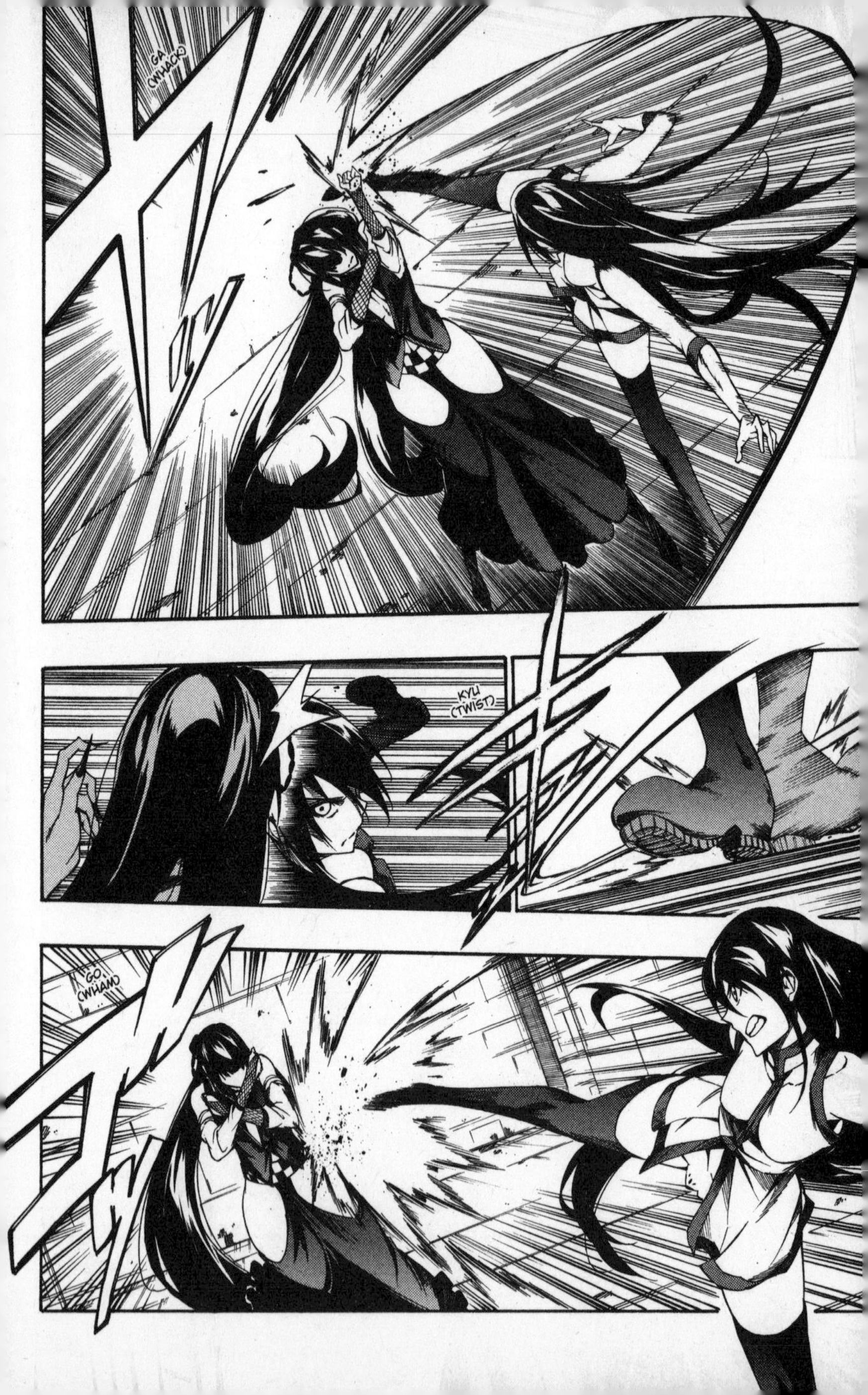
GA (WHACK)
KYU (TWIST)
GO (WHAM)

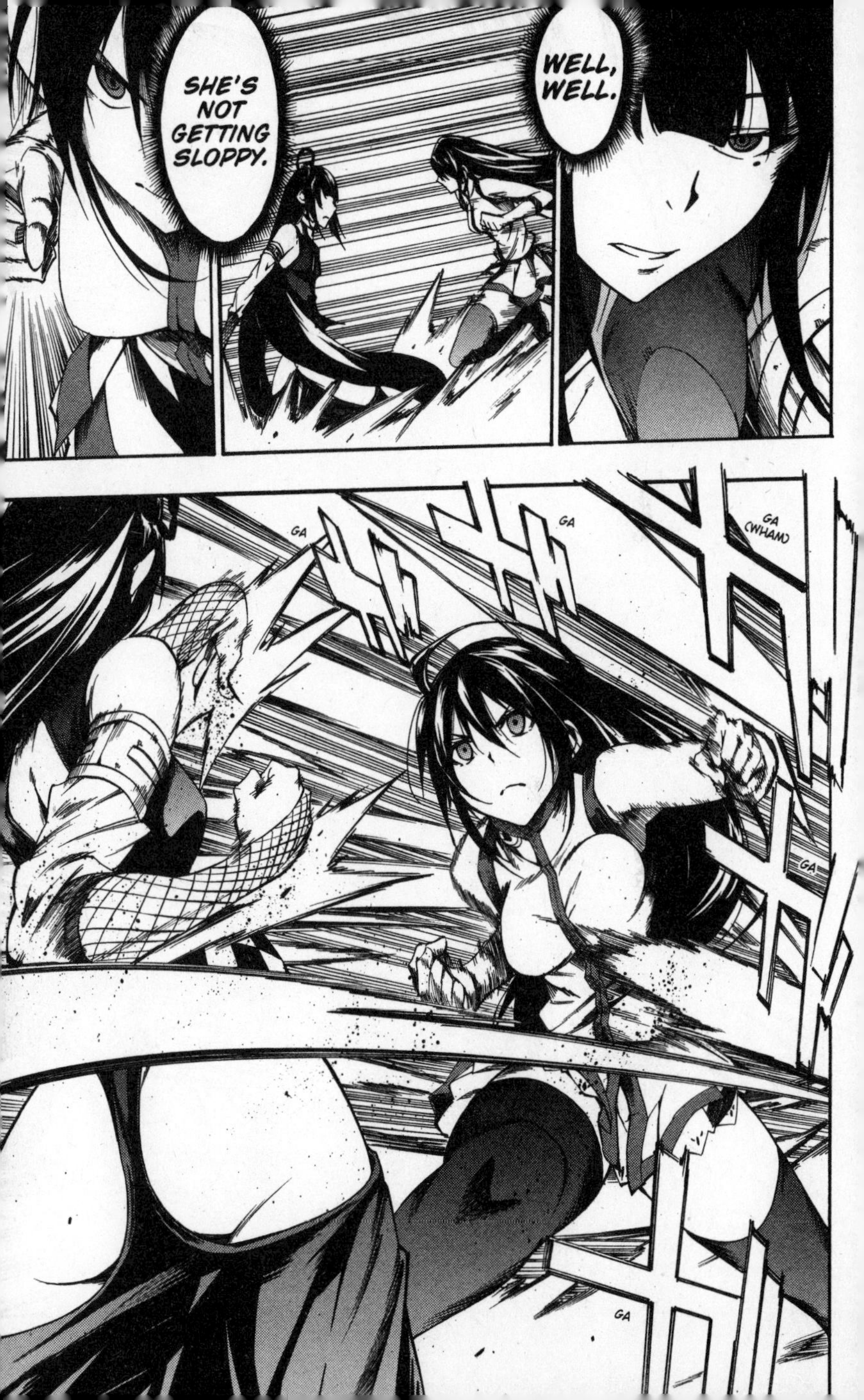
WELL, WELL.
SHE'S NOT GETTING SLOPPY.
GA (WHAM)
GA
GA
GA
GA

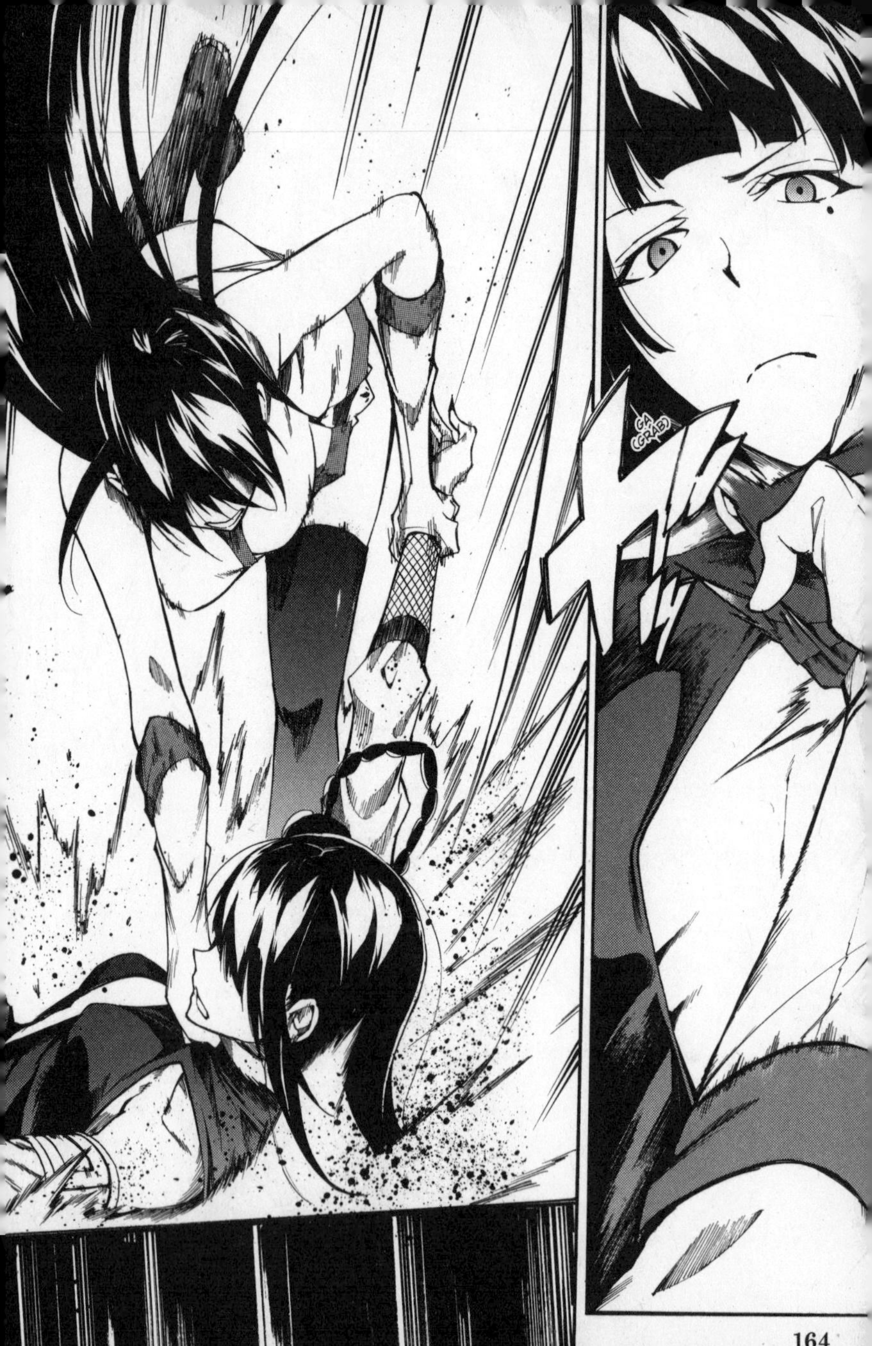
GA
(GRAB)

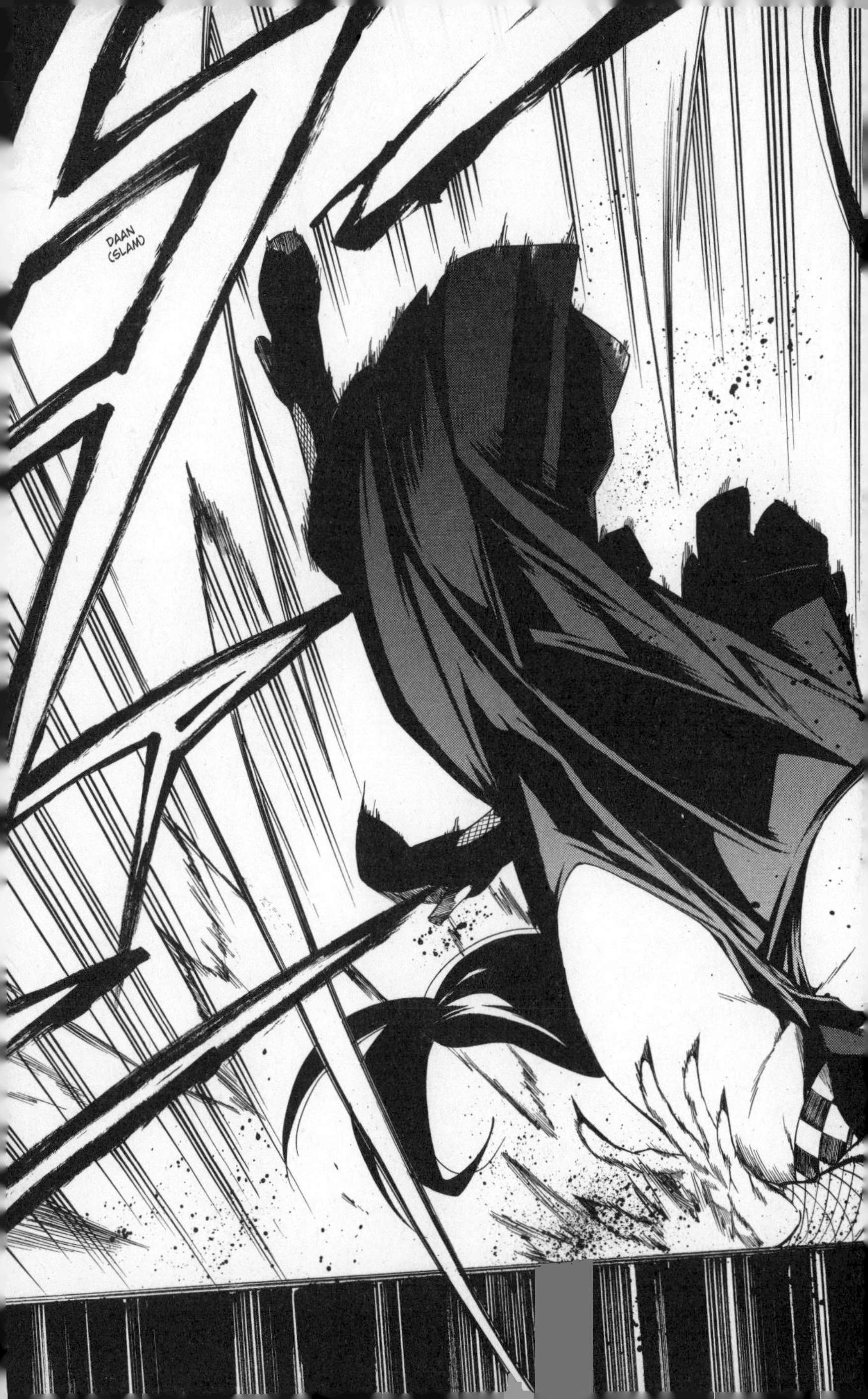
DAAN (SLAM)

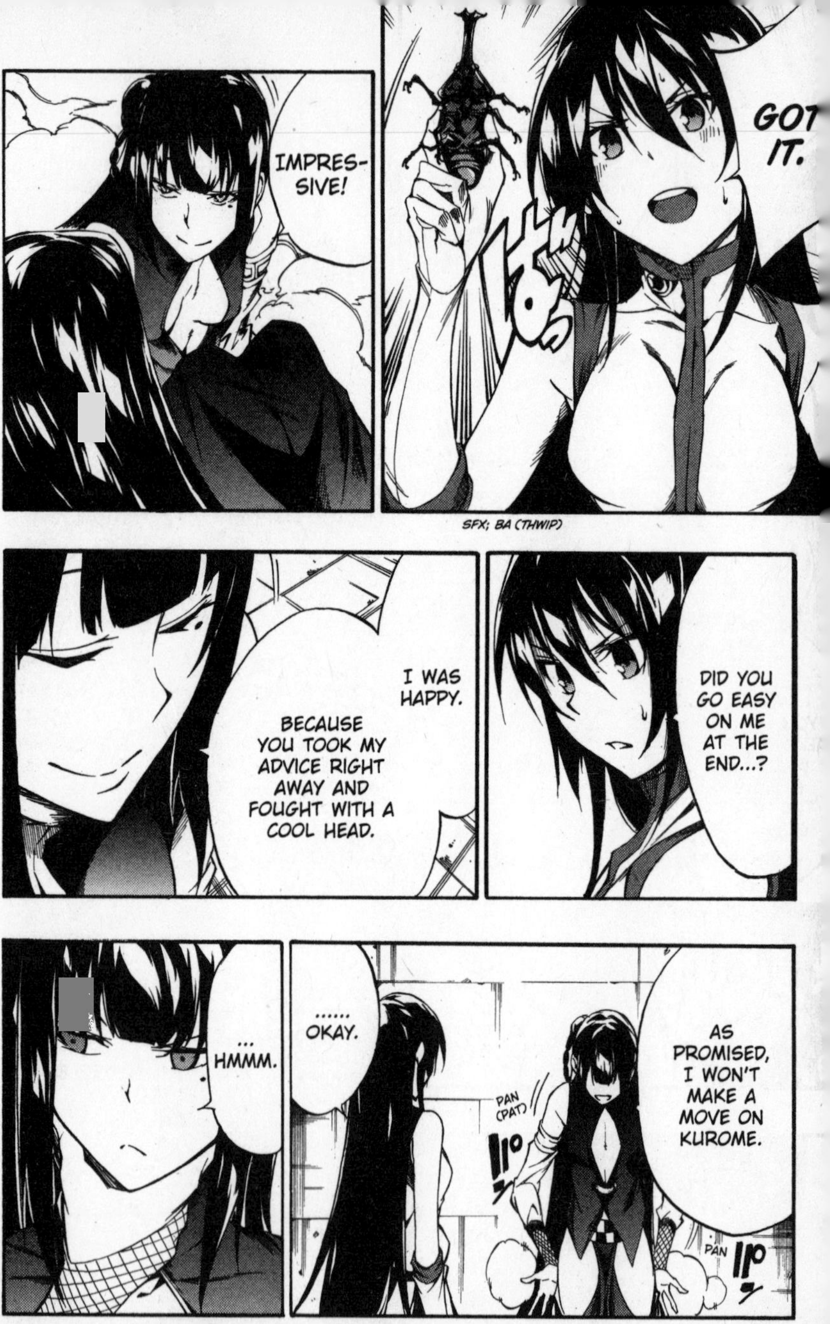
GOT IT.
IMPRES-SIVE!
DID YOU GO EASY ON ME AT THE END...?
I WAS HAPPY.
BECAUSE YOU TOOK MY ADVICE RIGHT AWAY AND FOUGHT WITH A COOL HEAD.
AS PROMISED, I WON'T MAKE A MOVE ON KUROME.
PAN (PAT)
PAN
......OKAY.
...HMMM.

SFX; BA (THWIP)

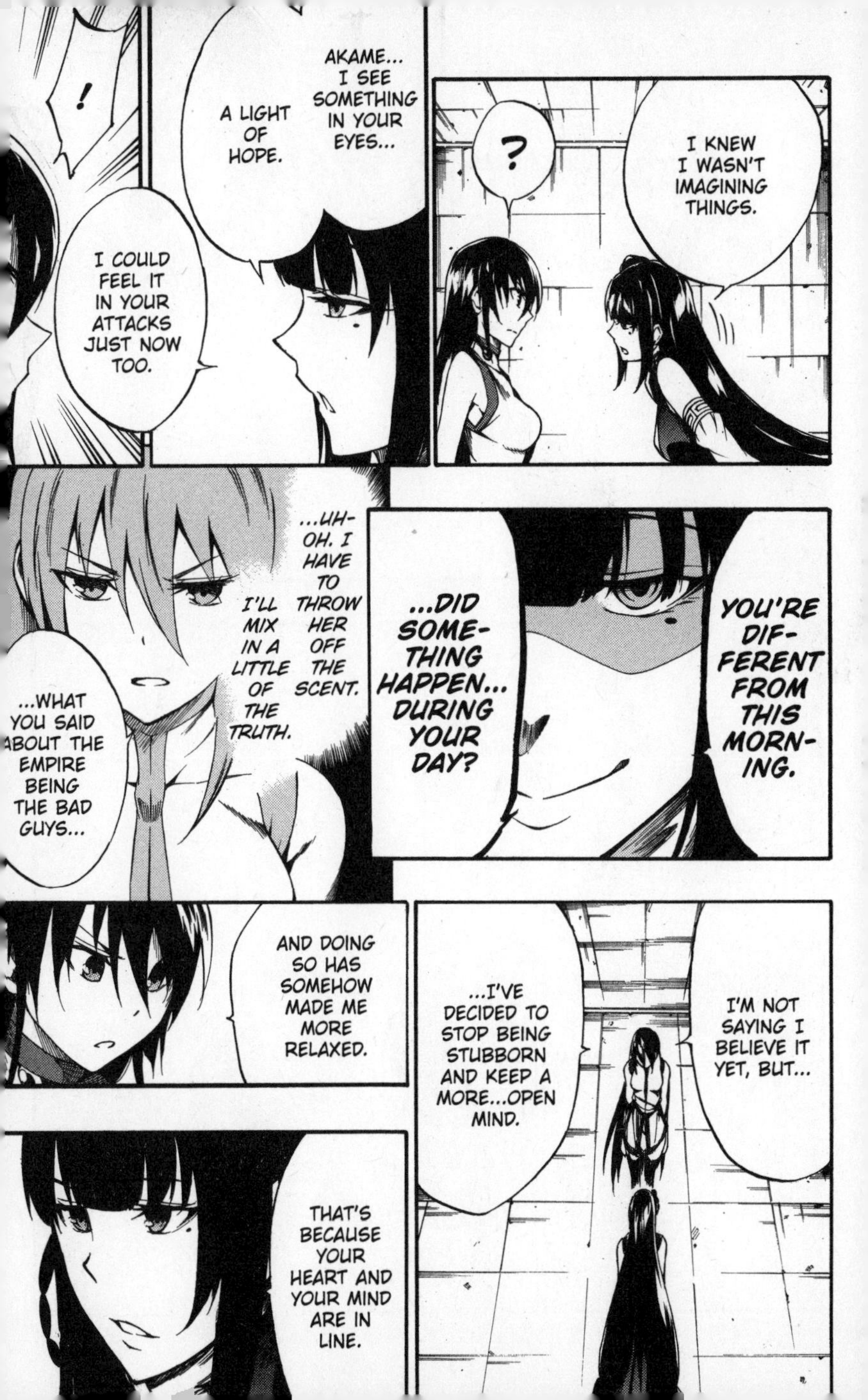
I KNEW I WASN'T IMAGINING THINGS.
?
AKAME... I SEE SOMETHING IN YOUR EYES...
A LIGHT OF HOPE.
!
I COULD FEEL IT IN YOUR ATTACKS JUST NOW TOO.
YOU'RE DIFFERENT FROM THIS MORNING.
...DID SOMETHING HAPPEN... DURING YOUR DAY?
...UH-OH. I HAVE TO THROW HER OFF THE SCENT.
I'LL MIX IN A LITTLE OF THE TRUTH.
...WHAT YOU SAID ABOUT THE EMPIRE BEING THE BAD GUYS...
I'M NOT SAYING I BELIEVE IT YET, BUT...
...I'VE DECIDED TO STOP BEING STUBBORN AND KEEP A MORE...OPEN MIND.
AND DOING SO HAS SOMEHOW MADE ME MORE RELAXED.
THAT'S BECAUSE YOUR HEART AND YOUR MIND ARE IN LINE.

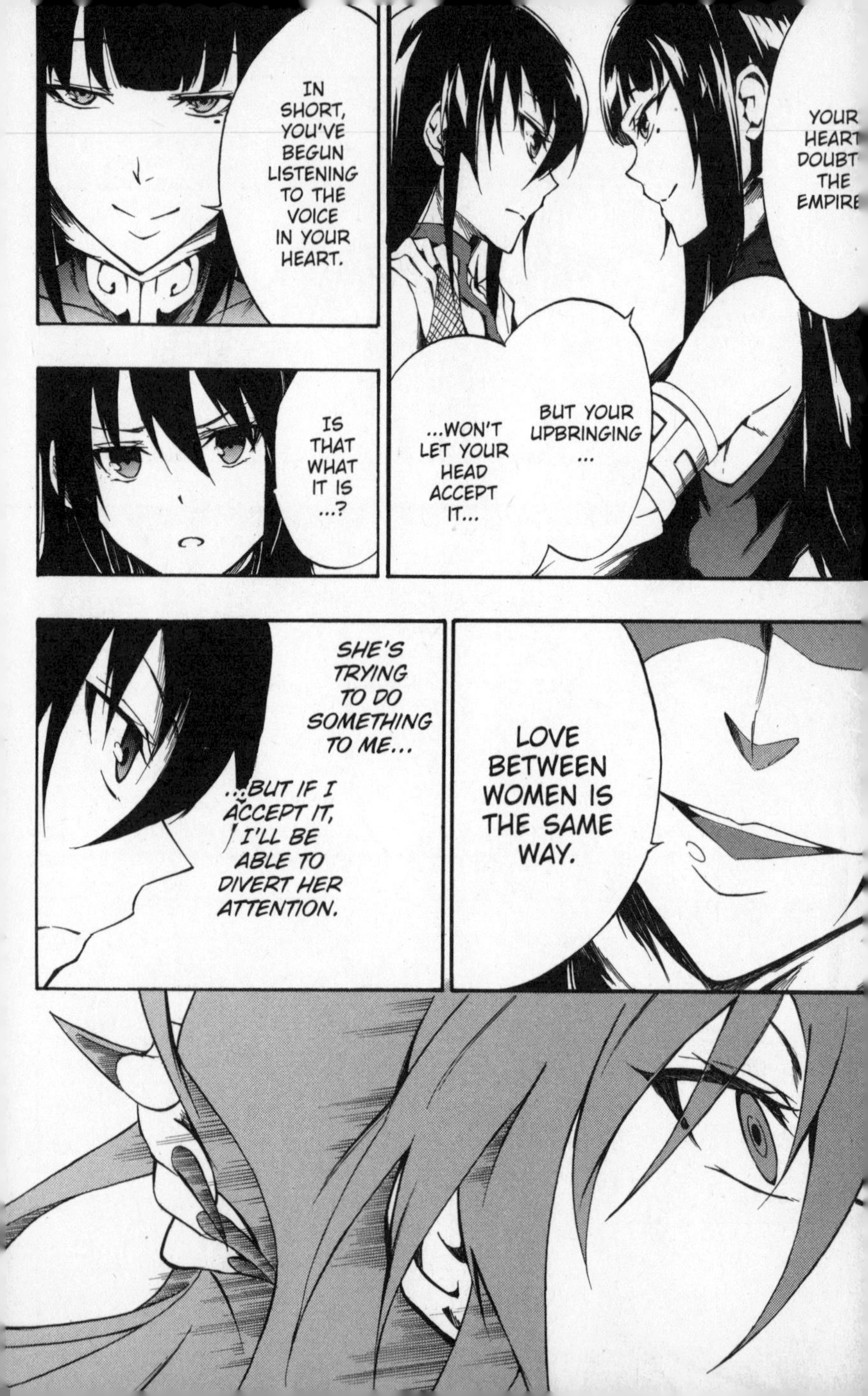
YOUR HEART DOUBT THE EMPIRE
BUT YOUR UPBRINGING ...
...WON'T LET YOUR HEAD ACCEPT IT...
IN SHORT, YOU'VE BEGUN LISTENING TO THE VOICE IN YOUR HEART.
IS THAT WHAT IT IS ...?
LOVE BETWEEN WOMEN IS THE SAME WAY.
SHE'S TRYING TO DO SOMETHING TO ME...
...BUT IF I ACCEPT IT, I'LL BE ABLE TO DIVERT HER ATTENTION.

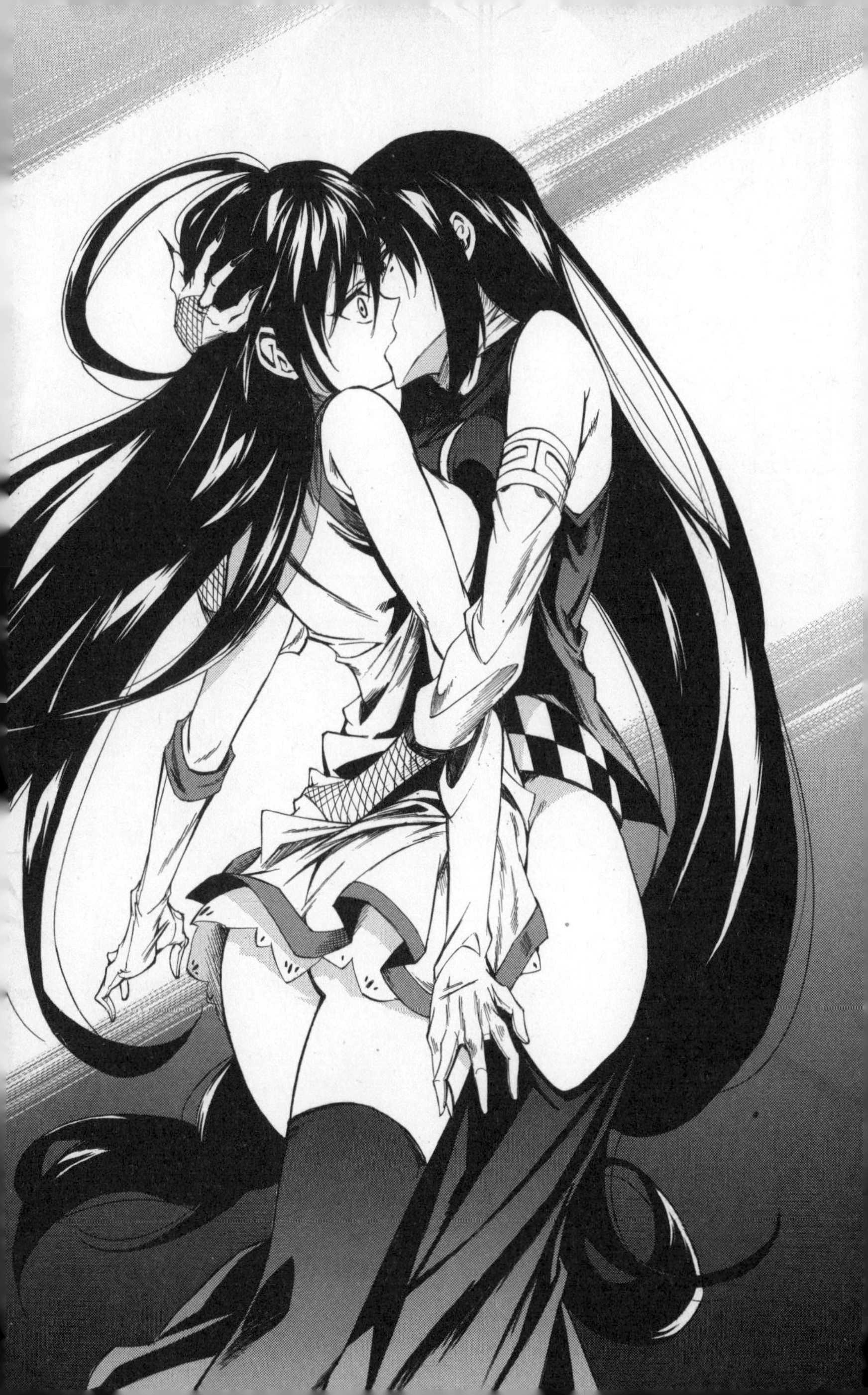

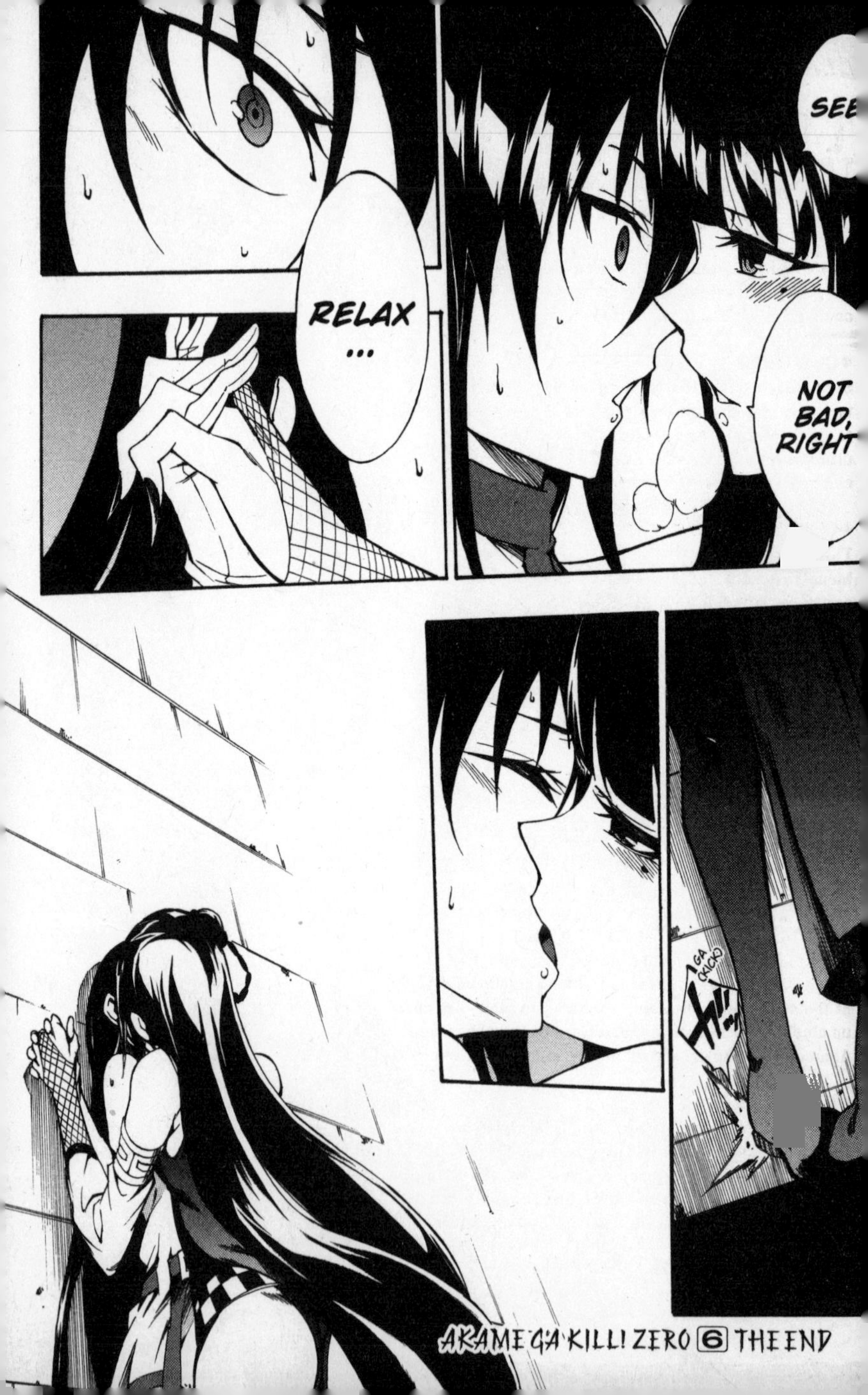
SEE
NOT BAD, RIGHT
RELAX ...
GA CKICK

AKAME GA KILL! ZERO 6 THE END

TAKAHIRO's PostScript

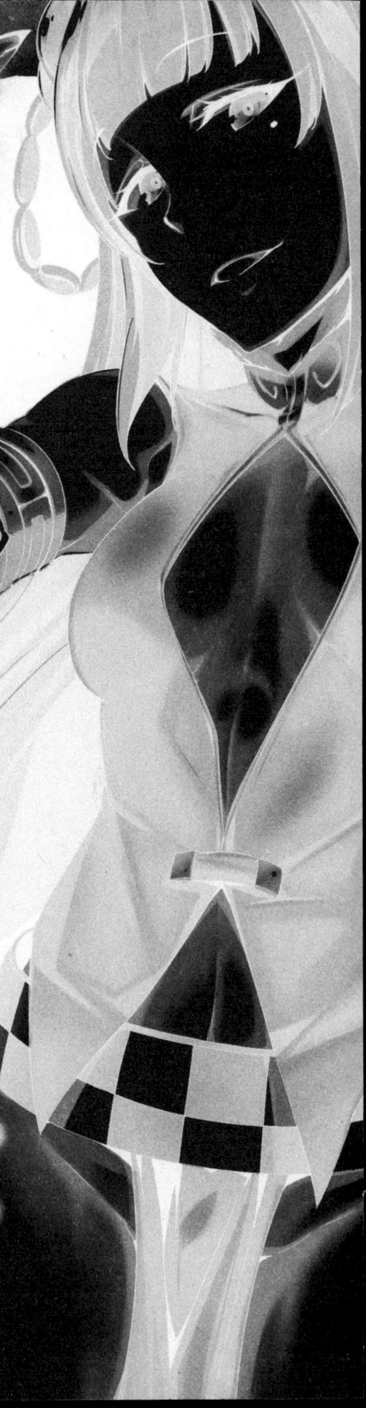

Hello, this is Takahiro with Minato Soft.
I'm going to provide some additional
commentary on each chapter in volume 6.

◆Chapter 32
Suddenly, it's all about big battles. The fight between
two very capable fighters, Mera vs. Gozuki, was fun
to write. Akame's one attack worked on Daniel and
ultimately saved Green's life in the end. I love Green's
commitment to doing whatever it takes to survive.

◆Chapter 33
This chapter deals with Mera's past. The fact that
Mera would attempt making a move on Esdeath is
a testament to her courage. I think the way Toru-
san draws girls is even cuter now. You can only see
Esdeath and Mera as children here in *Zero* (I think).

◆Chapters 34–35
At long last, Akame is seeing the Empire's dark side,
which she's suspected for some time. It's also a very
crucial chapter in her evolution as a character as
Mera prompts her to strive to be calmer and more
levelheaded in battle. Akame also has her first kiss.

◆Chapter 36
Since this chapter came out the same month that the
main *Akame ga KILL!* story ended, we linked it to that
main story a little bit. The Four Rakshasas also show
up as allies, and things are more boisterous than usual.
When Chelsea first conversed with Akame in volume 5
of the main story, she said, "Akame, you really are cute
up close. ♪" That was because she had first observed
Akame from afar, as shown in this chapter of *Zero*.

◆Chapter 37
In this chapter, Mera gets to completely have her way. The
Four Rakshasas are a little playful, aren't they? And the
reader should feel more acutely how central a figure Dr.
Stylish was to the Empire. Green has become more manly,
but In the end, he's still who he is: prone to delusions.

That's all. I'll continue the rest in the next volume.
Thank you very much.

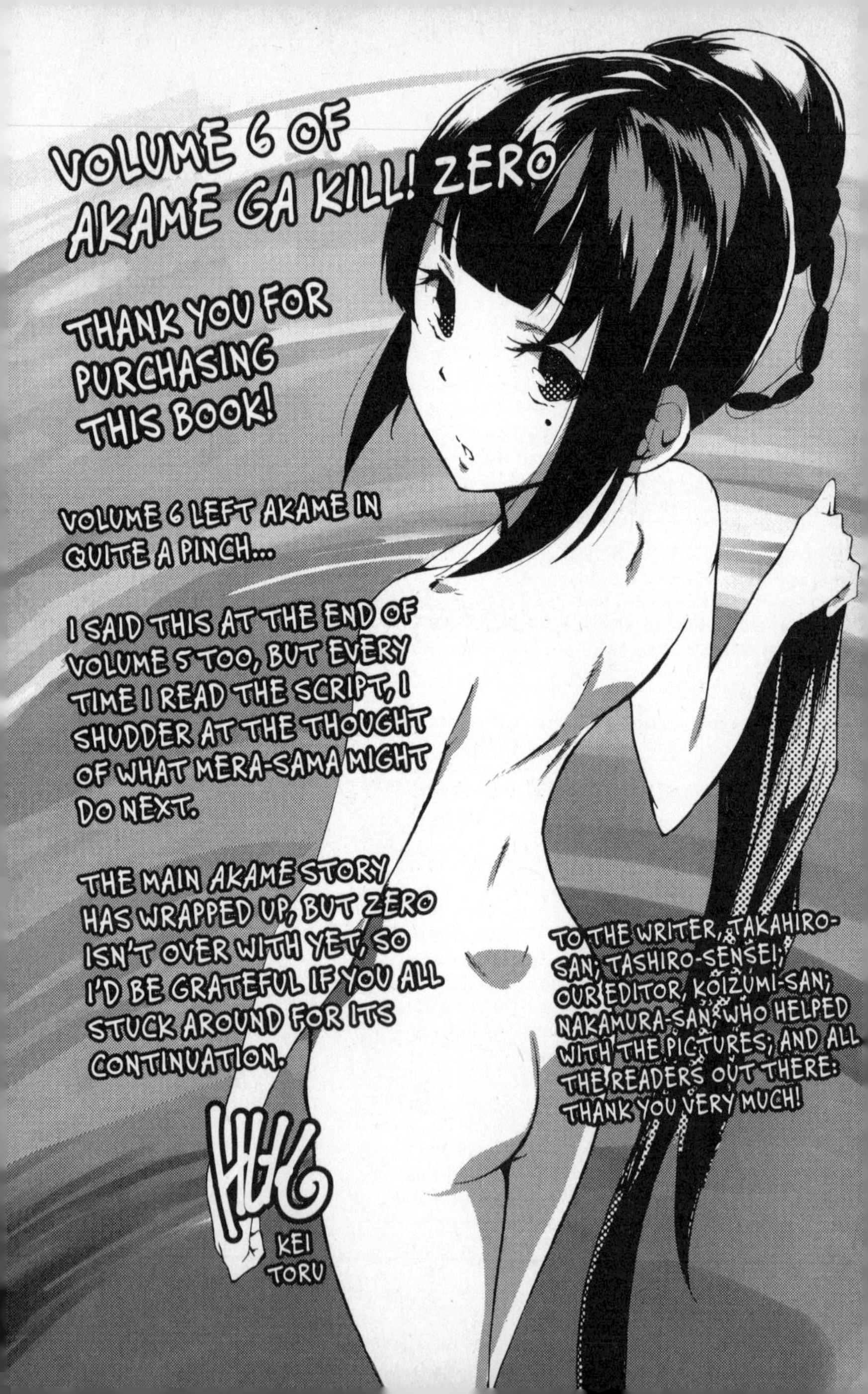
VOLUME 6 OF AKAME GA KILL! ZERO
THANK YOU FOR PURCHASING THIS BOOK!
VOLUME 6 LEFT AKAME IN QUITE A PINCH...
I SAID THIS AT THE END OF VOLUME 5 TOO, BUT EVERY TIME I READ THE SCRIPT, I SHUDDER AT THE THOUGHT OF WHAT MERA-SAMA MIGHT DO NEXT.
THE MAIN AKAME STORY HAS WRAPPED UP, BUT ZERO ISN'T OVER WITH YET, SO I'D BE GRATEFUL IF YOU ALL STUCK AROUND FOR ITS CONTINUATION.
TO THE WRITER, TAKAHIRO-SAN; TASHIRO-SENSEI; OUR EDITOR, KOIZUMI-SAN; NAKAMURA-SAN, WHO HELPED WITH THE PICTURES; AND ALL THE READERS OUT THERE: THANK YOU VERY MUCH!
KEI TORU

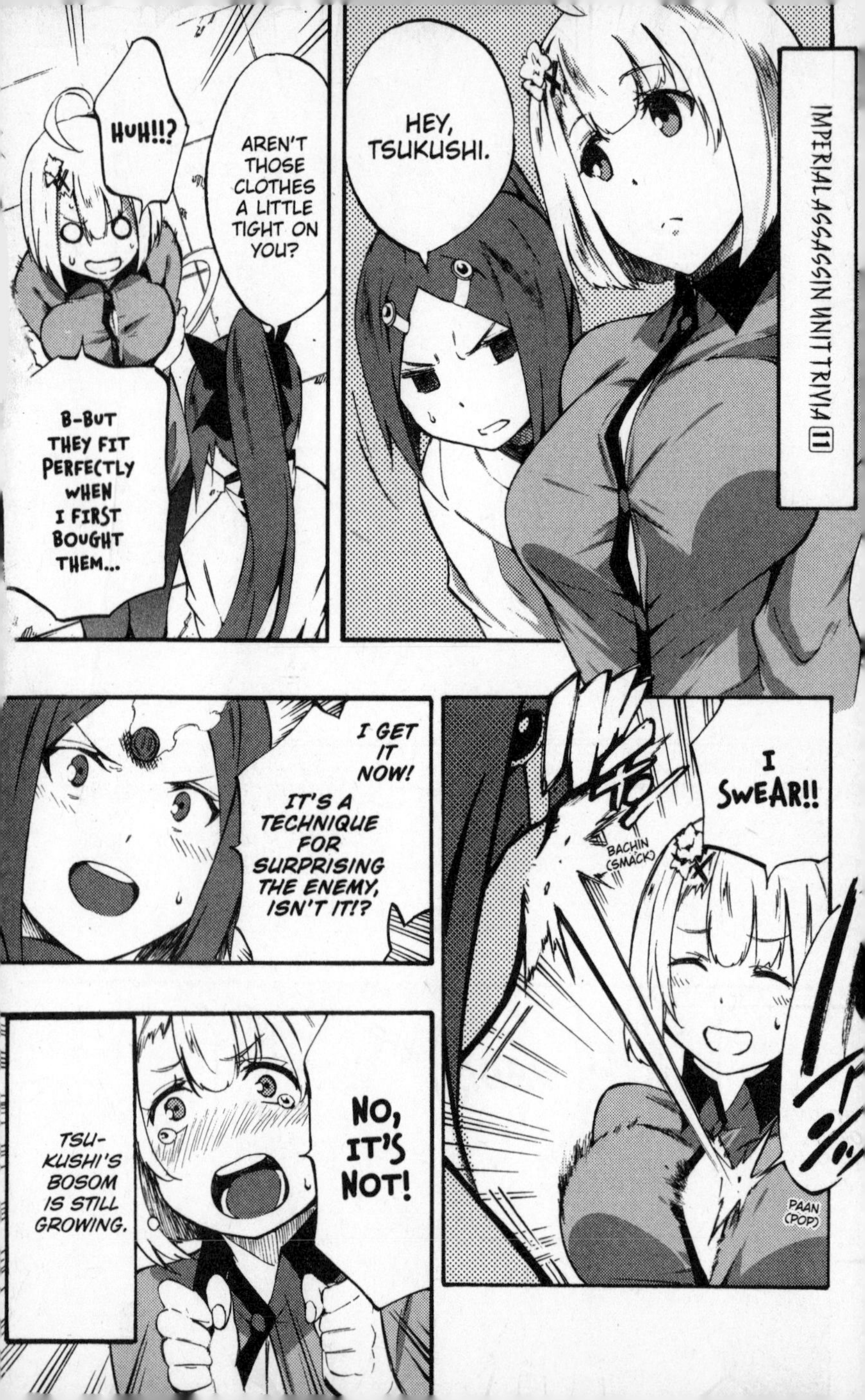
IMPERIAL ASSASSIN UNIT TRIVIA 11
HEY, TSUKUSHI.
AREN'T THOSE CLOTHES A LITTLE TIGHT ON YOU?
HUH!!?
B-BUT THEY FIT PERFECTLY WHEN I FIRST BOUGHT THEM...
I SWEAR!!
BACHIN (SMACK)
PAAN (POP)
I GET IT NOW!
IT'S A TECHNIQUE FOR SURPRISING THE ENEMY, ISN'T IT!?
NO, IT'S NOT!
TSU-KUSHI'S BOSOM IS STILL GROWING.

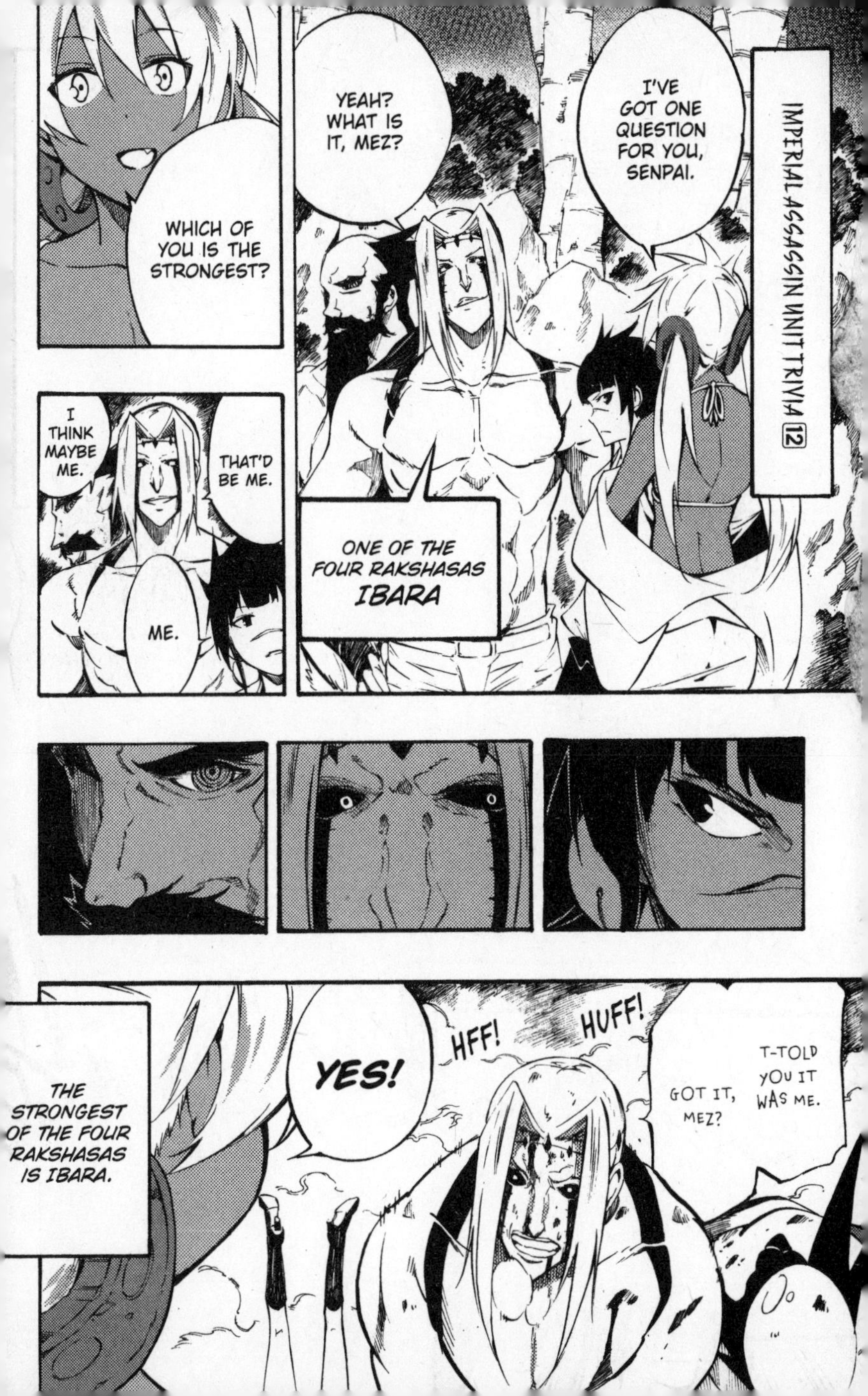
IMPERIAL ASSASSIN UNIT TRIVIA 12
I'VE GOT ONE QUESTION FOR YOU, SENPAI.
YEAH? WHAT IS IT, MEZ?
WHICH OF YOU IS THE STRONGEST?
ONE OF THE FOUR RAKSHASAS IBARA
THAT'D BE ME.
I THINK MAYBE ME.
ME.
T-TOLD YOU IT WAS ME.
GOT IT, MEZ?
HUFF!
HFF!
YES!
THE STRONGEST OF THE FOUR RAKSHASAS IS IBARA.

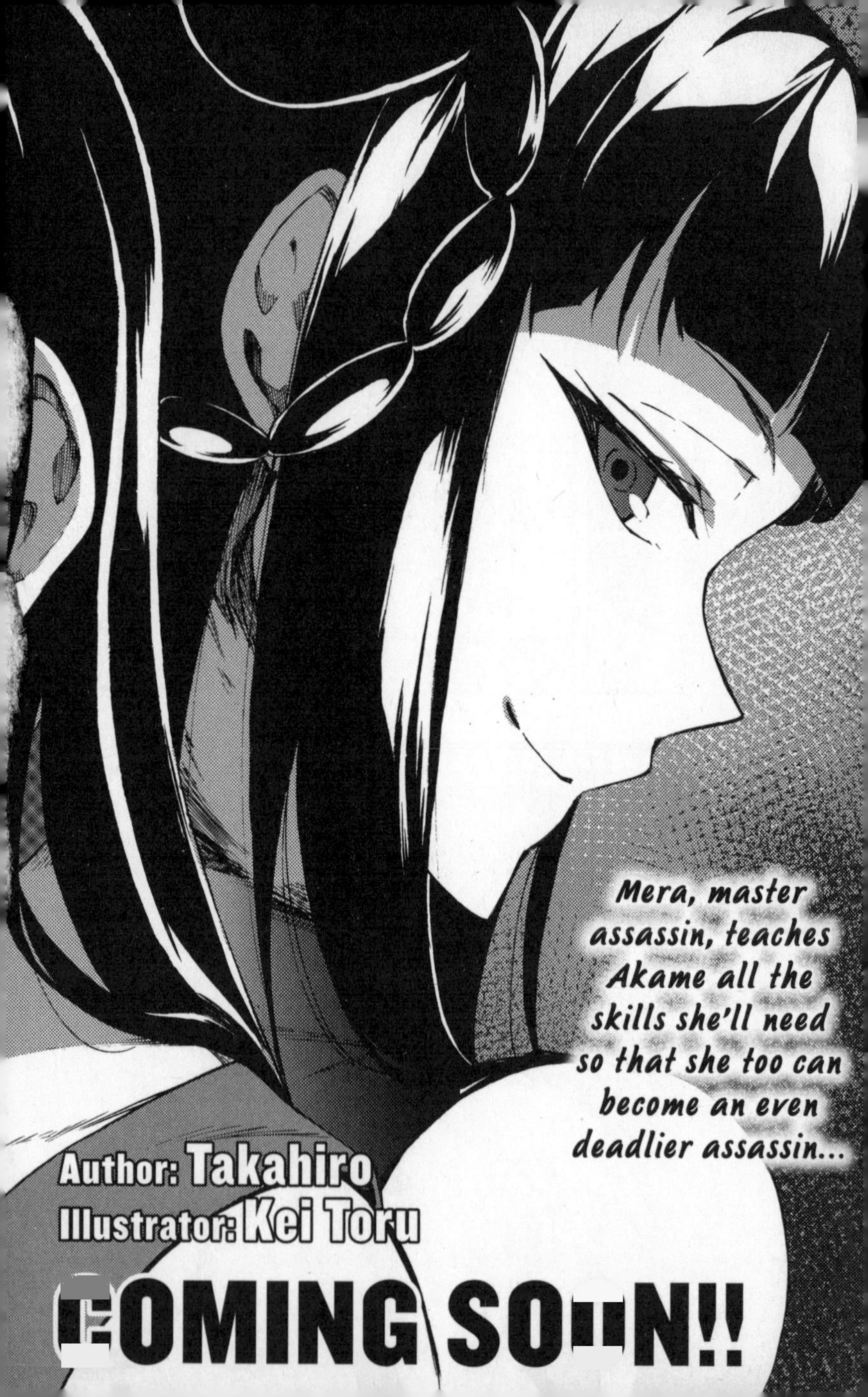
Mera, master assassin, teaches Akame all the skills she'll need so that she too can become an even deadlier assassin...
Author: Takahiro
Illustrator: Kei Toru
[redacted]OMING SO[redacted]N!!

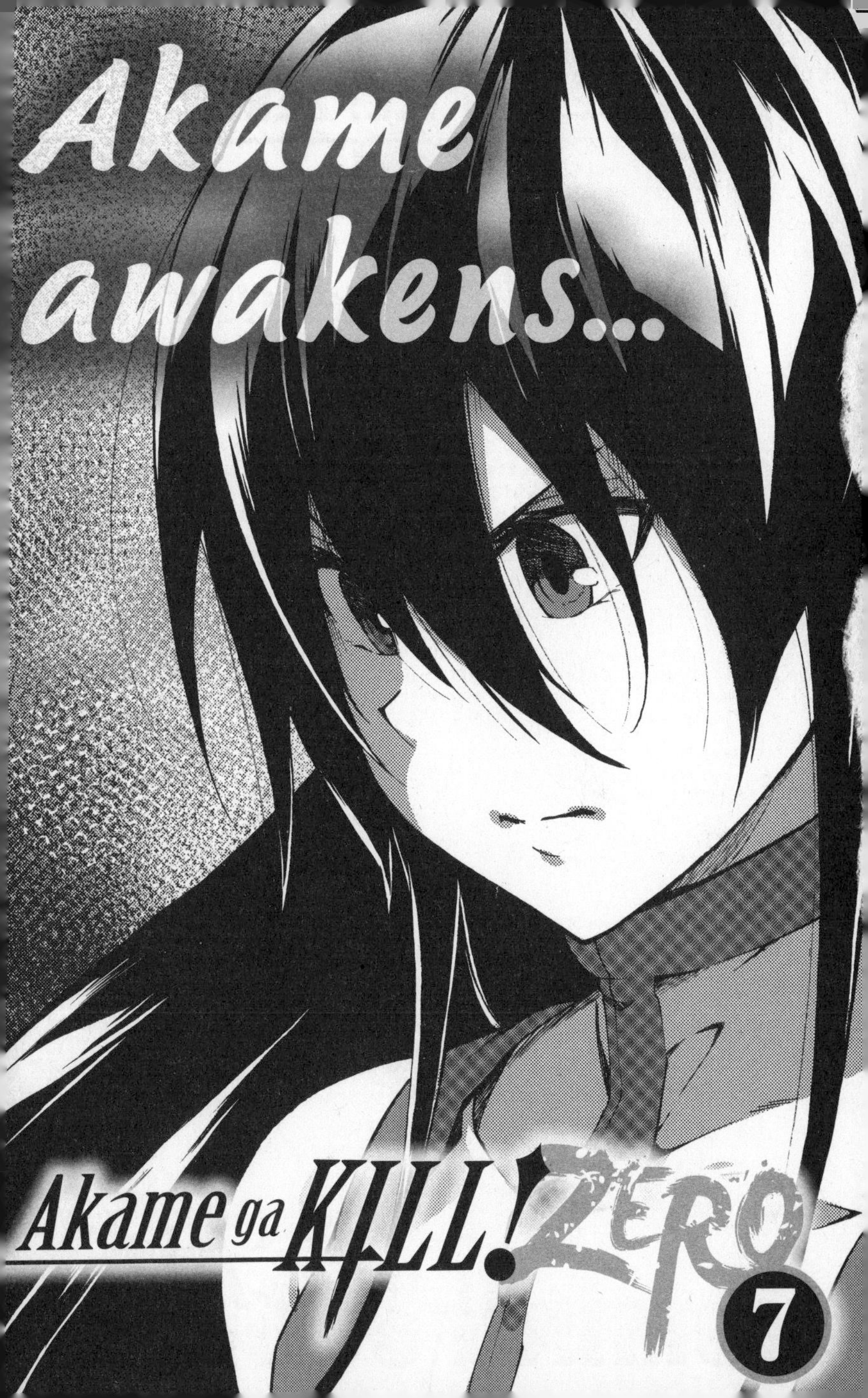

Akame awakens...
Akame ga KILL! ZERO
7

AKAME GA KIL

Takahiro
Kei Toru

Translation: Christine Dashiell   •   Lettering: Michele Lee

AKAME GA KILL! ZERO Vol. 6
© 2017 Takahiro, Kei Toru / SQUARE ENIX CO., LTD. First published in Japan in 2017 by SQUARE ENIX CO., LTD. English translation rights arranged with SQUARE ENIX CO., LTD. and Yen Press, LLC through Tuttle-Mori Agency, Inc., Tokyo.

English translation © 2017 by SQUARE ENIX CO., LTD.

Yen Press
1290 Avenue of the Americas
New York, NY 10104

Visit us at yenpress.com
facebook.com/yenpress
twitter.com/yenpress
yenpress.tumblr.com
instagram.com/yenpress

First Yen Press Edition: December 2017

Yen Press is an imprint of Yen Press, LLC.
The Yen Press name and logo are trademarks of Yen Press, LLC.

Library of Congress Control Number: 2015956843

ISBNs: 978-0-316-41414-2 (paperback)
       978-0-316-44786-7 (ebook)

10 9 8 7 6 5 4 3 2

WOR

Printed in the United States of America